D1421075

138633

Octavia Hill

Also by Gillian Darley

Villages of Vision (1975)
Dictionary of Ornament (with Philippa Lewis) (1986)

OCTAVIA HILL

Gillian Darley

Constable London

First published in Great Britain 1990
by Constable and Company Limited
10 Orange Street London WC2H 7EG
Copyright © 1990 Gillian Darley
Set in Linotron Bembo 11 pt by
Rowland Phototypesetting Limited
Bury St Edmunds, Suffolk
Printed in Great Britain by
St Edmundsbury Press Limited
Bury St Edmunds, Suffolk

British Library CIP data
Darley, Gillian
Octavia Hill
1. Great Britain. Environment. Conservation.
Hill, Octavia, 1838–1912
I. Title
333.7′2′0924

ISBN 0 09 469380 3

For Michael

Contents

Illustrations

[9]

Acknowledgements

My first debt is to the Ouvry family for their interest and support in my delvings into the life and achievements of their great-aunt: Romilly who loaned family papers and answered many questions; Jonathan, his son, who sent a mission into the recesses of his firm's archives and retrieved Octavia's tin box of papers; also the late Arthur and his wife Susan, and Ursula Cash (*née* Ouvry). At Crockham Hill the Revd Richard Ames Lewis was both helpful and enthusiastic. For lending me books or photographs, passing on information or for exchanging impressions and opinions (both in person and on paper) on Octavia Hill's life and legacy I would like to thank the following: Dame Jennifer Jenkins, David Graham, Robert Nuttall, Tony Richardson, Richard North, Freda Levson, Clare Ungerson, Jane Lewis, Robert Thorne, Alan Crawford, Andrew Saint, Kathryn Skrine, Mary Lynn McCree Bryan, Jacqueline Leavitt, Michael Rose, Robert Kaufman, Marjorie Cleaver, Andrew Patrick, Nick Mansfield, Margaret Wolfit and Nancy Slote.

I also received unfailingly generous help from librarians, curators and archivists of the following collections; the Wisbech Museum; the local history sections of Peterborough, Chester, Marylebone and Holborn Public Libraries; the Ecclesiastical Commissioners; the National Trust Registry; the Fawcett Society; the Ruskin Gallery, Sheffield; the Working Men's College; the Housing Centre Trust; the Octavia Hill & Rowe Housing Trust (as it then was); the Open Spaces Society; the Greater London Record Office; Senate House and University College Libraries (University of London); the LSE; the British Library; and, as ever, the London Library.

I am grateful to Lady Pickthorn for hospitality and for allowing me to use material from the Gow papers in her possession; to Belinda Norman Butler for permission to quote from the Booth material in the University of London, and to Felicity Ashbee for permission to quote from the Ashbee Journals, King's College, Cambridge. Permission to quote from MS collections in their charge (see Notes, page 345) was given by the Corporation of London – Greater London Record Office, the Local History Librarian, Marylebone Public Library, the Librarian of the British Library of Political and Economic Science (LSE) and the State Archives of Darmstadt, the Housing Centre Trust (Upcott papers), and Swarthmore College (Jane Addams papers). I owe a great debt to my meticulous and perceptive editor, Prudence Fay, and to that most expert of indexers, Douglas Matthews, Librarian of the London Library.

Finally, my deepest debt is to those family and friends who chivvied and encouraged me forward with this biography, through a personally difficult period, and beyond: above all, for that and much more, to my husband, Michael Horowitz.

G.D.
1989

Preface

Octavia Hill had the faults and qualities of many who achieve great things. She was obsessive and dogmatic, inflexible and harsh. Equally, she was sensitive (above all, to her own faults), highly intelligent, generous and profoundly self-effacing. She held the bonds of family and friendship as the highest possible trust.

Despite her own deep Christian faith, she was remarkably tolerant to those of other beliefs or denominations. Advantages of birth or wealth left her profoundly unimpressed: she judged men and women by their instincts and their actions. Uninterested in party politics, she won the admiration of figures at the furthest extremities of the political divide, from Lord Salisbury to William Morris. The only superiority Octavia acknowledged was moral superiority.

Octavia Hill's perspective on the role of women is a confusing one. She fought hard for women's rights in education and property ownership, and encouraged the women she knew, friends and family, to take public office where they could. Her own public achievements – the first woman ever invited to sit on a Royal Commission, and her role in framing legislation (both formally, in evidence, and informally through her valuable network of contacts) – were hardly negligible. Yet she was adamantly opposed to suffrage for women and envisaged the working-class woman staying at home and forming the stable world from which their children would take their standards.

Because of the contradictions in Octavia's character, and sometimes in her actions, she has been consistently misunderstood. With her individualistic creed and strong faith in human perfectibility, she was convinced that everybody could rise above his or her situation. She took an impossible position and sustained it – not, as the Council of the Charity Organization Society did, in a closed room in central London, but face to face with people in desperate straits. No one should underestimate how hard was the path she took. It needed immense physical and moral courage to face the world in which she worked – the poorest section of the population, ignorant and embittered, often met outsiders with hostility, even violence.

[13]

She was tiny, dressed as inconspicuously as possible, and as a young woman covered desperate shyness with an unattractively brusque manner. Her assets, in public life especially, were a particularly beautiful speaking voice and a powerful sense of timing, so that when she made a comment, it was at the right moment, brief and to the point. Her written style, however, both in delivered speeches and on the page, was much fuller and could be emotionally powerful. Addressing large public meetings, talking to Cabinet Ministers and Princesses, negotiating her way through committees, writing thousands of letters, and supervising the detail of her work as it expanded, was a colossal task.

Octavia Hill never spared herself. She never tired of picking up her pen or addressing one more crowded meeting to achieve something she believed in, not for herself, but for the public good.

Her blind spot lay in her inability to see the limitations of both the scale and the approach of her work. She resisted with improper vigour the introduction of social-welfare provision, whether in the form of old age pensions, free school meals, public housing or unemployment benefit. By the time she became a Poor Law Commissioner she was implacable and of a cast of mind which is difficult to enter in the late twentieth century. Even today's harsh reappraisals of the modern Welfare State show a greater tolerance of misfortune and poverty than had Octavia and her COS colleagues. Yet at a time when the political emphasis is unbendingly placed on the curtailing or severe limitation of State intervention, whether in housing, education, employment or even the arts (all areas that concerned Octavia greatly), there are parallels to be drawn between her personal myopia and the blindness caused by implacable adherence to dogma.

Decent housing, dependable employment, opportunities for recreation, a protected wider environment, enjoyment of the arts: to Octavia, all those were connected, and were reasonable expectations for all. Her achievements include the principles of social casework (if not the practice) and of modern enlightened housing management, with its return to a local approach. She encouraged community activity in theatre, literature and music. She supported the involvement of tenants in the decisions that directly affected them in their housing and their amenities: clubrooms, playgrounds, public gardens. She was a lifelong believer in co-operative ventures, whether in the workplace or in housing. She supported rehabilitation against demolition, preferred the building of cottages or small blocks of flats

[14]

to industrial dwellings. She set up a campaign against smoke pol-
lution, fought for the maintenance of rights of way and commons,
and set up the National Trust, which is currently rediscovering its
founders' principles.

As a tally of achievements by one small woman without advantage
of birth, wealth or formal education, in an age when women were
granted few favours, it is remarkable.

CHAPTER I

Beginnings

O
FTEN in biography the winding road through the genealogy
and antecedents of the subject turns out to have been a long
journey taken in vain, offering little or no insight. In the case
of Octavia Hill, her character was formed by the complementary influences of three powerful personalities, all members of her
immediate family.

At first glance there was little to suggest the direction Octavia's life
would take. Tucked well down the line in a family numbering, in
total, eleven children – ten of them girls – she might have been
expected to spend her time polishing the ladylike accomplishments
gained in the course of an undemanding education and suitable to a life
of bourgeois respectability, until marriage claimed her.

But circumstances, almost from the moment of her birth, conspired
against such an outcome. The hardships of her childhood brought out
a character of a very different cast. It was her own experience of
poverty and misfortune, together with her personal observations of
the conditions under which the very poorest members of society lived,
that pointed Octavia Hill to social reform. She knew from the example
of her grandfather the potential power of an individual fighting for a
cause; like her father and mother, he had used the pen and the platform
to drive home the truth to an indifferent and complacent public. These
three people contributed the ingredients of a personality which, from a
remarkably early age, was single-mindedly bent on bettering the
conditions of the poor, achieving that objective through tireless work
and absolute conviction.

The first of the three major influences upon her character was her
grandfather Thomas Southwood Smith. He was born in 1788 at
Martock, in Somerset, and in 1802 he was granted a scholarship to

Bristol Baptist College. Most unusually, it was extended for a further five years. However at Michaelmas 1807 it was abruptly withdrawn, since he had deeply disappointed his superiors, accused of 'entertaining opinions widely different from ours on most of the doctrines we consider to be essential to Evangelical Religion'.[1] Southwood Smith's training as a Baptist preacher came to an abrupt end.

Finding the Calvinism of the Baptists distasteful, he then turned to the Unitarians. His change of faith led to a permanent rupture with his family who broke off all contact with him. Despite such a bitter outcome, his farewell sermon at Taunton in 1808 was entitled 'The Benevolence of God displayed in the Revelation of a Future State of Perfect Happiness'.[2] Thomas Southwood Smith was an incurable optimist.

Losing the support of his own family, he found a new one. That year he married Anne Read, daughter of a Bristol stoneware potter who, although an ardent Baptist, was prepared to overlook any religious differences with his son-in-law. It says much for Thomas Southwood Smith's considerable personal charm that he was so readily accepted by his wife's family. Thomas and Anne's first child, Caroline, was born in 1809, and Emily followed a year later. But the pleasures of marriage and family life were to be tragically short-lived for the couple. Anne died in 1812.

Left a widower with two small daughters at the age of twenty-four, Thomas Southwood Smith took an immensely difficult decision. Leaving his children behind in Somerset with their mother's family, he went the following year to Edinburgh to study medicine. After a short time he could stand the separation no longer and went back to Bristol to collect his eldest daughter, Caroline, aged four. They travelled to Edinburgh by sea, much of the way through a fearful storm which pummelled and battered their boat, and so terrified the little girl that she could remember it vividly eighty-five years later.

For a father to bring up his daughter on his own was a highly unusual arrangement, especially for someone without the means to employ much domestic help. In fact, it was an extremely successful experiment and led to a lifelong intimacy between father and daughter, and an exceptional common purpose between them. Thomas Southwood Smith gave his daughter, Octavia Hill's mother, an invaluable legacy: he taught her that a combination of human sympathy, faith and a powerful sense of purpose could move mountains.

She in turn ensured that her own children never forgot that lesson.

His biographer, his granddaughter Gertrude, Octavia's sister, wrote that when he arrived back in Edinburgh with his daughter: 'Much interest was felt in the young pale student and his little girl . . . Caroline lived with him, cheering his home-coming from the university to their rooms and drinking in from him at a very early age – as I, her daughter, was destined to do many years after – lessons of self-devotion to great ends'.[3] Despite his high moral aims, Thomas Southwood Smith was very far from being a joyless prig. No one who recorded an impression of him over the years failed to mention his enormous personal warmth and irresistible conviviality. Gertrude's childhood recollections are of his being the perfect companion, bursting with fun and never too busy to throw himself into her games and schemes.

In Edinburgh Southwood Smith combined his studies with preaching – at Skinner's Hall Canongate.[4] The Unitarians in Scotland were a tiny minority in the midst of Presbyterianism, and although the punitive laws against them were repealed in England in 1813, in Scotland 'the law making the profession of Unitarianism a *capital crime* was still on the statute books, though of course obsolete. It was then repealed.'[5] Thomas Southwood Smith had chosen a difficult path, and his life in Edinburgh cannot have been easy in any respect.

It was probably at this time that he met Margaret and Mary Gillies,[6] two gifted sisters who had been brought up in Edinburgh by their uncle, Lord Gillies, following the business failure of their City merchant father. They were then in their late teens and taking their first steps towards distinguished careers as, respectively, a miniature painter and a writer. The friendship and emotional support they offered Thomas and his daughter made the sisters immediate honorary members of the family. In later years they were known by Octavia and her sisters as 'the aunts'.

In 1816 Thomas Southwood Smith left Edinburgh with his MD and a published collection of his sermons entitled *Illustrations of the Divine Government*. He moved back to Somerset, to Yeovil, planning to combine the practice of medicine with his vocation as a minister. 'The double capacity of physician to body and soul does not appear to be incompatible, and how the plan will succeed can be determined only by the test of experience.'[7]

Here he married again, Mary Christie, who gave birth to three children: Spencer and Christina who both died in childhood, and Herman, who was born in 1819.[8] Mary was from London, and the Southwood Smith family moved back there in 1820. Dr Southwood Smith took up appointments at the London Fever Hospital, the Eastern Dispensary and the Jews' Hospital, working from consulting-rooms in Trinity Square, close to the Tower of London, and practising exclusively in the East End.

Horrified by his observations and experiences, Southwood Smith found that simply to practise medicine was not enough. He had to reach a wider audience and persuade those in positions of power of the desperate need for public health reform and proper sanitary legis-lation. His fluency as a preacher, particularly the experience gained in promoting an unpopular creed in an unreceptive location, stood him in good stead when he began to write and lecture. Despite a fun-damental misunderstanding of the nature of infectious disease (he followed the universally held idea that the atmosphere was contamin-ated by contagious miasmas), Southwood Smith and a handful of colleagues did begin to connect appalling living conditions with the outbreak of disease. Accidentally, they had pinpointed the cause of recurrent fatal epidemics.

Ironically, in view of future events, Southwood Smith was caught in the financial crises of the mid-1820s. Trinity Square was given up, 'retrenchment became a duty; Mrs Southwood Smith went abroad with the three children . . . to carry on their education.' Caroline and Emily, daughters of Thomas's first wife, were by then already teaching away from home – Caroline had taken a post in Wimbledon and Emily was living and working in Italy, where she remained for the rest of her life.

Her father's financial crisis offered Caroline Southwood Smith her first taste of misfortunes which she was to experience in far more acute form in the years ahead. Personal poverty was a constant reality in Octavia Hill's childhood and endured well into her adulthood; the worry of repaying debts and living on the genteel brink of disaster was a spectre which haunted her all her life.

Following the dispersal of the family, Dr Southwood Smith dis-tracted himself with work. In 1824 he met Edwin Chadwick, a barrister in the Middle Temple who was developing an interest in sanitary reform. Southwood Smith and Dr Neill Arnott provided him with medical details, pointing him towards the East End fever dens and convincing him of the urgency of finding the causes of the spread of disease. Chadwick's own achievements were built upon the foundations of the doctors' expertise, although as an arrogant and domineering man he gave them little credit. In the following years Southwood Smith published his own findings widely, his steady professional observations filling countless reports and contributions to official documents. *The Treatise on Fever*, published in 1830, was the result of a painstaking survey of 2,500 patients whose symptoms were recorded on each of three daily visits over a four-year period.

Friend and doctor to Jeremy Bentham, it was Dr Southwood Smith who persuaded him to leave his body for dissection, the first such medical legacy. R. H. Horne described Southwood Smith in 1832 giving Bentham's memorial lecture over the body 'with a clear and unfaltering voice, but with a face as white as the dead philosopher before him'. Later, looking presentable with a wax facial mask and a suit of clothes, and lovingly housed in a purpose-built mahogany cabinet, Bentham's 'homely figure, with its long snow-white hair, broad-brimmed hat and thick ash-plant walking stick, *resides* with Dr Southwood Smith'.[9]

While Southwood Smith was establishing himself as a leading figure in the battle for both social and sanitary reform, his daughter Caroline was becoming something of an expert in her own field. No doubt aided by her father's connections in the literary world – he had helped Bentham found the *Westminster Review* – she began, in the early 1830s, to publish articles on educational theory in the *Monthly Repository*, while still continuing to teach. Her special interest was in the liberal and even radical educational theories of J. H. Pestalozzi,[10] the eighteenth-century Swiss educationalist who was convinced that observation was the only sure basis for learning and that a child's development should be allowed to follow a natural course. After a few of her articles had appeared, the editor of the *Monthly Repository* had a letter from a reader, asking for the name and address of the writer. Soon afterwards Caroline received a visit in Wimbledon from this admirer of her articles, who on the spot offered her the position of governess to his children. James Hill, a corn merchant and banker, was a recent widower and himself a determined advocate of Pestalozzian education.

Caroline, no doubt duly flattered, accepted, and found herself looking after the younger members of a family consisting of five daughters and a son,[11] the issue of two marriages. James Hill's first wife had been Ann Jecks of Norwich, whom he had married in 1818.

[21]

Following her death he had married her sister Eliza, who had died in 1832. The second marriage, under the tables of affinity, was illegal in ecclesiastical law.

Caroline's engagement as governess led, not surprisingly, to marriage. Indeed the progressive interests which she and James Hill shared made the development almost inevitable. They married at St Botolphs, Bishopsgate in the City of London, in 1835, and the Gillies sisters were Caroline's bridesmaids. The couple settled down in Wisbech in one half of a substantial double-fronted Georgian house, Number 8, South Brink, which had been built for the Receiver-General of the land-tax of Cambridgeshire, Charles Vavazour, in 1720.[12] Later in the century it had been fashionably refronted. It was a house which denoted status.

Seventeenth-century drainage of the fens had led to a boom in Wisbech based upon the growing and processing of oilseed rape. Inland lay some of the best farmland anywhere in England. Much effort had gone into improvements to the area's waterways, to keeping the North Sea at bay and improving access for barges and other craft. James Hill and his fellow merchants were benefiting from the foresight of earlier generations.

South Brink faced North Brink across the Nene. The riverbanks were lined with fine eighteenth-century merchants' houses, many of which stand today, notably Peckover House. Elsewhere in Wisbech the Castle (remodelled in fashionable Gothick dress) and the Crescent (a sophisticated development for a country town) show that the town continued confident and prosperous into the nineteenth century. The Museum – built in 1846 but established as a learned society some years before – points to the literary and cultural aspirations of Wisbech people. Superficially, then, the setting was solid, but despite James Hill's position as a leading merchant in Wisbech no one mistook him for a conventional pillar of local society. A number of question-marks hung over his head.

James Hill had moved to Wisbech from Peterborough around 1818. His father, also called James, had built up a business dealing in corn, wool and coal and, as was the practice, had become a banker too. Before long James Hill and Son owned a fleet of steam barges plying between Wisbech and Peterborough. Caroline Southwood Hill, writing many years later, remembered hearing that by the age of twenty-one James had a personal fortune of £30,000, a large house and a sizeable acreage of land.

In his bachelor days he allowed himself £10 a week for housekeeping and as he was at that time a vegetarian there was a large surplus which he regularly devoted to the purchase of books . . . He had genius and immense business talent – industry & energy almost superhuman; but the corn business in those days was susceptible to gambling – 'every shower of rain makes me a thousand pounds richer', he said on one occasion – but added after a few moments' reflection – 'one hates that it should be by the People's food becoming dearer'.[13]

It was inevitable that, with these ideals, James Hill would plunge into politics. In 1819 he was nominated, and elected, a Capital Burgess, standing as a radical Liberal. At his swearing in he refused to take his oath on the Bible and was forced to stand down in favour of his Tory opponent, who presumably showed no such hesitation. On 8 December 1820 a 'loyal address' drawing the King's attention to 'the Mis-rule of your present Ministers' went up in Wisbech: '. . . they have betrayed their King – insulted their Queen – despised the People – violated the Constitution – exhausted the Treasury – impoverished the Nation – disgraced the Church – demoralized the Land – scandalized Christianity and cast a Stain upon their Country which time cannot easily efface.' The protest could be signed at Mr Hill's Counting House, near the Bridge, Wisbech.

On 19 December 1825 another, less buoyant, bill was posted. It mentioned the 'temporary suspension of our payments occasioned by the inability of our London Bankers to meet their engagements', and thanked the creditors for their 'handsome and liberal conduct . . . and their unshaken confidence'. The Hills had been brought down in a nationwide banking crash. In April the next year, Thomas Hill of Uppingham agreed to pay the creditors six shillings in the pound – subject to their ability to prove the debt.[14]

Although the Hills soon bounced back, the shadow of the 1825 bankruptcy was to follow young James Hill and prove an invaluable weapon in the armoury of his enemies. He was a firebrand who espoused almost any radical cause which might benefit the working class. His son Arthur described him as a friend and supporter of Richard Cobden, 'whom he greatly assisted in the anti-Corn Law agitation', but also a 'thorn in the side of the Bishop of Ely, with whom . . . he was on terms of almost perpetual quarrel'.[15] He was muddle-headed in his idealism, passionate and utterly irrational. He was a natural political activist but a most unlikely businessman.

By the mid-1830s, James Hill had moved to the outer fringes of the political spectrum, endorsing the socialism of Robert Owen. At the meeting of the Wisbech Museum Society (founded 1835) on 26 February 1836 he was put forward as a candidate for the committee, proposed by Mr Weatherhead.[16] On 4 March the President, the Revd Henry Fardell, various members of the Peckover family (local grandees) and the Revd Jeremiah Jackson were amongst the majority who rejected him. As far as anyone knows, James Hill was the only man ever blackballed by the Society.

In 1836, taking advantage of the Newspaper Act which reduced tax on newspapers to a penny, and no doubt encouraged by the support of his young and capable wife, James Hill launched a newspaper, the *Star in the East*, or the *Wisbech and East of England Gazette and Advertiser*, motto 'the truth, the whole truth and nothing but the truth'. In its pages the two strands of his personality merge – the passionate reformer and the argumentative campaigner. The first editorial, on 17 September, set out the objectives of the paper:

> To advocate these principles, to help forward the cause of humanity – to vindicate the claim of the oppressed, and to place in their true light the influencing causes of social suffering and social enjoyment, shall be the grand aim of all our labours as journalists, and in this arduous but satisfactory undertaking, we anticipate the full sympathy and aid of 'all good men and true'.

The *Star in the East* ensured that there was no complacency in Wisbech. It brought news of Chartist insurrection in Birmingham (reported sympathetically), it chronicled the Owenite movement and colonies such as Ralahine, and included scientific reports and literary reviews. The newspaper was a remarkable achievement, particularly given the many other calls on the time of its editor.

James Hill argued endlessly in print, running the gamut from the puerile to the courageous. Vendettas were being waged against him, he knew; 'two lawyers, two divines, one mayor, two aldermen, two town councillors, nine Christians up in arms to put down one poor infidel', as he put it. A polemicist, he thrived on verbal combat. Often the leading article took the form of a letter, perhaps from a detractor such as the hated Unitarian minister, J. T. Cooper, followed by a signed reply from Hill. He attacked church and chapel, aristocracy and the privileged, local or national figures. He believed in Free Trade and household franchise. In 1837 he stood as a parliamentary candidate for Peterborough, and also as a churchwarden, though he was not a member of the Established church and was a sworn enemy of the vicar.

In all that James Hill fought for, his wife stood beside him. It must have been an exceptional partnership, based upon respect for each other's work and ideas, as well as on genuine affection. Before long, their family expanded. Caroline gave birth to her first daughter, Miranda, Octavia's eldest sister, on the first day of 1836. Gertrude was born on 28 July 1837.

Despite the birth of her children, Caroline continued to write and was instrumental in the setting up of James Hill's pioneering infant school which was based upon Robert Owen's New Lanark school, run on Pestalozzian principles.[17] It was housed in the Hall of the People, which James built in 1837 and which still stands.

The newspaper was very much a family enterprise, and included regular articles on education, signed simply 'C'.[18] Caroline seems to have written on all sorts of subjects well beyond her own field, such as the iniquities of Poor Law administration. One case she chronicled concerned a girl she employed at the school, who was forced to follow her mother into the local workhouse. Caroline fought the Wisbech authorities tooth and nail. They may have underestimated her connections; when she wrote to the Poor Law Commissioners to complain, the reply was signed by the Secretary – Edwin Chadwick, her father's close colleague.[19]

The newspaper also contained articles by Dr Southwood Smith and reviews of his books, whilst a lecture he gave in London was reported by someone obviously very familiar with him – his daughter, no doubt. The earliest piece by 'C' was a description of the appalling state of many dame schools. Its author described vividly the filth and degradation she had seen, in an account as potent and disturbing as her father's observations on the East End. Octavia inherited a strong and immediate written style and the ability subtly to conjure up images that would shock a comfortable public without resorting to exaggeration or melodrama.

The *Star* was a record and a barometer of Hill's activities. From its columns he drummed up interest and support for his ventures, as well as offering ammunition to his detractors. On 3 February 1838 there was a party at the Hall of the People, a regular event. The *Star in the East* reported: 'Late in the evening Mr Hill joined the party, when the subject of his plan for the amelioration of the Working Men of Wisbech being introduced, he was questioned as to some of the details, which enquiries being answered in his usual clear and clever manner, many persons came forward to put down their names as members of the New Society.' Such activities were grist to the mill of the Tory *Wisbech Gazette*, which watched Hill like a hawk. The *Star* referred to the 'imbecility and bigotry of the *Wisbech Gazette*' for calling the New Society 'impracticable and impossible and Utopian and visionary'. These were gentle opening skirmishes in what soon became a virulent war of words. Hill thrived on it.

By the end of March a membership of over 300 was claimed for the United Advancement Society (its name changed from the New Society). Members could buy their groceries wholesale; items offered included green and black tea, flour, coffee and soap. In effect it was just a co-operative marketing operation but it allowed those that were with James Hill to stand up and be counted. He saw the members as the cornerstone of his projected Owenite community. In the summer of 1838 Robert Owen himself visited the town at Hill's invitation to give a series of three lectures, lending credence to his host's radical qualifications and promoting his own plans. Owen also visited March and Peterborough; the Fens were fertile ground for agrarian radicalism.

The third of Caroline's daughters was born on 3 December 1838. Since she was James Hill's eighth daughter she was named Octavia. Her arrival coincided with the accelerating downturn in her father's fortunes. She could have hardly chosen a less auspicious moment to be born.

A few months earlier James Hill had earmarked a 700-acre estate at Wretton in Norfolk for his own agricultural colony. With his younger brother Thomas, his patient lieutenant in these ventures, he visited it in the autumn of 1838 on behalf of the United Advancement Society (President, Thomas Hill). The venture was financially unrealistic and Octavia's birth saw the dashing of all hopes for any experiment on that scale. Instead, in March 1839 the Society took possession of a mere ten acres just outside Wisbech, on the river. On 13 April the members celebrated, at tables laid out in the orchard, 'an event which, though small in its commencement, shall, ultimately, be found to have been the beginning of an important change in society.' But it was no time for such political statements, as Chartist unrest seethed and the social order looked dangerously unstable. By May the country was in crisis and few working men were in the mood to draw attention to themselves. By November members had begun to withdraw their money from the Society. The investment in land had absorbed funds and 'caused the trading part to move on with less advantage to the members'. The co-operative store was a failure and there was little support for the 'colony'.

Hill had ploughed substantial sums of his own money into his many schemes and had openly aligned himself with revolutionary causes. As far as the town was concerned, he was neither creditworthy nor trustworthy. Yet the final denouement, his bankruptcy, must have been sudden. The last issue of the *Star in the East*, of 11 April 1840, gave no intimation of its imminent demise. The paper was as full of features and discussion as ever – compared to the *Wisbech Gazette* it was a civilized, intelligent read – and little parochialism, beyond the local plans of its publisher James Hill.[20] But on 25 March *The Times* published the notice of bankruptcy of James Hill and his partner Thomas, merchants. A hearing was announced for 5 May at the Hotel, Stamford.

In April 1840 the *New Moral World*, the official Owenite newspaper, carried an advertisement from a lady in Wisbech, an experienced teacher, who was looking for a position as governess. Perhaps the advertiser was Caroline, still hoping to salvage the family fortunes? However on 3 June 1840 a sizeable auction was held at the Saracen's Head Inn, Peterborough 'by order of the Commissioners in a Fiat of Bankruptcy against James and Thomas Hill, merchants, brewers, and co-partners, and under the direction of the Assignees of the said bankrupts'.[21] The sum realized was £12,941, a great deal more than was expected.

Even if he could have salvaged his financial position, James Hill's reputation had reached its nadir in Wisbech. The family left and set out on what became a many-staged progress around the country. Since Caroline was then expecting another baby, her father and the Gillies sisters settled her in a cottage at Loughton in Essex, on the edge of Epping Forest, where Emily was born. Seeing his daughter in such desperate straits, with four small children and no financial security, Dr Southwood Smith, though well over fifty, offered to bring up his granddaughter Gertrude. She lived with him from the age of three until his death twenty years later.

Dr Southwood Smith must have been struck by the turn of fate that found him again in charge of a small girl, just as he had been thirty years earlier in Edinburgh. As always the Gillies sisters rallied round, and from the moment that he took responsibility for Gertrude they shared with him a succession of homes. In many ways Gertrude had the most loving and stable upbringing of all her sisters.

When she was older, Octavia once went back to look for the Essex cottage, accompanied by Anna Mary Howitt and her cousin Mary Harris, both of whom became lifelong friends.[22] They found an old-fashioned village, odd-looking because all the trees were pollarded. Octavia only just recognized the white-painted house, for it had lost its romantic disguise of creepers, roses and jasmine, and the shrubs and trees she remembered had been cut down and replaced by vegetable- and flower-beds. Despite the memories the charm was gone for her. The girls gathered primroses and oxalis in the woods before turning their backs on Octavia's past.

In the early 1840s there were more moves for the Hill family. After Emily's birth they lived successively in Hampstead on Pond Street, in Gloucestershire and in Leeds, where in 1843 the youngest child, James Hill's tenth daughter, Florence, was born. The Leeds address suggests that James may have been hoping to get support from Owenite contacts who were now publishing the *New Moral World* from there.[23] He might have expected encouragement, for in June 1838 the *New Moral World* had enthusiastically noted that 'the spirited proprietor of the *Star in the East* is now making common cause with us'.

Some time around the time of the move to Leeds James Hill had a severe nervous breakdown. Despite his recovery, the family never lived together again. Yet for a while the financial worries seemed to have passed: by 1843 Thomas Hill had returned to business in Peterborough and soon his brother began to appear once more in the annals of co-operation and agrarian community experiment, first in Leeds and then in London. In August 1845 James Hill bought the entire plant of the *New Moral World*, including the title, for £180. This was hotly contested by another Owenite, Fleming, who continued to publish the renamed *Moral World* from Harmony Hall, an Owenite community. Meanwhile James Hill, after three issues of his 'new series' *New Moral World* (between 30 August and 13 September) changed the title to the *Commonweal*.

The *Commonweal* was a small-format promotional sheet for Hill's latest venture, the National Land and Building Association. By now at loggerheads with the Owenites (Owen himself was in America), Hill began to sound increasingly unstable. Those who wanted to be members or shareholders of his Association (who were assured a 4 per cent return) were asked to address themselves to Mr Arthur Hill – presumably James' son. The address of the Association was 2, Bartlett's Buildings, Holborn; James Hill lived alone at 50 George Street, Euston Square. The Association continued shakily until 1847, by which time the Chartist Land Company had seized the initiative.[24] At this point the trail on James Hill runs cold, whilst his financial miscalculations came home to roost with a vengeance on his unfortunate wife and daughters.[25]

In a family with mental illness, its shadow always hangs heavily on succeeding generations. A veil was drawn over James Hill's shaky enterprises in the mid-1840s. The family ensured that in all later accounts of Octavia's upbringing, James Hill left the stage at the time of his breakdown. This was not strictly true. Emily Hill and her husband tidied up the later pages of Caroline's memoir of her husband as assiduously as they were to tidy up Octavia Hill's own life.[26] However, one scored-out section can still be deciphered and shows that Caroline was doubtful about the personally harsh solution to her husband's problems.

> By the advice of Dr Conolly and other physicians after his recovery he continued to live apart from his wife and her children, and although in this particular instance it may have been an over corrective yet it was grounded on a too little observed fact in human nature, that persons who will be perfectly sound in mind under some conditions, give way if exposed to exciting causes of disease. How many a tragedy might never happen if care were taken to avoid these – if the pressure of pecuniary anxiety for children's sake were lifted off a man for instance or he were kept away from the object of hopeless love or groundless jealousy.[27]

The comment suggests that the dispersal of the family had not been inevitable and only occurred in such a definite fashion because of medical advice. Caroline, it seemed, deeply regretted that it should have come to that. Until James' death almost thirty years later the devoted couple, the parents of five daughters, who had worked as one

[29]

for the causes they believed in, were kept apart in order to spare James any strain and to avoid a recurrence of his breakdown. Caroline's comment adds a sad note to the family history.

Although future meetings between James and his children were few, Octavia told another close friend, Mary Harrison, of once being sent to her father with an important message. She came to a lonely cottage and knocked in the silence, shouting, 'Your little daughter Octavia has come.' James Hill was a tragic, absent figure who held continuing significance in his children's lives. His name occurs from time to time in their letters, and at intervals in the 1850s they would hear that he was poorly and rally round to visit him or send money.

James Hill, the lost father, haunted them all. For Octavia there were many repercussions. She idealized the family as a solid unit in which each individual had his or her allotted place, despite the fact that her mother had been brought up without a natural mother and she herself had scarcely known her father. More tangible was the constant burden of debt; Octavia was still working to pay off her father's and the family debts in the late 1850s and her legacy from her grandfather went to settle the last outstanding bill in 1861. James Hill lived on until 1871, in later years living with his widowed daughter, Margaret Whelpdale – one of the step-children with whom Caroline always kept in close and fond contact.

On leaving Leeds, and her husband, Caroline lived with her daughters for some years in Finchley, then a country village well north of London. All financial support was provided by her father, who lived with the Gillies sisters first in Kentish Town and then in Highgate. That house, Hillside,[28] in Fitzroy Park, their home between 1846 and 1856, was a welcoming second home for Caroline and her daughters.

Hillside was situated in a glorious spot on rising ground on the edge of Hampstead Heath and Kenwood, with the open hayfields, hedges and lanes of Highgate offering the children endless possibilities either for intent exploration or exuberant games. In spring there were wild daffodils in the rolling field next to the house and all the year round, as their mother pointed out, the flowers changed with the seasons. When Octavia first went abroad her letters brimmed with the names of dozens of wild flowers that she recognized. Later, when she planted her own country garden, she chose the plants that grew in neighbouring fields in preference to garish Victorian favourites.

But already in the 1840s that idyllic scene was threatened. Development was marching on and the peaceful atmosphere was being constantly shattered by the felling of venerable oaks and the insidious encroachment on ancient meadows. The campaigns that Octavia mounted in the 1870s and 1880s to preserve Swiss Cottage Fields and the extension to Hampstead Heath were given added intensity by her treasured memories of Hillside and its unspoiled rural setting. Yet the house and its neighbours were in themselves part of London's expansion outwards, into and over the surrounding villages.

In 1838, the year of Octavia's birth and the subsequent crisis of James Hill's bankruptcy and collapse, her grandfather was in the eye of the public health storm, embroiled in a massive amount of work and becoming a figure of national standing. He was not, however, a wealthy man and the financial strain of supporting his daughter and her family must have been immense. The typhoid epidemic of 1837 had been a turning point, and had plunged Southwood Smith into action, both as practitioner and theorist. In an important contribution to the public health debate, he presented the Poor Law Commissioners with 'Reports on the Causes of Sickness amongst the Poor which are capable of Prevention'.[29]

Although the Commissioners' investigation was prompted by worries about the rising burden of the poor rate, rather than humanitarianism, the observations of Southwood Smith, together with those of his colleagues Drs Arnott and Kay, were valuable prompts to the Commissioners. Southwood Smith's own contribution, in the shape of documentary accounts of Bethnal Green and Whitechapel, was graphic. He described, just as he often did to important visitors, the cupboard-sized rooms, eight foot by ten or even less, in which up to six people lived and worked, day and night. He told how open drains surrounded these warrens of filth and degradation, how sick people lay in the same room as healthy members of the family, ensuring continued contagion, and how dampness and darkness compounded the horror. He wrote in a matter-of-fact tone that was far more shocking than a highly coloured account would have been.

The abysmal sanitary conditions in the miserable housing then available to the poor were, the doctors knew, at the root of the contagion. Southwood Smith pointed both to cause and effect. His report prompted the Bishop of London to call for a parliamentary Select Committee into the Health of Towns. The committee met in 1840 with Dr Southwood Smith as its first witness.

In 1842 Southwood Smith, who had been responsible with Edwin Chadwick and Thomas Tooke for the pioneering 1833 report of the Commission of Enquiry into Factories,[30] published another report on child labour, this time in mining. In a brilliantly imaginative gesture, Southwood Smith commissioned illustrations so as to make the maximum impact, and catch the attention of Members of Parliament who were either too lazy to read it or inured against shock by the constant perusal of worthy reports and blue books on social conditions. The remarkable pictures of women and children at work in the mine shafts, crouched like caged animals in the confined blackness, were drawn by Margaret Gillies.[31]

The Gillies were also close friends of the Howitts,[32] a redoubtable and distinguished Quaker couple who lived first in Clapton and then in Highgate, and whose house was another in which the Hill girls were made to feel completely at home. Octavia and their daughter Margaret, known as Meggie, became firm friends and Charlton, their son, was a regular playmate. Mary Howitt liked Caroline Southwood Hill's way with Meggie. Miranda Hill remembered that her mother 'seldom gave a distinct order or made a rule . . . the children learnt from early infancy . . . that if a thing was right, it must be done; there ceased to be any question about it'.

At the end of one of Octavia's visits, Mary Howitt wrote to Caroline: 'We are all charmed with her, and know not how we shall part with her.' The pleasure was reciprocated. 'I shall never forget the atmosphere of love,' Octavia wrote. Holidays with the Howitts must have been a relief from the strains around the Hill home as Caroline struggled to make do without the support of either a husband or a father for her children, and utterly dependent on her own father's generosity from his limited funds. Caroline's own worries, exhaustion and unhappiness must have meant that there was little time for warmth or the demonstration of affection at home. Throughout her life Octavia was drawn towards families who were close and loving like a moth to a candle. Margaret Howitt's memory of Octavia was of:

a very ardent, eager child, with a quick sense of the ludicrous that was partially hidden under a precise determined manner . . . Octavia enforced an exacting discipline of high aims and self-improvement, against which I . . . often chafed; and more especially because her lofty standard was coupled with a quite startling humility . . . When Octavia visited us later on, her sense of humour was as keen as ever, but life seemed already to have for her a set purpose . . .

The Hill girls became her 'cherished friends for life'.

Octavia was, from childhood onwards, especially close to her older sister Miranda. Gertrude, growing up elsewhere, was more like a favourite cousin than a sister, but Miranda (known as Andy) was always at home. Already the sweetness and gentleness that marked her as an adult were evident. She was a perfect foil for her intense, purposeful younger sister. In these years in Highgate and Finchley, while the two youngest sisters, Emily (known as Minnie) and Florence were still tiny, Miranda and Octavia developed the intimacy that strengthened and illuminated both their lives.

Caroline Hill's writings on education, some of which Octavia published after her mother's death,[33] offer revealing insights into the way the children were brought up. Her Pestalozzian ideas were very unconventional and far from the mainstream of early Victorian thinking. Caroline held that no mother should decide 'what sort of human being it is her object to fashion'. She objected to rivalry, to struggling for prizes and the rigidities of pointless discipline. She saw the danger which lay in damping down a child's spirit: 'life begins with happiness . . . we ought to endeavour that it should go on.' Indulgence, however, was not the same as happiness.

Education, Caroline Hill wrote, was both an art and a science and the care and development of body should be matched by that of the mind. Endless repetition of particular sayings or principles ensured that the child would grow up hating them – even in religion, where 'the constant reiteration of sacred truth, before the experience of life enables the child to understand the words, is one of the causes of the lifelessness of many people's religion'. Octavia remembered, and followed, this broad-minded approach to religion all her life.

A mother should always be learning, to keep pace with the child's curiosity, Caroline felt. Yet she should make it clear that she had her own interests and work to pursue – assuring the child of her continued and constant affection whilst encouraging independence. Results were not everything. Forcing a child without athletic abilities towards sporting achievements, or one without intellectual prowess into academic pursuits, was pointless. A child should be encouraged in its natural talents: 'there is nothing which cannot be obtained by means of affection'. As an educational theory it is hard to fault.

[33]

The Hill daughters struck people as lively, delightful little girls who were clearly benefiting from their mother's liberal principles – love, freedom, obedience and health were a child's requisites, she wrote. Caroline later described these years.[34] There had been no money for toys, but 'the consequence was they invented games – their invention was inexhaustible'. One energetic game came unstuck. Octavia was the leader, as she often was; 'they were all fastened by a cord tied round her waist, and she ran them down the meadow and leaped over the brook there, reached the bank safely, but forgot that her tail would assuredly not be beside her but drop into the water, which they did to her great surprise and remorse.'[35]

Certain of Octavia's qualities keep recurring in all accounts of her childhood. Chief among them were her absolute sureness of her own convictions and her dominant personality, oddly at variance with her shyness and uncertainty. She also seems to have been particularly physically lively; she behaved as if she had limitless energy, and drove herself impossibly hard, which led to a series of major nervous collapses later on.

To the younger ones, Octavia was the dominant elder sister, despite being the third child. As often happens with children who show unusual maturity, she rapidly became entrusted with responsibilities and tasks which she took on without complaint. Miranda was thought by her mother to be less practical ('dreamy') and less strong, despite being the eldest, and thus was never given the adult burdens that fell upon Octavia, even in her early teens.

The Hill girls were encouraged to read voraciously, whether classics or poetry, plays or novels. Their mother fed them a diet of Milton and Shakespeare; as she put it: 'Whatever teaching they did get it may truly be said they "bettered the instruction", they were all so clever they learnt without difficulty.' Octavia retained a love of poetry all her life; some of her happiest times were spent discussing the merits of Tennyson, Browning or other favourites. As a form of relaxation it often came to her aid in her worst moments of stress and tension.

Their mother provided the rest of their lessons on an irregular basis. Her priority was that the children be outdoors whenever possible and not be tied to the exigencies of a rigid timetable. She considered that formal education ought to begin around the age of sixteen, an age at which learning becomes interesting for its own sake. However informal their education, the Hill girls had a remarkable range of intellectual contacts. Robert Browning was one of many literary figures who met Southwood Smith and his granddaughters in High-gate. He told Octavia many years later that a literary friend had commented, of herself and Gertrude, 'Those are wonderful children; you can talk to them about anything'.[36] Perhaps it was this easy, mutually respectful relationship between adults and children which stood Octavia in good stead when, still in her teens, she met, and argued with, towering figures of the age such as F. D. Maurice and John Ruskin.

Other figures in the close-knit Highgate circle, none of whom were remotely conventional in either thought or way of life, were W. J. Fox, the Leigh Smiths (Barbara Leigh Smith and Octavia continued the connection for many years), and Charles Dickens. Dr Southwood Smith had asked both Dickens and Wordsworth for support for a Sanatorium he was planning[37], and Dickens found him very per-suasive; 'the reasons for such an Institution and the advantages likely to result from it, could not have been more forcibly or eloquently put'.[38]

Dickens was soon turning to Southwood Smith for help with detailed backgrounds for his novels. In the summer of 1841 they planned to travel north together to visit some mines. Dickens being unable to go, he asked Southwood Smith to note what he saw, on his behalf. The following year, Dickens again wrote for help, this time in finding a suitable Cornish mine for him to visit, as background matter for a future novel. In tribute to the geniality of Dr Southwood Smith he ends the letter: 'I ought to make many apologies for troubling you, but somehow or other I don't – which is your fault and not mine'. In March 1843 Southwood Smith sent his friend the report of the Commission on children's employment in trade and manufacturing. It impressed Dickens deeply, who wrote in reply: 'It must be a great comfort and happiness to you to be instrumental in bringing about so much good. I am proud to be remembered by one who is pursuing such ends and heartily hope that we shall know each other better'.[39] It is hardly a coincidence that the hero of *Bleak House* is a doctor working in a slum district.

A distinguished foreign visitor to Highgate was Hans Christian Andersen who was staying with Mary Howitt, his translator from the Danish (which she learned expressly for this purpose). 'We had taken him, as a pleasant rural experience, to the annual hay-making at Hillside, Highgate, thus introducing him to an English home full of poetry and art, of sincerity and affection . . . Immediately after our arrival, the assembled children, loving his delightful fairy-tales, clustered round him in the hay-field, watched him make them a pretty device of flowers; then feeling somehow that the stiff and silent foreigner was not kindred to themselves stole off . . . Soon poor Andersen, perceiving himself forsaken, complained of headache, and insisted on going indoors, where . . . he remained irritable and out of sorts.'[40] It is easy to picture the disappointment of the children, when the author of the magical stories turned out to have such feet of clay.

Much better humoured than the self-important Dane were the Harrisons. Anna Harrison was Mary Howitt's sister and the family moved south from Liverpool to Romford in the 1840s. They too were Quakers. Mary, the eldest of their twelve children, was to remain close to Octavia, and later became a regular correspondent, travelling companion and worker in the housing field. Described by her niece as gifted and handsome, Mary Harrison had had an accident in infancy which left her lame but unbowed. 'Aunt Mary . . . had a flair for interesting people'; it did not take her long to decide that Octavia was exceptional.[41]

The Highgate circle, Unitarians and Quakers almost without exception, shared the Nonconformist radicalism which lay behind both Hill and Southwood Smith attitudes. Conventions were not the point; high principles were. Margaret Howitt remembered that as a small child Octavia did not take sugar, since it was the product of slave labour, and that she was also moved to write a poem about the Irish potato famine. If the Hill daughters should ever have been tempted to forget the misfortunes of others, their grandfather's admirable and tireless work stood as a constant reminder of what had to be done, there on the doorstep, in London.

Dr Southwood Smith's campaigns were finally bearing fruit. In 1848 the first Public Health Act was passed but it was too late: in 1849 a terrible cholera epidemic began which raged intermittently until 1853. In the early months of 1849 Southwood Smith himself contracted the disease. He, Edwin Chadwick and Lord Shaftesbury worked tirelessly to ensure that this horror spurred on reform. The pressure to set up a Board of Health in every town was largely Southwood Smith's: 'These miseries will continue until the Government will pass measures which shall remove the sources of poison and disease from these places . . . These poor people are victims that are sacrificed. The effect is the same as if twenty or thirty thousand of them were annually taken out of their wretched homes and put to death; the only difference being that they are left in them to die.'[42] With the Board of Health's formation, he became its medical member, working without payment for the first year.

Despite the troubles that still lay ahead for Dr Southwood Smith, he offered his granddaughters an inspiring example. So far as the other family influences were concerned, as her sister Miranda put it: 'Octavia seems to have inherited her father's extraordinary energy of mind, and keen business instinct, with a caution which was all her own. From her mother she inherited the imaginative sympathy which so distinguished her.' Awareness of her grandfather's achievement and a steady progress towards his goals, contrasted with her father's utopian ideals and impracticality and backed up by her mother's impressive strength of character and resolution in the face of awful misfortune, guided Octavia towards adult life.

CHAPTER 2

Guild work

IN 1852 Caroline Hill was offered a job, and, as her elder daughters had reached the age when they too could work, she moved from the cottage in Finchley into central London. Octavia, nearly fourteen, found herself wrenched from the pleasures of rural life to a harshly urban one. In her mind, childhood and freedom from responsibility were always inextricably connected with the open countryside, whilst adult cares and desperate financial worries corresponded with city life. The key to many of Octavia's views lies in that short journey between two worlds.

Octavia, her eldest sister Miranda remembered, developed into a woman with a remarkable suddenness. 'From playing in the fields at Finchley she became at once interested in all the great questions of life. At the age of 14 the condition of the poor, the efforts of the working people by co-operation and by their Trades Unions to improve their condition, occupied her thoughts.'

The girls had been brought up to be deeply conscientious. As early as 1850 Miranda was enlisting her half-sister Kate's support for a cause: 'I shall have great pleasure in working for the Peace Society . . . Will you tell me . . . what are the doctrines of the Peace Society? I know very little about it though still enough to engage my sympathies.' Margaret Howitt later remembered Octavia, aged twelve: 'Awakening one night, I saw by the light of a lamp in the road a young statuesque figure seated with folded hands in the sister bed. "What are you about, Ockey?" I said. "Praying for Poland", was the reply.'[1]

The girls' grandfather, Dr Southwood Smith, who used his professional expertise enlightened by his personal and religious morality to bring about a quiet revolution, stood as a reminder of how ideals could be combined with practical endeavours. The family followed his progress with pride. In later life Gertrude remembered her grand-father's address to one meeting; 'when his speech came, towards the end of the meeting, I felt the thrill of his voice, and liked all those other people to hear it too – I liked them to feel *what* he was.'[2]

In 1850 Dr Southwood Smith gave up professional practice to become the permanent medical member of the Board of Health, a position he held for four years. Possibly it was this move, which must have curtailed his income and hence his ability to support his daughter's family, that precipitated Caroline's search for a job.

These were difficult and saddening years for the doctor. Even with a fatal epidemic raging the way forward was blocked. *Laissez-faire* was the spirit of the age. Yet in the brief tenure of the Board, while Edwin Chadwick was to become a deeply unpopular figure, Southwood Smith attracted wide admiration both from the press and medical profession. 'The simplicity and integrity of his character won over for the cause many who were repelled by Chadwick's demoniac reputation.'[3] Chadwick was sometimes contemptuous of his col-league, who was muddled in his office work and a slower thinker than himself. Also many of Smith's supporters knew, and made it known, that he, and not Chadwick, was the father of sanitary reform.[4] Nevertheless the *Lancet*, spurred by the jealousy of professionals watching lay members of the Board of Health operate outside their remit, retaliated by sneering at the 'zymotic gibberish' of the Chief Medical Inspector, Dr Southwood Smith.

The weight of parliamentary opinion fell against the Board. Ben-jamin Hall made a swingeing attack, accusing Lord Shaftesbury of being a 'mere pliant tool of Edwin Chadwick and Southwood Smith', whilst the latter had proposed 'mischievous vagaries and extrava-gances'. To enact public health reform flew in the face of the free market and would inevitably raise levels of rent and rates, they held. The argument raged from both sides of the political divide. *The Times* joined in; running a leader on 12 July 1854 which fulminated: 'these gentlemen have contrived to overwhelm a good object with obloquy and hatred and to make the cholera itself scarcely a more dreaded visitation than their own.'

Later that month the Board of Health fell. *The Times* leader of 31 July crowed: 'Esculapius and Chiron, in the form of Mr Chadwick and Dr Southwood Smith, have been deposed and we prefer to take our chance of cholera and the rest, than to be bullied into health.' *Laissez-faire* had triumphed.

When the three men resigned, Chadwick, to his credit, took up the cudgels for his old friend. Aged sixty-six, Dr Southwood Smith 'without fault proved and indeed after extraordinary and successful labour, is dismissed a ruined man without any compensation whatsoever,' wrote Chadwick the following month. Despite a letter on Lord Palmerston's behalf referring to the 'full approbation of Her Majesty's Government of the zealous, able and indefatigable manner in which you have performed the important duties which have belonged to your official situation,' it was some time before matters were put to rights, and Southwood Smith was awarded a pension of £300.

In 1854, just as he was preparing to move from Hillside to Weybridge, to a new house built for himself and the Gillies sisters, Dr Southwood Smith became ill and had to have a major operation. He had hardly recovered when Emily Hill contracted scarlet fever. Characteristically he delayed the move to nurse her through it. However, despite these misfortunes, the move to The Pines at St George's Hill took place before the end of the year.

From London, Octavia wrote to Gertrude. She would remember Hillside all her life, she assured her, the 'bright happy hours . . . a vision of beauty connected with it which can never be affected.' But, she wrote, 'it seems to me it cannot be very sad for you to leave it, because you carry with you that which will make another home the same, love.'[5] She hoped that Gertrude did not feel she was leaving life behind, moving so far away to Weybridge, and promised to write to her.

Mary, Southwood Smith's second wife, returned from abroad around this time, and died at The Pines in 1858. In that year a memorial bust – possibly the one sculpted by his daughter Emily and of which he commented 'I do not like to know I look so savage as *that*' – was presented to him in recognition of his achievements and as a gesture of apology for his shabby treatment. Dr Southwood Smith was not embittered. As if to underline the quality of his personality, subscribers to the memorial bust, headed by Palmerston, represented a roll-call of the enlightened Establishment and the cream of philanthropic and intellectual England. Chadwick's name was thought to be too contentious and was omitted from the list, 'lest it ruin the proceedings'. Lord Shaftesbury's tribute to Southwood Smith at the time of the fall of the Board of Health, was magnanimous and clearly heartfelt: 'No work ever seemed too much for him if it were to do good. His great services will not, I fear, be appreciated in this generation.'

The Hill family difficulties in the early 1850s were more acute than merely genteelly reduced circumstances. In later years Octavia occasionally summoned up the memory of this time to remind her tenants that she had known the privations of poverty, too. Support offered by her father and other friends had enabled Caroline Hill to keep the family together through childhood but immediately the girls reached their teens the obligation to repay Dr Southwood Smith's loans (as well as James Hill's debts) was pressing, particularly since the doctor was now approaching retirement. The further education that Caroline Hill had planned for her daughters was out of the question and the family ethos pointed them towards work which could benefit others.

As always, Dr Southwood Smith's friends rallied round them. Margaret Gillies offered to train Octavia as an artist, whilst a Hill half-sister, Margaret, offered her a post as pupil-teacher.[6] But according to Caroline Hill, the turning point came in the form of an invitation to an exhibition in Russell Place – 'a show of painted glass, consolidated, so as to make it suitable for tables & other purposes'. Mrs Hill thought it might just be the kind of work that would suit her eldest daughter, Miranda, who seemed to her in danger of becoming 'too dreamy and poetical', and she wrote to Mrs Wallace, who had invented and patented the process, to inquire about lessons for Miranda. But it was Octavia who benefited.

As Caroline Hill put it, this request 'led to the formation of a Society for the Employment of Ladies' – the Ladies' Guild, founded in 1852. In fact, it seemed to have coincided with her own ideas, for the year before Caroline had written to the recently founded *Christian Socialist*, to put the case for a Society of Lady Promoters.

The Ladies' Guild was a crafts workshop for generally unskilled women and girls. Edward Vansittart Neale, one of the newest members of the Christian Socialist group,★ personally supported the Guild, adding a number of other ventures to the original glass-making, including the making of toys – dolls' furniture constructed out of wire and chintz, another of the ingenious Mrs Wallace's inventions. The Guild, as it was set up, was run on co-operative principles and Caroline Hill was appointed manager and book-keeper. She took the

★ See p. 45.

post, for which 'no one could have been less fitted both by faculties and experience', in order to find employment for her daughters. Despite her modesty Caroline was hardly a nonentity, being known through her own writings and as the daughter of the eminent doctor.

Neale soon found Octavia a job managing the toymakers, who were a rough group of girls from a Ragged School. Hardly more than a child herself, Octavia was a confusing mixture, her adult sense of duty and mature grasp of organization infused with a still childish spirit.

At the age of fourteen Octavia became, in effect, the business brains of the enterprise; book-keeping, designing and pricing all fell to her. She also had to act as quality controller, but when something failed the test it took courage to say so. For the first time, Octavia was experiencing how thin the line between poverty and ruin could be. On one occasion Clara, a toymaker, had her work returned. 'She burst into tears, and said that her mother would beat her if she did not take back the money expected of her.'

The post at the Ladies' Guild was an invaluable first step for Octavia. She had 'a little room, all to myself', as she wrote to Gertrude. Busy with writing, her pot plants, drawing and reading, she was forming the enthusiasms and formulating the ideas that would guide her for life. Significantly, she had been reading Ruskin's *Modern Painters* ('it was so very beautiful'), and had plans to visit the Dulwich Art Gallery. It was a fertile and intense period for her. In a single leap, she left childhood for adult life, very much as a working-class child would have done. There were few enough glimpses of adolescence.

Octavia formulated in this first job the principles of a lifetime. Although she was nominally the manager of the little enterprise, she also undertook to educate the rough children and instil in them the aspiration to break out of the trap of their impoverished lives.

A glimpse of the toymakers' day was given by a writer in Charles Dickens' *Household Words*. The familiarity of the anonymous writer with the subject is easily explained; it was Caroline Southwood Hill.[7] The article, entitled 'Ragged Robin' after the child whose story is woven into the piece, opens with a description.

There is a large, light, lofty workshop, situated in one of the best thoroughfares of the town, in which are occupied about two dozen girls between the ages of eight and seventeen. They make choice furniture for dolls' houses.[8] They work in groups, each group having its own department of the little trade . . . A young lady whose age is not so great as that of the majority of the workers – only whose education has been infinitely better – rules over the little band; apportions the work; distributes the material; keeps the accounts; stops the disputes; stimulates the intellect, and directs the recreation of all. The Autocrat of all the Russias has not a sway more despotic than Miss O.P.Q.; but the two potentates differ in this, that the one governs by fear, the other by affection.

It is not hard to guess the identity of their ruler.

Caroline Hill described the toymakers as 'singing in chorus, as they sat at labour, a song about buttercups and daisies', and the entry of a little girl, dressed in a pair of boys' boots, familiar to the other children from the Ragged School. She was soon fitted out and joined the workers. The children ate together, putting a shilling of their wages back towards 'a wholesome and sufficient meal' – a stew and hot potatoes. 'This was an arrangement of Miss O.P.Q.'s; who had remarked with sorrow the unwholesome food brought by the children, and that even sometimes they brought with them none at all.' After lunch they tended their gardens, and within three-quarters of an hour were 'all happily seated again at their work'. Other people come and go. 'Edith' was Emily and 'Miss Anna' who took lessons at four o'clock was Miranda. They started with writing, then geography and history.

It was a sunny story, with a poignant tale within it. Robin was sent home with a message to her mother, that she should come dressed cleanly. She never came back to work but visited the workroom, burdened with three small children, some weeks later. 'Miss O.P.Q.' was not there but later went to look for the child at home. 'It looked too dirty to enter: but one of the girls who acted as guide mounted the stairs and on a dark landing Robin was found washing sheets, with which she stood upon a three-legged stool to struggle.' Then, Caroline Hill wrote, 'she was seen no more.'[9]

By contact with these girls, and such glimpses of their lives as she gained from visiting some of their homes, Octavia was learning first-hand about the conditions of the very poor. Measuring the pinched simplicity of her home against the utter poverty of these, she was aghast. As she grappled with these new impressions, always against the background of F. D. Maurice's inspiring sermons and

Ruskin's magnetic writings, she was turning over in her mind what she could do. 'I must bring home to them some of the gladness which they see around them . . . There is time enough for Christmas to become solemn, when it has become joyful and dear.' That year Miranda wrote a play, the first of many she was to write for later generations of children and tenants, [10] and Octavia helped the toy-makers to perform it. She tried to read to them for three hours a week, and encouraged them to go to Sunday School. Octavia offered the children organized Saturday outings, parties, and chances to learn; their welfare, in the fullest sense, became her concern. She was also increasingly aware of the connection between the education and employment of children; 'principally because, unless you can develop the minds of your workers, they never can become intelligent, or qualify themselves to fill better situations.' [11]

The Ladies' Guild had brought Caroline, and soon brought her daughters, into the orbit of the informal group known as the Christian Socialists. Alongside various publishing enterprises, and the running of a night school for poor boys, the Christian Socialists were becoming increasingly involved in similar co-operative associations. Caroline Southwood Hill found herself once again on the fringes of a radical circle.

The Christian Socialists were a heterogeneous group centred upon the influential figure of F. D. Maurice. [12] Noted as a preacher who had turned from Unitarianism to an idiosyncratic position close to the Church of England, he combined the academic with the apocalyptic. [13] The question of whether his theology was universal or obscurantist occupied many leading minds of the day. Some people found his sermons uplifting – 'spiritual champagne' was one phrase – but not everyone agreed. The nine-year-old Mary Hughes was taken to hear him; 'while Father was listening with rapt attention, or else asleep, I never could feel the slightest interest in the sermon, as Mr Maurice used to speak all the time as if he were weeping.' [14] Many, adults included, found him baffling – among them Gladstone, who considered him 'difficult to catch, and still more difficult to hold'. Aubrey de Vere considered that listening to Maurice was 'like eating pea soup with a fork'. [15] One lady admirer wrote, years later, to another with some of her worries about the great man. Although he had 'one of the most saintly natures that ever were condemned to sojourn in the world . . . the rhetorical character of his mind . . . jars against me; the pouring out of his indefinite, and yet vehement ideas, as it were, *over* all the difficulties that they do not touch, which always stirs in me an almost bitter sense of all the difficulties.'[16]

In early 1848 John Ludlow,[17] a lawyer, Charles Kingsley,[18] then still an unknown country vicar, and F. D. Maurice had decided to publish a newspaper, inspired by Cobbett's *Political Register*, in which to express their disenchantment with the state of society. It was called *Politics for the People*. It did not last long but it sowed the seeds for its successor, the *Christian Socialist* which Ludlow edited, with Maurice effectively as editor-in-chief and Kingsley a contributor. Miranda recalled that Octavia carried copies around and slept with one under her pillow.

Although the earlier paper foundered after a few months, it gave rise to an informal discussion group around Maurice. Potential members were taken to tea with Maurice and to hear him preach at Lincoln's Inn Chapel where he was chaplain; if interested, they were invited to join the weekly meeting in which readings from the Bible were used to focus on contemporary social problems.[19] Maurice was 'Master', or 'Prophet' – titles which his disciples used without any sign of embarrassment.

As a more practical contribution to social reform, the group set up a night school in Little Ormond Yard in Holborn, which opened in September 1848 and soon expanded to offer daytime classes for both boys and girls. The school, needing teachers, attracted new adherents to the Christian Socialists. Two barristers joined their ranks: F. J. Furnivall,[20] who brought exuberance and eccentricity to the movement, and Thomas Hughes,[21] who despite his disarmingly hearty manner was deeply committed to social work. There were at first no working-class participants, but this was rectified when the Scottish tailor, Walter Cooper, an active Chartist, joined them in 1849.[22] A series of fortnightly public meetings between working men and gentlemen were instigated, held at the Cranbourne Coffee House off Leicester Square. According to Ludlow, 'The result of the conferences was to satisfy us that social and not political questions were what lay nearest to the heart of the thinkers among the working class.'[23]

When Kingsley could manage to get there from his Hampshire parish, he cross-questioned the Chartist men ceaselessly, collecting material for his novel, *Alton Locke* (published in 1850) a powerful indictment of sweated labour and insanitary conditions.[24] *Yeast*, the novel he published the following year, took the theme of neglectful landlords.[25] Maurice was unable to express his ideas clearly

[45]

on paper and Kingsley had a fearful stutter. As a result Kingsley's writings had much of Maurice in them, as Maurice's public utterances did of Kingsley.

To cement the links with Chartists and working men, the Christian Socialists decided to promote a network of workers' co-operatives. Despite Maurice's stated dislike of organizations, he did not object. Walter Cooper was the key figure in the first Association, the Working Tailors' Association. Maurice, in his son's phrase, wanted 'to Christianize Socialism, not to Christian-Socialize the universe'. It was perhaps symptomatic of Maurice's confusing theology and thinking that he should have become the architect of a movement which he did not, intrinsically, support.

The Associations gave the Christian Socialists their sense of purpose and identity. About ten were formed in 1850, though not as speedily as the promoters expected, nor any outside London. The central figure in this movement was, relatively, a late-comer, Edward Vansittart Neale.[26]

Neale, a wealthy man from a landowning family which counted Oliver Cromwell amongst its forebears, and whose uncle was the abolitionist William Wilberforce, eventually ruined himself in his support for the co-operative movement. It was estimated that he poured over £40,000 – some said £60,000 – into the Associations.[27] Despite the ethos of self-help, the main support thus came from a philanthropist. Some observers saw the irony. John Ludlow considered that 'Neale's purse gave a premature and factitious expansion to the movement. It soon became known – and all such knowledge leads to exaggeration – that there was money to be had at the office of the Society for working men who chose to set up Associations, and applications poured down upon us for help.'[28]

The Council of the Promoters of the Working Men's Associations did not approve of this untrammelled offer and it was left to Neale to make the advances on an individual basis. That was unsatisfactory, for 'if the Council lent £50 from its funds, and Neale lent £500, it is obvious that he became . . . ten times as important as the Council at large.' In Ludlow's view, 'Neale's liberal purse was one great means of flooding the field of Association with mushroom bodies devoid of all self-reliance.'

The Ladies' Guild was just one among the many co-operative associations that bloomed, and then withered, in the early 1850s. But for Ludlow, it had an important result:

[46]

It brought into our movement Mrs Hill's daughters, one of whom was the now well-known Miss Octavia Hill, one of the ablest, most self-devoted and most admirable of the distinguished group of female workers in the latter half of the 19th century. When it is recollected that Mrs Nassau Senior, another member of that group, was Thomas Hughes' sister, I think it may be claimed for Christian Socialism that it has been a powerful leaven in the work of both sexes.

Caroline Hill's own retrospective judgement was not dissimilar. Despite the failure of the Guild, which she claimed to have foreseen from the beginning, the co-operative initiative as a way of organizing women's work turned out to justify faith in the idea. In 1883 Mary Llewellyn Davies, daughter of the Revd John Llewellyn Davies, founded the Women's Co-operative Guild, which by 1930 would claim 1,400 branches and 67,000 members.

The Hills were often in F. D. Maurice's congregation at the Lincoln's Inn Chapel. Octavia was an avid listener, and an impressionable one. Where Maurice was, Octavia was often to be found. 'I walked twice to Mile End to hear Maurice and Kingsley preach. I never leave London when Mr Maurice is here.'[29] One Christmas she asked her mother if she might join the family later, so as not to miss his Christmas Eve sermon.

Soon they all got to know Maurice personally. As Caroline later wrote: '*Now* [Octavia's] religion – which purposely had been left untouched by her mother – took definite shape.' Octavia enjoyed fixed services and forms of prayer, as she told Mary Harris later when comparing the structured service to the freer Friends' Meeting. Writing to Gertrude in 1854 she told her she had just come back from church. 'Mr Maurice has been speaking today of sacrifice as the link between man and man, and man and God, it was such a sermon, one feels as if all peace and quiet holiness were round one, everything appears to have a beauty and calm in it . . . and to shed a light on all dark, and difficult things, on sorrows, and loneliness.'

Maurice's particular kind of preaching appealed in a highly emotional way to his listeners. Octavia's religion, a strong core to which she held with increasing faith, was not a questing one; it laid down principles, of service, duty and of individual responsibility which she applied to herself and her family and those with whom she worked. The idea of service was often the way in which Victorian women philanthropists expressed their religious impulses, rather than in more contemplative or purely doctrinal fashion.[30] Miranda observed that, in Octavia's case, 'all the depth and ardour of her nature were called out by her faith which was ever the underlying motive and guide of her whole life.'

Miranda, Emily and Octavia were all baptized and confirmed in the Church of England. Maurice was Octavia's sponsor for baptism, presumably since it was under his influence that she had followed him out of the Unitarian congregation and into the Established church. She was confirmed in 1857 by Bishop Tait.[31] Gertrude and Florence remained, with their mother, Unitarian.

Octavia in her teens was very prone to uncritical admiration, and several of the Christian Socialists became her heroes. She admired Neale enormously. He gave her a copy of Maurice's *Prophets and Kings of the Old Testament* for her fifteenth birthday, and she declared: 'It seems such a glory that he does look upon us . . . not merely as receivers of wages, that he considers us workers with him.' It set the model for her idea of fellow-workers.

Some of the Christian Socialists attracted by force of personality; Frederick James Furnivall was one such. 'Mr Furnivall I admire more and more the more I know and read of him; and, as to Mr Ludlow, certainly there is not (excepting Mr Furnivall) such a person in the whole world. He has the largest, clearest, best-balanced mind joined to the truest most earnest wish to help the working classes,' Octavia wrote to her closest sister, Miranda, in June 1852. Not everyone thought as she did. John Ludlow described Furnivall as 'a terrible thorn in Mr Maurice's side . . . I believe that there are few men who, meaning so well, have done more mischief.'[32] Ludlow was intensely religious and his antagonism towards Furnivall was largely because Furnivall was irreligious.

In 1854, a meeting took place of the Council of Promoters of the Working Men's Associations, at which Maurice was the President, Charles Kingsley was the speaker, and Caroline Hill, Miranda and Octavia were in the audience, together with Mary Rogers and her father.[33] The sixth member of their group was Emma Cons, exactly Octavia's contemporary and whom she regarded as something of a protégée.

Emma was of German descent; her mother had seven children, the youngest of whom was Elizabeth, Lilian Baylis' mother. She was hoping to be an artist and had been a student at the Art School in

Gower Street before coming to Mrs Hill's to help at the Guild. As in Octavia's case, Emma Cons's family had to earn for itself, since her father was sick; and soon she was helping with the toymakers too. She seems to have released Octavia's adolescent high spirits with her own carefree personality, which was underpinned by an equally powerful sense of moral purpose.

Of all Octavia's friends, Emma was to be the one who mirrored her own achievements most closely and gave her the sense that she was not working alone. Writing to Mary Harris in 1857, Octavia told her something of Emma. 'She has now thoroughly established herself, and has begun to study, walk, think, draw, be entirely independent of me . . . whoever cares to break through her shell will be well rewarded . . . I find in her a strength and energy which is quite refreshing, and consign to her much which I should otherwise under- take myself.'

The slightly patronizing note, remarkable in one aged seventeen, is lightened by admiration.

> I feel, in Miss Cons, whose growth I have watched eagerly, an amazing perseverance, a calmness, a power, and a glorious humility before which I bow, and which I feel may be destined to carry out great works more nobly. I am particularly glad that she has friends, as I find that now instead of giving her my society, I can only give her my friendship and sympathy.

Octavia's work and sense of purpose were coming together; the intensity that the Howitts, amongst others, had noticed in her even as quite a small child was now dominant in her personality.[34] On a visit to the Howitts' cousins, the Harrisons in Romford, she wrote to Emily describing an enjoyable evening: 'gathered round the fire . . . we talk of the Guild, of Ruskin, of the poor, of education, of politics and history.' It was hardly carefree chatter.

In July 1855 some friends of the Harrisons asked to come and see the toymakers' work. Octavia described it all in her letter, as it had developed. 'It is a wonderfully interesting work, at times a difficult one; thrown so much together as we all are . . . we have at last broken thro' the wall of ice that has surrounded these children's hearts, threatening to shape them into machines, not to educate them as human beings, having individuality, powers of perception and reflec- tion.' She continued: 'I do not think the influence that the rich and poor might have upon one another has been at all understood by either. I think we have all taken it too much for granted . . . that the giving is all on one side, the receiving on the other.' But, she ended the long letter, it was God's work.

In Mary Harrison Octavia had found another kindred spirit. 'Your letters have given me much pleasure because they are assurances that we are not working utterly alone.' She described some of the inherent conflicts in her work. 'Fancy appealing to a child's sense of duty to do something which will delay her work, prevent her earning so much as she would otherwise have done, perhaps deprive her of a meal, very often of a new pair of shoes!' The work was both rewarding and impossible; 'they will do anything *for you*, they will do hardly anything because it is right.'[35] After the visit of the Harrisons' friends, Mary wrote again, suggesting that Octavia bring the children to Romford. Octavia was delighted to accept.

The outing to the Harrisons' pleasant house, Marshals, with its large gardens and lake, was a happy break in the routine and the children were thrilled by it all. For the first attempt at a longer outing, it was a good choice of destination. Typical Yorkshire people, the Harrisons had an easy sense of hospitality and made the children feel as much at home as possible. If the expedition had an impact on the children it also made a strong impression on the Harrison family. One of them remembered, years later, Octavia's arrival. 'She walked in, a little figure in a long skirt, seeming much older than her seventeen years, and followed by a troup of poor and many of them ragged children. They came from back streets and crowded hovels.'

Caroline Hill described the same expedition in her article in *Household Words*. The Harrisons had had twenty-five visitors. 'Unfortunately they had a wet day: but all enjoyed the drive, and kept up their spirits by loud choruses. Many of the girls had scarcely ever – some had never – seen the country. So far all had been laughing and talking; but, on entering a fine elm-tree avenue leading to the house they visited, they were subdued and became silent.'

Given umbrellas and overshoes, they went out to explore, fascinated particularly by the great conservatories. There was a generous meal, and someone played the piano. One of the Harrison sons wanted to capture the visit in a photograph; 'when all was settled, great misfortune got among the chemicals, and the photograph did not succeed.' The youngest Harrison daughter, Lucy, rowed the children

around the lake.[36] Back in London the toymakers talked of little else –
the boat, the water, the garden, the flowers. But the spell had gone and
the children, Octavia found, were up to their old tricks. They were
constantly quarrelling and she had no idea how to stop it.

In Caroline Hill's view the Guild transformed her family's fortunes,
even though 'the articles manufactured were not saleable and after
enormous pecuniary sacrifices on the part of one of the most generous
of men the institution was closed.'[37] In fact there had also been other
difficulties.

Neale had objected to Miranda reading the Bible to the children,
although she was sure that they enjoyed it. F. D. Maurice had offered
to take a Bible class for the toymakers but he had become a rather
suspect figure in religious circles. As early as 1853 Octavia had written
to her sisters: '(don't tell *anyone*) that they have discovered heresy in
Professor Maurice's last book, and he will probably be expelled from
the Church.' He was not, but that year saw him lose his post as
Professor of Theology at King's College, because of the views expressed in his *Theological Essays*. The prospect of Maurice coming to
the Guild therefore horrified the evangelical ladies who supported it,
and who sent to it the toymaker children from the Ragged School
Union. They threatened to withdraw all support if Maurice gave his
Bible class. Caroline protested, and she was dismissed in late 1855.
The Guild did not last long after her departure, although the toymaking, which was at the centre of the dispute, carried on a few
more months.

As the future for the Guild began to look increasingly precarious,
Octavia was weighing up her options. On her seventeenth birthday
she wrote to Mary Harris: 'If I leave here, I intend to continue to
support myself if possible, if I can keep body and soul together. I have
just completed some work for Ruskin. When I take it home, I intend to
learn whether he thinks it any use for me to go on drawing; whether
there is any hope of employment . . . If *not* I intend to begin to study
with all energy, to qualify myself as a governess.'[38]

Octavia had first encountered John Ruskin in the pages of *Modern
Painters*.[39] For years she had been reading his resounding phrases,
memorizing pages at a time, but he had remained a distant idol. In
November 1853 she defended him to Gertrude: 'If . . . *The Times*
accuses him of affectation of style and want of humility, I entirely deny
the first charge; as I think there is never a single word he writes, which
could have been left out without loss, or changed without spoiling the

idea.' A week later Ruskin met his fifteen-year-old apologist for the first time, when he came to visit the Guild.

Octavia reported the meeting. 'Ruskin has been here. All went as well as I could possibly wish . . . he offered to lend us some things [i.e. pictures] to copy.' He impressed her deeply and, 'you would have said with me that it was utterly wonderful to think that that was the man who was accused of being mad, presumptuous, conceited and prejudiced.'[40]

In 1855 Ruskin suggested that he should train Octavia as a copyist. There was a considerable demand for careful copies of old master works and Ruskin used them as aids in teaching and to illustrate his own writings. Before the introduction of cheap colour printing, copies served the function of modern reproductions and posters of works of art. It was in this year that he had first thought of founding a working brotherhood (which he referred to for some time as the Protestant Convent Plan) along the lines of a medieval scriptorium, to copy illuminations.[41] He wrote to Octavia suggesting that she and Emma Cons might 'pay a little visit to my MSS here, they would feel themselves, as far as age and parchment admit of feeling, very much honoured, and I think they and I together might give you some useful hints.'[42]

Octavia told Emily, rather breathlessly, about the first visit to Denmark Hill, in the spring of 1855.[43] 'At last we arrived at a green gate with a lodge . . . Imagine a handsome mansion or large villa, a broad sweep of gravel road leading to it, bordered by a lawn . . . a footman came and showed us upstairs; we entered Mr Ruskin's study, and he was there.' The holy of holies was dark, with heavy furniture, walls covered with pictures, the table covered with papers, a cabinet of shells and a couple of dead ferns. He showed them illuminated manuscripts and criticized Octavia's drawing for its poor colour sense but otherwise complimented her. They discussed beauty and pleasure, country and city, and much more.

Octavia had high hopes 'that, well-used, this friendship(?), so happily begun, may be a long and growing one; that I have seen a world of beauty; and that this might be the opening to a more glorious path; and that I would give years, if I could bring to Ruskin "the peace which passeth all understanding."?'

As the future of the Guild looked increasingly unsure, Octavia turned to Ruskin for support for it. He offered partial support in his reply. 'I will do what I can. I hope I *can* be of use . . . I *hate shares*, and abhor anything in that form to the uttermost. I can only help you by taking work, or subscribing. That I will do, but at present I would rather take work, because I don't want my name to be connected with too many *new* plans at once; it weakens my influence.'[44] His gesture was to commission a consolidated glass table from the Guild, ornamented with bramble leaves surrounded by a rousing passage from one of the psalms.

Despite the inevitability of the closure of the Guild, which happened in early 1856, it came as a grave disappointment to Octavia. She referred to 'the utter failure of that for which we have all struggled so long and hard'. The experience hardened her resolve to work for others. 'I care but little for any system of division of profits, although it may bear witness for a great truth . . . That which I *do* care for is the intercourse, sympathy, self-sacrifice, and mutual help which are called out in fellow-workers.'[45]

She considered colouring in photographs or engraving watches, which Emma Cons had now begun to learn,[46] and which she felt 'affords a prospect of establishing a Guild gradually'. Whatever she was going to do must not 'separate me from that social work which I have learned to prize so highly'. She also had high hopes of employment vested elsewhere. 'One other path is open. I have to write to Ruskin this week . . .' Within a few days, Ruskin had offered Octavia paid employment, copying illuminations.

Although there was an age difference between them of twenty years and she was now an employee, Octavia assumed the role of one of Ruskin's older women friends, to whom he turned for advice, rather than that of one of his innumerable adolescent 'pets'. He was soon addressing letters to 'my dear Octavia', and she confided to Mary Harris: 'I rejoice very much in the words themselves . . . I think they show he wishes to know more of us.' She and Ruskin were developing a relationship of a rather special order.

CHAPTER 3

Classes

EARLY in 1856 F. D. Maurice offered Octavia the post of Secretary to the women's classes at the Working Men's College, for £26 a year. It was timely and practical support, for although Edward Vansittart Neale continued to finance the toymaking venture, its situation was increasingly precarious after the collapse of the Ladies' Guild, and Octavia had been looking out for extra paid work which could be combined with supervising the toymakers, so that she could give them her services free. (Another economy was to move the toymakers from Russell Place to a room in Devonshire Street.)

Maurice's offer was a partial solution. Octavia was also trying to continue her own studies, with a view to teaching. When Octavia was at the College, for two hours each afternoon, Emily stepped in to keep an eye on the children. It was the beginning of a lifetime of deputizing for her sister.

The Working Men's College had grown out of the experience of the Little Ormond Yard school, as well as the lectures and classes given to members of the Working Men's Associations. In particular it was inspired by the People's College in Sheffield, founded in 1842. (There women attended the classes alongside the men.[1]) The Christian Socialists as a group had turned with relief to the setting up of a Working Men's College and away from the thankless task of organizing producer co-operatives.

The College now brought others into the Christian Socialist ambit, notably John Ruskin, whom F. J. Furnivall had described a few years earlier:

A fair man, with rough light hair and reddish whiskers . . . how vivid he is to me still! The only blemish in his face was the lower lip, which protruded somewhat: he had been bitten there by a dog in his early youth. But you ceast to notice this as soon as he began to talk. I never met any man whose charm of manner at all approacht Ruskin's. Partly feminine it was, no doubt; but the delicacy, the sympathy, the gentleness and affectionateness of his way, the fresh and penetrating things he said, the boyish fun, the earnestness, and the interest he showed in all deep matters, combined to make a whole which I have never seen equalld.[2]

Ruskin taught at the Working Men's College from 1854 to 1858, and sporadically thereafter. John Ludlow remembered him as a teacher: 'Ruskin in his class was charming, so long as you were towards him in the position of a disciple – so long as you were in the looking-up attitude . . . but you must walk on his lines, do as he bid you.'[3] Before long Ruskin began to view the College, with its largely artisan students, as a useful source of labour at Denmark Hill.

Ironically enough, Ruskin was among those who failed to appreciate Maurice's profundities. Emily wrote to Florence about Ruskin's birthday visit to Octavia in 1858, when the main topic of conversation seems to have been Maurice. 'Ruskin . . . said he did not know much about Mr Maurice; he had not read much of his, he found it such hard work . . . He seemed like a man who did not see clearly, and was always stretching out, moving on in the right direction, but in a fog.' Octavia had disputed this view: 'Mr Maurice quite understands what he means himself; and the difficulty which people find in understanding him, arises partly from his style, and partly that people require to understand his way of putting things.' Ruskin countered: 'I had always thought that the very greatest men were essentially simple. The only great man I know who is not, Dante, throws out a word or two quite knowing what he means, and says "Think out that," and people do not know which end of the things they have got, and so quarrel over what he does mean. But when he says anything directly, it is very clear and simple.' And so the argument had continued, with Emily taking Maurice's part with particular enthusiasm.[4] Ruskin enjoyed his status as a hero and did not appreciate sharing it.

Maurice's fall from official grace over his theological views meant that he was available to be the head of the Working Men's College. His opening lecture at their premises in Red Lion Square was given on 31 October 1854. George MacDonald was in the audience. The Scottish poet, future novelist and author of fairy tales was himself enmeshed in theological doubts about the unremittingly Calvinistic interpretation of Christian doctrine, and had recently given up the ministry. Dogged by bad health and financial worries, he was looking for work and was taken on to teach poetry at the College.

As early as 1855 the question of classes for working women had been raised. In the event these classes began in January 1856, at Red Lion Square. Emily Winkworth, who had helped arrange the introductory lectures, described the timetable: 'Two hours every afternoon. The first hour gentlemen are to give lectures to the women on history, Bible, domestic economy, and health. The second hour ladies are to teach them writing, needlework, geography, arithmetic etc . . . Mr Maurice does manage everything so nicely about these classes. I like him because he is so despotic.'[5]

One of the earliest lecturers to the working women's class was George MacDonald, who addressed them on poetry. Octavia and Emily were there, obviously attentive amidst a rather unresponsive audience. MacDonald noted their interest and invited them to visit him and his wife. It was the beginning of a close and lifelong friendship.

Her post at the Working Men's College cemented Octavia's friendship with Furnivall and Ludlow, and of course ensured that she was never far from Maurice. Furnivall fascinated Octavia; it is clear that his gaiety and carefree personality were highly attractive – later on he was revealed (or so his detractor, Ludlow, wrote) in a less upright light.[6] Furnivall was the organizer of social events at the College and planned some fairly punishing excursions. The half-day Sunday walks had the following schedule; 'meet King's Cross at three, walk to Epping – 16 miles – by seven, tea till eight, and back at King's Cross by twelve, all done to the minute, whatever the weather was.' St Albans, forty-four miles there and back, was another destination. Tea with Ruskin, also on the College social calendar, must have been a welcome respite.[7]

The Revd Llewelyn Davies,[8] brother of Emily Davies[9] whom Octavia would later support in her campaigns for women's higher education, became Vice-Principal of the College. He had been brought in following a letter he had written to the *Spectator* refuting Kingsley on 'the state of mind at Cambridge'. Before long, he became in Ludlow's view at least, an authoritarian exponent of 'Mauricianism'.[10] He came to Christ Church, Cosway Street off Lisson Grove in 1856 after serving as a curate at St Anne's, Limehouse and St Mark's, Whitechapel. Later on he was to be a pillar of the Charity Organization Society, much influenced by what he had seen in these poor parishes.

Tom Hughes had become a friend, too. He taught gymnastics at the College, fittingly for one whose faith was decidedly muscular, and joined Furnivall in organizing the social side of the College. Octavia quickly read *Tom Brown's Schooldays* which, she told Mary Harris, was one of the noblest books she had read, although she conceded that people might raise objections to it. Hughes, she told Mary, was 'one of the brightest, best men in the world'.

The status of women in the College was a contentious topic. 'I hear that . . . it was proposed that women should be admitted to the General Meeting. The idea was laughed at. Someone then proposed that the women's classes should be held in the evening; and the question was referred to the Council.' Whatever the governing members of the College thought, Maurice recorded that 'pupils . . . would have been quite willing that the women should have been instructed, if we had thought fit, in the same classes with themselves. This plan, after careful consideration, we determined not to attempt.'[11]

Significantly, the women's classes – which in the event took place in the afternoon between three and five – were never envisaged as being for the working classes. They aimed, Maurice wrote, to 'bring different classes more into fellowship with each other, which should educate ladies for occupations wherein they could be helpful to the less fortunate members of their own sex . . .' The prospectus emphasized that the teaching hours of the women's classes had been chosen 'because they do not interfere with the hours of the classes for Working Men'. It also offered, in addition to the more academic subjects taught by women, a selection of domestic subjects which for some bizarre reason would be delivered by gentlemen. They included 'the Management of Children', 'the Management of Houses', care of health and sickness, 'the duties we owe to each other' and 'what women may do to make their sons good citizens and good men'.[12]

Octavia's own firm and unequivocal view of these classes was given in her first published work, a two-part article for the first volume of the *Working Men's College Magazine*, written a few years later in 1860. The first part was on the general benefits of education for women, although not those 'commonly called Working Women'. A woman should hold her own in matters of education. 'The man who has felt himself benefited by the study of mathematics, or philology, or natural science, desires that his wife, or his sister, or his daughter, should share the gain with him. It is for her own sake, as well as for the pleasure which will accrue to him from her learning to sympathize in his tastes, that he urges her to go to the afternoon classes at his own College.' Such a woman, having finished her household tasks, 'enjoys the quiet of Great Ormond Street, enjoys the notion of having got into an intellectual atmosphere for a brief space of time.' After all, 'One tough little bit of study . . . must be more beneficial to a young woman's mind than any amount of desultory rambling or scrambling through cheap periodicals.'

In the second part Octavia wrote 'Hints on a few principles of Instruction of working women, suggested by a teacher'. Education should not be a class luxury. She believed in 'opening out . . . fresh sources of joy, both by revealing facts new and wonderful to them, as in natural history and geography; by calling out new powers, as in arithmetic; and by cultivating such feelings as the delight in music and colour.' Why not organize 'singing classes . . . into choirs to give concerts in wretched neighbourhoods?' Drawing, as Mr Ruskin had pointed out, leads to observation and then delight. Reading and writing are the prelude to the pleasures of English Literature, which can be as instructive as it is enjoyable. 'What class reading the description of the storming of Front-de-Boeuf's castle in "Ivanhoe" . . . but would wish to understand the plan of a Norman castle, and would retain a clear idea concerning it?'

'OH' ended her piece: 'there is a tendency to relax study in the sense of usefulness, and new-found delight in teaching. This should be guarded against, and those who have commenced teaching should be strenuously exhorted to continue learning.' Octavia had begun to add teaching to her administrative duties at the College and so she was here expressing her own sentiments.

Barbara Leigh Smith,[13] a friend from the Highgate days, had also turned to teaching, founding the radical Portman Hall School in 1854. Octavia remained in contact with Barbara, and in 1856 she helped her orchestrate the campaign for a Married Women's Property Act in order to remedy the inequitable situation whereby women lost all property rights on marriage. Octavia felt that women's education and property rights were entirely reasonable expectations. They collected 24,000 signatures and the names on the petition presented to Parliament on 14 March included most of the old Highgate circle – Anna Mary and Mary Howitt, Elizabeth Barrett Browning, Eliza Fox – as well as Barbara and Bessie Rayner Parkes, Jane Carlyle and Mrs Gaskell.

Anna Mary Howitt wrote to her sister Margaret to tell her it had been announced in Parliament. 'The London signatures are within a small number of three thousand . . . Yesterday evening, as it was growing dusk, Octavia made her appearance, looking so bright and happy. She had been taking her Ragged School children for a walk in the Highgate fields; and dismissing them, came here. She helped mother to paste the signature sheets, which have all been sent in today.' Despite the backing of Lord Brougham and the Law Amendment Society, that campaign achieved no change in the law.[14] The Act was finally passed in 1870 but was not fully comprehensive until a further Act of 1882.

Octavia was by now already taking the role of the head of her own household, despite her youth. Caroline Hill had left London for some months after her abrupt dismissal from the Guild, and Octavia found herself in charge. In her mother's words, she 'was found to possess such excellent judgement and management of money that her grandfather gave into her hands the money he allowed the family and from that time forward the whole direction of its affairs very much devolved on her, she was the moving spirit. The trust was nobly carried out. She never incurred a debt, she never in her whole life borrowed a penny.' She had even paid off 'two rather substantial debts of her mother's, debts which could not legally be cleared, but which certainly ought to be paid.'

Each of the sisters had begun to contribute towards the accumulation of debt, as well as current expenses, as they started work. Octavia's £100 legacy from her grandfather, when she was twenty-three, allowed her finally to clear a debt which, according to Miranda, had been incurred before she was born.

Octavia was deeply respectful of money. Early on she was struck by the fact 'that to one the shilling was of as much importance as the pound to another.' She was a believer in want as a stiffener of character and lived strictly and abstemiously herself. It was significant that she exercised discipline among the toymakers by means of fines. 'Somehow personal poverty is a help to me,' she wrote, much later. 'It keeps me more simple and energetic, and somehow low and humble and hardy, in the midst of a somewhat intoxicating power.'[15]

Yet her family underestimated the burden that such responsibility cast upon a deeply conscientious character. By July 1857, when she was still only eighteen, she wrote to her confidante Mary Harris: 'I feel sometimes frightened at what I have undertaken. I have learnt since the autumn of 1855 many things, and among others that we undertake more than we know when we say, "Leave us alone, we ask no more help from you . . ."' Money was a constant worry. Writing to Gertrude in November 1857, Octavia confessed that she was out of spirits having found even more debts than she knew about; she wanted to ask Gertrude's advice about it all.[16]

Nor were Dr Southwood Smith's own financial worries yet behind him, as he told his daughter Emily in a letter enclosing a letter of credit. 'Margaret [Gillies] has been very successful with her pictures this year which have all sold excepting one . . . This success has come just in time to save us from the pain of giving up The Pines for the summer. We had made up our minds to do so, the necessity of which was imperative.' He was relieved not to sacrifice the house and glad that 'we shall be enabled to live here as well in the beautiful as the rough part of the year.'[17]

In many ways Octavia took over more than just financial responsibility for the family. Her mother was cheerfully engrossed in her writing, and Octavia found that when 'you have taken on yourself the wants, longings, desires of people, you are bound not only to let them live, but to live happily.' They wanted amusements, holidays, to see their friends and give them presents, 'and if you do your duty you will give it to them, without their seeing that it is any trouble, in the smile or the puzzled thought as you promise to do it.' When she was small, her sisters had teased her and called her their 'brother' – that ability to bear responsibility for other people until her back broke under it misled people into imagining that there was no limit to her strength.

The copying for Ruskin proved both arduous and enjoyable.[18] He was a stern taskmaster; accuracy was everything, he considered, and 'you yourself are nothing near the mark yet. The Claude foreground, is, however, a step in advance.'[19] Octavia had to fit all her other activities around it – teaching and administrative duties at the College, her own studies, and work with the toymakers, although Emily continued to help out there. But contact with the great man was not to be taken lightly, and she believed that assiduous copying would make a real artist of her. Ruskin, on the other hand, did not want his copyists to entertain unrealistic aspirations as artists.

[60]

Octavia sent Florence some of her paintings, done over the summer and autumn of 1857. Ruskin had just been to see her:

> You do not know how pleased he was with all I had done, or how happy I was that he was pleased. He said I had done an immense quantity of work, and that I was far more accurate than any of his men at the College, whom, you know he teaches every week. He said of one of my drawings, 'This is quite a marvellous piece of drawing, Octavia.' And when I showed him one of my Albert Dürers he exclaimed, 'Is that yours? I was going to say you had been cutting up my print.'[20]

But the worries about the toymaking business were now wearing Octavia down. There had already been alarms about the venture, but always cause for optimism as well. Securing regular orders was only one of her headaches. Some children were dilatory workers, in her view, and she had to complain to their mothers in the hope that they would exert discipline. She had been to a meeting about Ragged Schools. Caroline's ideas spring off the page, though the words are Octavia's: 'I'd rather be a table than a Ragged School child. Not an attempt made to show how the teaching influences the children themselves, plenty of statistics about numbers of Bibles given away etc.'[21]

At best, Octavia's two worlds – the College and the toymakers – could be made to connect. In July 1857 she took the toymaker children to the British Museum ('Oh, these delicious little breaks in the routine, they are so refreshing!') since the elder ones had been to natural history classes at the College. She told Mary Harris: 'I am getting on very well at the College now I have the teaching . . . it was the same with the Toy Workers once. I could not sit down and teach them what twice three was, till they knew how much three flowers or three friends were worth . . .'[22]

The College provided Octavia with stimulus and entertaining company, a welcome respite from the sometimes recalcitrant toymakers. For the autumn, she was to teach reading, writing and arithmetic there: 'all the classes . . . except singing'. It also exemplified a place in which the classes could meet each other in a relaxed way. She described a College *conversazione* as 'a meeting-point for the divided classes, of friendship and mutual help, of earnest study and hard work brightened by all three . . . There stood Mr Maurice, his grave face lighted by a smile of delight and sweetness in the realization of much that he had worked for. And here and there and everywhere glanced the fire of Mr Furnivall's intensely joyous eyes, delighting in all things . . .'[23] So bound up was Octavia now in her London life that she turned down a seaside holiday with her mother and stayed in town for the summer.

The final failure of the toymaking came in the autumn of 1857, not long after Octavia had confidently placed a large order with a wholesaler. Either a default in payment or a fall in orders signalled the end. A nurse from the old Wisbech days undertook to distribute the rest of the toys, agreeing to wait for payment. Caroline Hill wrote: 'I am proud of her, and look upon her as a fellow-worker.' Mrs Wilson, as she had become, was married to a tailor and was a haven for more than toys, for she took in little Amelia (the Ragged Robin of Mrs Hill's article) on one occasion. Other friends also rallied round; notably Mary Harris who had written to inquire how much was needed to keep the enterprise going for another year. But Octavia accepted that it had failed.

Her mother wrote to Emily: 'Ockey begins to-morrow to work at home. I mean to read some nice book to her, and do all I can to make her happy. She is my own brave, beautiful, good, tender Ockey; and it's a hard trial to lose one's post in a Cause.'[24] The work for Ruskin, both so stimulating and so exhausting, was important in carrying Octavia through this demoralizing failure.

There seems to have been a move to bring James Hill, Octavia's father, to London in 1858. Writing to her grandfather ('dearest Booie') Octavia told him she and her sisters had 'been seeing and thinking a great deal about Papa lately', and that 'having seen the utter loneliness and wretchedness of his life, we cannot but feel that it would be well if some of us could be with him.' She wanted to consult him about the plan and declared, 'I cannot write all I have to say.' As a postscript she added that she was sorry to bother him.[25] Nothing further came of the plan.

In January 1859 the family moved from 4 Russell Place. After a short interlude in Francis Street, they settled in an unfurnished house at 103 Milton Street (now Balcombe Street), off Dorset Square. There were three rooms which suited the needs of the reduced family, consisting of Octavia, Caroline Hill, who had returned to full-time teaching, and Emily, who had won a scholarship to Queen's College, Harley Street (set up by F. D. Maurice in 1848 as a foundation of the Governesses' Benevolent Institution).

Mrs Hill wrote to Miranda, who was staying in Florence with her aunt:

> I only came to this house today. It is so very pretty; you and Florence would be enchanted with it. Dear Ockey and Minnie [Emily] must have worked so hard, they would not let me have any trouble but arranged it all, and beautiful indeed it looks: the crimson table cover and chair cover and green carpet and white muslin curtains and white walls with roses, make such a lovely combination, and I enjoy the nice square high rooms.[26]

Dr Southwood Smith had once again come to the rescue, lending the money for the furniture and decoration, and would have to be repaid promptly; so the enjoyment of a prettily furnished house only intensified the pressures of continuous financial worries.

In July 1859 Octavia was in the presence of her grandfather and his old friend Lord Shaftesbury, at the founding of the Ladies' Sanitary Association. Charles Kingsley gave a stirring speech, some of which Octavia reported to Miranda: 'What will be the result, if you succeed in accomplishing your aims . . . very dangerous aims some people would tell you that they are; nothing less than saving alive of some four out of every five (?) children that die annually.' Then in a part of the speech which evidently lodged fast with Octavia, 'he looked upon the legislative part of sanitary reform with something more like despair than ever. They were not reasons connected with this Government, or with any possible Government, but resulted from his consideration of the character of the individuals, into whose possession small houses were passing more and more . . . Therefore he hoped women would go, not only to the occupiers, but to the possessors of the house, and influence people of "our own class."'

This was the germ of Octavia's idea to target and influence landlords, and it was heady stuff. 'It is in the power, I believe, of any woman in this room to save three or four lives, human lives, during the next six months. It is in your power, ladies, and it is so easy.'

Kingsley later reported to Lady Hardinge that the meeting had gone well. The last two speeches had been 'dear old Southwood Smith, the father of all us sanitary reformers, and Lankaster's. I am going to throw myself into this movement. I am tired of most things in the world. Of sanitary reform I shall never grow tired.'[27]

The Ladies' Sanitary Association began by distributing material on

[63]

health legislation to cottagers and artisans. In common with that of other bodies such as Ellen Ranyard's Bible Women, the work depended on visiting, and its strength lay in personal observations of actual conditions.

At this time Octavia was showing the first signs of one of the succession of nervous illnesses that periodically laid her low over the next twenty years or more. She had already had warnings.

> Miss Sterling had a very long conversation with me on the way I am ruining my health, but especially about Sunday work . . . She mentioned it to Mr Maurice . . . He thought that rest was as much a part of God's order as work was; that we have no right to put ourselves out of that order, as if we were above it . . . it is very self-willed to try to do without it; it is really hopeless to try to exist, if one is for ever giving out, and never receiving; nor does he think that the doing of actions rightly, brings with it enough of this receiving.[28]

Octavia found Maurice's advice hard to take and harder still to follow.

By 1859 Octavia's daily schedule was crushing. She had had to stop her own studies, she told Mary Harris, but she was still up at five in the morning to do needlework. After the copying at South Kensington or Dulwich,[29] which might take four or five hours, she had to get back to Great Ormond Street for the Working Women's classes. She often walked there and back to save the fares. She was also giving drawing lessons at Barbara Leigh Smith's Portman Hall School.* On Saturdays she did the mending and accounts. She was driven by desperation to earn the money to clear her father's debts and to pay back her grandfather and free him from the burden of financial responsibility for the family. She also still longed to be an accomplished artist.

Ruskin got her a student's ticket to copy some Turners 'in outline' in Marlborough House.[30] A copy of Bellini's Doge Leonard Loredan from the National Gallery (now in the Ruskin Gallery, Sheffield) was one of the great Venetian works that he encouraged her to copy in watercolour.[31] Despite his unremitting pressure, Octavia often got short shrift from Ruskin. In February 1859 he wrote: 'Any time will do for the Salvator. I thought you would come to a smash with all that sentimental business of teaching and what not – no wonder you've

* See p. 68.

[64]

been ill, but what's the matter that you speak so seriously? Perhaps you oughtn't to work for the present. Let me know. Truly yours affectionately, JR.'

Octavia was now at breaking-point. The physical symptoms of her exhaustion were eye-strain (doubtless exacerbated by the long hours of close work, in particular the copying for Ruskin) and severe back pain. In April 1859 the family persuaded her to go abroad. She viewed the prospect with timidity for she had never left England before. 'It will seem very strange to you, but I dread it. I have been working so long, I don't feel as if I knew how to stop.'[32] The sisters were anxious that the trip would go well. As Emily wrote to Miranda:

> You may think what a state of excitement dear Ockey was in yesterday with seeing Ruskin and with the thought of her journey . . . Her costume looked so pretty and suitable. Gertrude made her a present of such a beautiful black silk dress, so nicely made that it has disclosed to me, what I did not know before, that Ockey has an extremely pretty figure.[33]

In the event Octavia's holiday, in company with the Howitts' niece Mary Harrison, was an unmitigated success. 'I am quietly, splendidly happy,' she wrote to her mother from Dieppe, a very rough crossing notwithstanding. All her verve and vitality returned, almost as if a switch had been flicked on. She missed nothing – the architecture and the landscape, the odd people she met along the way and her attempts at speaking French, which 'increases the fun very much,' as she enthused to Emily. 'I have laughed more since I came to France, than I have done for years, I think.'

She wrote to Gertrude on her return, listing the wild flowers they had seen at Mortain: 'million of flowers, wild hyacinths, cowslips, stellaries, robin hood, orchises, speedwell, buglos, toadflax and numbers more, and all shadowed or lighted by apple and pear trees in full blossom and poplars swaying gently to and fro.' She had scrambled over the moors until she could see Mont St Michel in the distance. 'I delighted in the diligences, we always took the coupe . . . we took off our hats and the wind blew over all those lovely hills . . .'[34]

It might not have been such a restful interval had she chosen Italy as her destination, for Emily had written a vivid series of letters from

Florence at this time, describing the Tuscan revolution, the Grand Duke – 'poor old Hyena' – procrastinating while the crowds proclaimed revolution. 'There is something so beautiful in *unity*, in men forgetting for a time their petty cares and dislikes, enmities, passions, interests, uniting in the great common feeling.' The Hills always stirred to the sound of fellowship.

On her return from Normandy, Octavia launched with new enthusiasm into the old tasks. The most time-consuming of these was, as before, her work for Ruskin. Artistically Octavia was to fail Ruskin's high standards, but he had seen far more in her than a rather average student or apprentice, and he found her sufficiently responsible to be delegated certain tiresome tasks, and people. One of these was Anna Blunden,[35] who was determined to make her way as a painter with Ruskin's help. In 1859 he told her to contact Octavia: 'I have told her to take some charge of you – she is another pupil of mine – quite as good as you are – and much wiser.'

Six weeks later, as Miss Blunden became ever more persistent, he wrote, 'No possibility of seeing you for some days yet. Ask Miss Hill how often I can generally see my pupils . . . meantime paint a single nut – out of shell – from nature as well as you can.[36] I am never angry at your letters – only can't generally read them, and should consider it necessary to stop correspondence if they came often.' That day he also wrote to Octavia: 'Find out if Miss Blunden wants some money and try to explain to her absurdityship how often I can generally see pupils or what time I can spare to them.'

Octavia must have enjoyed the feeling of complicity; Anna Blunden continued to plague him and Ruskin continued to hide behind Octavia's skirts. In March 1860 he sent Anna along to South Kensington to copy Turners, wanting her 'properly paid, as Miss Hill is'. But by May 1860 he had lost patience. 'What in the world should make you think I like talking to you, or letting you talk to me – more than anybody else of my friends of pupils . . . be assured once for all that if you go on in but *one* letter more with any nonsense, I will positively break off all correspondence but through Miss Hill.'[37]

Despite Ruskin's dependence on Octavia's goodwill in these exchanges, he was very sparing in praise for her help with his own work. *Modern Painters V* was published in July 1860, 'with four of my own scraps in it and a word or two in the preface about me,' wrote Octavia to Mary Harris. 'It implies no praise whatever of power or skill, but just says that my help has been, what I hope nearly everyone's is "disinterested". . . . I know no more of what he thinks about my work than I did before.'[38] The bald acknowledgement was to 'Miss Octavia Hill, who prepared the copies which I required from portions of pictures of the Old Masters.'

In her work for him, which continued for ten and a half years, Octavia was rarely encouraged and was often reduced to confusion by his reactions; one day, positive, the next, negative – which were more a reflection of his mood of that day than anything specific. She was often puzzled. 'I wonder why he should speak *so* despisingly of all copies, and yet set me to do them; but some day I shall understand it.'[39]

Ruskin's inconsistent behaviour, raising hopes with praise or promises, and then dashing them, was one of the least attractive aspects of his character. J. W. Bunney, another Working Men's College pupil (who sometimes deputized for Ruskin in teaching Octavia), had far worse experiences than Octavia. Ruskin could be massively insensitive. He was wealthy and enormously gifted and was completely unable to enter the minds of vulnerable people who possessed neither advantage.

Before long Octavia sought other work, where Ruskin's mercurial temperament would not interfere with her progress. In 1864 she took on a difficult drawing for the Society of Antiquaries – a copy of the earliest dated portrait of an Englishman, from 1446. The subject was a Grimstone, an ancestor of Lord Verulam. 'It is rather a grand piece of work; and is to be kept in the gallery of the Society, after being sent to Germany, to be chromolithographed for publication in their "Archaeologia". The Secretary of the National Gallery had noticed my work, and recommended me to the Secretary of the National Portrait Gallery, to do the work. It is expected . . . to lead to much more, and would really make me rich, in spite of myself.'[40] If Ruskin failed to encourage her, she now had independent proof of her abilities.

Despite all the strains in her life, Octavia had a streak of gaiety in her character and Furnivall, the dashing ladies' man, seemed to know how to bring it out. In the summer of 1859 he had given a 'delightful dance', inviting the men and their friends and herself. 'I went with Louisa and Henrietta[41] and a glorious evening we had!' she told Miranda.

The dance did not present Octavia with the same problems of conscience as Sunday outings in Furnivall's company. This was a matter she found increasingly troublesome. Reluctantly, she told Miranda: 'I have been convinced of the necessity of keeping Sunday as a day of rest . . . My own impulse would have been to hold this very firmly and yet go [on the outing], of course attending service but claiming for the remainder of the day the blessing of seeing God's works and friendly intercourse.'[42] She wrote on the subject to Emily, too. 'I'm a little weary of thinking over the Sunday question . . . of course I told Mr F. that I should never dream of entering into a plan involving habitual absence from church; tho' I didn't tell him now how much I can sympathize with the spirit of some people who do.'

Octavia discussed the question with Maurice. 'I have been very much impressed by the good and joy Mr Furnivall's Sunday excursions seem to be giving to the men and to their wives, sisters and friends who from time to time accompany them . . . I imagine, perhaps incorrectly, that you disapprove of these excursions . . . but is not refreshment by seeing friends and change of scene right?'[43]

Maurice's reply was in the negative. She wrote again, as befitted a faithful disciple. 'Your letter has shown me a much deeper meaning in Sunday than I had ever perceived in it; and I see the difficulty about the excursions very clearly, as not speaking to people as spiritual beings, called to full rest in trust in God.' She decided she would not go on the Sunday excursions since Maurice felt so strongly on the subject, but clearly she was far from convinced.

In 1859 Octavia had added to her teaching hours by giving French and drawing lessons at the Portman Hall school. It had been founded in 1854 by Barbara Bodichon and Elizabeth Whitehead.[44] It had remained very much a family enterprise, with two Leigh Smith sisters, Isabella and Anne, helping Barbara, by then Madame Bodichon, who was spending half the year in Algiers with her French husband. The founders had prepared themselves thoroughly for the undertaking – Elizabeth Whitehead had studied at William Ellis' Birkbeck schools in Peckham.

The school's opening had been regarded with some trepidation by traditionalists in education, for it was inspired by the educational ideas of James Buchanan, a Pestalozzian. Pupils wore no uniform and were not punished. It was strictly non-denominational and admitted boys and girls, Jews and Christians, each paying sixpence per week. The school set out to be international, and Garibaldi's son was a pupil. Pupils spent some of their time visiting museums and art galleries and, in line with the genuinely radical nature of the school, ethical readings were substituted for prayers and hymns.

Caroline Hill, with her interest in Pestalozzian education and Robert Owen's ideas, must have supported Octavia's involvement with the school. Barbara Bodichon was an impressive woman, a close friend and confidante of Marian Evans (George Eliot). Elizabeth Whitehead (Mrs Malleson as she became) was, with her husband, the prime mover behind the Working Women's College which opened in 1864 in Queen Square. Octavia joined the Council of its teachers, and presumably continued with the classes she had previously delivered in Great Ormond Street.[45]

Disingenuously, Octavia wrote to Miranda in Italy:

> I do not know how you think or feel about the Portman Hall school. You know that I do not think the omission of all religious teaching a sufficient reason for disapproval to counterbalance the immense good which I consider they are doing there, especially as the teacher and three of the monitors are earnest believers . . . I would not give my whole or main strength to the school unless I were obliged; but I would and do very willingly help.[46]

Octavia, who was missing her sister very much, thought she had found a way to inveigle her home.

> You will wonder why I write all this. It is because they are trying to find a lady to help there; and I have mentioned you to them . . . They first wanted a person's entire time for £100; but now they have resolved to divide their fund, and would probably like to have you for about two or three hours daily except Saturday. I do think that a permanent work of this sort, and among that class of children, would be deeply interesting; that it would make a nice change from private pupils; that you would find Mme Bodichon and Mrs Malleson delightful people to work under.

But, she added, 'I mean to learn what Mr Maurice thinks. Oh, darling, you must come in spring somehow.'

Octavia also wrote about the school to a new friend, Emma Baumgartner, clearly torn between the evident worthiness of the cause and its radical rejection of religious instruction – 'wherefore, say many wise people to me, you as a Christian should not accept it at all. So I have *not* thought; but I suppose I hardly feel sure enough about whether I ought to give my sister advice . . . I think the tendency is . . . to think our faith cramps our labours and narrows our hearts.' But, she added, 'I never would deny faith. I care very little to express it anywhere but in life . . .'[47]

[69]

As usual, Maurice gave a strong opinion. Octavia wrote to her sister with his response: 'He decidedly thinks you ought *not* to undertake it. He says, what one sees at once, that you could not bind yourself not to speak to the children in any way that seemed best to you . . . He was so good, and took a great interest in all our plans.'[48] It was predictable that the Revd Maurice should unequivocally veto the idea for Miranda – he had a much firmer influence there than with the purposeful, and, when necessary, headstrong Octavia.

What kind of person was Octavia, as she approached her twenty-first birthday? She had an extraordinary intensity of purpose, and that purpose was what seemed a God-given task to better lives. Never a theoretician, she had nevertheless spent the previous years listening and talking to John Ruskin and F. D. Maurice: few young women had had such an education. In Miranda's words, 'It is impossible to realize how much of what her life was is due to their help and influence.' Maurice was her spiritual mentor and she turned to him for help with many hard decisions. Ruskin was her aesthetic guide and the confidant with whom she shared her wider hopes. On the practical level, both of them had offered her material help in the form of employment at moments of crisis.

If in many respects the adult Octavia had been formed at fourteen, her views had been leavened by experience, for work with the toymaking children was a hard school. She had met an enormous range of people, from the intellectual giants of the age to humble people living in a degree of poverty of which she had, hitherto, been unaware. Octavia had told Ruskin that she felt much changed, but 'he laughed very kindly, saying, "Oh no, you're not; you're just the same as ever; only you know more."'

Octavia's range of occupations, and the contacts she was making, helped her to gain confidence with all sorts and classes of people. She wanted Mary Harris to join her on the tailors' 'beanfeast' –

It is an annual holiday for the two Associations of Tailors . . . The tailors, their wives and children and friends form the body of the party, and invite Mr Maurice, Mr Neale, Mr Furnivall, Mr Ludlow, Mr Hughes etc. They come, most of them in vans to the Roebuck Inn at Woodford, where they spend the whole day, cricketing, swinging, riding, shooting with bows and arrows etc. After dinner,

Mr Maurice and Mr Cooper and others speak. You know my opinion about classes in society sufficiently to know why I go and why I should rejoice that you should go.[49]

Octavia's own views on class were very determined. 'I don't know what there is in the word "lady" which will connect itself with all kinds of things I despise and hate.' It spoke to her of feeble attitudes, and much 'I would if . . .', as she put it.[50] She wondered what Mary Harris felt on the question – 'how far you approve of intercourse between classes, how far you would do work which is usually done by a lower class, if it were useful but not necessary. Oh, what a power for good anyone has, who does go among people, as if he was one of them, entering into all their thoughts.'

In fact, Octavia was much less narrow in many of her views than Miranda, who hid, under a gentler exterior, a very strict personal code. In a letter to Mary Harris, written around the time of her confirmation, Octavia reported an evening at the house of Mr Spottiswood, a printer who held services there. 'The clergyman, who entoned [sic] the service, was evidently a Puseyite, which Miranda in her bigotry had been mourning ever since . . . but I saw too much in the large, sad, earnest eyes to care whether he preached in black or white.'[51]

In matters of religion Octavia was refreshingly open, and in a letter to Mary Harris, who was one of her several Quaker friends, she commented: 'Thou and I are not further off from one another because we have not attended the same place of worship. God, not churches and creeds, binds us together.'[52] She did not believe in misplaced missionary zeal either, admiring her friend Mary Rogers who worked with Moslem women in Palestine while respecting their faith. 'I have no sympathy with, no admiration for, those who try to *force their* notions, *their* faiths on every one; who decidedly set to work to convert people.' Later on in the same letter she adds, 'People wonder that I will recommend teachers for Unitarian Sunday Schools. The result be on their head not mine.' Many years later she was energetic in dissuading a god-daughter from entering an Anglican order. Her own family, divided between Anglicans and Unitarians, harboured no dissension in these matters, and later on Octavia was to be very sensitive also to the fact that many of her tenants were Roman Catholics.

Octavia's friendships were intense, based upon a shared sense of purpose. There was little opportunity to break out of her zealous circle, bounded by charitable work, religion or education. The sophisticated radicalism of the Portman Hall ladies was foreign to her and her closest friends tended to mirror her own earnest character. She delighted in acquiring new friends and invested a great deal in them. She was rarely disappointed. Emma Baumgartner invited her to stay with her family in Godmanchester:

> As I went down there a perfect stranger, knowing nothing about who they were, and we had no mutual friends, we had to be specially communicative; and so, I suppose, our friendship sprang up more quickly than otherwise it could have done. Then, except at meals, we were quite alone, drawing, walking, rowing or resting. But the principal thing that drew us together was my delight in finding in her a great nobleness of judgement and of sympathy, right views about work, and all religious and social questions; and I think she found a great pleasure in my companionship. We taught her night-school for men and boys together. We attended her men's reading-room. We taught in the Sunday school. We drew. We talked of Ruskin and Mr Maurice, as well as of her brothers, my sisters, architecture, and all kinds of things. I have had a delightful visit; and she says she does not know when she has enjoyed a week so much.[53]

The Baumgartners' home was, to Octavia, the embodiment of a happy family life. Emma's mother was a stern but kindly old lady, her father was elderly, and her brother fond of flowers. The warm brick house stood almost opposite the church, the hall was hung with old pictures, and a delightful garden ran down to the river Ouse. After the visit, Emma became one of Octavia's regular correspondents.

At the Hill home frivolities such as food and dress were not discussed, and the sisters grew up 'abstemious in the one, and all skill in dress was acquired in after years'. As far as Octavia was concerned, 'she had no lack of judgement or taste or even of wish to dress nicely and suitably, but life was too hurried and more weighty matters pressed.' Her mother, regretting that she had not helped her earlier in these things, felt more optimistic about Octavia after her sisters described her at a party looking lovely in a white dress, a scarlet sash and scarlet net. For some reason she had made a big effort on that occasion, as her mother told Miranda. 'Ockey, tho' looking so ill, is unusually nice genial and merry. She has met with some amusing people lately, and it is as good as a play to hear her relate her dealings with them.'[54] On the whole dressing-up was like parties – an inessential distraction from the austere business of life.

Birthdays were the exception. Octavia's twenty-first birthday party was a gloriously happy event. She spent 3 December 1859 surrounded by friends, family, gifts; such a good day in fact that 'it was almost too much to bear'. It all seemed to confirm how much her, and her family's, life had changed for the better. Gertrude came from Weybridge and stayed in their grandfather's consulting-rooms at Southampton Street, since Mary Harris was sleeping at Milton Street. Only Ruskin failed to materialize, but he sent a letter with a parcel of books, thus quite redeeming himself. 'I never have seen any but specially nice people on my birthday,' she told Emma, apologetically once, when her friend was spending her own birthday on some dutiful task which could not be confused with pleasure.

As if to confirm the feeling that life was moving forward as she wished, Octavia had at this time just read an inspiring book, *The Missing Link*.[55] 'It is an account of the Bible Women, of whom you may have heard,' she wrote to Emma. 'They are quite poor women, sent by ladies to sell Bibles . . . They have reached the very lowest class, seen and helped them in their homes. They give nothing away, but get people to buy beds and clothes, for which they pay gradually. They encouraged women to take a pride in keeping their children and homes neat; and living among them, can do so much. Mr and Mrs Maurice are so deeply interested in the plan, that they have lent me the book . . .' Ellen Ranyard's Bible Women suggested a way in which Octavia might one day be able to work. But for the moment she was looking for more paid work, 'copying or other untiring work' as she told Gertrude.

Octavia spent Christmas 1859 in Weybridge with her grandfather, mother and sisters, and she went out riding until her horse fell. But never far from mind was Ruskin who was behaving, again, increasingly oddly. Caroline Hill had warned her of his capriciousness, but Octavia was under his spell, and wrote to Miranda, 'I am certain he is not.' On her visit to him that Christmas, he worked the usual charm, as she wrote to Emma. 'With his own exquisite elegance and ease, which enables him to do the oddest things in a way that one can't feel rude, instead of rising, he threw himself back in his chair and shook hands with me, as I stood behind.'[56] They talked about what she had been doing, and even touched on the subject of the education of working women: 'he asked much about it, seemed greatly interested.' His father had been horrified to hear rumours of a Working Women's College some years before – fortunately Ruskin was not influenced by his father's prejudices.[57]

Ruskin gave Octavia in person the insights which the Victorian intelligentsia had to learn from his books. They discussed religion, society, nature, literature as well as art. He summed up his beliefs in a resounding phrase in *Modern Painters III*: 'the greatest thing a human soul ever does in this world is to see something, and tell what he saw in a plain way . . . To see clearly is poetry, prophecy, and religion – all in one.'[58]

Unfortunately Octavia suffered in one respect from reading Ruskin. Her writing style became increasingly prolix and ornamented with purple passages. Ruskin and Octavia shared a love of literature, especially contemporary writing, and their talks on the subject gained from the fact that Ruskin knew many great literary figures personally, whilst Octavia remembered several of them from Highgate days. He thought Elizabeth Barrett Browning 'the only entirely perfect example of womanhood he knows', and had asked Octavia to illuminate 'Caterina to Camoens'. Octavia was particularly excited to hear that Florence had met Mrs Browning in Italy. 'I wish it were possible, or would be of any use, to thank her thro' you for all she had taught me.' She often found herself repeating 'Isabel's Child', she wrote, as she tramped up and down the New Road to Dulwich.

It is hard to realize how influential Ruskin's teaching was, chiefly through the medium of his books, in the drawing-rooms of Victorian England. One disciple admitted: 'I always look at the waves with a sense of gratitude to Ruskin; there are so many details in that picture that I never should have seen without his magnifying-glass; and when one has once looked through it, one can see them without it. I think the man who has taught us to look at the waves and the clouds ought to be allowed to talk a little folly without being sneered at.'[59] Many leading figures in the artistic and intellectual circles of 1860s England would have agreed with Miss Wedgwood.

Nobody got to know Octavia without meeting the family, and Ruskin became fond of the other sisters. On one occasion Emily and Octavia went to lunch with Ruskin and 'it seems M[innie] said some very pithy things, which delighted him extremely, and which he afterwards quoted. He spoke of O's painting powers *very* highly – he was all kindness.' He had also, so Mrs Hill reported, become very emotional as the sisters described how they had nursed Miranda through a severe illness. Caroline continued: 'M says he seems so impressed with O's greatness and he told someone she was the best person he knew.'[60]

Acutely, Ruskin had spotted Octavia's real potential. If he was to concern himself with practical reform, Octavia Hill was an ideal vehicle. In one of their heart-to-hearts Ruskin and Octavia had discussed social injustice. She told Emma Baumgartner:

> We spoke about the wickedness of rich and poor people. Ruskin spoke of the little children like angels he saw running about the dirty streets, and thought how they were to be made wicked. I spoke about the frightful want of feeling in all classes; but added that I thought rich people were now waking up to a sense of their duties. 'Yes' he said, '. . . I think we may live to see some great changes in society.' 'I hope at least' I said, 'to see some great changes in individuals before I die.' 'Oh no' he said, 'that's quite hopeless; people are always the same. You can't alter natures.'[61]

By 1860 Ruskin was disillusioned, depressed and lethargic, stirred by intense emotions about an impending catastrophe in society. Two years before he had become 'unconverted', plunging into spiritual turmoil, and had also met the nine-year-old Rose La Touche – the beginning of a fifteen-year obsession. He planned to stop writing and teach more. But the Working Men's College was not holding his attention, lectures to working men in both Oxford and Cambridge had met with mixed responses, and much of his teaching consisted of a peculiar correspondence course, often running to dozens upon dozens of letters, by which he taught drawing to mainly young lady amateurs such as Anna Blunden.[62] But Ruskin's state of mind, his growing disquiet with the state of society, would one day be to Octavia's direct advantage.

Meanwhile, in a letter to his father in 1861, written from Bonneville, Ruskin presented Octavia as just another assistant. 'Miss Hill is a very useful copyist and an estimable person and I will not throw her off until she finds other employment.' He asked his father to write to Octavia and find what she was owed: ' – (it *is* as she says "nearly all the summer –") and pay it her. She had leave to pay 10 shillings a week lately to the eldest girl of an orphan family – the girl was dying of consumption, she will say if dead or not . . .' He thought she was owed at least £20 – for Octavia a sizeable sum. Her salary was 20 shillings per week, and Ruskin listed her as being among the select band of five assistants to whom he paid a total of £400 per annum. George Allen,[63] the most trusted of these, received £78 a year. Octavia, though driven hard, seems to have been paid a fair wage, measured against the others.[64]

Ruskin was not worried about this continuing expense because, with his characteristic perception, he could see where Octavia's future life's work lay. 'Ruskin had said, "If you devote yourself to human expression, I know how it will be . . . there will be an end of art for you. You will say '*hang* drawing!! I must go to help people.'"' I told him it would not be so.'[65] For once, Octavia was wrong.

CHAPTER 4

Nottingham Place

A NEW friend came into Octavia's life early in 1860 – Sophia Jex-Blake, 'a bright, spirited, brave, generous young lady living alone in true bachelor style'. Miss Jex-Blake wanted some book-keeping lessons and always invited Octavia to dinner afterwards. She noted in her diary, after the first lesson on 26 January: 'Clever, pleasant girl – much nicer than I thought. Dined with me. What and how the deuce am I to pay her? £1 1s. I suppose . . .' The following day, she noted that Miss Hill might be a friend, or at least an ally: 'Very good worker, I expect.'[1]

Within a couple of months, Sophia was teaching Octavia Euclid and, as Octavia wrote to Miranda, 'Miss J.B. and I are great companions. I'm always doing things with her . . . We went to see Holman Hunt's picture . . .'[2] Octavia was taking a night-school class for girls and added that she was getting into parish work. 'Miss Sterling and Miss J.B. give me almost unlimited money help for poor people; the only question is how to use it wisely.' Sophia was generous with her money well before she took up her salaried post as a mathematics tutor at Maurice's Queen's College.

Octavia's curious way with her friends was to lecture them. Only a couple of months after she had met Sophia she was chiding her that 'turning away from so many important thoughts with a half joke, you are refusing God's means of grace as much as in staying away from ordained services. It is no good my writing sermons, however.' Once Sophia wrote, a little pained, to remind Octavia that 'she was neither nurse nor parson'.

Despite Octavia's high moral tone with her new friend, it was Sophia who dominated the friendship. Octavia capitulated before the extraordinary force of Sophia's personality, in particular a tempestuous emotionalism which seems to have been permanently on the boil. Even her lowering dark looks contributed to this sense of a temperament poised on a constant seismic fault. Elizabeth Garrett, who met her a couple of years later, found her enormous generosity and intelligence overshadowed by a manic personality which allowed for few calm moments. Sophia's character was, Elizabeth Garrett told her mother, marred by certain 'peculiarities'. Although it took Octavia longer to recognize the immense difficulties of dealing with Sophia, it was this temperamental imbalance that contained the seeds of the destruction of their friendship.

In the early months of 1860, the friendship between Octavia and Sophia was heating up. By May Sophia was planning a holiday for them in Wales and telling Octavia about it, her heart 'beating like a hammer'. Discussing the trip further, Sophia confided to her diary that '[Octavia] sunk her head on my lap silently, raised it in tears, and then such a kiss!' While the language is that of the passionate friendship enjoyed by many innocent young Victorian women, on Sophia's part it was clearly more intense, a love affair – if only of the heart.[3]

The holiday in Wales, Sophia wrote to her mother, was 'such a happy time without a single blot I never remember in my life . . . we have been everywhere and have had no dischance, no annoyance of any kind. Octa looks five years younger, and as bright as a sunbeam. And I am in so thoroughly happy a state of mind as hardly to know myself. I really almost think I should be good-tempered now.' Her mother, a long-suffering victim of Sophia's temperamental outbursts, must have been surprised by such a promised transformation.

The journey ended with a marathon return journey; they came back from Llangollen, forty miles by coach and almost 200 by train – 'not a bad journey for one day'. Sophia was astounded by Octavia's energy – 'after that tremendous journey not reaching home till 10.30 she was off to Lincoln's Inn at 7 a.m. the next morning for the early communion, and went again, and I with her in the afternoon. Her Mother and sister were so delighted with her account of all her doings.'

In August Sophia was abroad with another friend, a fellow teacher at Queen's College, Martha Heaton. Octavia was miserable without her. 'London feels strangely desolate, the lamps looked as they used to look, pitiless and unending as I walked home last night, and knew I could not go to you . . .' She hoped that Sophia might visit Italy and see her sisters.

In early September Sophia wrote in her diary of 'a plan on foot of my taking part of a house with the Hills and having Alice for a servant. That would be very jolly. But rents high about here – at least £120.' The location of that house is not recorded, but the figure alarmed the Jex-Blake parents and when Sophia mentioned that they would need to find a tenant for the drawing-room, the scheme looked more hare-brained than ever. Her father wrote: 'You cannot surely mean to take a house and let lodgings in direct opposition to your dear Mother and me . . . I had no more idea of your becoming a lodging-house keeper than of your keeping a shop. You cannot suppose that I would assist Miss Hill in such an exceedingly blameable transaction. I would *with real pleasure* assist her in all possible ways . . .'

In the coming weeks houses in Harley Street and Bentinck Street were considered, Mrs Hill being insistent that any house they took should be near the park. Octavia wrote to her 'darling treasure' that if they could secure the Harley Street house, then they (the new household) should pay all the taxes, 'whatever they may be'. For one who was generally so careful in financial matters, Octavia was acting oddly out of character; Sophia's customary imprudence had, it seemed, momentarily overruled Octavia's better sense.

Finally, a suitable house at 14 Nottingham Place was decided upon. It had plenty of backyard space and stabling which was to prove a considerable asset. Octavia had difficulty in securing the lease of the house, being without existing property, young and a woman. But her references from Ruskin and Maurice attested to her maturity and capabilities, and a formal guarantee from a Miss Wodehouse (drummed up by Sophia) completed the business. With her usual pleasure in such tasks, Octavia set about arranging it all. As Emily reported to Miranda, still in Italy, Octavia was 'immensely busy, and quite in her element, buying things, and reading over schedules of fixtures, and examining the plans, and carpentering'. By now she was experienced – having moved the family into Milton Street and fitted it out only two years before.

They planned to keep some rooms for the family, and let the rest. In case that scheme did not immediately work, Octavia had, as Emily told Miranda, put aside the first quarter's rent. The house looked over Marylebone churchyard and was close to Regent's Park and Queen's College, Harley Street, convenient for both Sophia and Octavia.

Octavia wrote to Miranda that their new home had wide stone stairs, and large, light, quiet rooms. Miranda never saw the house in

Milton Street and had not yet met Octavia's new friend who was to join the household. Looking back, a year later, Octavia remembered leaning out of the window in the new house on the last day of the old year, full of plans and hopes.

As before, Octavia's sterling efforts on behalf of her mother and sisters took their toll of her strength and health. Her Quaker friend Mary Harris was now living in Cumberland, looking after five small nieces following the death of their mother. She had given up her work at Newgate gaol, where she had been a prison visitor along the lines established by Elizabeth Fry in the 1820s. In January Octavia went to visit Mary for three weeks. She was, the sisters reported, writing ecstatic letters and planned to go back 'again and again'. By May she was indeed back again, for Mary Harris was ill herself and Octavia was far from well. She stayed in the north from then until October. It was 'five months' parting – hard it seemed then, but painless – heaven – to what came after,' Sophia wrote later.

Once again the sisters had kitted Octavia out for her travels; as Gertrude had bought her the dress for the journey to Normandy, so this time Miranda had made her a skirt which was greatly admired. As usual, Octavia was hugely appreciative of her holiday. 'I've had such a summer as I shall never forget. The unbroken peace of it, like one long unclouded day!' Probably the absence of Sophia and her tantrums and emotionalism was one ingredient of that peace. Octavia loved the Harrises' happy home life, the mountain scenery, the garden, and the chance for lots of reading. But she did not do any walking after the first few days – it wore her out and she then had a fever. Instead she convalesced on the terrace. They toured, looking at all kinds of historic sites and landscapes. They went down a coal mine. In July they took the five exuberant little nieces (whom Octavia described a little crustily as always running wild) to the seaside near Maryport, from where they sent lavender and heart's-ease and seaweed to Emily, to mark her birthday.

In Octavia's absence Sophia had made the acquaintance of the two sisters finally back from Italy. She remembered her 'unwilling acquaintance ripening gradually into love for Frid [Miranda], called forth perhaps first by her great love for me.' Miranda's was a generous spirit. Sophia had taken various household responsibilities upon herself which had not endeared her to the family, and in truth she was a cuckoo in the nest. As her biographer put it: 'She never saw her own personality from the outside; and of course hers was not the only "temperament" in the house. No member of the family could have been described as a mere cabbage.'

Octavia faced her return to London, after the becalmed months with the selfless, gentle Mary Harris, with some trepidation. Suddenly the prospect of living with Sophia, a constantly threatening tidal wave of temperament, alarmed her. In July she had written: 'All my life long this dread and misery about even the slightest contention or estrangement had taken the form of misery, continually saying in itself, "I cannot bear it". Since physical strength has left me so far, this wretched dread has increased tenfold . . .' Sophia's incessant temperamental outbursts, though they passed quickly enough, were disruptive to the atmosphere in the house in general and to Octavia's fragile nervous state in particular. Her mother, a perceptive woman, talked to her immediately on her return from Cumberland. In the watches of the night, as Sophia's biographer puts it, Caroline told Octavia that the situation could not go on; someone had to leave, and that someone could hardly be a member of the Hill family. Even though, as Jex-Blake's biographer terms it, Octavia's relationship with her mother was 'less fervent' than it became afterwards, 'she had a strong sense of filial affection.'

At just this point, in October 1861, two Hill sisters accompanied by a formidable-looking dark woman were seen at a lecture in South Kensington given by T. H. Huxley. Elizabeth Garrett, who was attending the lecture as part of her extra-mural medical training, invited the three, the third of whom was Sophia Jex-Blake, back to 22 Manchester Square, where she was living with her sister Louisa and family. It was the first meeting between the two future leading women in nineteenth-century medicine. Elizabeth Garrett was to be the first British woman doctor, qualifying in Paris in 1870; Sophia Jex-Blake the founder of the Edinburgh School of Medicine for Women, qualifying in Berne and Dublin, and registering in Britain in 1877.

Presumably the Hill girls had already met Elizabeth Garrett at F. D. Maurice's Bible classes, where she was a regular member. She had originally met him as a member of his congregation at St Peter's, Vere Street, where Octavia also was often to be found. Maurice's enlightened views on education for women did not include the medical profession, but Elizabeth was still prepared to call him 'prophet' and attend his classes, as well as his services. She also taught at the Working Women's College for some time.

The Manchester Square evening was not a success. Elizabeth

noticed that Sophia Jex-Blake was at loggerheads with the Hill girls and made things worse by derogatory remarks about Maurice. In fact, unwittingly, Elizabeth had met them at the height of the crisis between Octavia and Sophia, precipitated by Caroline Hill's ultimatum.[4] Sophia had been told that she could keep her room at Nottingham Place 'as a matter of business', but not surprisingly neither she nor her mother agreed to this.

Sophia never recovered from Octavia's abrupt rejection of her, and soon left London for Edinburgh to pursue her mathematics training and start on a medical career. When Elizabeth Garrett came to Edinburgh the following year, Sophia was unstinting with helpful introductions and useful contacts. Elizabeth saw a great deal of Sophia but found her as difficult as ever. They holidayed together in the Trossachs in temperance hotels and third-class railway carriages for economy, Sophia choosing the most precipitous routes for their climbs and Elizabeth sticking to safer paths, but there was always a distance between them. In the end, it became a professional antagonism in which Sophia's impossible temperament played its part.

Although Octavia replied to Sophia's letters from time to time, she had no wish to fan the flames of their friendship. Sophia, however, tended them for the rest of her life, making a succession of wills in which she left everything to Octavia.

The Jex-Blake ability to overwhelm did not diminish with the years. Many years later, William Morris wrote to his wife, telling of Dean Jowett's meeting with 'the two Miss Jex-Blakes . . . they are very learned ladies and when they got hold of him they talked up and they talked down, on the most abstruse of subjects, so that the poor man, who is himself a great talker, could not get a word in edgeways: so when he was asked afterwards how he had enjoyed his evening he said: "Well, I have known for long that LEX was the Latin for LAW and I now conclude that JEX should be the Latin for JAW." '[5]

After Sophia left Nottingham Place, a large part of the house was let out, but meanwhile a plan was emerging which would avoid the necessity of letting rooms. The sisters would run a small school at Nottingham Place for the children of close friends. Octavia and Emily would be in charge. Two of Mary Harris's nieces, Annie and Edith, were to come south and live and learn with them.

The school began with four boarders and a family of fatherless children ('dear, earnest, thoughtful, gentle, well-trained girls') who came as day pupils. There was always one free place offered. Amelia 'Robin', the toyworker whom Octavia had taken care of since 1857, sending her for training to an Industrial Home in Brighton, was now sixteen and came to Nottingham Place to work as housemaid.

Octavia was, in effect, the headmistress. Miranda, now back from Italy, was at this time fully occupied running a day school for the children of tradesmen and artisans. Octavia 'gave the school its start and impressed it with her character.' Caroline Hill was in charge of the children's health, a kind of matron, and when she was in England Florence taught music and languages. Emily was qualified from Queen's College, and in 1864 Octavia gained her certificate in mathematics.

At the end of the first year in the new house, Dr Southwood Smith died. Sophia Jex-Blake noted the fact in her diary, and Octavia broke her own rule to visit her, wrapped in what Sophia called 'the utter stupor of misery'.

When Lord Shaftesbury heard the news of Southwood Smith's death, which happened in Italy on 10 December 1861, he noted in his diary: 'my valued friend and coadjutor in efforts for the sanitary improvements of England is gone – the learned, warm-hearted, highly-gifted Southwood Smith.'[6] His gravestone under a cypress tree in the Protestant Cemetery at Porta Pinti in Florence bore lines by another old friend from Highgate, Leigh Hunt:

Ages shall honour in their hearts enshrined
Thee, Southwood Smith, physician of mankind;
Bringer of air, light and health into the home
Of the rich and poor of happier years to come.

In his professional life and in the extraordinary devotion and time he paid, despite everything, to his daughter's family and family diffi-culties, Dr Southwood Smith left a flawless memory behind him. Even the *Lancet*, which had treated him so shabbily over the Board of Health, honoured him with a lengthy obituary referring to his family as 'the objects of his protecting, self-denying affection'. In his will he left £600 to his daughter Emily, £200 to Caroline and £100 each to the granddaughters – except for Gertrude, who had a little over £300. There were also generous legacies to the Gillies sisters, as well as a list of items payable to Miss Hill, 'for the maintenance of her sister' – perhaps for Florence, who suffered from recurrent ill health.[7] Right up to the end of his life he had helped out with family finances; the legacies were what remained from a generous stream of assistance.

In her notes Caroline Hill, writing many years later, noted that Dr Southwood Smith had left 'touchingly little for so great a life and there was a great blank when his affection, his counsel, and his supporting influence were gone, which nothing ever filled up. The head of the family was missed and none could take his place.' He was never far from the family's thoughts. Forty-two years later, Gertrude wrote to her daughter Elinor, a day or two after Elinor's wedding, that she had unwired her bouquet and put the flowers, with some asparagus fern 'into the Dr Southwood Smith dear old dishes. (I thought that would be nice) . . .'[8]

Well before his death his granddaughters' lives had begun to show promise. He took much comfort and happiness from, as Gertrude put it, 'the opening out of the lives of . . . Miranda and Octavia Hill; for it was at this time that they – at the ages of nineteen and sixteen – took the responsibilities of their lives upon themselves, and began the great and good works which they have since carried to such wide issues.' He would have been delighted by the setting-up of their little school at Nottingham Place.

The school opened its doors in 1862. In Octavia's approach to teaching, Caroline's liberal principles were somewhat diluted in a search for a more disciplined regime. Octavia wanted to inculcate 'habits of neatness, punctuality, self-reliance and such practical power and forethought as will make them helpful in their homes'. She had her own upbringing in mind, wanting to encourage the older children to teach the little ones: 'I think it would deepen their interest in their own studies so much.' But then she added, 'I do mean to be so very careful not to overwork them.'[9]

On the other hand, Miranda helped to soften the regime; returning from a hard day at her own school she delighted Annie and Edith by singing to them in the evenings and reading to everybody. She derived great satisfaction from her own teaching, however tiring; in late 1863 her school moved into the very rooms in Russell Place where the Ladies' Co-operative Guild had been in 1851.

Octavia found sharing the pleasures of others difficult – at least when she was working at full stretch, preoccupied by all her many concerns. During the summer of 1862, when Caroline Southwood Hill was in Italy staying with her sister Emily and her daughter Florence, still mourning her much-loved father, Octavia wrote to her:

'I often reproach myself so much, dear Mama, now that you are gone, with the way I never entered into your plans for joy . . . I wish this letter, or anything else I could do, would make you feel how entirely I rejoice with you in all you are seeing; but perhaps you do know it partly.'

Octavia tried to brighten up the household, and make it more sociable for the children. Florence had sent a message about letting the children rest for half an hour after dinner, and this had been attended to. Her teaching, Octavia wrote to her mother, was showing up her own ignorance, especially in Latin: characteristically, she was planning to rectify it. Then she planned to learn physiology, keeping one lesson ahead of the children. The truth was she found the teaching easier than joining in with the more light-hearted side of children's lives. Octavia's gentle sisters seemed to show up her own limitations. She wrote, with commendable self-knowledge, to Florence:

> I often long for you, dear, with all your sympathy with people in general, and power of making children happy. You know I've a dampening cool sort of way that just stabs all their enjoyment. I don't think I've any child nature left in me. However, it will injure them less, that what they all want is to grow up.[10]

Those were the thoughts of a black day, however, and Octavia sometimes had more self-confidence; as far as her own 'little flock' was concerned, she later wrote, 'somehow the bond between us seems to grow deeper, and I fear it is not that I have learnt to understand them better, but they me . . . Why the children love me so now I cannot tell.' Perhaps it was because her attention was often elsewhere and 'children are so much better if they do not feel themselves the main object of actions and words, and yet are regularly attended to and made to fulfil all their duties.'[11]

The next year, 1863, was easier in one respect – Ruskin went to Switzerland and so the demands from Denmark Hill ceased for a while. However he had given Octavia some good advice: 'Don't be proud and foolish; remember your strength is worth keeping. Rest for months or years, if you ought, but don't lose it.'[12] Ruskin, retreating from his own nervous exhaustion, was offering her the fruits of his experience.

But it was Miranda who fell suddenly ill in the summer of that year,

with some sort of severe fever. For some days the doctors offered little
hope of her recovery. Octavia and her mother did almost all the
nursing; the children behaved impeccably, the little ones being quiet,
the pupils getting on with their own work. They 'waited with gentlest
service on us; and poor old women who sent daily to ask, and teachers
who offered all service to set us free, and friends who drove in to bring
flowers and grapes, and servants who were like rocks of strength:
there wasn't one person who didn't show love and helpfulness far
above what one could have dreamed or hoped.'[13]

Despite Octavia's misgivings over her relationships with children,
she enjoyed tutoring, and at Christmas Tom Hughes begged her to
come to the country for a month and help his children, who had
developed a hatred of lessons. The prospect of a month in the
Bedfordshire countryside was enough to persuade Octavia. She also
greatly enjoyed the Hughes's company: 'Mr Hughes is cordiality and
politeness itself and does so like to talk about Co-operation. He speaks
to Mr Neale, but has not seen him lately.' She added: 'I am *very* happy
here, getting on capitally, especially with Mrs Hughes, whom I like
extremely.'

(Of the numerous Hughes children, the youngest Mary (known as
May) born in 1860 and therefore too young at this time to be one of
Octavia's charges, later became a dedicated worker for the poor in the
East End, living simply as a Quaker in considerable personal pov-
erty.[14] Another, Arthur, became the close friend and correspondent of
John Bailey, Octavia's colleague at the National Trust many years
later. A third, Lilian, married the Revd Ernest Carter who became the
vicar of St Jude's, Whitechapel, after the Barnetts left there to set up
Toynbee Hall.[15])

The combined pleasure of common interests, in particular their
shared admiration for F. D. Maurice, and the pleasant atmosphere of a
happy home, were a great boost for Octavia, who showed the same
response to a warm, relaxed atmosphere as she had in the past with the
Howitts, Harrisons, Baumgartners and Mary Harris. Such households were, it seems, very unlike her own childhood home, even
given the happy days at Hillside.

The confidence that the enjoyable stay with the Hugheses gave
Octavia was reflected in successes at Nottingham Place. Octavia
willingly involved the school in Emily Davies's and Barbara
Bodichon's experiment which was spearheading a campaign for the
extension of University Examinations and places to girls, and some of

her pupils sat for the Cambridge Local Examinations in 1863. Other candidates came from Queen's College and the North London Collegiate School, run by Frances Buss. In total, those sitting the examination numbered an impressive eighty-three. In the spring Octavia reported the success of Mary Eliza, who had passed although two years under age and with only six weeks' preparation behind her.

There was, however, a high failure rate in mathematics, which, with the other problems that the entrants encountered, were all to the advantage of the campaign. It emphasized the fact that girls' education was carried on without any overall standards being applied. Once girls were officially accepted for these examinations, as they were in 1864 after a signed Memorial was sent to the Vice-Chancellor of Cambridge, they had to be taught a curriculum which conformed with that of the boys. The isolation of women's education ended with this breakthrough.[16]

Emily Davies asked Octavia for her reaction, and Octavia replied: 'I was *extremely pleased* with the effect on our pupils. I thought they were much invigorated by the examination; it interested them much; the intercourse with other students gave them a feeling of working with a large body of learners all over England, which was very good; and I think the examination tended to raise their standard somewhat.' In general, she continued, 'there are better things to be learnt than ever can come out in an examination . . . learning for the sake of learning and knowing, is the only legitimate course; but a standard, that will test our knowledge at last, is almost invaluable.'[17]

By 1866 Emily Davies' campaign for a Cambridge College for women had begun in earnest; twenty-five years later Octavia would be much involved with both Girton and Newnham students at the Women's University Settlement. In the meantime she joined the London Schoolmistresses' Association, formed in March 1866. Emily Davies was the founder and remained its Secretary for the twenty-two years of its existence. The twenty-five members, who included Miss Buss, Mrs Malleson – Octavia's old colleague from Portman Hall days – and other key campaigners for women's education, met in one another's houses every two or three months.[18]

The intellectual weight of the argument against them may be gauged by a comment from the Dean of Canterbury, Dr Alford, who was considered friendly to their cause. He thought that 'personal eminence would be dearly bought at the sacrifice of that unobtrusiveness which is at the same time the *charm* and *strength* of our

Englishwomen.'[19] But Octavia was not deterred by unreasoning objections. 'Some such plan *must* be adopted before the education of our girls will improve. It is next to impossible for ladies [i.e. employers] to know what their governesses know . . . we want just such a standard as this offers.'[20]

Another way in which Octavia helped to broaden the educational prospects for women was through her involvement with the Working Women's College which opened in October 1864. It was housed in self-contained premises at 29, Queen Square, with 157 students on the roll and here Octavia consolidated her earlier work with the women's classes at the Working Men's College. In March that year Octavia had received her certificate from Queen's College so she now had paper qualifications to add to her undoubted ability and enthusiasm for teaching.

Elizabeth Malleson was the principal of the Working Women's College, having campaigned for an establishment which could provide 'the same sort of educational advantages for them [the women] that the men enjoyed'. It was non-sectarian and among the fellow teachers were Elizabeth Garrett and Arthur Munby, the esoteric diarist.[21] Octavia was pleased to report that she had eighteen students for her drawing class. In 1874 it became a mixed college and later was incorporated within Morley College.

A few years later Miranda described the Hill sisters' own school,[22] which changed little in the thirty years that they ran it. There was no prospectus, since the pupils were either the daughters of friends, or came by personal recommendation. There were fourteen boarders, aged twelve to eighteen, and another ten or so day girls. 'Our reason for not increasing the number of our boarders is that we wish to keep the arrangements those of a home rather than that of a school.' This allowed for individual attention; for the same reason, they preferred pupils to stay at least three years.

Those who stayed longer, 'our most satisfactory pupils', went on to pass the senior Cambridge examination (by then open to women) and often attended lectures at the Royal Institution. The school curriculum included 'English subjects (that is, history, modern and ancient, geography, grammar and arithmetic), Latin, French, Italian, German, music, part-singing (not solo-singing), drawing, the elements of Euclid and algebra, and also of botany, chemistry and natural philosophy.' The latter subjects were only touched on in first principles, but 'we find them valuable as well as interesting to girls.' Astonishingly, all the subjects except dancing and gymnastics were taught by the sisters themselves, and Miranda listed their qualifications.[23]

Terms were seventy guineas a year for boarders, and twenty-five for day girls. The only extras were for laundry, books and stationery. The girls' health, Miranda assured her correspondent, was in good hands and there were daily walks in Regent's Park; they had the key to a private section where the girls played running-games in winter and croquet in summer. In summer, too, dancing and gymnastics were replaced by rowing on the lake and weekly visits to a swimming bath.[24] (Not all parents approved of these physical exertions.)

Octavia's work with the poor was instrumental in:

> interesting our pupils in actively benevolent work, and they help in it to some extent, after school-hours. One evening a week is given to assisting to teach needlework, and to cut out for a class of poor women which meets in our school-room [the tenants from Barrett's Court, see p. 132]. We value this part of the training for our pupils as much as any. They also frequently help at concerts for the poor, and entertainments of various kinds.

It bore out Octavia's wish to 'imbue the young with her principles . . . a Nursery of Fellow-Workers'.[25]

Evenings were free from study, which stopped at six. Dinner was taken together and then the evenings passed 'either in social occupations, such as chorus-singing, and needlework with reading aloud; or else the girls take their own occupations – read – write letters etc.' There was, on the whole, 'a very delightful feeling of mutual confidence and friendship between us and our pupils'.

Although Octavia handed on the day-to-day running of the school to her sisters as she became increasingly involved in other matters, she was still much in evidence up to the day the school closed in 1891.[26]

One twelve-year-old pupil, Sina Card, remembered the school around 1890, with slightly less enthusiasm. Lessons took place in the stable behind Nottingham Place.

> Miss Octavia took us in drawing and accounts. Of course we took back to school 'tips' and during term time had 6d a week pocket money. We had to keep account of all this and Miss Octavia OKed it. She was strict over it and I fancy many 'forgets' must have meant sweets! I was the youngest there, and slept at the top of the house in a

[89]

room with two of the oldest girls – great pals, so that I was a bit 'out of it'. . . . I believe I was a bit afraid of Miss Octavia; she was inclined to be stern, and a bit uncompromising – sometimes a bit sarcastic. Miss Miranda I loved; she was so gentle and understanding, and always ready to help.

She also remembered Caroline Southwood Hill, who seemed very old indeed (she was then about eighty), joining the school for dinner which was served in a long room in the front of the house. Sina Card only stayed a couple of terms, since the Hills gave up the school in March 1891, but as Mrs Meyrick-Jones she was asked back to one of the Hills' 'afternoons', with her baby daughter. 'These afternoons were interesting. As far as I remember we sat around the room and had tea. One might sit next to a peer or a chimney sweep!'[27]

CHAPTER 5

Ruskin: practical help

R USKIN did not want to be personally involved in Octavia's schemes. But he sensed that her deep sense of the practical, her apparent (if not actual) limitless energy and her forthright and developed views would be the germ of something remarkable. He wanted to be a patron, to enable her to put into practice what he knew she could do. On the death of John James Ruskin in 1864, his only son inherited £120,000 and some property. Now his financial help was a possibility.

For a long time Octavia had been considering the housing question. The conditions she had seen within the toymakers' homes and when trying to find accommodation for poor families she knew, indicated an area in which action was desperately needed. Her grandfather had been involved in philanthropic housing so that Octavia knew what provision existed in that form. Almost twenty years earlier, Dr Southwood Smith and Lord Ashley had reformed the Labourers' Friend Society, which had originally been a largely rural enterprise, into the Society for Improving the Conditions of the Labouring Classes.[1] The return on loans was set at 4 per cent.[2] The SICLC's first exercise was a block of model dwellings in Lower Road, Pentonville, designed by the architect Henry Roberts, who later built the model cottages for the Great Exhibition under the auspices of the SICLC and Prince Albert. The model dwellings at Streatham Street, near the British Museum, built in 1850 (which still stand) were the most advanced of Roberts' schemes for the Society.[3]

'I have long been wanting to gather near us my friends among the poor, in some house arranged for their health and convenience, in fact a small private model lodging-house, where I may know everyone, and do something towards making their lives healthier and happier,'

Octavia wrote to Mrs William Shaen,[4] wife of the solicitor friend who was already helping her look for premises, 'and to my intense joy Ruskin has promised to help me to work the plan.'

Although her initial idea was to find a suitable house for her scheme, the vendors soon withdrew from any negotiations once Octavia's purpose became clear. It became evident that she would have to buy already tenanted courts in poor condition and put them into order around the existing tenants.

Ruskin urged a gradual approach. 'My father's executors are old friends, and I don't want to discomfort them by lashing out suddenly into a number of plans.' That Ruskin was spending a small part of his father's fortune on a social scheme was ironic, given John James Ruskin's view that his son was apt to lose direction and, potentially, influence, when he tried to find solutions to social and economic problems.

Octavia was now busily learning about housing management. Mr Harlow, the landlord of Nottingham Place, took her to look at his model lodging-houses and she reported to Mary Harris that: 'The appliances are excellent and the good will perfect; but alas, the condition simply bore out my belief that appliances are almost worse than useless without energy, and energy is often not to be found among the poor.' So she concluded: 'it needs supervision, which can only be given by a friend.'

Octavia was tending to the conclusion, based on what she knew of Ellen Ranyard's Bible Women and others like them who carried out their work by personal contact, that money spent on bricks and mortar alone was money wasted. But she had to find a property, in order to test her theories. A friend told her of a group of houses to let or for sale in a street known colloquially as 'Little Hell'.

Octavia decided to talk to the Secretary of the Marylebone Association for Improving the Dwellings of the Working Classes. The Association had bought and cleaned up eight similar houses, which were paying a return on the investment. As far as the three houses available to her were concerned, 'more awful abodes for human beings I never entered,' Octavia wrote. 'The stairs broken, the walls bulging and tumbling, the dirt, the darkness, the utter absence of all attempt at ventilation.' Nor was there any open ground around them to speak of.

The ludicrously named Paradise Place (now Garbutt Place) was tucked off Marylebone High Street and only a hundred yards or so from Nottingham Place. The houses stood on the Duke of Portland's estate[5] and were subject to a ground rent of £4 per house. There was a 56-year lease and the asking price was £750.[6] Legal complications meant that completion was delayed until April 1865, whilst the resident landlords were not due to move out from each of the three houses until midsummer of that year. Octavia, fired up in the enthusiasm for her new enterprise, found the delays frustrating.

However she could start with the human foundations of the scheme and 'do much small personal work among them, so that we may get to know them'. To this end the stable block behind Nottingham Place was handy, and could provide a tenants' meeting-room; Octavia spent the sizeable sum of £78 on improving it. Above that was a little flat where a blind man and his family lived. Emma Cons and Octavia personally whitewashed the rooms and glazed the windows, so that once she gained full possession at Paradise Place Octavia would have some practical experience to help her direct the building works.

Octavia had worked it all out.

I see no end to what may grow out of it. Our present singing and work[7] will, of course, be open to any of our tenants who like to come. We shall take the children out, and teach the girls; and many bright friendships, I hope, will grow up amongst us. The servants and children here are trained for the work and longing to co-operate.

Octavia did not want to be encumbered by committees and group decisions at this stage and so opted for tight management. Ruskin 'showed me . . . it would be far more useful if it could be made to pay; that a working man ought to be able to pay for his own house.' They decided upon a 5 per cent return on Ruskin's money, his argument being that if the venture started on a sound business footing, then she could encourage others to follow his example and contribute to the expansion of her work.[8] That the payment of rent might prove a major problem had not occurred to her. She had not yet fully grasped the extent of poverty and the uncertainty of employment that faced even the steadiest of her tenants.

Once the new work began Octavia feared she would be unable to go on copying for Ruskin, yet she desperately needed the money. She was dependent on that and her teaching, both at Nottingham Place and at the Working Women's College, for her income. She always argued that the best work for others was undertaken on a voluntary basis and, since she had ways of earning her living, she preferred to apply her own rule to herself – gruelling as it was. She talked to Ruskin about it.

> I offered to resign my salary, urging that the house would take so much of my time. 'As you like,' he said, 'but it is yours now, as long as you want it, for you are doing some of the work that I ought to do'. 'I'm afraid I shall always want it, there is so much to do'. 'Then always have it,' he said, with one of his sweetest smiles.[9]

By the following summer the copying work for Ruskin had come to an end, no doubt because of the pressure on Octavia's time, now that the houses were hers. 'I know it will seem all right in time, perhaps better than ever, but it feels so sad now. For ten years and a half I have worked for him, and been so proud of my work, and now it is all over.' Nevertheless, 'I dare trust our friendship to take care of itself.'[10]

So excited was she by her hopes and aspirations for Paradise Place that family business sometimes slipped her mind. Shamefacedly she admitted as much, telling Emma Baumgartner as an afterthought that Gertrude, her elder sister, had married Charles Lewes, the stepson of George Eliot. With hindsight she might have given the news more weight, because she gained an influential friend and great moral support in this new member of her family.[11]

The engagement excited great interest on both sides. George Eliot's letters were full of it. She confessed herself surprised that anyone could have fallen for 'our amiable bit of crudity' but it was indeed the case.

> She *has* fallen in love with him and it is very pretty to see their fresh young happiness. She is in my opinion remarkably handsome and has the rare gift of a splendid contralto voice. She is four years older than Charles, which under all the circumstances is an advantage, for she seems to have been brought up in such a way as to have preserved all that is best in youthfulness while she has had much domestic experience.

The particularly beautiful voice which her future mother-in-law mentioned was a gift shared by several of the sisters. For a while Gertrude had considered pursuing a professional singing career. Sadly, marriage put paid to these plans.

In another letter George Eliot described Gertrude's background: 'the granddaughter of Dr Southwood Smith – *the* granddaughter whom he adopted when she was three years old, and brought up under his own eye. He left her to the care of the two Miss Gillies – (you have heard of *Margaret* Gillies) and these two elderly women dote upon their Gertrude which is one good testimony to her character.'[12] On the Hill side there was equal pleasure in the match. Octavia told Mary Harris about it all. 'I have such faith in Gertrude's goodness as really to expect great happiness for her. It is all very wonderful . . .' The families had met, Charles Lewes had impressed them with his gentle, open manner, and Mrs Hill was very happy about the engagement.

After Christmas Octavia went with Gertrude to visit the Leweses. 'I am very glad that I went. Mrs Lewes was very nice; a softened nature of great strength showed itself in all her words and looks. Best of all in her I liked a nervous intensity of expressive power in her hands, as she held mine for a second or two at parting. We spoke of Mme Bodichon. It was a bond, I know.'[13] In a second letter, referring to another visit, hardly a week later, she describes a talk with George Eliot; they argued about poetry,[14] Thackeray, Ruskin and:

about Dickens, and much did I enjoy it. Then we got into talk about Dissenters and the hold they had on the poor; its ground and tendency. You will know that she told me much that was interesting. Then we talked of Nottingham Place and the work here. I asked her what kind of help she had meant I was to ask her for. She told me that if I saw something she could do with money, and I could ask her more easily than anyone else, she should be so happy to give it.[15]

The wedding took place on 20 March 1865. The small party at the Rosslyn Hill Unitarian Chapel[16] in Pilgrim's Lane, Hampstead, was lacerated by an icy east wind. George Lewes was surprised that although only close family and the 'aunts' (the Miss Gillies) were invited the church was quite full. The absence of Dr Southwood Smith must have been felt by everybody. George Lewes, Mrs Hill, Florence Hill and Margaret Gillies signed the register. Afterwards they went back to Church Row – where the Gillies and Gertrude were living – and had a 'quiet and pleasant talk with them all'. 'Happier prospects never smiled upon a marriage,' George Lewes noted in his journal.[17]

For Octavia, the wedding was a brief interlude in the run-up to taking on the houses. As soon as the first one became available,

[95]

Octavia began her work. The tenants, she told Mary Harris, 'seem to respect me so deeply because I have bought the houses. It makes me almost shudder to see what a mighty power money has.' She hated the subservience of the women; they seemed 'deadened to all sense of order or cleanliness or self-respect'. In a letter a few days later she described taking possession of one house. To clean it, 'we have turned out the bad old tenants, in spite of tears and prayers.' Unhappy about this, she mused that perhaps she should not have been able to do so.

'I went over the emptied house with builder, surveyor, sweep and broker, such a ludicrous train! thou wouldst have laughed to see me stalking about with the great rusty keys of the desolate rooms, and a newspaper parcel of rent, £13 in silver, under my arm.' But Mary's smile would have faded to see the conditions, Octavia added. 'I think I should have fainted in one room had not Mr Stokes quickly stepped forward and thrown open the closely shut windows.' The drunken widow with four children who had lived there had begged to be allowed to stay. 'I was so weary and sick at heart, but went to hear [George] MacDonald lecture, which did me good.'

From now on Octavia did not need to rely on published accounts of poverty, whether the journalistic reports of Mayhew or Hollingshead, or the fictionalized ones of Dickens or Kingsley. There in central London, a stone's throw from the elegant terraces around Regent's Park, she had all the evidence of poverty she required.

Number 3 was soon finished, 'every corner of the house having been thoroughly cleaned, and old mess cleared away, and windows perpetually open; and we having placed a ventilator at the top of the staircase. The house felt like one belonging to a different class of people.' Octavia's plan was to give each family two rooms instead of one: families moved into their larger quarters and hung curtains, pictures from the *Illustrated London News*, even new coloured blinds. Despite all this, Octavia realized the house would soon be dirty again 'without almost superhuman efforts, but these we must try earnestly to get the people to make. I do hope we have rescued them from two evils forcibly brought before me – overcrowding, and a tyrant vixen of a landlady (unless I turned into that, Mary).'

Once the first property had been acquired, Octavia began to link the strands of her life together. She assigned each of the pupils at Nottingham Place a child from the buildings, as her responsibility. One or two of her oldest friends started to help with the rent collection and supervision of the buildings, Emma Cons in particular, although she was still illuminating manuscripts for Ruskin to earn money. Octavia was busy trying to make the outside of the houses nicer, too. She wanted little railed spaces, and there she would plant some Virginia creeper brought back from a stay in Cumberland with Mary.

She now began to note down her impressions and experiences, as a kind of working handbook to housing management. Once the tenants were a known quantity, she began to broaden her contact with them, much as she had done by taking the toymakers for their outings. Hardly had she taken on the houses when she took the children on a boating trip. They came back with treasures: feathers, sticks, leaves, clover.

For the last year, 1865, everything had gone better than she could have hoped. The housing work was under way, and her teaching, both at home and elsewhere, was going well. She had the personal support of two nationally famous figures, Ruskin and George Eliot.[18] She had secured a new literature teacher for Nottingham Place, George MacDonald, and her friendship with him, which Ruskin had encouraged,[19] was flourishing. One evening in June 1865, Miranda, Emily and Octavia went home with George MacDonald and sat talking in his garden until the moon rose. His cheerful household full of lively children was exerting the customary hold over Octavia and her sisters.

While there were new friends, though, some of the old circle were no longer part of Octavia's life. The Christian Socialists had dispersed, although the Working Men's College flourished. F. D. Maurice and Tom Hughes and his family remained close friends ('I like Mr Hughes more and more,' she wrote in March 1864). Two Hughes children came to the Nottingham Place school for drawing, arithmetic and Latin lessons. But others from the old Christian Socialist circle, such as Neale and Furnivall, had drifted away. When in 1864 Octavia met Furnivall again, she found him 'not the least changed. Just that seraph brow, and sweetly happy mouth, and the great dark eyes, and just that provoking, self-willed, arbitrary way of behaving.'[20]

Octavia encountered Neale again a little later, with his wife and two daughters in West Wickham church. She wrote to her mother:

the service was very beautiful and set me thinking much about him, and his life, and its apparent failures and real successes . . . I had such a sense of his being looked upon by many people, if not as foolish, at least as having utterly failed. As if that unbounded, because entirely unselfish, generosity could fail to leave its impression on the world. His own retreat from all the people who would have reverenced his spirit seems, too, as if he himself had a sense of utter failure.[21]

In the September of that busy year, 1865, Octavia went to God-manchester to rest with the Baumgartner family. She had grown very fond of Emma's mother and listened to the old lady reminiscing about her childhood home, hoping 'to learn something of what that deep attachment is to an inherited spot of this old earth, rich with memories of days long ago, and people long dead, and I wonder silently at the death of all this feeling in this change-loving age.'[22]

Another visit to a favourite family took place in December when she went to Offley, to the Hughes's. She returned:

> with quite wonderful vigour and mirth. Mr and Mrs Tom Hughes were kindness itself, and, as they were alone, I saw a very great deal of them. Mr Hughes is really quite charming, that deep, true, undercurrent of earnest faith running perpetually under his beaming sympathy and bright fun are simply delightful. I had many a long interesting talk with him about the future of the working classes, about the new 'Broad Church' books . . .

Then Hughes read *Pickwick* aloud till the children went to bed. Through Hughes, Octavia met several leading painters; Holman Hunt[23] and G. F. Watts[24] in particular.

At Christmas that first year, Octavia asked the tenants' children to a party at Nottingham Place, an event which was to become an annual affair.

> One family touched me most. The mother and father were out, and five children left at home, the eldest only eleven. She was vainly trying to clean the dirty faces and awful room; a bright quick child, whom I know I shall like. I feel as if I hardly knew what to appeal to to raise these people, there is something so fallen in all around them. I don't quite know how to nerve them to self-help and decency. Well, we shall see.

Then she and Florence took the children to the Zoo. Again she painted the scene for Mary's benefit: 'If thou could have seen us, such a troop! The children with torn dresses revealing *such* petticoats, hats all bent and broken, cloaks fastened with pins all twisted round. I had one child clinging to each arm, one grasping each hand, and fourteen clustering round.'

Desperate as it all was, it invigorated Octavia enormously. The months and years of dreaming, the spirituality of her thinking, had hardened into a plan, and a practical one which embodied a Christian ethos. It made her feel quite young, 'planning what we will make of it all in the years to come, and how we shall watch the children grow up, and think that perhaps we shall see them grown women returning to make better homes than they knew as little children . . . and how succeeding sets of our Nottingham Place pupils will be bound to these by inherited work and a history.' She was twenty-six.

CHAPTER 6

Freshwater Place onwards

WITH the work at Paradise Place under way Octavia turned her attention to the equally ill-named Freshwater Place,[1] Ruskin's second contribution.

The five Freshwater Place houses, and one in the Marylebone Road, were bought freehold for Octavia by Ruskin in the spring of 1866 for £2,880.[2] She described Freshwater Place, in a published retrospective view:[3] 'a row of cottages facing a bit of desolate ground, occupied with wretched, dilapidated cow-sheds, manure heaps, old timber, and rubbish of every description. The houses were in a most deplorable condition – the plaster was dropping from the walls; on one staircase a pail was placed to catch the rain that fell through the roof.' Her catalogue went on; the banisters had been used as firewood, the washhouse was locked, the dustbin in front of the houses spilled garbage all over the court, the drains were blocked, there were filthy puddles on the broken paving, one large dirty waterbutt provided fresh water. Yet she did not provide new fittings immediately, 'as we had determined that our tenants should wait for these until they had proved themselves capable of taking care of them.'[4]

Rooms were distempered and painted, the drains put in order, a slate cistern was provided, the washhouse cleared out and opened on certain days to each tenant. Windows were glazed – broken panes had been sealed with layers of paper and rag, and Octavia, with her passion for detail, observed that out of 192 panes, only eight were intact. New grates were provided and the roof, plaster and woodwork were repaired as necessary. Later, in 1873, an extra storey was built on to the cottages and outside staircases, which led up to a common balcony on to which the rooms opened.[5]

The Freshwater Place landlord was a small tradesman, not particularly wicked but unable to withstand the attrition of bad debts with no capital behind him. Before taking over, Octavia went around with him to collect rents; a man accompanied them 'whom, as he confided to me, he wished to pass off upon the people as a broker.' The man was a threat – the broker being, in effect, a bailiff. Many tenants owed six to eight weeks' rent, some much more. Since she had taken over 'I have *never* allowed a second week's rent to become due.'[6]

The tenants were not artisans but were those whose employment was intermittent, seasonal or particularly low paid. Octavia recognized that the fluctuations of work caused difficulty in payment even for the thriftiest, and tried to deal with this in two ways: either by encouraging tenants to save, or by employing them herself. For example older girls could earn something by scrubbing the passages three times a week.

Poor as the tenants were, bad debts were minimal (Octavia knew to the last farthing what was owed). 'Extreme punctuality and diligence in collecting rents, and a strict determination that they shall be paid regularly, have accomplished this.' Then she added tartly, 'as a proof of which it is curious to observe that £1 13s 3d of the bad debts accumulated during two months that I was away in the country.' She was unflinching in her determination to evict tenants who did not pay. 'I believe it to be better to pay legal expenses for getting rid of tenants than to lose by arrears of rent – better for the whole tone of the households, kinder to the tenants.' In the first months there had been just one eviction – a threat was usually sufficient. She would not house those leading 'clearly immoral lives'.

Once Octavia had taken on the management of a house, the wider work could begin. In the case of Freshwater Place, it was the provision of a playground that concerned her most immediately.

It is indeed an almost desperate undertaking . . . The people . . . are as low as I have ever seen, wild, dirty, desperate, full of bitter passions and jealousies and imaginations. The wall that we have been building round the ground has been advanced so far with the greatest difficulty, bricks stolen in the night, broken and thrown about by day, but it was slowly rising until Thursday, when I went round and found the place . . . quite deserted, and there lay the wall one tumbled mass of ruin. A bitter hopelessness filled my heart.

But she pressed on. A night watchman was employed and the wall rebuilt. 'I have resolved not to go near there today. I can do no good,

[101]

and as we are to have our opening meeting there on Tuesday I must keep quiet or I shall be unfit for it.' Ruskin provided trees and creepers, and the services of his gardener, Downes – a devoted supporter and friend to Octavia.

Once the playground was open, she engaged a superintendent. One afternoon the children were entertained by an organ-man: 'The whole ground was covered with tiny dancing figures.' Moments like that kept her going. Then, too, Mrs Simeon, the woman looking after the ground, proved a great success and was working wonders. When Octavia helped there she found it arduous; four hours at the playground felt like four years.

The sheer grind of administration prevented her establishing a friendly relationship with the tenants, she felt. They were besieging her with requests, 'most of which I am unable or unwilling to grant; they seem to feel that I am strict, in fact they say so, and two of them have left.' The problem was not the rent but the rules. 'I fancy I must err in setting the right before the people too harshly . . . Many people I fail to touch and lead, and am powerless even to make them feel that I love them.'[7]

In undated notes for a talk to tenants, she asked them what they wanted and gave them her views on indiscriminate charity – no doubt to their utter bewilderment. She referred to the time,

> before you knew me when we became *very* poor, even you would have thought us poor. I have never before spoken to you of that time, because I remember it with a sort of awe it was such a desolate terrible time. I learnt a great deal in it though, and I never forget it . . . it often makes me understand you better than you know . . . I daresay I often seem cold, and rough and harsh and in a hurry, I know I do here at home, and I am very sorry . . . you will never know how thankful I am to you that you have trusted me so much in spite of my sternness.[8]

It was the same worry that she had with the pupils at Nottingham Place. She knew her own faults and had recurring bouts of self-doubt, not alluded to in print but often referred to in letters to close friends, above all to Mary Harris.

Octavia's work was of considerable interest in Denmark Hill. Ruskin wrote to send another £10 from his mother and noted, cryptically, that 'the account of the quarrels and economies of your poor people under just government is very valuable to me.'[9] Later in the year he wrote: 'I'm particularly happy that my mother has taken to you so; it's very good for her, and gives her a new interest and admiration.' Their friendship, his mother's approval securing it, went particularly smoothly at this time.

Octavia often joked about her affinity with elderly ladies and with this one she became a favourite. The redoubtable eighty-five year old widow told her that she had but once drunk tea away from her husband in forty-seven years of marriage, and recalled her nine-year engagement.[10] She took a lively interest in Octavia's schemes, sending gifts, both money and useful items such as knitted shawls, and before long had persuaded their cousin Joan Agnew[11] to go out rent-collecting for Octavia.

In 1866 Octavia reported that the scheme had yielded 5 per cent on capital, some £48.[12] Tenants with large families had been persuaded to take two rooms for hardly more than the rent of a single room, 4s 6d for two rooms against the 4s that most were paying for one. No sub-letting was allowed.

The houses had been repaired, and tax, ground-rent and insurance paid. The rates, which were to rise steeply over the coming years as the implementation of public health reform increased the burden, together with the mounting Poor Law rates, were paid by a device known as 'compounding'. This meant that the landlord was responsible for payment but in the case of an annual rent below £7 4s he could claim a 50 per cent reduction.[13] In later years Octavia campaigned against this responsibility and ensured that her tenants paid their own rates (with an appropriate reduction in the rent).

As in Paradise Place, any surplus over the 5 per cent return was accumulated to be spent as the tenants chose. Various classes were being held in the tenants' room at Nottingham Place; twice weekly for boys, once for girls. There was a singing class and a sewing-work class for married women and older girls.[14]

The ground in front of the houses was organized as a drying-ground during school hours, so that damp clothes should not be hung out of the windows as before. Out of school hours it became the playground and provided, in addition, the drill parade for the boys as well as practice for a drum and fife band. Octavia did not care for the games that the children chose for themselves. 'For instance,' she expostulated, 'what is to be said of a game the whole of which consists in singing, "Here comes my father all down the hill, all down the hill" (over and over again), and replying, "We won't get up for his ugly face – ugly face" . . . then come the mother, the sister, the brother, to whom the same words are addressed. Finally the lover comes, to whom the greeting is, "we will get up for his pretty face."' The song was lost on her – her customary difficulty in entering into children's minds was aggravated by the vulgarity of the refrain.

Most important was the weekly contact between the lady rent-collector and the tenant. 'First, there is the mere outside business – rent to be received, requests from the tenant respecting repairs to be considered,' then tenants had to be corrected, rebuked for untidiness or bad behaviour. 'Then came . . . the little histories of the week.' Tenants would ask for advice, whether a daughter should go into service, should a sick child be taken to hospital? Reconciliation between warring neighbours was another task, as Octavia saw it.

In May, 1866 Octavia organized a celebration, with maypole and band. It became an annual occasion for the next twenty-one years.[15] After the addition of the extra storey in 1873, the balcony would be threaded with gorse and laburnum and the maypole itself twined with a rich mixture of wild flowers.

Octavia's efforts were aimed at inculcating a love of beauty in the tenants' minds. 'Intervals of bright joy' were part of the plan; Christmas celebrations and summer expeditions would help to bind the tenants together and absorb good influences. Seventy tickets were issued for the May festival but Octavia was worried because of the 'dense population of people, who break and destroy and steal, and heave stones, and bricks, so that one feels as if living in old times, when all things were decided, not by right, but entirely by might.' Old friends, including the Revd Llewelyn Davies and Mr Maurice, came. The police were little help, but support was given by a handful of women who attended her classes and by the children.

Mary Macaulay[16] (later Mrs Charles Booth), who had first met Octavia in 1862, when she was a schoolgirl at the Miss Harrison's establishment,[17] later remembered Octavia and Miranda at one of the festivities organized for the tenants:

Among the people moved two small figures, very plainly and even poorly dressed with no advantages of height, figure or toilet to distinguish them from the poor women whom they served, until one looked into their faces and heard them speak – but never shall I

forget them and Miranda was lovely with a most powerful sweetness of expression. Octavia had beauty too but the enthusiasm which
inspired her and shone in her eyes was the chief characteristic of her
appearance.[18]

Distributing the tickets nearby had shown Octavia more of the
horrors of the life of the poor.

Awful dens of darkness . . . narrow, filthy dark places, winding
stairs, where light never comes, three, four and five children and
their parents living, of course, in one room only; oh, but such
rooms! And the children! their eyes all inflamed with continued dirt,
their bare feet, their wild cries, their disordered hair, and clothes
looking as if dogs had torn them all round, and carried off great
jagged pieces.

They had met a wandering simple-minded orphan girl, been abused
by a raving Roman Catholic madman – there was no telling what any
door would reveal.

As Octavia accumulated experience she asked Ruskin whether she
should publish an account of her work. He encouraged her idea
(though not a suggestion that she was considering nursing cholera
victims[19] – 'I fear for the strong helpful instinct,' he wrote); characteristically he could see advantages in such publication for himself, too.

State your own views in beginning this thing; say that I furnished
you with the means in order to prove and practise one of the first
principles of my political economy: that proper use of money would
give proper interest, and that no one could otherwise than *criminally*
take more. Make the thing short, but put in *some* distinct and
interesting stories about your tenants, and I doubt not the immense
good you will do, and probably induce others to do.[20]

Octavia's article, an account of the work on Paradise Place and
Freshwater Place to date, appeared in the *Fortnightly Review* of
November 1866, entitled 'Cottage Property in London'. Ruskin was
well pleased. Later on, it appeared as the first essay in *The Homes of the
London Poor*, published in 1875 in London and New York, and later in
translation.

The piece is a crisply written record of the fruition of Octavia's plan, which 'I had long contemplated'. She did not have a precise scheme, but

> my strongest endeavours were to be used to rouse habits of industry and effort, without which they must finally sink – with which they might render themselves independent of me, except as a friend and leader. The plan was one which depended on just governing more than on helping . . . That the spiritual elevation of a large class depended to a considerable extent on sanitary reform was . . . proved; but I was equally certain that sanitary improvement itself depended upon educational work among grown-up people.

Interestingly, she was already setting aside a contingency sum for paid rent-collectors, although at present she was doing it herself and 'finding it most important work'.[21]

The account also contains the germs of Octavia's thinking on charity, which she was beginning to define under Ruskin's influence:[22] 'They expected a greater toleration, ignorant indulgence, and frequent almsgiving, but in spite of this have recognized as a blessing a rule which is very strict, but the demands of which they know, and a government that is true in word and deed.'

Then she turned to the matter of landlords and landladies, who in general held, she felt, more power than schoolteachers. The lodger who drank most with the landlord received preferential treatment and his debts were overlooked; this resulted in a rent rise – 'the steady and sober pay . . . to make up for the losses.' She gave case histories of various tenants: of an Irish family who had patched up a feud for her sake, of a man to whom she had given notice to quit because he would not send his children to school and had overcrowded his rooms. He protested that he had paid his rent – to which Octavia replied that 'it isn't quite the only thing I insist on. I cannot allow anything so wrong as this neglect of the children and overcrowding to continue where I have the power to prevent it.'

She concluded that there had been many minor difficulties and disappointments but the tenants' 'energy and hope amid overwhelming difficulties have made me ashamed of my own laziness and despair'. There were endless 'annoying small perpetual cares' – dealing with dustmen, lawyers, repairs to the nine houses and the like – but 'it is only when the detail is really managed on as great principles as the whole plan, that a work becomes really good.'

In the summer of 1867 Octavia fell ill, and went north to Mary Harris. It was to be a more prolonged absence than she at first imagined. But there was a high point: in his diary Ruskin noted that he had driven around Derwentwater with Octavia and her friend. Mary Harris, who knew the Lake District so well, was a useful guide for Ruskin who was hoping to find a house in the area. On this excursion Octavia bought a seventeenth-century oak chest, always one of her most prized possessions.[23] Ruskin's search culminated in the purchase of Brant-wood, on Coniston Water, which he bought unseen in the autumn of 1871. Octavia visited him there at least once, in 1873.

After her stay in Cumberland she joined George MacDonald's family in Bude. Ruskin was behind the plan and wrote to them offering help: 'I can't put things into polite form just now – but what expense she is to you, I should like to replace to you as far as her illness has increased it – and I should be glad if she could stay with you and near you – under present circumstances till you return to town.'[24]

Her visit was a great success, Octavia reported to Mary Harris. 'The coach drive of twenty-four miles was delightful. Bideford was so lovely and the profusion of flowers glorious. There everyone was so kind and there was such a sense of solitary freedom. The whole rocky coast and upland moor are so wild, my room is wholly my own, and I am expected to do exactly as I like.'[25]

Nevertheless she felt an obligation to give something in return for all the pleasure she was receiving and she decided to do some teaching. Greville MacDonald,[26] the MacDonalds' eldest son who suffered crippling deafness from the age of ten, benefited in particular from her impulse. He described himself as a dull, indolent schoolboy. 'Every morning she took me out alone with her on to the Chapel Rock at the end of the breakwater, our delightful solitude shared only by the gulls and the Latin Grammar, which, so long my enemy, she soon taught me at least to respect . . . Her personality overruled all adverse suggestive influences, and I went back to school finely grounded in my Latin, my stupidity no more insuperable.'[27]

There were outings, including one to Tintagel Castle, which Octavia must have recalled when, in 1896, the National Trust mounted an appeal to buy the headland. When she wrote to Greville MacDonald on the occasion of his parents' golden wedding anniversary in 1901, she recalled 'those wonderful old days in your parents' house, Bude and its breakwater, Hammersmith and the garden and the river and all the sweet and high converse of the good and wise in which you all grew up.'[28] She enjoyed the MacDonald children, of whom there were eventually eleven (including one called Maurice, after F. D. Maurice, and another pretty little girl called Irene who delighted her with her dark colouring, and a black dress trimmed in red). When Octavia was relaxing, her painter's eye came back into play – whether it was observing people or countryside.

In the autumn Octavia came back to London but she was no better and was persuaded to go to Italy to visit her aunt, Emily Southwood Smith, for some months. Although she delighted in the journey, she found herself lonely in Florence, since Emily was busy all day teaching. Then she met a fellow Englishwoman, Miss Mayo, and her days became much more cheerful.

Knowing that Emily and Miranda were holding the fort at home, and a former pupil at Nottingham Place, Alice Collingwood, was helping with the tenants, Octavia fought back thoughts of home and of her work just begun, by remembering that she was away from it all in order to gather her strength. 'I try to pretend to myself that the things [here] are very engrossing and sufficient; and in a way they are.' She was transported by the beauty of Florence and its surroundings, the Certosa and Fiesole, the autumn light, the flowers and the music; she joined the Cherubini Choral Society and sang Bach and Mozart.

By March she was admitting to Emily the recuperative powers of careless pleasures. 'I am thriving in the most unaccountable way . . . This week I really *have* had dissipation, and it has done me all the good in the world.'[29] She went to a fancy dress party in a borrowed and magnificent Eastern dress.[30] 'It was the admiration of the whole company; in fact, I am never to hear the last of it, I think. It was pronounced very becoming.'

Letters from home reassured her. 'It is wonderful how smoothly things go on,' Emily wrote, 'and I am able to do the most important part of the work. The thing I have to neglect is going to see the people; but I spent nearly two hours with them; and they all welcomed me.'[31] Tom Hughes's sister, Mrs Nassau Senior, was helping out with the accounts.

When Octavia returned in April 1868, she found that in her absence all had gone remarkably well. She wasted no time, and was immediately back collecting rents and enjoying talks with the tenants after the long interval. 'I meet these details with less intensity of thought than of old. My sisters are such a rest and joy to me; I could never tell anyone what they are . . .'[32] But her health was still not

good, and they had persuaded her to leave the school teaching to them
– 'I have little temptation to meddle.'

When the May festival came round, Octavia was away again but her
mother wrote describing a successful day. The improvement in the
children was remarkable and many of them had spent the evening
before making wreaths from flowers provided by Ruskin and Mrs
Gillum.[33] The May Queen, a girl called Nelly Kinaly, sat upon a
throne in the midst of it all. 'The children looked so pretty – their
untidiness only went for picturesqueness.'[34]

Octavia was back at Derwent Bank with Mary Harris for the
summer weeks, and in early August she was staying at a health hydro
near Leeds, Ben Rhydding. Victorians, firm believers in the healing
powers of the waters, treated a wide range of illnesses, physical and
psychological, with an unremitting regime of hot baths, long cold
drinks and controlled diet. For some years Octavia was a regular
visitor to Ben Rhydding. Writing to Gertrude she reported how
effective the treatment was. 'All my pain has gradually decreased, my
head grown clear and capable, my back does not ache and I sleep
soundly, this is only wholly true of the last twenty-four hours but I
have been getting steadily better.'

She loved the solitude:

I wander on and out farther and farther over the wide high moor-
land, or I hurry up to my little eyrie in the doctor's quiet house and I
think and draw, and read, and write, and lie down and do exactly
what comes into my head. If I want a little change I swoop down
into the drawing-room where I am quite absurdly lionized. What
won't idle people amuse themselves with? But besides the idle ones
of course there are all those who are earnest about better things, or
glad to know of them and the great awkward but genuine sympathy
of the rich for the poor . . .

In 1869, when she was at Ben Rhydding again, Octavia managed to
visit a housing scheme of a different order. This was the remarkable
West Riding industrial settlement, Saltaire, outside Bradford: 'a
model village near here which has grown up round a manufactory
belonging to a Mr Titus (now Sir Titus) Salt; no beer shops there, only
model cottages, schools etc.' It was the kind of new beginning that she
would have loved to give the tenants of her London courts, but it was
utopian and required bottomless resources.

A valuable new friend whom she met at the hydro in 1871 was Sydney Cockerell, a City businessman. He described her to his sister:

> First and foremost of all the guests at Ben Rhydding, in my opinion, comes Miss Octavia Hill; an unobtrusive, plainly dressed little lady, everlastingly knitting an extraordinarily fine piece of work, whose face attracts you at first, and charms you, as you become acquainted with the power of mind and sweetness of character, to which it gives expression; a lady of great force and energy, with a wide, open and well-stored brain, but, withal, as gentle and womanly as a woman can be; and possessed of a wonderful tact, which makes her the most instructive and the pleasantest companion in the establishment. Miss Hill has done great things among the poor, in her own district of Marylebone.[35]

In 1868 Octavia was asked by her half-brother Arthur to be godmother to her niece, Constance Ida Hill, which re-established her contact with that branch of the family, from then on to be a great support to her. Arthur had begun his business career with Morton Peto, the railway magnate, and had built up a successful coal business. Later he was an important figure in civic life in Reading, becoming mayor.

Staying with Arthur and his wife, Octavia wrote to Mary Harris, 'it is very strange here. I feel so very near and yet so far off.' She watched her seven little nephews and nieces with interest: 'It is curious to see the Hill nature in them, and to see what it becomes under training and circumstances to me quite new.' The children have 'abounding energy, intellect and will. Margy [Whelpdale, their aunt, Arthur's full sister] says that they are very affectionate. I dare say they are, but they are not caressing children, not fond of animals.' Octavia was probably not exactly a cosy aunt. Once again, she looked a little plaintively at family life. 'The complete home-life is very lovely, not rare, thank God, but strange to me; the children's confidence in their father's love and strength, his joy in helping and planning and working for them, brings tears into my eyes.'

Octavia, nearing thirty, was watching her own opportunities for marriage and children slipping inexorably away; her life was full of other things but the longing for domesticity seemed to haunt her. Of her full sisters only Gertrude was married. Before long she managed to convert these feelings into the bedrock of her social work. Like many other Victorian reformers, in particular those who did not marry, she developed an ideology of domesticity. A few years later she wrote an article on the insights which the home offered.

> Is not she most sympathetic, most powerful, who nursed her own mother through the long illness . . . who entered so heartily into the sister's love and marriage; who obeyed so perfectly the father's command when it was the hardest? Better still if she be a wife and mother herself and can enter into the responsibilities of a head of a household . . . Depend upon it, if we thought of the poor primarily as husbands, wives, sons and daughters, members of households, as we are ourselves, instead of contemplating them as a different class, we should recognize better how the house training and high ideal of home duty was our best preparation for work among them.[36]

The home-based school at Nottingham Place merely developed Octavia's ideas of these links. That autumn term of 1868, it was at capacity, '. . . mainly under my sisters' care, who enjoy the work and thrive in it. I only teach the girls a few things . . . give a few drawing lessons and am managing my dear houses which are getting into such excellent order as to be a great joy, and but little painful care.'[37]

Everything was looking brighter. Work with the tenants did not engross her to the exclusion of all else. She went to hear John Stuart Mill, her grandfather's old colleague, giving his election address for a seat at Westminster. Although admiring him, she could not agree with all his points.[38] She was busy reading George Sand's *Countess of Rudolstadt*, and also finding time to draw again, seeing friends and catching up on news after her long absence. Approaching her thirtieth birthday she was able to sum up that 'it is a quiet, beautiful, thankful, busy, but not oppressed, life.'

Ruskin was immersing himself with new energy in the arts. Octavia wrote to Mary Harris, 'I cannot but be glad. They [Ruskin's drawings] are in many ways quiet, interesting, and freer from pain than the details of social work . . . he asked about me, and I told him concisely of our various successes in the houses.' She dined with him early in the new year, and he noted in his diary that William MacDonald and Miss Hill had been among the guests – 'all nice'. She was there again on 1 March. On another social occasion, the guests were treated to the remarkable sight of Octavia and Ruskin leading off a set of Sir Roger de Coverley.

Comparatively new friends were the Ducies – Octavia had taught Lady Ducie's daughter and niece drawing a few years earlier and in autumn 1866 Octavia was invited to stay, to continue the lessons. As a result, the Ducies became firm friends, as usual the bond being an interest in the same work. In early 1869 Lady Ducie invited Octavia to lunch, where she met Lady Amberley, Bertrand Russell's mother. Lady Amberley recalled: 'a very good little woman, who has courts in London she buys with money Ruskin lends her and then becomes landlord and keeps them in good repair and has built a play ground.'[39] She also noted:

> Lady Ducie is such a wonderfully energetic woman in good for the poor and all so very sensibly and not from the pauperizing and charitable point of view. She has now started a Co-operative store and it answers wonderfully though the place is purely agricultural and the houses very scattered – Lady Ducie lent books about it and talked and urged etc. and then there was a meeting about it and they elected a Committee, Lord and Lady Ducie keeping quite out of it then that it might be worked entirely by the people . . .[40]

Lady Ducie's other ventures were a convalescent hospital and a scheme of training midwives. Visits to Tortworth, the Ducies' house in Gloucestershire, became a regular event in Octavia's year – her only close contact with the world of the aristocracy.

In the spring of 1869 Octavia described her activities, apart from housing and the tenants, to Emily Shaen:

> I have hardly any of the teaching at home; dear Andy [Miranda] and Minnie [Emily] having thrown their strength fully into it; so Flo and I only take special classes; but the bright young life round one is very refreshing; and I grow much attached to some of the girls; – not the old sense of being any longer their head . . . My work now is mainly teaching drawing, which I enjoy much.

It is not easy to piece together the sources of Octavia's income in these years. Teaching, even with regular outside pupils, cannot have provided much of a living. The school at Nottingham Place must have provided salaries for all of the sisters, but Octavia's scruples prevented her ever paying herself a salary for the housing management work.[41]

She wrote to Mary Harris at this time:[42] 'How I should like to introduce you to some of my newer friends, Miss Rowland with her high aspirations and child-like reverence and energy; stately Mrs Duckworth,[43] magnificent in all she does, but strangely reverent and beautifully simple . . .'

Henrietta Rowland, who was working for Octavia, was for some years an intimate friend. In her late teens she had started working in one of Octavia's housing ventures, her 'pioneer schemes' as Henrietta put it. Her sister Alice Hart was also to become a stalwart; in particular as the organizer of concerts and ballad evenings. Henrietta's brother-in-law, Ernest Hart, was a Jewish surgeon and journalist, editor of the *British Medical Journal*, who was involved in numerous charitable organizations, from the Association for the Improvement of London Workhouse Infirmaries to several which were close to Octavia's heart – bodies campaigning for open spaces and smoke abatement. In the early 1880s he was co-founder of the Metropolitan Public Gardens Association.[44]

Henrietta saw Octavia as a heroine, and recorded her impressions of her friend on the evening that she first met the Revd Samuel Barnett, whom she was to marry. It was Octavia's birthday party in December 1870. Octavia was thirty-two, Henrietta nineteen. 'I remember going early to help Miss Octavia with the arrangements, and doing her beautiful hair in a more becoming way than in the tight twist at the back, which was where she usually carried it on her shapely head.'[45]

The guests came in shyly from the back door, and Henrietta noticed 'the rather exaggerated cordiality of Miss Octavia's greeting in the effort to make them feel welcome; and Miss Miranda's bright tender way of speaking to everyone exactly alike, were they rich or poor; and old Mrs Hill's curious voice with its rather rasping purr and pride and pleasure and large-heartedness, as she surveyed her motley groups of friends.' Also present were the two Miss Harrisons, 'those beautiful and generous artistic souls, the one so fat and short and the other so tall and thin, and their duet, purposely wrongly rendered to provoke the communion of laughter, ending with the invitation to everyone to say "quack, quack" as loudly as each was able, if only to prove they were all "ducks".'

Other guests that Henrietta could identify were Miss Florence Davenport Hill, daughter of Matthew Davenport Hill the Birmingham prison reformer (no relation), Mr C. E. Maurice, and Emma Cons. She was not introduced to the Revd Samuel Barnett but found herself sitting next to him at what she described as a generous, homely meal with its mixture of guests both rich and poor.

Henrietta was soon enmeshed in a correspondence with the young curate of St Mary's Bryanston Square. She was taken aback to receive a proposal of marriage from him in early 1872, 'as I had taken his many communications as representing his anxiety for the success of Miss Hill's social experiment and the consequent frequent supervision of one of her young workers.' In any case, she added, 'he looked so very much older than his age – twenty-seven – that I had accepted his interest as that of a kindly elderly gentleman, with small sensitive hands, a bald head and shaggy beard . . . far removed from a girlish idea of a lover.'

Her view was echoed by Kate Potter, Beatrice Webb's sister, who recalled her first meeting with Samuel Barnett in 1875: 'the young man – for he was young then, though he never looked it – struck me as plain and insignificant . . . In fact, what in my old hunting days I should have classed as a "poor thing".'[46] Despite that, he became to Kate Potter, as to Octavia, a 'dear and honoured friend'. Despite her slightly disparaging comments, Henrietta accepted Samuel Barnett's offer of marriage. Two other guests at that 1870 birthday party were also to marry in 1872: Emily Hill and Edmund, one of F. D. Maurice's sons.

There was little enough light-heartedness in general in these years around 1870. Octavia was occupied in evolving a stern view of the effects of indiscriminate charity. She was now engrossed in bringing into a coherent system her own work and wider endeavours under the umbrella of the Charity Organization Society and within the parish of St Mary's Bryanston Square. She had chosen a punishing path.

CHAPTER 7

Charity Organization Society

OCTAVIA's ideas on the limits and organization of charity were already firm when she embarked on her housing work; they scarcely changed in the next forty years. She set them out starkly in an article in 1869 for *Macmillan's Magazine*. 'Where a man persistently refuses to exert himself, external help is worse than useless.' Octavia's support for and sympathy with the objectives of the Charity Organization Society were fundamental to her own work, in all its areas. The COS reinforced and enhanced her emphasis on individual responsibility and her abhorrence of state-assisted services.

The Charity Organization Society, which Octavia supported steadfastly, came into being to deal with what was seen as a thoughtless, unco-ordinated reaction to poverty. Like Octavia, it took as its creed the possibilities inherent in the individual and his responsibility to himself and his family. The apparent rise in pauperism was seen as an indictment of the system of outdoor relief. Profligate expenditure on charity – conscience money given without thought – Octavia believed had nothing but a demoralizing effect.[1]

The COS did not at any point admit the accident of circumstance or the outcome of exploitation – yet Octavia readily acknowledged that much of the distress that she came upon was the result of bad housing management (landlords who merely increased rents for all to cover non-payment by some) and the uncertainties of seasonal employment. As it happened, Octavia was developing her own methods of dealing with both these problems.

The COS's guiding principle was to decentralize, and to target those in need; the COS was to be a referral agency, not a distributive body.[2] Visitors, the COS suggested, could obtain information as to the circumstances of those applying for financial aid, then charity could be directed to the 'deserving' – while public relief was for those who fell through that net. No allowance was made for those too proud to ask for public assistance.[3]

As the historian of the COS, Charles Loch Mowat, put it: 'The "organization" of charity, which began as an attempt to co-ordinate the work of charitable societies and the Poor Law, thus became a movement to reform the spirit not only of charities but of society.' Moralistic and inflexible in practice, the COS line was attacked constantly during its existence.

The most vivid illustrations of the disorder of charitable giving were the appeals mounted for national disasters. At a time such as the Lancashire cotton famine the middle classes were moved to give enormous sums, but where did it go? Fraudulent claims were believed to take a large proportion of all such appeal funds. Many who gave charitable donations on a regular basis did so through their churches. But the clergy were depleted in numbers and the church was itself falling out of touch with the majority of the population. The COS was born in an atmosphere of panic, which was exacerbated by the frequent abuses and corruption within the vestries and the disorder of private almsgiving. It operated from a standpoint of defensiveness, and from a deep fear that pauperism would get wildly out of control. The COS may have shared Christian concern and involved a number of churchmen, but it had little or nothing in common with Christian Socialism or the clergy in general, who were largely unpersuaded by COS claims.

In 1869 Octavia set out her opinions in a paper entitled 'The Importance of Aiding the Poor without Almsgiving', which she delivered to the Social Science Association in Bristol. It was a courageous act in view of the fact that women then rarely addressed large public meetings.[4] Octavia began: 'There are two main principles to be observed in any plan for raising the poorest class in England. One is that personal influence must be brought strongly to bear on the individuals. The other that the rich must abstain from any form of almsgiving.' Her four years of work with 'about forty families of the very poor' had demonstrated to her that the approach worked.

'No one can over-rate the urgent need of organization. Every worker among the poor could give instances of the present waste of the donors' money, energy, and time.' Definite rules were needed; either the registration of each individual and assessment of his or her need, or the 'assignment of definite places or families to the care of individual workers, answerable, if need be, to committees, but left in the main to use the invention, perception, power of adapting plans to character, and the might of personal influence, both or either of which are impossible to committees.' Above all: 'Do not trust any plan of relief, however methodical which leaves intimate personal action out of account.' Octavia's own approach was founded on personal appraisal. 'For by knowledge of character . . . more is meant than knowledge of whether a man is a drunkard or a woman dishonest; it means knowledge of the passions, hope, and history of people.' Once the worker had become a 'friend', then help could be given 'friend to friend'. She did not want to deny the poor, or 'sacrifice even the least of them to a theory.'[5]

The audience was so large that the meeting had to adjourn to the Bristol Library, ten minutes walk away. 'I started with a few friends, and the audience came streaming behind. I never saw anything so absurd . . . I wasn't the least nervous, but was uncertain how to measure the distance my voice would travel. I understand it was easily audible. My paper was a great success.' The audience wanted to hear about the housing work, and 'several capital questions were asked, to which I replied. Never was anything simpler or easier, but the amount of feeling it took out of me was considerable.'[6] In the midst of the philanthropic society of Bristol she had considerable support and several friends, in particular the Winkworths. The interest in her work gave her courage: 'I am more and more impressed with the work opening before me.'

Where did Octavia get her own firm, if not rigid, ideas, which she had so polished by 1869 that she could lecture and publish articles on charitable organization? She always claimed to have been a member of the COS since 1867; but it did not then exist and she must been referring to one of its immediate forebears, the London Association for the Prevention of Pauperism and Crime, whose prospectus had been drafted by Ruskin.[7] It changed its name to the Society for Organizing Charitable Relief and Repressing Mendicity in April 1869. By the time of its first annual meeting, it was known in shorthand as the Charity Organization Society.

Octavia anticipated the COS line, with its dislike of dependency, to such an extent that one might almost see the COS as the mirror of her ideas. Certainly, the influence of John Ruskin can be detected. Ruskin was a member of the first Council of the COS, and remained a member and Vice-President for many years. According to C. S. Loch, he also was generous with financial support in the early days when the COS nearly foundered for lack of funds. Ruskin may have introduced Octavia to an organization of those who shared her views, but her views were entirely her own.

There were precursors for the COS. Dr Thomas Chalmers' work in Edinburgh was one. From 1819 until the late 1830s he ran a system of parish-based visitors who disbursed the funds raised by the church. Another scheme, the Elberfeld system in Prussia, was based on a network of unpaid almoners who distributed funds which were a mixture of public and private charity.[8] Octavia frequently referred to this as a model for her own approach.[9]

Various organizations which operated by friendly visiting existed before the COS; Ellen Ranyard's Bible Women, or 'native reformers' as she preferred to call the helpers whom Octavia admired so much;[10] the Metropolitan Visiting and Relief Association, begun in 1843; and the Society for the Relief of Distress, set up in 1860 specifically for London problems, which used a system of voluntary almoners.

Edward Denison[11] is often cited as the father of the COS; his work preceded the Settlement movement by twenty years when he moved into the East End, off the Mile End Road, in 1867 to see poverty at first hand and at close quarters. The combination of an ineffective Poor Law administration, what he saw as the effects of indiscriminate charity, and the absence of professionals or the upper classes to carry out voluntary work, gave him the idea of organizing what charity there was on a local basis.

The COS itself was born out of a series of committee meetings in the early months of 1869. Lord Lichfield was the first chairman on the Council, a post which he held until 1877. An office was set up in Buckingham Street, which ran down to the Thames behind the Strand. Several of those involved had had experience in some of the earlier charitable organizations but by the time of the first Annual Meeting, held on 30 March 1870 the committee had swelled to include the Marquess of Westminster, Lord George Hamilton, Archbishop Manning, Mr Gladstone, and Octavia herself. The COS used its influential friends to best advantage, and the list of Vice-Presidents which appeared the following year was highly impressive.

The central figures in the early history of the Organization were a tight-knit group, several of whom had been COS volunteers. Work with the COS became a lifetime's commitment for many of them — which was one explanation of their inability to alter its views even as the world around them changed. C. S. Loch, who became secretary in 1875 – and held the office until 1913 – was drawn in after he graduated from Balliol, in 1873. Charles Bosanquet was the first secretary of the COS and his son, Bernard, was a contemporary of Loch's at Oxford. In later years, Bernard Bosanquet and his wife, Helen Dendy, promoted the organization's views widely through books, lectures and membership of committees. Helen Bosanquet sat with Octavia on the 1904 Poor Law Commission.

Sir Charles Trevelyan,[12] the co-author of the Northcote-Trevelyan report on the Civil Service, and who had carried out practical social reforms during his years in India, was another prominent figure in the early days of the COS. As an administrator *par excellence* he was an important member. Edward Peters was another Council member; his daughter Sophia later married C. S. Loch and was Octavia's assistant in the early 1870s.[13]

From its early days the main Council of the COS seems to have seethed with disagreements and personal antipathies. Nobody agreed with any but his own account of its founding, nor about the way in which it should proceed. Quarrels reverberated for years.[14] Some of the members were strongly anti-clerical. A major difficulty concerned the inequality of available aid to rich and poor areas: Octavia supported the idea of centralizing the system, on the grounds that this would enable the strict COS line against indiscriminate charity to be held. The majority of the Council thought otherwise.

Edmund Maurice was by this time Octavia's brother-in-law, having married Emily in the late summer of 1872 at a quiet church service with many of the tenants in the congregation. 'I like to think that the blessing of the poor rested on them,' Octavia wrote.[15] Edmund became another of Octavia's dependable inner circle, an honorary member of the family, although she sometimes felt he was narrow-minded.[16] He was often with Octavia at the COS meetings, so his reports of these fallings-out are first-hand. As he put it, with detached understatement, 'Her sympathies with the enquiry traditions of the Society, and with the restrictions on reckless relief, often startled and repelled some of the more impulsive philanthropists.'

The COS plan was to set up an office in each Poor Law division, staffed by an agent and supported by a local committee. Each COS office would keep a record of all charitable cases in the district and investigate those that had not been helped to date. An individual applying for charitable assistance would undergo a rigorous test for suitability. According to Loch Mowat, the plan failed from the first.

The operation of the Poor Laws depended on the Boards of Guardians, elected (following the 1834 Poor Law Amendment Act) by ratepayers of each union, or group, of parishes. These people had complete powers over the social provision for the poor, and could consign families to the workhouse on the slenderest of pretexts. One priority for the COS leaders was to seek office as Guardians, in an attempt to reform the administration of public relief by inconspicuous infiltration.

In 1875 the first woman Guardian was elected, in Kensington, and thereafter an increasing number of women joined their number.[17] In three East End unions, St George's-in-the-East, Whitechapel and Stepney, the Guardians and the charitable agencies, in particular the COS, agreed to co-operate; outdoor relief was abolished and the voluntary bodies dealt with those paupers whose case was not hopeless.

Significantly enough, the only example of the COS system in full and effective operation was the Marylebone District Committee, Octavia's own, but from which she resigned in 1874 after a series of disagreements. Octavia described this committee in some detail in her report to the Local Government Board. Four agencies were involved: the Guardians with their relieving officer; the Relief Committee; the District Visitors; and then the COS. It was an elaborate system, made complex in order to 'administer relief to the necessitous in the wisest and most really helpful way'. It was of course, far too complex, and has all the marks of Octavia's dangerous obsession with detail. She seems to have created an unwieldy structure which led to misunderstanding, disagreement and solved little. It also depended crucially on Octavia herself, queen bee in the midst of it all.

Octavia had been approached by the Revd Fremantle,[18] a friend of her great supporter Lady Ducie, to join his Marylebone District Committee in June 1869. It was founded at a meeting in the parish: Archbishop Manning and the Revd Llewelyn Davies (Emily's brother) were there. As Octavia wrote to Florence Davenport Hill before the important meeting: 'very opposite creeds will be represented.'[19]

Octavia was soon organizing District Visitors, eventually some thirty-five of them, who distributed the funds from the St Mary's Relief Committee, on which Octavia also sat. She assumed the role of referee and 'personal' link between the two bodies. Samuel Barnett, who was Fremantle's curate, was one of her helpers in these early days.

The Revd Fremantle's views were in advance of his time. He felt that a parish should function as a community – a divinely established microcosm, as he put it – and while 'we cannot . . . expect the parish church to be a spiritual home of all the parishioners . . . we can still make it a centre of good in which the rich may help the poor, and the school may become a nursery for the Christian family, and various institutions may arise for mutual good and for common interests beyond our own narrow boundaries.' Looking back, he continued:

> I had many excellent assistants, and cannot repress a sense of pride in the fact that two of the greatest efforts for the good of the poor of London sprang up in the parish of St Mary's Bryanston Square, namely, that which was carried out by Miss Octavia Hill under the inspiring impulse of the great thinker Mr Maurice, and that of Toynbee Hall and its adjuncts under Mr Barnett, who worked with us at St Mary's for seven years before he began his great work in the East of London. These two great works had a common source and were begun under the shadow of St Mary's Church.[20]

The Revd Fremantle had been amazed by Octavia's forceful and developed views about the organization of charity although, when they first met, she was little known and without influence.

In his 1870 Pastoral Address and Report of Charities, an account of the uses to which donations of £611 had been put, the Revd Fremantle included an Appendix written by Octavia about her Walmer Street Industrial enterprise.[21] This, a new undertaking, served the tenants in the Walmer Street and Walmer Place properties, the poorest in Fremantle's parish, consisting of around 200 families. Octavia had begun to manage the houses in January that year.[22]

Henrietta Rowland described Octavia's objectives:

> Counting that the only method of improving social conditions was by raising individuals, she held that it was impertinent to the poor and injurious to their characters to offer them doles. They should be lifted out of pauperism by being expected to be self-dependent, and, in evidence of respect, be offered work instead of doles, even if

work had to be created artificially. To this end, and with the support of the Rector, Miss Octavia Hill had recently started a workroom for women, and created an odd-job department for the houses she managed.[23]

This idea had grown out of the earlier work with the women from Paradise Place, and their employment in the small workshop behind Nottingham Place. Octavia, as District Visitor for the Walmer Street area, was stepping out of line with her colleagues, who were presumably dispensing charity in the usual way – gifts of money or tokens for coal or groceries. Octavia would have none of that. For Octavia, the mechanism of employment was the perfect way to ensure that charitable donations were focused upon need. She was willing to provide work for everyone who needed it in the area, as long as they could make a case for needing it.

For the men the range of jobs included carpentering, whitewashing, window-cleaning, portering; for women, washing, upholstery and needlework. For younger girls and boys she found positions as under-servants and errand boys respectively. In 1870 she had 133 applicants, of whom 90 were offered work and 51 accepted it. Families where the father was fully employed or where the family 'were in receipt of private gifts' were excluded. Some applicants wanted 'free gifts and not honestly earned wages'; they got short shrift, and there was often much bad feeling. There were also a number who were ill and too old to work, and here she dispensed loans or pensions, the latter being designed to keep the elderly out of the workhouse. 'There is a charm about a little home of one's own, which the rich may fairly provide for those who have worked hard as long as they were able.' These pensions, Octavia added, were from a special fund provided by a friend.

George Eliot was a generous supporter, perhaps even the friend in question. She wrote to Mrs Richard Congreve, regretting that she could not give any more money to a pensioner:

I would rather not apply any more money in that direction, because I know of other channels – especially a plan which is being energetically carried out for helping a considerable group of people without almsgiving, and solely by inducing them to work – into which I shall be glad to pour a little more aid. The repugnance to have relief from the parish was a feeling which it was good to encourage in the old days of contra-encouragement to sturdy pauperism; but I question whether one ought now to indulge it, and not rather point out the reason why, in a case of real helplessness, there is no indignity in receiving from a public fund.[24]

In 1872 Octavia wrote an updated account of the Walmer Street experiment.[25] Her organized plan had, she said, 'succeeded beyond my best hopes'. Initially, she admitted, there had been misunderstandings and 'a bitter sense of resentment among the people', but she thought there had been a great change. 'No doubt individuals still feel annoyed . . . but . . . we have come to know each other better, and sometimes the bitterness of feeling has seemed to me wholly gone.' It had been hard and needed courage to enforce her system. Now the Industrial Experiment was to be merged into a general scheme; the workroom for women would be made available for anyone from the parish and the work for men 'will be at the disposal of the St Mary's Committee of Poor Relief'. There had obviously been disagreements; but 'my position now differs from that of all Mr Fremantle's district visitors in no way, except that I am in more constant communication with the Committee than most of them have hitherto cared to be.' She had also set up a playground in the area near her houses, and laid on excursions and winter entertainment – 'to cheer and brighten . . . a few hours of lives which are habitually ground down by care and monotony.'

The alliance of the Church Council with the district COS had achieved another of Fremantle's objectives – widening the aims beyond the confines of the Church of England. The committee included at least one non-conformist, and the secretary was a Jew. One of Fremantle's innovations was to entertain the entire parish, street by street.[26]

Octavia soon involved the young curate, the Revd Samuel Barnett, in her work in the parish. Barnett ran a Club at Walmer Street and Octavia found him congenial. According to another colleague at St Mary's, the Revd Young, 'the effect of her coming was to cause [Barnett] partially to throw off the reserve which his modesty had imposed upon him, and together they became the driving wheels of Charity Reform in our parish.'[27]

Octavia enjoyed the work. She wrote to Mary Harris on the first day of a new year, 1872; 'Oh, we are getting on so beautifully at St Mary's! I cannot tell you of half our successes, or the vistas of hope that open out before me. May I only have a long life and many fellow workers!'

Much of her optimism was due to the pleasure of working with and forming lasting friendships with Samuel Barnett and Henrietta Rowland, whom he soon married. Henrietta, immensely impressed by Octavia's achievements, remembered her as she was then:

> She was small in stature with a long body and short legs. She did not dress, she only wore clothes, which were often unnecessarily unbecoming; she had soft and abundant hair and regular features, but the beauty of her face lay in her brown and very luminous eyes, which quite unconsciously she lifted upwards as she spoke on any matter for which she cared. Her mouth was large and mobile, but not improved by laughter. Indeed Miss Octavia was nicest when she was made passionate by her earnestness.[28]

Despite their close working relationship, Barnett did not introduce Octavia to his family or friends. 'To old Mrs Barnett, who had only heard of her, she was a source of continual fear,' wrote Henrietta:

> and I attributed part of her warm welcome to me, after our engagement, as due to relief of mind. Though no names were mentioned, her inability to understand such a friendship was evidenced in her congratulations on my youth, and her strongly expressed opinion that men should marry women younger than themselves, and not older ladies whose views were all settled, and who liked the work they had given themselves to do better than taking care of their husbands and their homes.[29]

Another new and valuable friend who helped Octavia with the accounts – a trusted position usually conferred upon men – was Tom Hughes's sister and daughter-in-law of a political economist, Jane Nassau Senior. Soon after Octavia met her, Jane was appointed the first woman Poor Law Inspector. James Stansfield, President of the Local Government Board and an ardent supporter of women's rights, wrote: 'I did the thing which they hated the most. I imposed a woman on them, I made a woman a Poor Law Inspector.' More than that, before stepping down he made her post a permanent one.[30]

Jane had enormous experience, having for many years been a

workhouse visitor. She was well connected in circles concerned with social work; she knew Louisa Twining, the eminent pioneer of workhouse visiting, and was a close friend of George Eliot whom she helped through the terrible last weeks of her stepson Thornie's illness.

Jane's appointment was an important step towards breaking down the barriers to women in the civil service. In January 1873 Stansfield asked her to carry out an enquiry into the barrack schools for pauper children and to give 'the woman's view' of their influence on the girls who were educated there. A year later Jane produced her report. It was a most impressive piece of work, based on a survey of some 650 pauper girls who had gone into service, and full of her own enlightened ideas and suggestions.[31] She was highly critical of the scale of these 'monster' schools – the largest, Sutton School which served the South Metropolitan district of London, had almost 1,600 children – and considered that boarding-out was a satisfactory solution for orphan children.[32]

Her various recommendations fell on deaf ears. Stansfield lost office with the fall of Gladstone's administration and Jane Nassau Senior had to resign because of illness. But her example as a woman penetrating the closed world of government and the civil service remained an inspiration to many others moving in that direction.

In 1872 Octavia started her annual 'Letter to Fellow-workers' which gave a detailed picture of her progress, a kind of descriptive balance sheet. The Letters followed the same formula as the two accounts of the Walmer Street Industrial Experiment, and effectively replaced them. Addressed to those who financed her endeavours as well as to those who worked with her – 'fellow-workers' were sympathetic people, whether directly or indirectly involved – they were accounts of failure as well as of success. Begun as personal letters written to each individual helper, they were, from 1872 onwards, in recognition of their swelling numbers, privately printed and circulated to supporters. She was always adamant that they were not to be published.

All the houses, she wrote in 1872, were paying a minimum 5 per cent dividend, and offers of capital were pouring in – faster than they could train the workers to manage more houses. 'It is extremely important not to advance beyond the sphere which can be managed by trained and tried workers, which naturally contracts our operations.' In one case, a 'spirited lady' – Lady Ducie – had invested a magnificent £7,000 in order to buy a block, but intended to superintend it herself, with a trained worker paid from the rents. (Lady Ducie's property was in Barrett's Court,⋆ where Henrietta Rowland was, as she described herself, 'the volunteer and inefficient rent-collector'.) Although the credit and debit columns at the end of the Letters do not include salaries, there were by now a number of paid workers, funded through the commission the owners paid for rent-collection. Emma Cons, for example, was salaried, whilst the wealthy Henrietta Rowland was a volunteer.

Any return in excess of 5 per cent was invariably reinvested for the permanent improvement of the property. Some of the owners of the houses had also been involved in offering summer excursions and winter entertainment to the tenants – 'thus not only giving pleasure, but deepening the sense of a personal relation and responsibility'. Octavia also described the experiments in providing work – 'to my mind the most useful possible help'.

Donations were meticulously listed against expenditure in the back of each Letter, and the accounts always balanced to the last halfpenny. From the beginning, the names of donors are a roll-call of those active in social welfare in the Victorian period. Although Octavia's housing work was limited in scale by her difficulties in delegation, and by her insistence on a personal approach which necessarily constricted what could be done, her influence on middle-class thought was immense. Whether she provoked agreement or disagreement, she formed opinions and brought the whole housing issue into the limelight.[33]

Disagreements always caused her unhappiness. On 1 November 1875 she sent a long, pained letter to the Revd Fremantle, offering her resignation from the Marylebone District Relief Committee. She had confided in Samuel Barnett and he had advised that resignation was her best course. However, 'I remain painfully impressed with an immovable conviction that it [resignation] is the wrong [decision] which comes no doubt from an overweening sense of my own importance and of . . . living down misunderstanding.'[34] She was disappointed by the calibre of the Visitors – 'the real link between rich and poor which shall last when the miserable "cash-nexus" of dole-giving shall have ceased' – and by lack of support from the members. 'Your Committee has always appeared to me only the first step in a system which may do almost anything for the people if it is well followed up, but the living individual influence must be brought to bear by the Visitors.'

⋆ See Chapter 8.

She proceeded, without apology, to give Fremantle her views on what should be done: she felt that any denial of an offer for assistance should be fully explained, for 'the refusal can hardly be a help to the man unless it is again and again gently explained, unless advice is given, information procured, and the right moment noted and acted on when it comes for the man to do what the Committee advised.'

The trouble seems to have lain in the discrepancy between the hard line taken by the committee and the Visitor's own judgement when faced with someone whose plight seemed desperate. Octavia's faith in her theories allowed her to look beyond the immediate misery to a resolution based on self-help and individual effort, but understandably many of the Visitors could not do this. 'Many of them at present need help to understand why the committee so often think refusal of immediate help the best permanent help.'

One example of the difficulties on the ground was represented by Emma Cons's experience. She tried never to give money, only gifts in kind such as holidays and employment. But once she broke her rule. Entering a room, she saw a stiff figure under a sheet, a weeping huddle of children and a stricken widow chopping up a chair for firewood. Moved by the tragic sight, she emptied her purse. A little later she realized that she had forgotten her umbrella. Going back into the room she found the corpse up and about in the best of spirits, and the family taking turns with the gin bottle. She told the story against herself, as a cautionary tale for the credulous.

In her letter of resignation, Octavia described herself to Fremantle as 'one of the first leaders in an unpopular movement'. It was to become a far more unpopular movement later on, at a time when Octavia herself was considerably less pliant.

By the mid-1870s two camps in the war of charities were locked in conflict. There were people:

a little hard and dry in their manner of urging their views [on social welfare] and but few of them have real, living, personal intercourse with the poor. On the other hand, there exists a large body of kindly, liberal, devoted workers among the poor, who *never* look beyond the immediate result of the special gift, who are injuring them irreparably by ill-considered doles . . . these two sets of people must be brought together and learn to understand one another, and that quickly.

The former group consisted of the 'young officers, merchants, noblemen, lawyers, bankers' of the COS; the latter the willing but over-impulsive women visitors from the District Visiting societies. Octavia pinned her hopes on the clergy becoming the intermediaries between the two groups – there was so much to do.[35] But the difficulties which she encountered at St Mary's were endemic in the organization and its relationship to the world outside it.

At its period of strength – the early 1870s to the 1890s – the COS was enormously influential, even if highly controversial.[36] Octavia never wavered in her general adherence to its letter, but others veered from its moralistic and severe line from early days.[37] Among philanthropists and social reformers, Emma Cons and Eleanor Rathbone both later abandoned COS principles, as did the young Beatrice Webb, the Barnetts and Cardinal Manning. By the 1890s the exodus was gathering momentum and even Octavia had her doubts, fearing that those at the centre had little sense of the realities encountered by those who had to confront, and justify, their actions to the poor. She often referred to the members of the main committee as 'hard'.

Her own housing work was going exceedingly well in the early 1870s. She wrote to Henrietta Barnett (always known as Yetta),[38] telling her of a meeting that she had gone to at which was discussed the subject of housing the poor.

> It was to me a very impressive meeting, it was beautiful to see so very many earnest men all setting their heads and hearts to work to root out the evil . . . I could not help wondering whether my grandfather could look down at all and see us. My memory of work among the poor as I heard of it in childhood was so different, the pioneers . . . sacrificed so much, met with such obloquy, somehow our actions seem to me so cheap in comparison with theirs.

Octavia sat on a number of COS sub-committees in the 1870s. In 1871 the subject was unemployment relief. The committee, chaired by Sir Charles Trevelyan, reported along rigid lines, emphasizing the distinction made between 'improvement schemes' which offered regular employment and wages, and 'relief schemes', paid at subsistence level, for the sick and helpless. It echoed Octavia's Walmer Street Industrial Experiment to the letter.

The following year a major committee was set up to investigate the whole topic of the dwellings of the poor in the metropolis. It was a

BOROUGH of WISBECH CAMBRIDGESHIRE.

Octavia's birthplace in Wisbech, Cambridgeshire – the house on the right by the bridge over the River Nene.

James Hill, Octavia's father.

Dr Southwood Smith, Octavia's remarkable grandfather, drawn by Margaret Gillies.

Caroline Southwood Hill (1808–1902), Octavia's mother.

The drawings by Margaret Gillies of women and children at work in the mines, which illustrated Dr Southwood Smith's report on child labour (see page 32).

The Hill sisters in 1864: from the left
they are Gertrude, Octavia,
Miranda, Florence and Emily.

John Ruskin (left, photographed by Charles Dodgson) and F. D. Maurice the Christian Socialist. Miranda wrote, 'It is impossible to realize how much of what her life was is due to their
help and influence.'

No 4, Russell Place (now demolished) where
Caroline and the girls lived when they first
moved into central London.

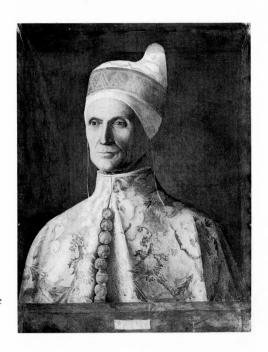

Octavia's watercolour copy of Bellini's Doge Leonardo Loredan, made for Ruskin (see page 64).

The Revd Samuel Barnett (1844–1913) and his wife Henrietta (1851–1936) – lifelong friends and colleagues of Octavia's.

This picture of Freshwater Place was taken in the 1950s: it is now demolished and replaced by Octavia House, a block of old people's flats. Note the balcony and top floor, added in 1873 (see page 104).

A slum family making brushes at home, around the 1890s – a scene Octavia would have been familiar with.

Walmer Street, now demolished but here photographed in the 1950s.

Octavia at the age of 39, drawn by Edward Clifford.

weighty committee, chaired by Lord Napier, and loaded with peers, MPs and distinguished figures in the housing field, including Lord Shaftesbury and Sir Sydney Waterlow. There were old friends such as Tom Hughes and forty COS representatives, including Octavia.[39]

The committee held sixteen meetings and one of its conclusions was the inadequacy of the industrial dwellings companies' provision for the needs of a dramatically overcrowded city. Only 27,000 people had been housed through their efforts – less than half the annual increase of population in the metropolis. The report, submitted as 'Dwellings of the Poor' and sent with an accompanying memorandum to the Home Secretary, was to be of great importance when the government framed the next major piece of housing legislation – Richard Cross's Artisans' Dwellings Act of 1875.

Octavia was consulted in great detail over the drafting of the bill. As Mr Kay-Shuttleworth MP, later Lord Shuttleworth, recalled:

> Miss Octavia Hill was pre-eminently fitted for contributing an exceptional amount of practical knowledge, experience, and wisdom at the meetings . . . on a subject which she made her own. She would quietly listen to a discussion of some point, and at last say a few weighty words in her calm, impressive, tactful way, which would carry with her the general assent of all, or nearly all who heard her, and would thus promptly bring the debate to a sound conclusion.[40]

Octavia was eager to point to the example of Glasgow where an Act had been passed which allowed the municipality to demolish tenements and to rebuild. But by contrast with London, private enterprise there had succeeded in replacing the demolished dwellings with an equal amount of new housing.[41]

Octavia had now assumed a highly influential position – that of policy-maker. Her opinions and experiences, formed over the last ten years, were in demand by those who were framing the laws of the country. As she wrote to Mary Harris, she was busy dining and talking with men such as Kay-Shuttleworth, Sir James Stansfield and Mr Shaw-Lefevre. 'Mr Cross has accepted nearly all we submitted to him. So far all is very satisfactory,' but there were fears of dissension from Mr Fawcett, 'representing extreme political economy', and Mr Cawley on behalf of the vestries. 'We are much afraid of clogging amendments being carried; and no one knows what the Lords will do.' Her man in the Lords was Lord Monteagle, 'who will really master the details, and may secure more powerful allies in the world's opinion; though I believe in the careful whole-hearted work of young men really in earnest, much more than in the chance of a few words from a man of influence. Dost not thou?'

She was in the House for the second reading of the Bill, since she was being consulted over the proposed amendments. She was tasting power. 'I was sitting quite alone in the gallery belonging to the Speaker's wife; it was very late, and she and her friends had all gone home . . . I had been listening intently, but, when Mr Kay Shuttleworth began to speak, I thought I knew all that he was going to say, and was leaning back thinking, when suddenly my own name caught my ear.' Shuttleworth was reading out sections of her article on Blank Court (Barrett's Court) which had appeared in *Macmillan's Magazine*. 'Somehow it seemed a blessed thing to have half suggested, and wholly anticipated the feeling on the part of that bright, promising young man, and thro' him to the whole House. One felt so small, so alone and out of sight; and there were thoughts bearing fruit in ways of which one had never dreamed. I can't tell how tiny it made me feel.'[42]

The Artisans' Dwellings Act of 1875 empowered town councils, or the Metropolitan Board of Works in London, to make improvements, to acquire property, to demolish and re-erect houses on the sites. Octavia was optimistic. 'If only the first schemes are well made and carried through, this bill will do as much as even I had dared to hope.'[43]

In fact the bill was utterly ineffective. The flaw lay in the arrangements for compensation; landlords were effectively encouraged to run down their properties (already desperately unprofitable through non-payment of rents) so as to receive compensation once they were deemed uninhabitable. The local authorities then failed to carry out their part of the bargain, which was to rebuild the housing to a decent standard. The overall effect was thus further to deplete the housing stock, and overcrowding and lack of sanitary facilities became ever more dire.

When the COS set up a committee in 1880 to consider why the bill had so signally failed, Octavia was again Shuttleworth's confidante and helper. The resulting COS report, produced in 1881, led to much disagreement; the outcome was a rather feeble retreat, relying on the hope that workmen's trains would spread the population over a wider suburban area and thus reduce the pressure on the centre.

With her membership of the Council of the COS and of its various committees, Octavia was much engrossed in the development of the COS itself. Its influence upon her and on many with whom she worked, continuing into the 1890s with Charles Booth[44] and into the 1900s with the Poor Law Commission, meant that the ideology of the COS was interwoven throughout Octavia's life and achievements.

Hearing that Octavia was to be a member of a special Sanitary Committee of the COS, her mother recalled Dr Southwood Smith. 'All the men who have worked from the beginning are there and many others besides. Is it not wonderful that Octa should be among them, and able continually to say a word in season. Dear child, the mantle has fallen on her.'[45]

CHAPTER 8

Barrett's Court

IN 1870 George Eliot forwarded to Octavia a copy of Lady Amberley's speech given at the Stroud Institute on 'The Claims of
Women', advocating suffrage and equal rights in education, professions, employment and wages, as well as property rights for
married women. Mrs Lewes could find 'little of which I cannot say
that I both agree and keenly sympathize with it'. Octavia's response is
not recorded, although her record on a number of campaigns, including the 1856 petition on married women's property rights and for the
extension of further education to women, was an enlightened one. By
the end of 1870 the Married Women's Property Act was on the statute
book.[1]

This was welcome news for married women, many of whom gave
Octavia financial help in the form of investing in properties which she
and her fellow workers could manage for them. During 1869 and 1870
friends of Octavia's bought a number of such houses, amongst which
were some of the worst properties she had ever encountered.

The Sterling sisters, Hester and Julia, purchased Walmer Street and
Walmer Place, off Seymour Street: Emma Cons was to manage the
thirty-eight houses and live on the spot. Although dependent on
Octavia for the channelling of funds, Emma was in all other respects a
trusted and autonomous worker. It showed Octavia that, in the right
hands, she could devolve the management of housing completely.[2]
Nevertheless Octavia remained critical of Emma's lack of care over
detail. Referring to a neatly kept rent book she noted that 'Miss Cons is
sure to consider it quite thrown away labour. Why is this in her, I often
wonder? She would do a thing of the kind any day to spoil me, but she
would think me quite mad to care, all the time.'[3]

Emma Cons also helped Octavia at Barrett's Court, one block of which had been bought in 1872 with Lady Ducie's munificent £7,000. Another block had been purchased by Mrs Stopford Brooke, who as an invalid was unable to take a personal interest in the tenants (as Lady Ducie did), but was unfailingly generous in her financial support.

Emma, significantly for the future status of the profession of housing management, became a paid worker at Barrett's Court rather than the occasional assistant she had been at Paradise and Freshwater Place. Remembered by the tenants as 'a pleasant-faced young woman, with bright rosy cheeks', she threw herself into her new occupation with characteristic gusto.

Barrett's Court, to which Octavia gave the pseudonym of Blank Court in her writing, and which was later officially renamed St Christopher's Place, was in an appalling state, but the tenants made her hopeful. Octavia described them as 'almost the poorest class of those amongst our population who have any settled home . . . when unruly and hopeless tenants were sent away from other houses in the district, I had often heard that they had gone to Blank Court . . .' She planned to treat the tenants courteously and carefully, and was confident that they would respond to her approach.

Barrett's Court immediately presented Octavia with a grave embarrassment. The Medical Officer of Health had condemned the original group of houses, and it was a test of whether her scheme of carrying out initial minimal repairs and low-cost improvements could stand its ground against the public health standards – low as they were. The first hurdle came when the COS sub-committee on housing decided, in November 1871, to enquire into Octavia's system of housing management. They gave her an endorsement in their findings, published in February 1872, but the attentions of the Medical Officer of Health for Marylebone were to dog her until 1875.

An early first-hand account of Octavia's housing management – never to be referred to as rent-collecting – was given by the Hon. Mrs Maclagan, who was taken on, after a brief interview at Nottingham Place in November 1871, to look after Mrs Stopford Brooke's seven houses in Barrett's Court. The new worker was required to go to the Court every Monday 'armed with a bag, an account book and an ink bottle slung round my neck, and call on every tenant for the weekly rent. What a boon a fountain pen would have been! but they were not invented and I never found any ink bottle that did not leak!'

Each house contained a shop, a parlour and six bedrooms. The cellars were let with the shops for storing goods, and Octavia was firm that they should not be used as living accommodation.[4]

Every house had its own small yard with a water butt and other 'conveniences' such as they were. The entrance passage was by way of being kept clean by children of the tenants, to whom 1s a week was paid if the work was well done, and the tenants on each floor were responsible for cleaning their staircase. Miss Hill began by repairing and strengthening all the front doors, and supplying latch keys to the tenants, but this had soon to be abandoned, as the tenants lost the latch keys and the drunken people in the Court burst the doors open if they were bolted, and slept in the passage or on the stairs, leaving them often in a state of indescribable filth.

Forty-five tenants and their families lived in Barrett's Court, in forty-nine rooms. Given the size of most families, the population must have run into several hundred. To those who would take a second room, Octavia offered a reduction of 6d and 3d per week respectively on the first and second floors. The tenants seldom availed themselves of the offer. Mrs Maclagan remembered a family, 'a man and his wife and seven children including the baby, who lived, cooked, slept and did the family washing in a single room.' Most of the tenants were Irish, 'Roman Catholics of a very low type, the prevailing trade being that of a "handy man" . . . who could do nothing really well, and was frequently out of work.'

Among my tenants I had 3 or 4 very decent artisans in receipt of good wages and with regular steady work. Also one retired soldier, a nice old man, whose room was always scrupulously clean. I found the people ready and eager to pay their rent when they had the money, but a curious custom prevailed among them – every man in full work gave his wife £1 a week, apparently it made no difference whether he earned 25s or £3, or whether the family was large or small. With this pound the 'missus' was expected to pay the rent and the schooling and feed and clothe the family . . . no man would ever help with the rent. Miss Hill had a penny bank in the Court and I have known men to bring 2s, 3s or even 5s on a Saturday evening, when the rent of their room was two or three weeks in arrears – in theory Miss Hill never allowed arrears for more than a fortnight without threatening, or a month without putting in the broker, but like many theories, hers were not always put in practice and I have known tenants in arrears for as much as eleven weeks. Probably she knew that they had a good deposit in the Penny Bank which she, or one of her chief workers, always managed in person.

On Thursday, the volunteers went to look for those tenants who had been out on the Monday. Where possible reliable tenants were employed to carry out the repairs; Mrs Maclagan had £2 every quarter to spend on the seven houses, which returned an average weekly rent of 28s each. She also ran a small school on Sunday afternoon in the club room.

Every quarter she had to call in her rent books and balance the accounts 'to a penny'. Records were kept in a large folio volume, with two pages per tenant, headed by a COS printed table,

in which I was to insert every scrap of information I could collect about the number, occupations and earnings of each family, with a monthly record of their history, a line for each month. These books with the rent books were presented and carefully examined every quarter at a workers' meeting at Miss Hill's house. The admirable part of this system was that every worker, paid or amateur, was bound to keep her books so that a stranger could pick up the threads with ease, and this really was done as I and my various substitutes could testify . . .

The work was much more interesting than it sounds, for the weekly visit, on business, gave ample opportunities for making acquaintance, and the tenants who stayed soon learnt to look on me as their friend, and listened willingly to good advice, even if they did not follow it. [They never asked to see the accounts] but were amazed and delighted when I produced from 10s to 15s to help the Christmas dinner or Whitsuntide outing . . . but there were those who didn't stay – idle drunken ne'er do weels, who drifted about from tenement to tenement . . . these were the people who tore off the wooden banisters for firewood, and 'disappeared' on Sunday evenings, leaving no trace behind them, the 'residuum' who baffle all the theories of political economists.

I worked at first under Miss Emma Cons, the most genial and kindly of women, and I may add the most courageous. I have seen her plunge into a street row, and forcibly separate combatants, men and women who slunk away from her indignation like whipped hounds. Later on, when she went to Drury Lane, my companion was Miss Rowland.

The workers whom she knew were all total abstainers, so appalled were they by the effects of drink. But Octavia's sensitivity in religious matters was shown in the fact that Mrs Maclagan was not allowed to say prayers or read the Bible at the night school or Sunday class, 'lest the susceptibilities of the Roman Catholic tenants or their priests should be wounded'.

When 'her' houses were condemned in 1873 some eighteen months after she had begun the work, Mrs Maclagan left 'the dear, dirty court' and took up work in another parish. 'My last official act was to give notice to all my tenants, whose grief at leaving their tenements was almost incredible. "Oh Miss, find us a room, do, *anywhere*, so as it is in the Court" . . . The Barrett's Court I knew is now quite a respectable alley, rather darkened by the tall model lodging houses, and it is called St Christopher's Buildings.'[5]

The replacement for Mrs Stopford Brooke's houses, only one section of the large block of property that Octavia managed at Barrett's Court, was her major rebuilding programme to date (albeit forced upon her by the circumstance of the closure order). Octavia was full of hope; 'when these houses are completed we shall have really good rooms to offer those of our tenants who strive to live quietly, and keep their homes tidy and clean . . . until the inhabitants had been trained to some degree of care, we could not trust them in new houses.'[6] However, Mrs Maclagan reported that the model lodging-houses were unpopular – 'the staircase, the laundry and the water tap served for 6 or 8 houses, and the "privacy" such as it was of the tenements, was deeply regretted.' (Possibly it was this reaction that made Octavia so vehemently opposed to model dwellings in later years.)

The new block was designed by Elijah Hoole,[7] who worked closely with Octavia from now on – even designing her gravestone. He seems to have been that rare thing, an architect who was prepared to be guided by his client. According to Miranda, 'his knowledge and conscientiousness made [Octavia's] reliance on him very great and the way in which he adapted and altered plans so as to carry out her wishes rendered all that part of her work much easier.' It was a harmonious relationship which grew into a close family friendship.

Octavia was often asked to take people round the courts but was careful to guard her tenants' privacy. On one occasion she wrote to

Mrs Nassau Senior: 'Five of us could not well invade a small room unexpectedly; also . . . in areas, yards, and courts, one can't talk so well to a large party, to point out what has been done, or tell what was.' She suggested that they met beforehand for a briefing and then she could take three of the party and Emma Cons two, for 'she can and does tell and show as well or better than I.'[8]

When Florence Nightingale's trainees visited her uncle Sir Harry Verney, they were often taken on an 'outing' to one of Octavia's courts. Florence Nightingale was a cousin of Barbara Leigh Smith (Bodichon) and perhaps knew of Octavia through that connection. Reading *Middlemarch* in 1873 she was immediately struck by the parallel between the idealism of Dorothea Brooke and 'close at hand, in actual life . . . a woman – an Idealist too – and if we mistake not, a connection of the author's who has managed to make her ideal very real indeed.' Determining to what extent George Eliot had Octavia in mind when she wrote *Middlemarch* is a fruitless task, but it is interesting that Florence Nightingale should have seen a possible connection.[9]

In Octavia's scheme of things good behaviour had its own rewards. The Barrett's Court Working Men's Club came into being, as one of the original members wrote,[10] housed in a little shop at 24 Barrett's Court, which Octavia made available to the tenants. The club was for the free use of male tenants on Monday evenings only. Attendance was never more than a dozen. In 1872 the members decided to organize a proper club, with committee, a penny subscription, a reading room and savings bank. It was open on Monday and Thursday evenings. Soon the premises had become too small; 'the atmosphere on a winter's night, with some twenty or thirty men smoking not the mildest of tobacco, was a little trying.'

Octavia, delighted by their initiative, offered them larger premises at No. 20–two rooms were linked by double doors, which made it useful for concerts and performances. By January 1873 the membership was nearing sixty and the members had painted, papered and decorated the rooms. Edward Bond, a 'nice young lawyer' whom she had recently met as a visitor on the district committee of the COS, and who had enthusiastically offered to help her with the club, was elected President. The club was open every evening including Sunday, from 7.30 to 10.30.

That year the indefatigable Sydney Cockerell, whom Octavia had met at Ben Rhydding, began to help her, in particular with the Working Men's Club at Barrett's Court. His advice in matters ranging from detailed financial points to general practical or organizational details was unfailingly calm and wise. Octavia fired off a ceaseless battery of letters, to which Cockerell replied promptly, keeping her informed as to how the club was progressing when she was out of London. He had written out a list of rules, some of which mystified Octavia, and she was worried about the increase in entrance fee from 1d per week, to 2d, fearing it would change the character of the club – 'but perhaps all good things must rise with their original elements and other new organizations meet the wants of the lowest, beginning again and again till the whole is raised.'[11] It was, in fact, exactly what she had hoped would happen.

Club games included bagatelle, cards and dominoes; the reading room offered newspapers and books, most of which were lent and were 'not always the most suitable; for instance Herodotus in Greek, Chaucer in early English are neither of them much appreciated by our members,' it was noted wryly. History and travel were popular subjects and Sir Edward Creasy's *Decisive Battles of the World* was eagerly read, 'by many to whom literature of that class must have been quite unknown hitherto'.

Mrs Maclagan recalled (in addition to the school at which she helped and the lending library) a night school for boys and, later, a mission service for men and women on Fridays, conducted by the Vicar of St Thomas, Portman Square. 'I cannot say that any of these were well, or regularly, attended.' Emma Cons, indefatigably pursuing the cause of temperance, organized regular meetings of 'The Blue Order of the Sons of the Phoenix', and Edward Bond, a helper upon whom Octavia would become increasingly dependent, talked to the men, presumably on some morally improving subject, on Sundays.

One outright failure was the co-operative shop; inexperienced managers, the new system of cash payment and no Sunday trading all contributed to its failure. 'The Store is doing very badly, and I wish you would send me a prospectus of the Manchester Store', Octavia wrote to Mary Harris.[12] The band, on the other hand, was a great success. There was a bandmaster, and concerts and dances, including step-dances to the bagpipe, were open to wives, daughters and friends.

By June 1874 the Working Men's Club had moved to the New Building; membership was almost one hundred, although attendance was much higher in winter. General meetings were quarterly, and the officers were elected each time, while committee meetings were held once a fortnight. New members were proposed at these meetings, and had to be over eighteen, presumably to meet the licensing requirements. Difficulties at the club seemed to stem from the clashes between those who came to drink and the strict teetotallers.

The move of the men's club to new premises freed the two rooms at No. 20. With a little bit of furnishing and improvement to their appearance, they were ideal for use by the women, who paid ten shillings a week for them. The first Annual Report of the Institute for Women & Girls recorded the activities for 1874–5.

Women members had to be aged twelve and over. One penny a week bought full privileges. It was, the Report admitted, a small membership – forty-four, of whom seven had then gone into positions as residential servants and had left the Court, one had gone to an Industrial School, and seven had ceased their membership. Of those who remained, seven were married women, nine young unmarried women and thirteen aged between twelve and sixteen.

The Institute was 'social and secular in character'. Classes were held every night, including Sunday; twice weekly in reading, writing and arithmetic, once a week each in singing and needlework. Needlework was practical because it trained women in paid work that they could do at home, and they brought in their own work and materials. They had lessons in cutting out and making dresses, in mending, trimming, and use of the sewing machine. There was good support for singing and some pleasant voices, and it was hoped that they would learn to read music.

Four lectures had been held during the year. Mrs Buckmaster had spoken on 'Cheap cooking with practical illustrations', Miss Frith on the management of babies, Mrs Johnstone on infectious diseases, and, breaking new ground, the Revd Mr Geary on the Arctic, with magic-lantern illustrations. Mrs Lankester had promised lectures to working women on homes, health and children for next summer. Evenings devoted to amusements had been given over to games, reading, singing or dancing, whilst winter Saturday evenings were for set entertainments – of which there had been twenty. Among the plays produced was *The Winter's Tale*, and two works by George MacDonald.

The MacDonald family theatricals were to become a regular event, held in the basement entertainment room at Barrett's Court, and elsewhere. There were winter performers too, sometimes of music, sometimes plays. At Christmas the MacDonalds laid on a carol concert, George MacDonald punctuating the singing with dramatic renderings of his own nativity verses.[13] Later on Mrs Baylis, Emma Cons's sister, provided operettas. In summer the club members were offered outings; they went to the South Kensington Museum, Hampton Court, the Zoological Gardens, Hampstead Heath and the other London parks. Twice they were invited to tea. On these occasions members paid their own expenses.

The first Report appealed for presents to improve the rooms; chairs, a carpet, bookcase or shelves, a second-hand piano would all be welcome. Books were needed for a small lending library of 'readable books'. Miss Dunlop was thanked for her loan of watercolours, Mrs George Lewis (sic) – in fact George Eliot – had given a Wilcox & Gibbs sewing machine. Alice Hart, Henrietta Rowland's sister, was Honorary Secretary and Treasurer of the Institute. She had done well – under Octavia's eagle eye, the credit and debit columns came out neatly, each level at £44 13s 11d.

The activities centred on the clubs give a glimpse of the fuller world of opportunity that Octavia so zealously desired for her tenants. Now that their housing was improved and she could offer the neediest some kind of employment, she wanted to raise their aspirations. For example she wanted to offer them beauty, and for that she relied on contact with the countryside. 'I brought up from the country ninety bunches of flowers; there was one for each family in three sets of houses. I had such a work distributing them; those in Barrett's Court had to be given at night, when we went to collect savings. I got such a delightful greeting as I went from room to room.'[14] All these endeavours were linked and indivisible parts of regaining a human existence for those whose lives had offered little more than utter deprivation.

The number of girls going into service must have pleased Octavia, for that, in itself, was an improvement over indigence and the other evils that lay in wait for the poor if misfortune overwhelmed them. But the picture of life around the courts that Mrs Maclagan left gives some sense of the intractability of the social problems Octavia had set herself to solve.

Sydney Cockerell's support became increasingly important to Octavia. 'Thank you very much indeed for – well so many things it becomes very difficult to say which most or first,' she wrote to him in November 1874. Objections to the state of the Barrett's Court property had been once again raised by the vestry, and substantiated by Dr Whitmore, the local Medical Officer of Health. She decided to call a meeting with the tenants and 'consult as to how *they* can keep things in better order, keep front doors shut, etc.' She had to try and explain the complexities of Public Health legislation and entreat them to help her prevent the likely closure order – which would be a resounding failure for her methods. Miranda wrote to Emily that Octavia 'fears the tenants will be in a very bad state . . . She wants to get co-operation; and the people think she is only to hear complaints.'[15] Octavia hoped that Sydney would chair the meeting, rather than Edward Bond – 'it would be fitter and pleasanter to have you than him.' Perhaps he had a lighter touch or greater authority with the tenants?

The Public Health problems at Barrett's Court turned into a war of attrition between Dr Whitmore and Octavia, and, Edmund Maurice suggested, led to Octavia's lifelong hatred of officialdom.[16] Henrietta Barnett's brother-in-law Ernest Hart, a surgeon, tried to intercede on Octavia's behalf and show Whitmore 'how utterly untenable his position was. Mr Hart looked into the matter thoroughly . . . he thought she had a *very* good case.'[17] Whitmore agreed to retreat.

But he returned to the attack in April 1875 – 'Dr Whitmore is by no means "squashed"'[18] – and Octavia reported that he was 'serving notices for covering disused cisterns in which no water comes and other similar things, but one doesn't mind when one is well!!' By October the new legislation, the Artisans' Dwellings Bill, was law, but Octavia had won her argument. 'Dr W. has reported to the Metropolitan Board of Works as to districts requiring to be dealt with in Marylebone under the Artizans' [sic] Dwellings Bill and has *not* included Barrett's Court. I think he has chosen the right spots and am glad, though I was prepared for the other course being adopted.'

Octavia was torn; on the one hand she had triumphed over interference, yet she knew that the new legislation was framed to be effective in just such a case as Barrett's Court. 'I should have felt it a gain in some ways to have had the bill brought to bear there . . . *we* ought to rebuild by rights, and then we should keep all this and get better houses too.'[19] If the decision had gone that way, Octavia could have claimed compensation and used her example as a demonstration of the efficacy of the bill. As it was, it was later shown to be toothless.

Edward Bond had found Octavia a new assistant, since Sophia Peters had left on her marriage to C. S. Loch. Mrs Allen was another COS stalwart but Octavia was not sure about her: 'I do not heartily like her myself but there is *much* very much in her favour, and the work *may* be a great blessing to her individually, also the people are *sure* to object to any one new, still I am grateful for all who will tell me what impression is created by work or workers of mine.' Cockerell was her trusted lieutenant in these matters. 'We might talk the matter over a little on Saturday perhaps.'[20]

By March 1876 Octavia was complaining to Sydney about Mrs Allen's slowness and inaccuracy in book-keeping. She 'dreads to be found out in it . . . and she hopes things will come right if they are kept quiet. I, on the other hand, abhor and detest unbalanced uncompared books, and I feel wretched till the mistakes [are] hunted down.' Nevertheless, 'She has the elements of a good book-keeper, however, all except moral courage to face and clear up a mistake at once.'[21]

Octavia's own manner was a problem of which she was still all too aware. Writing to Mary Harris in 1875 about Barrett's Court, she told her how much she was enjoying contact with the tenants. 'I am sensible how much I lack swiftly turning perception, and unfailing gentleness, and a certain cautious reservation of speech . . . I have no powers of diplomacy; these I don't regret, but the power of non-expression might be an advantage.'[22]

One surprise was that the Barrett's Court band had decided to become teetotal. Octavia was sorry that it should be so, but this was clearly Emma's doing for she was the moving spirit behind the band, as well as being an activist for temperance. Octavia, although she admitted the dire effects of drink, was never as inflexible on this subject as Emma Cons.[23] While Emma would take her tenants on country outings and plan with great care routes which would not pass a public house, Octavia trusted that distraction would do the trick.

Octavia was nevertheless moved when Mr Smale, one of her helpers at Barrett's Court, decided 'to take the lead there in the teetotal cause. It was very touching and very beautiful to see him take the pledge. He looked so young and so good, and took it wholly for the sake of the people.'[24]

The strains on Octavia were mounting again. She wrote to Cockerell in July that she was 'completely knocked up and am fit for no place but home. I feel almost as if I could *not* go among people, specially strangers . . . I daresay one will get through this as one does through other things somehow . . .' Not everyone realized how overwrought she became, she told Cockerell.[25]

One sign of Octavia's condition was her decision to exclude tenants from her 1876 birthday party. She wrote to Henrietta, 'I daresay you will feel as if I were falling away from my old life in deciding this . . . I want, and always wanted, my annual party to gather in those who stood nearest to me in my daily life, or so many of them as space allowed.' But there were too many and she had so many friends 'who have gone side by side with me through difficulty and pain, friends who have given me of their best, friends who have kept alive in me the memory that life meant more than work . . . shall they be less precious to me than my dear poor?'

In a surprising admission, Octavia continued, 'The many poor . . . are dear to me because they are poor and needy, but . . . are not individual living men and women to me.' The tenants from the original courts were different, 'living beings to me'. Octavia's individualistic approach had its roots in her own affection for poor people as individuals. Some of the disparities between her theories, as argued along COS lines, and her practice, which often seemed to break her own rules, can be explained by her real sensitivity and humanity – qualities which she often did her best to disguise.

CHAPTER 9

Eastwards

OCTAVIA took great pleasure in the progress made on the original courts. By 1873 Freshwater Place, the first freehold, was transformed.

The cottages look so neat and clean and the whole place so fresh and substantially good . . . I looked at my cottage with its heightened rooms – taking off the weight from above that presses down, in order that the human being may have room to breathe, to expand, to rise. Then how the children have improved! As to my singing-class, it was quite delightful. I had a troop of them round and about marching and singing 'Trelawney'. It was capital. Such days are worth living for.

To celebrate the achievements at Freshwater Place, Octavia decided to install a tiled inscription, designed by William de Morgan, with each letter paid for by supporters, fellow-workers and family. She had taken the idea from Ruskin. In *The Seven Lamps of Architecture* he had admired the way in which, in parts of Germany and Switzerland, a builder would inscribe blank stones 'with a summary of his life and of its experience, raising thus the habitation into a kind of monument'. She wrote to some of her supporters, enclosing the Ruskin quotation and suggesting the tiled ornament to commemorate their joint achievement.

The wording was 'Every House is Builded by Some but He that Built All Things is God'. Allotting the letters and words to each of the subscribers took on an almost religious significance, and Octavia gave it deep thought. They represented her inner circle of supporters and special friends, such as Ruskin's gardener Downes; and she wrote to Sydney Cockerell listing them and telling him about the discussion between herself and the designer William de Morgan. Octavia wanted blue, de Morgan either copper lustre or deep crimson. It was agreed that he should try 'different colours and designs, on his own responsibility, and for his own pleasure.'[1]

Sadly de Morgan's expertise did not extend to setting the tiles properly; the frost got behind them and before long they began to drop off and break. A later inscription, placed on the church of St John's, Waterloo and overlooking the garden, was carried out in small mosaic pieces and remains intact.

Ruskin had taken very little active interest in Octavia's work for some years; he was lethargic and had lost all interest in her housing schemes. (Canon Scott Holland in his brief sketch of Octavia's life recorded an apparently well-known incident in which Octavia took Ruskin down to one of the courts: it seems he was sickened by what he saw and could not wait to escape.) But he supported her idea for the inscription and gave his letter. He was at this time in a state of almost constant depression. In 1872 first his beloved dog, Wise, died and then his mother. Intermittent letters from him followed Octavia; one from Arezzo damned her with faint praise. 'I am a *little* cheered by what appears to me your naive hopes; the proper and natural result of great personal success,' but, he continued, 'I solemnly and with all my mind believe that the catastrophe coming on Society cannot now be averted, though I have faith absolute in final victory of what I have taught. I sometimes think that you are too successful to be quite right!'[2]

At Octavia's birthday in 1874, however, Octavia received a present from Ruskin: a heart-felt compliment from Thomas Carlyle. 'You can't get faithful people,' Carlyle had said; 'they're quite exceptional. I never heard of another like this one. The clear mind and perfect attention, meaning nothing but good to the people, and taking infinite care to tell them no lies.'[3] Octavia was delighted and thanked Ruskin. 'It was very kind and showed me, – what I cared for most about it – that you had not given a bad account of me to Carlyle; for, as he does not know me, he must have judged me from your account . . .' The words 'came to me like the blessing of a prophet'; they also 'soothed me for present troubles, and helped me to see how ephemeral they were.'[4]

Ruskin corrected her: '. . . what Carlyle said was absolutely his own gathering and conclusion from what he had seen and read of you, or heard in various general channels.'[5] Octavia had not yet grasped how her fame was spreading.

She continued to send Ruskin scrupulous accounts of both Paradise Place and Freshwater Place. The former had netted him £20 5s 8d, she wrote in the autumn of 1875, after having received from him an unexpectedly positive letter. 'I had no idea you could have honestly spoken so of work which I have always thought had impressed you more with its imperfections, than as contributing to any good end. That it actually was in large measure derived from you, there can be no doubt.' She had been rereading, for the first time since she had known Ruskin, the first volume of *Modern Painters* which Edward Bond had lent her. She was, once again, much impressed and told Ruskin how profoundly the book had influenced both her work and her life.[6]

Octavia had not abandoned her painting. She wrote to Henrietta: 'I have no excuse now for not making my life very complete and I wanted to keep in it always some time for learning and I thought of drawing at the National Gallery one morning weekly between Christmas and Easter . . . Till Christmas I am working at the School of Art.'[7]

Summarizing the affairs of 1874 for her fellow-workers, Octavia told them that she now managed fifteen blocks containing between two and three thousand tenants. She described the organization, which bore no name except her own:

Each block belongs to a separate person or company, who entrusts me with the collection of rents and management of the houses. Each block is placed by me under a separate volunteer worker, who has the duty of collecting, superintending cleaning, keeping accounts, advising as to repairs and improvements, and choice of tenants. [In addition they offer] all personal help that can be given to the tenants without destroying their independence, such as helping them to find work, collecting their savings, supplying them with flowers, teaching them to grow plants, arranging happy amusements for them, and in every way helping them to help themselves.

Of course, she added, it was the weekly collection of rent that gave the opening; 'the control of the house itself, judiciously used, gives power for good much greater than that possessed by the ordinary district visitor.'

The work was an acknowledged success and the localized informal shape of the organization mirrored her ideas. Ten years later, in 1884, she told the Royal Commission on Housing about it:

So strongly do I feel about the individual influence and work and relation that I have never formed a society. It would have saved an enormous amount of trouble in many ways as to accounts, because, for every one of these places, we have to keep a separate account now, as they are really separate bits of property. But then we get the whole interest and personal relationship of those various men of education and power and thought who have cared to take a small bit of London and see what they can make of it and its people.

Octavia was a figure of national stature by 1874 but her personal financial worries remained. That year a group of her friends set up a fund to free her from the necessity of earning money. Edward Bond was involved, and George Eliot and her husband George Lewes were generous contributors – they gave £200.[8] Lewes wrote to Bond: 'will you kindly let me know whether the plan we talked of has been making progress and what is the amount already assured?'

William Shaen was probably the prime mover in the scheme. He had helped Octavia search out the original premises, Paradise Place, and from then on had acted as her solicitor and business adviser. When Barrett's Court was causing her the most worry, Octavia wrote to Emily: 'We owe more to him than to almost anyone else who has helped us.'[9] Now, writing from his office at Shaen, Roscoe & Massey, William Shaen forwarded to her a message he had received.

Some friends of Miss Octavia Hill who desire that their names should remain unknown, understanding that you have for some-time past advised and acted for her in business matters, beg you to accept, in trust for her, the sum of three thousand pounds, invested in American and Russian Bonds. The gift is made in the earnest hope and confident trust, that she will accept and use it as intended to put into her life a feeling of rest and increased opportunity for leisure.

Octavia was overwhelmed. She wrote to Shaen:

In spite of the extreme kindness and beautiful feeling shown by whoever has given all this help, I must request you not to receive for me one penny more. The thing is done beautifully, efficiently and abundantly; there really it must rest. I have more than enough for holidays and everything I can possibly want. I do assure you I mean what I say. I can never want or have to earn again, I feel richer than I ever did, and able to do things I never dreamed of doing. But once more and most emphatically I decline more. I have enough.[10]

As she consolidated her work, Octavia carefully considered the organization. She found her workers by various means; a Miss Lacy, from Miss Selwyn's training school for girls near Birmingham, presented herself to Octavia. She was not young, wanted to devote herself to the poor freely and had had some experience in Bermondsey; 'wants to be right in the middle of an East or South district, doesn't like sisterhoods, peculiar dresses or nursing'. Octavia wondered if Henrietta could find her somewhere to live and take her under her wing? Other helpers came by word of mouth; not all were successes.

The personal qualities of the collectors was crucial. Emma Cons remained the rock among them and Octavia praised her work fulsomely. The courts near Drury Lane were making magnificent progress.

She has undertaken them wholly, makes her own centre quite independent of this house except as to funds, enrols her own volunteer workers, founds her own classes, clubs, savings' banks, keeps her own accounts, supervises all the business and personal work, and reports to the owners of the courts direct. I asked her to adopt this plan, because I saw that she was quite able to take the lead in any group of courts entrusted to her, that she might grow to be a centre of workers, and so be able to extend the plan to more courts than we could while she was only my lieutenant, and while all decisions came from me. I knew she would manage courts differently from me. I thought this a gain . . . Miss Cons had an ideal; left to herself she would gladly have sacrificed it to mine in a moment . . . That could not be. I set her free to work towards her own standard; I knew we should each learn from the other. I must say I have been astonished how little her work has differed from mine; still it *is* her very own . . . I see several courts full of people watched over, saved, cared for, all without me. I see a group of volunteers working with full energy, with deep devotion, some of whom I never knew . . .[11]

Emma was a stalwart friend to Octavia. On one of the many occasions that she offered to help, 'it made me feel how real her friendship was, whatever little clouds or freaks might obscure it; how it was something that might be depended on in need, and was real and true all the time.' And again: 'I have long watched and wondered at her goodness but really lately it has exceeded all I could ever have imagined in her. Such marvellous loyalty, such gentleness, such sweetness of temper.'

Yet Emma could never share Octavia's rigorous attention to detail or her adherence to theory. When Octavia lectured her, Emma did not seem to attend. 'Somehow to dear Emma words seem to me to confuse her more.' Emma's carelessness and more pragmatic attitude towards her tenants sometimes exasperated Octavia and led her to overstate their differences of approach. 'I have done my best to help her to see . . . and yet she sees literally *nothing* of what I am aiming at. What *must* she think me! And yet she is so perfectly gentle.'[12]

Meeting Emma Cons some years afterwards, Beatrice Potter (later Beatrice Webb), acute as always, confided her impressions of her to her diary. She noted that Emma had been trained by Octavia Hill and that she was 'not a lady by birth, with the face and manner of a distinguished woman, a ruler of men. Absolute absorption in work, strong religious feeling, very little culture or interest in things outside the sphere of her own action. Certainly not a lover of fact or theory. Was not clear as to total number of rooms, unlets or arrears. No description of tenants kept.' She was struck by the 'peculiar mixture of sympathy and authority which characterizes the modern class of *governing women*'.[13]

Octavia was finally learning to delegate. 'I am sure it is best for them that I should stand aside and let the local or appointed workers make some good thing of the work without my meddling.' Busy as she now was, she deeply regretted distancing herself from the tenants. 'I cannot suddenly throw all aside to spend, as one must spend, time at the exact moment to save this one or the other . . . I have little power with strangers and that seems to point to present arrangement [sic] of work and yet it is strange to know there's a girl I've never seen, but one of the Granby tenants, lying in Newgate now and I have done nothing except by letter to [illegible] her.'[14]

On one occasion she wrote to Cockerell, pleading on behalf of a man with a drunken wife who had left Barrett's Court, 'to try and place her where she might do better. He looks so battered and has eyes that look so hungry for a little help and sympathy.' Would Cockerell let him back?[15] Octavia's genuine sympathy for misfortune was never far below the surface.

A few years earlier she had admitted that 'changes always worry me. They are times that call for decisions and it is so hard to know when things are very near that one sees them rightly and clearly. When they are far past one can look back and weigh so accurately the relative importance of facts.' Her inability to stand back contributed greatly to the degree of the stress that Octavia seemed to create for herself. 'I suppose one will learn more quiet as one grows and that life will have less of passion and more of peace.'[16]

Octavia now began to feel that the work should slow down. Her health was not good, as she wrote to Henrietta who had invited her out for one of their walks. 'I am not fit to go out on Sunday, only to poke about in my small den and recover strength for the coming week's work which will be hard.'[17] A couple of weeks later the Barnetts did manage to tempt her out. 'That walk on Saturday did me so much good, though I had a dreadful time in Barrett's Court that night and on Monday. Still all went well at last.'[18]

1874 was the first year in which Octavia turned down chances to manage property, including one in Lisson Grove (although later she took on and built properties there, in Bell Street and nearby), 'partly because the price asked was high, but more because of the imperfections which still remain in our organization.' She wanted her workers, the visitors (she loathed the term rent-collector), to take complete control, 'as they would in their own house, garden or field', but according to her own exacting and meticulous standards. They 'must take the position of *queens* as well as *friends*'.[19]

It seems that some of the owners had proved difficult, wanting to take a larger part in work which their generosity had made possible. Octavia preferred, on the whole, that they should remain in the background. There was a constant tension in Octavia's work between her wish to let the projects become autonomous and also to keep the necessary control upon the venture as a whole. It is a tension that organizations often meet – as between central and local responsibility – and the COS dissensions and difficulties were a case in point. Octavia's delight in the detail and the personal approach was hard to reconcile with her desire to establish an approach that would be widely applicable. She never fully solved that problem.

In the early 1870s Octavia had still not touched the East End, but with the Revd Barnett, now the vicar of St Jude's, Whitechapel and

married to her friend and helper Henrietta Rowland, a perfect opportunity offered to attempt some kind of joint venture there. She had her
eye on a block at St Jude's which seemed ideal, 'with power to redeem
it'. Evidence of her increasing concern for the East End is her note to
the fellow-workers, telling them that several large sums had been
given on her behalf to the Whitechapel Baths and Wash-houses; 'once
set free from debt [they] will be self-supporting; they are situated in
the midst of densely-populated and poor districts and will be of great
value.' Around the same period, she took on the management of a
block in Lambeth – her first venture south of the Thames.

The housing situation in the East End was if anything worse than
that in Marylebone – it was merely less visible to the gentry. In July
1874 Octavia wrote to Samuel Barnett: 'I find the difficulties of
management in Whitechapel greater than ever I anticipated, property
and people being equally impossible to deal with so far in any
satisfactory way . . .'[20] Ruinous houses could be let for nine shillings a
week[21] and under the Artisans' Dwellings Act of 1875 things merely
became worse. The Metropolitan Board of Works had no powers to
compel landlords to spend money on repairs, so the landlords merely
waited for the compensation which came once a dwelling was declared
uninhabitable. The result was a stalemate; six years after the Act
Barnett wrote of the anomaly of houses condemned as unfit for
habitation, still standing and empty.

The Barnetts were not easily defeated. The sale of Henrietta's
jewels[22] and a donation from Edward Bond secured New Court for
around £500. Octavia reported to Jane Nassau Senior that the Barnetts
were planning to spend a legacy 'in rebuilding their worst court
irrespective of making it pay or waiting for the Bill [the Artisans'
Dwellings Bill]. Of course I said by all means; and now, if they can but
purchase, I think it will give new life to their future there, to see some
tangible and radical reform actually achieved.'[23] In Henrietta's words:
'So we bought the rickety dwellings, gave its degraded inhabitants the
chance of reform before turning them out, tidied up the property, and
used its rents to the day of its final destruction.' It became Kate Potter's
responsibility during her years in Whitechapel. Later the ground
became part of the Toynbee Hall tennis court.

Alongside New Court another piece of vacant ground was bought
by A. G. Crowder, and in 1877 a block of model dwellings was built
on the site. Opened in June, the tenements accommodated about fifty
families, paying around 2s 6d per room. Mr Barnett noted in his diary

that 'they will be under careful supervision, and we may expect that fifty families living respectably will have a great missionary power in the neighbourhood.'

The outcome was far from that universally desired, as Crowder wrote in an article in the *Pall Mall Gazette* in November 1883. He noted that the benevolent regime meant that no tenant who paid regular rent was disturbed, 'with the result that I became literally disgusted with the state of my property though managed by experienced and judicious ladies, visiting weekly. The vicious, dirty and destructive habits of the lowest strata have obliged me at last to decline them as tenants.'[24] Crowder, never one of the gentler spirits in the social welfare movement, became a COS stalwart at St George's-in-the-East. Whilst the Barnetts, faced with the reality of unmitigated poverty, moved steadily away from the COS line, Crowder was still peddling unreconstructed COS dogma as late as 1909.

The expansion of the housing work in the East End continued, in close collaboration with Octavia, but run independently by the Barnetts – very much the same arrangement she had with Emma Cons. Money came from both Octavia's fund-raising and from the Barnetts' own efforts; they pursued their own campaigns, ably assisted by Henrietta's brother-in-law Ernest Hart; and they had their own group of eight women housing visitors (several of whom were generously passed on by Octavia), who spent two days a week with the tenants. They carried out the work along their mentor Octavia's lines: 'Punctual payment is enforced, chiefly because of the element of order and regularity it introduces into families, the cause of whose trouble is generally disorder,' wrote Samuel Barnett.

Henrietta had a different approach to the work, even in the early days, but Octavia was perfectly understanding. 'There are many ways of dealing with people . . . each possible and natural to different natures, and you and I need not mind differing as to ways, we are one utterly and entirely in what we aim at.'[25]

By 1879 Samuel Barnett estimated that there were around a thousand people 'now living in houses which are under the control of those whose object is their real good. Mistakes may be made and their actions misunderstood, but the fact that those who own this property are moved by a desire to be helpful rather than to make a profit must have a distinct influence.'

Eventually, in 1884, the Barnetts' work became the starting point for the East End Dwellings Company, a conventional philanthropic housing company, of which both Edward Bond and A. G. Crowder were directors.[26]

In 1875 a selection of Octavia's essays was published, *The Homes of the London Poor*. According to Edmund Maurice, the American edition was the first, followed by an English one the same year and later a German translation. Octavia now had an international public. Although she had published many articles by then, she was touchingly delighted with the book. She positively crowed to Sydney Cockerell: 'my book has been so well reviewed, fourteen reviews in all, and all favourable! I don't now believe in its selling though, it is so dear!'[27]

Her publications and her spreading reputation brought an impressive list of distinguished names to join Octavia's original workers. Often it became a family concern, the interests of parents being passed on to the younger generation. The Stephen and Duckworth families represented the world of the intelligentsia. Caroline Stephen[28] (known as Milly in the family) was Leslie Stephen's younger sister. Octavia met her in the early 1870s when she was visiting the elderly in workhouses and teaching in a night school. She was also a district visitor for the Board of Guardians. 'I do not know a more depressingly bewildering experience than that which befalls a lady on first undertaking to visit a district of poor houses,' she wrote. In 1877 she bought a plot of land on Church Street, Chelsea, near her own house, and commissioned Elijah Hoole to design a block of artisans' dwellings.[29] She planned to be both owner and rent-collector.

It was a courtyard scheme, twenty-eight flats on three floors, reached by iron balconies. Hereford Buildings was governed by a number of rules: occupants had to hang lace curtains at their windows and look after geraniums by their front doors. There was a washhouse on the roof and an iron street gate which was closed every night. Over the entrance were inscribed the stirring words: 'Unto the upright there ariseth light in the darkness.' In 1879 Caroline Stephen joined the Society of Friends, and in 1881 she passed Hereford Buildings over to Octavia's care and went to live in Dorking.

Leslie Stephen's second wife, Julia Duckworth, was also a great admirer and supporter of Octavia's work. Her name is often listed on the donations list of the Letters to Fellow-workers. She had set before her children three daunting models: Florence Nightingale, Mrs Humphry Ward and Octavia Hill.[30] Not surprisingly, therefore, her daughter Stella, a gentle dutiful girl who uncomplainingly took on the burden of looking after her irascible stepfather following her mother's death in 1895, chose to become one of Octavia's workers. In 1897, she died. Octavia paid her a tribute in the 'Letter to Fellow-workers' of that year:

> The other new buildings just being finished are six more cottages. [near Lisson Grove]. They were undertaken by Miss Duckworth,[31] who had worked with us so devotedly, who was so beloved by all among whom she worked, who had taken up as an inheritance her mother's help to our donation fund, whose marriage and tragic death during the year filled us first with warm sympathy and then with deep sense of loss. These cottages, her last work for us, will come with all solemn sense of trust from her and as dear for her sake.

There is no doubt that working in poor areas was rough for hitherto protected girls, from middle- or upper-class homes. They had to steel themselves to witness horrors of every kind: drunkenness, starvation, the signs of physical abuse on women and children. (Sometimes men supporters were first drafted in to a new building to test the water.) A circuit had developed along which the trained housing workers were passed. Octavia was the key, whether they worked under her, or for the Barnetts or Emma Cons. Many of them went on to work either as Poor Law Guardians or in local government, when the doors began to open for women. The generation that followed them built upon those foundations.

In October 1875 Katherine Potter, Beatrice Webb's sister, came to live and work with Octavia – 'she wants to stay on for, possibly, two or three years. She is very bright and happy here; extremely capable, and has been through a good deal in her life, though she is young. She seems to fit in among us very well.'[32]

In fact Katherine, or Kate as she was known, had been getting on badly at home[33] and had been planning to leave, ever since the family returned from America in late 1873. 'After a last "season" in London during which many mistakes had been made, much trouble endured and some lessons learnt I made up my mind to leave home and go to Miss Octavia Hill to be trained for her work in London.' There had been two proposals of marriage – 'the pain drove me into a life of independent thought and action.'[34]

Kate's first evening at 14 Nottingham Place was 25 October. From then on she accompanied Octavia everywhere, to Barrett's Court, St Mary's and the Council of the COS; she acted as secretary and was filled with admiration. However as the weeks passed she found that Octavia did not reciprocate her affection, and she felt disillusioned. But the stay at Nottingham Place opened her eyes. 'It was while staying with her,' she wrote, 'that I first became aware of the meaning of the poverty of the poor.'[35]

She soon found that the work was very hard, with almost no rest or recreation. 'In work my relations with my chief thoroughly satisfactory but my enthusiasm for herself cools and I find the strain of life at Nottingham Place too much for me.' Before long she was nursing an attack of bronchitis at home in Princes Gardens – she had introduced Octavia to her family 'but they did not take to each other'. In return, Octavia had little time for them. She wrote to Henrietta about appealing to the Potters for some funds: 'I have *very* little faith in a £5 note from them unless the scheme is one likely to attract general or *particular* attention, but of course they can be tried.'[36]

By contrast, the friendship between Kate Potter and the Barnetts flourished, after a hesitant start, and the Barnetts spent some days around Christmas 1875 at Standish, the Potters' country house. They probably helped to harden Kate's resolve against her parents' indifference; 'father and mother kind and willing to let me take my own line but (naturally enough) without much confidence in it or me – the younger sisters approving and more or less interested.'[37]

Octavia had already sensed that she and Kate did not make an ideal working partnership and that Kate might be more help working for the Barnetts. She wrote to Henrietta: 'I can't help thinking you would be very wise to see Miss Potter and interest her quickly. She is taking up one thing and another here with vigour and energy and naturally won't like to give them up for East End work when once she has begun them . . . Mr B has already arranged for her to begin in New Court under Mr Leonard.'[38]

By the summer of 1876 Kate was collecting at George Third Buildings, one of the roughest in the East End,[39] and met Annie Townshend – who later shared her lodgings – and the Revd Brooke Lambert, who later took on St Jude's from the Revd Barnett. These fellow-workers were also invited to Standish. By October Kate had left Nottingham Place and had set up in two small rooms in Westminster at 7, Great College Street. She must have echoed the feelings of many other young women breaking the mould of the Victorian daughter and working for the proliferating organizations for the poor; it was 'rather lonely at first but I gradually get to like the complete independence of my life and get very fond of my wee panelled room.'

Kate Potter was active in the Westminster COS and received regular visits from Cardinal Manning – 'rather overwhelming, but he was very good to my people in Whitechapel and did me many little services there. At one time he evidently had hopes of my conversion.' Her sister Maggie stayed with her for Christmas 1877: 'we go about together a good deal – she comes down with me to Whitechapel where though she confesses it is not in her line she makes very suggestive [helpful] remarks.' The sisters were glad to be away from Standish, where the family had taken up spiritualism.[40]

Another pair of sisters, Rosamond and Florence Davenport Hill, were, as Samuel Barnett wrote to his brother, 'doers of the hard dull duty which a hard dull age imposes. It is good to be with them, to feel around one the breath of truth, the breezes of duty.' The sisters were often included in the Hill family circle (though not related) and their success in different fields from her own (Rosamond in educational administration and Florence working with juvenile paupers) must have given Octavia added strength in her own endeavours.

The Miss Winkworths from Bristol, whose sister Emily was married to Octavia's faithful solicitor William Shaen, were involved in work connected with women's education. However, as was so often the case, they were active in many branches of philanthropic works and Susanna Winkworth, much interested in Octavia's ideas, decided to venture into housing. Gathering support amongst the philanthropic business men of Bristol, she built a block of model dwellings known as Jacob's Wells Buildings in Dowry Square, Hotwells, in the mid-1870s. Later on she added Brandon Buildings. She arranged for rent-collection by a group of volunteer ladies and was herself the managing director. The financial return was disappointing because of the expense of the building and the failure of the contractor before completion.[41] The Miss Winkworths' brother Stephen and his wife were amongst the most consistently generous of Octavia's supporters, and their names appear year after year on the donations list in the 'Letters to Fellow-workers', always against considerable sums.

Octavia wanted to involve old friends in her schemes. One was John Ludlow, the Christian Socialist. Since he lived in Wimbledon, and she needed help with the 400 tenants whom she was planning to take out there to Caesar's Camp one Wednesday soon, his name crossed her mind – and she blithely wrote reminding him of the tailors' 'bean-feasts' of long ago.

> Though now my people are quite unconnected with the Associ-ations and founders of Associations, it yet remains true that it was the early connection with that body of 'Christian Socialists' to which much of my present work must owe its spirit. It had to find its own form, according to the needs and possibilities of circum-stances; but its spirit must have been influenced deeply by the deeds and words of all that group of men.

Now looking after 3,000 tenants, she told him, it was appropriate that she should look back and remind herself when her ideas had originated.[42]

The late 1870s, which brought so many other troubles, released Octavia from the financial burden she had carried for twenty years or more. The family debts were at last paid, and the trust set up by her friends in 1874 had provided her with her share of the £700 needed to buy the lease of Nottingham Place in the spring of 1876.

> I have a profound contempt for unquietness about money, hasty action, or meddling with things of which I know nothing and should like to do one of two things either, if I could, to have money in things (like this house) which I control, know about, and can calculate about myself, or in other good things managed by capable people I know; or else to take the best advice I can get, obey it literally, and with a quiet mind let things take their course.[43]

Better still, their small savings gave the family a novel sense of freedom. Octavia told Cockerell: 'I sometimes feel as if it would not be so *very* long before I should be able to tell Miranda it was for her to decide from pure interest in her work whether she would continue it or not.'[44] In the event, Miranda's school went on for many more years.

Octavia was elated about the prospects for her work, too. There was Lord Pembroke's £6,000 for the purchase and management of housing in the East End and she now had altogether 3,500 tenants and as much as £40,000 worth of property in her charge. 'I have more great bits of work on hand than I ever had at one time I think . . . please God, they will do, if we accomplish them, such a quantity of good.'

She was hardly finding time to see her family. 'It is well for me that in the course of work I do naturally see many of my friends; and that I do love and care very deeply for many of my fellow workers.'[45] The shared interests and the absorption in the work were bringing her closer to one fellow worker in particular than anyone could have suspected.

CHAPTER 10

A Royal supporter

ON 6 November 1876 Octavia wrote up some notes of a tour
she had made of her Marylebone properties. With a companion, she had visited Barrett's Court and met various tenants;
these included the Bristows – 'large family occupying shop – wonderfully improved. Man secretary to Workmen's Club. Boy very respectable, girl Mary Ann comes to singing-class, learning to read 18 years
old!' Next came the Marns, whom she noted were very dirty, and the
boy had got into trouble for stealing a tumbler in order to get 2d for the
music hall. Another tenant, Mrs Crimmins, with a very crowded
room, had reproached Octavia for not allowing her to sublet. Her
husband was on and off the drink. Upstairs in a neat, tiny room were
the Martyns; the husband made buttons and pins for footmen. She and
her companion visited the New Building, met the superintendent,
Flood – 'used to be a fearful drunkard' – and talked to others, including
a woman who had recently arrived from Manchester. At Freshwater
Place Octavia and her companion talked to the Sansome family
through the window, and to a Mrs Manders 'who spoke somewhat
hardly I thought of the baby dead since I was last there'. (Octavia was
curiously innocent, not realizing how inured against infant mortality
poor people had to be.)

Octavia frequently took interested visitors around her properties
but she did not usually note as carefully where they went or whom
they saw. But this was no ordinary visitor; Princess Alice of Hesse-Darmstadt, Queen Victoria's third child and second daughter, was her
companion, and that visit laid the foundations of a friendship quite
remarkable by the standards of the time.

The link seems to have been made through Colonel Gardiner,
Equerry to Queen Victoria and fellow-member with Octavia of the

Charity Organization Society. She also knew him as a Marylebone Guardian and he had persuaded an impressive list of aristocrats and well-known names such as Angela Burdett-Coutts to lend support to Octavia's campaign to buy Swiss Cottage Fields.* Presumably Princess Alice, on one of her infrequent visits to London from Darmstadt, had asked him to arrange a meeting with Octavia.

Before long, Princess Alice and Octavia were corresponding with complete frankness, without any formalities and with considerable warmth and enormous interest on both sides. While Princess Alice was avid to hear more of Octavia's work, Octavia eagerly asked for accounts of Princess Alice's own initiatives in Darmstadt. Princess Alice confided that she was tortured by her sensitivity to the problems of the poor, and that at home in Germany, bored by Court life, she would pay visits to the poorest areas of Metz. Her meetings with Octavia sealed a close friendship in which differences of station counted for nothing. There can have been few such friendships between a royal princess and a Victorian commoner – but Princess Alice was a remarkable woman, very much after Octavia's heart and style.

Although she had given birth to seven children (one of whom was Alix, later to become Tsarina of Russia), Princess Alice was unhappy, hating life in a provincial German city. Her marriage was far from satisfactory,[1] and it was a curiously purposeless existence, a long way from home. In particular her husband, Prince Louis, took no interest whatsoever in her activities, so that she found the supportive role expected of her when he later became the Grand-Duke a particular strain. Her father, the Prince Consort, remained a constant inspiration to her in her own work.

In 1872 Princess Alice wrote telling Queen Victoria about a series of meetings she had arranged, to discuss the education and employment of the poor, nursing and other topics of interest to women. These were to be known in Germany as the Parliament of Women. Princess Alice had called the conference to reinforce her own charitable endeavours, and, although it was largely a German gathering, she had invited a few English delegates. These were Mary Carpenter, with whom she exchanged ideas about education and penal reform, Catherine Winkworth and her sister Susanna, and Florence Davenport Hill.[2] They were the personal guests of Princess Alice, and stayed in the Grand-

*See Chapter 11.

Ducal palace. They all spoke impressively and 'greatly enhanced the importance of the meeting'.[3] Mary Carpenter, by then in her late sixties, was the doyenne of English women voluntary social workers and 'spoke on all subjects relating to women's work in England,' although she concentrated on the subject of the training of women in child-care.

The English visitors found Princess Alice a delightful person; pretty, animated and, thought Catherine Winkworth, 'a clever, *able* woman, clear-headed and gets through an enormous amount of work . . .' Prince Louis remained on the sidelines, making 'funny little half-quizzical remarks'. Catherine thought they seemed fond of each other.

Princess Alice treated her visitors to afternoon expeditions, taking them to some of her own foundations – schools, orphanages, hospitals. She was relieved to find that these women were not political radicals nor feminist agitators. Mary Carpenter, like Octavia, whilst firmly behind the improvement of women's status in terms of education, ownership of property and professional training and work opportunities, had no time for the battle for universal suffrage.[4] They were apolitical women who dealt with the system as they found it.

Before Princess Alice's visit to Octavia's London properties, a meeting in order to brief her was arranged. Octavia described it to Mary Harris. 'We spoke much of work among the poor, and I could see, from little stories that came out, how earnestly she had tried to get near them, and how the paraphernalia of her position has again and again thrown her back. It was touching.' They arranged to go the next day to Barrett's Court; Princess Alice would be alone and incognito, 'right down face to face with the people . . . Is it not strange? It is a profound secret, partly lest a crowd should gather, and the arrangements as to coachman, private doors, entering one place and escaping by another make me feel as if in a novel I was stealing a princess.' Despite the dramatic aspects of the arrangements, Octavia found her 'simple and sweet'. They shared an admiration for George Mac-Donald and his writing; Princess Alice considered him a refreshing example of a clever man who believed. 'I dare say I did hosts of incorrect things, but it didn't seem to matter. I thought it was best to be quite natural . . . and we sat and chatted.'[5]

After the visit to Barrett's Court and Freshwater Place, Colonel Gardiner wrote to Princess Alice enclosing a letter he had received from Octavia:

The enclosed was not meant for your Royal Highness's eye but I think you may like to see how your interest in the poor is appreciated by one who is reckoned *hard* and who in matters of feeling is apt to frame her words somewhat coldly – from observation of her for the last ten years I believe that there does not exist a more unselfish person and that her whole heart is given to the Glory of God and the good of her fellow creatures – though she never speaks of her motives.

While acknowledging Octavia's personally difficult manner, Gardiner gave a testimonial to the shy woman who he suspected shared all the aims and aspirations of Princess Alice. In fact Gardiner's encomium was hardly necessary; the Marylebone visit had been an astonishing success and Princess Alice had asked for another expedition, this time to the East End. A small logistical problem had to be overcome; Princess Alice had chosen the day of the Lord Mayor's processions and since there was to be the novelty of elephants that year, even larger crowds than usual were expected.

Just as her grandfather had taken Lords Shaftesbury and Normanby around the East End, so Octavia shepherded Princess Alice through the fetid alleys and courts around St Jude's.

> With a charming excellent lady Miss Octavia Hill; I have been this morning in some of the very poor courts in London, garrets and streets . . . such quantities of little children and so many living in one dirty room. It was sad to see them, in one way, but beautiful to see how these ladies worked among them, knew them, did business with them. I have been trying to see as much and learn as much as possible of what is done for the poor in every way and have heard of such good and unselfish noble people.[6]

In a letter written from Buckingham Palace the following day, Princess Alice described the expedition. Octavia and she had driven to Whitechapel, where she had met Samuel and Henrietta Barnett – 'both the most self-sacrificing excellent people, full of their work and having the best influence over the poor and often deformed people under their charge. I believe the Court I was taken to see is one of the very dirtiest and worst in the East End. New Court is narrow, very dirty, very low tumble-down houses.' They had gone into a room downstairs, where an umbrella-maker sat in the window, a sick child with heart disease lay in the bed and two 'half-naked' smaller children ran about.

After that grim sight they had gone to Wentworth Street, to look at a model lodging house. It was clean, well kept, with a reading-room and a large kitchen, where men made their own meals. Although some of the men looked idle to her 'and some are very late risers the woman of the house said, she said there was little risk in her house of drunkenness.' Octavia offered them some pictures for their common room, and the landlady 'did not object'. Then they went to Angel Alley, 'a horrid lodging-house'. There were dark rooms, disreputable people, 'but the children had dear little faces'. The little rooms had open fires and were littered with work. Octavia talked to them. An 'indifferent idle woman . . . had a long discussion with Miss Hill as to sending her girl to service which she did not seem to care about.' On the next stair were nice people, a woman nursing a four-week-old baby, another described as having water on the brain, and two more small children. The husband, a shoemaker, was working in the room too. From there they went to a block of newly rebuilt dwellings, 'with tidy staircases and a large balcony running along the second floor'.[7]

After the visit the Barnetts sent Princess Alice a note of whom she had seen and where; at New Court, George le Strange, umbrella-maker, sick child; Mitchell, tailor; Hayes, girl who won't go into service; Barton delicate woman, shoemaker. George Third building: Shateal, sailor from Bavaria. Lodging House, Wentworth Street, good. Lodging House, Angel Alley, bad. Castle Alley, O'Brien, sick woman, lazy sons. Perhaps the Barnetts did not appreciate how carefully Princess Alice was noting for herself everything she saw and everyone she met. The distance from Buckingham Palace might have been immeasurable, but she was as acute an observer as an experienced and practised rent-collector. She noted on a scrap of paper the differences between leasehold and freehold, and details of Octavia's role which she succinctly described as 'agent of the landlord – gathers the rent and is the friend of the poor and sees to repair and fair treatment.'

While Princess Alice remained in London, Octavia had another suggestion for her. Would she perhaps care to come to one of her tenants' parties? There was to be one the following Tuesday, at eight o'clock, at Nottingham Place. It would be a mix of tenants and fellow-workers, 'precisely as we usually do. Your Royal Highness will see what our ordinary parties are, which go on once or twice a week during the winter in various places, taking in once each year every one of our grown-up tenants.'

Alternatively there was the Monday evening gathering at the Club room. This was a concert at half-past eight, 'arranged wholly by the people themselves'. Tuesday evening would find Octavia as hostess and in charge. She could then,

> with a word or look decide all that shall or shall not be done, but on Monday the people themselves settle all and I am simply one of the audience, surrounded it is true by friends who are tenants but with some strangers and most desirous not to dictate or interfere in any way whatever with the development of the scheme as the Committee of the Club themselves wish. They have a standard, they do care to keep up to it, it is improving but I could not promise that you would not hear strange, rather low-toned songs, remarks on the rich and great, discontent with things as they are. The men smoke bad tobacco, the band plays deafeningly loud in a small room, the girls – oh, it breaks my heart to see the girls – they are so giddy and fond of rough ugly play, still there it is in all its native energy, vigour, roughness and to me deep interest. I care to be there that the slightest weight of influence may be on the side of good . . . I learn too more of the people's thoughts and views at these concerts than almost anywhere. I have told you frankly the advantages and drawbacks, because I cannot but feel you *do* care to pierce below the smoother surface to the human heart . . . If you care to see this also and send me a word I will call for you or meet you anywhere only too proudly and gladly – but probably it is all too rough.[8]

But Princess Alice had already shown herself to be game, and by return she notified Octavia that she would be there on the Monday. Octavia sent her a note: she would be at the Equerry's door at ten minutes or a quarter past eight, and would send in her card. She had already a plan of Buckingham Palace from her visits earlier in the month. She was able to reassure the Princess that the whole business would entail the strictest secrecy and discretion: 'you may trust me.' Princess Alice had also asked for a copy of the 1874 'Letter to the Fellow-workers', and Octavia wrote that she would try and find one for her.

And so Princess Alice set off, for the third time in a week, to see something of the life of the poor working-class in London. Since

Octavia was sworn to silence, no mention of this visit appears in any of her letters, nor in the accounts of her activities given to fellow-workers. However Emily Shaen was there and wrote to her sister describing the occasion. 'She came *quite* alone, in a big hat and old black gown, ran about like a young girl, and would not have the least notice taken of her.'[9]

On her return to Darmstadt, Princess Alice sent Octavia a life of the Prince Consort in thanks. 'The great exemplar of her father was always before her . . . a "leading Star" to her own,' as her biographer Theodore Martin put it. Thanking her for the gift,[10] Octavia told her that 'you would know that I *must* prize the book after what I have had the privilege of seeing of you, and what you said to me, very deeply indeed. I shall read it with the most solemn interest.'

After her thanks, she went on to describe the activities. 'My sister, all our pupils and about seventy ladies and gentlemen are singing at St Jude's tonight'; they were singing *Elijah*, to an audience of the poor. The following week they would repeat it in another East End parish. The Barrett's Court Club was doing a Christmas play, and that week there were three parties, which would include all the Drury Lane tenants. Octavia hesitated to ask Princess Alice (whom she addressed in letters as 'Madam') to trouble to write, but she did want to hear about what she was doing in Darmstadt. Perhaps there was a printed account?

There had obviously been plenty of personal conversation between the two: 'I like to think of the bright group of your children who would greet you when you return and of the eldest boy who is able to respond so readily to your thought. I feel it was very good of you so kindly to let me in to the human life which all have in common, still more perhaps have I to thank you for your sympathy for the lives of my people, believe me, the memory of it will not fade.'

Octavia apologized for dwelling on small things, but, knowing her interest:

I feel sure I am right in believing that even these small facts will interest you – I am writing to you also precisely as I should to anyone who had come forward and shewn real human interest in our poor, I do not think you would gain anything by my thinking much of forms to which I am wholly unaccustomed. I am not unmindful of what they mean . . . and I fancy I have not read your meaning wrong in thinking that for the sake of the poor who are

[165]

God's children, and our brothers and sisters, you would rather put up with queer, awkward forms, with ignorance of ceremony . . .

Octavia was testing the water; the experience of writing such easy, intimate letters to royalty must have come oddly to her, and she wanted reassurance that Princess Alice really did not wish for proper forms of address and other practices laid down by protocol. She sensed that Princess Alice found such formalities an obstacle between herself and those she felt sympathies with, and so Octavia excused herself accordingly: 'I do not think there remains in me any shadow of fear that you will think this letter rude because it is without them, or that I have interpreted your desire wrongly in believing you would rather have the facts and the thoughts as they come naturally.' As always when Octavia was worried, her writing style became increasingly convoluted as she attempted to explain herself.

Her birthday was approaching and as usual Octavia was surveying progress, which she shared in this letter with her new friend – amazed at how 'what was begun in solitary insignificance grows and grows'. There were wider gains too; 'the blessed sense of triumph in the nearer links drawn yearly between men different in class but citizens of one country.' It was a long letter, for which she hoped Princess Alice would forgive her but 'the quiet, the evening stillness, perhaps the sense of its being near the end of my own year have led me to run on at great length.'

A reply followed immediately and Octavia wrote again in mid-December. Princess Alice had sent special messages for the Mac-Donalds, which Octavia assured her had been passed on. They were very busy indeed with their acting. The purpose of Princess Alice's letter had been, however, to ask if Octavia would mind if she arranged for a German translation of *The Homes of the London Poor*. Octavia was delighted, and replied that there was no one better to oversee such a task: 'Oh surely you of all people will enter most deeply into what I feel.' Princess Alice had, Octavia told her, gone right to the heart of the matter: 'that the first and fundamental need is that of the person to carry out this work. Systems may be valuable, essential, but in most things, certainly in this, they are like machines useless or worse, unless the motive power and directing power are at hand and this human beings only can supply.'

Octavia proposed that Princess Alice personally should write the introduction to the German edition of *The Homes of the London Poor*.

Despite her own 'passionate longing . . . to creep once more *out* of sight' it was necessary to tell the story and she added: 'the history as to leases, finances, difficulties, successes are and must be the world's.'

Princess Alice's other request was evidently to be allowed to translate and arrange publication of the annual 'Letter to Fellow-workers', of which Octavia had sent her copies. This was less acceptable. Octavia was utterly firm, if apologetic.

> I fear I feel just a little differently about my letters to my fellow-workers, and that slight difference of feeling makes all the difference in action. Though they are printed, and pretty widely circulated among certain circles of people, they have never been published. I have refused more than once to let them be published either in America or here. For this reason. They are meant for, and written to my fellow-workers and though they contain passages which are entirely public, there are other parts I could not write exactly as they stand if I felt I were writing to the world in general.

They had begun six years before because of the sheer impossibility of writing individually to all of them.

> I hated printing, I hated a circular letter, instead of one addressed to one person only. You see my fellow-workers *are* my friends, their lives, even often in their secret recesses, their characters, their needs are known to me and I should have like to feel that we could speak to one another by letter from time to time . . . When I sit down as I shall do next Sunday to write my annual letter, I feel that I am writing not to the world but to my own friends . . . to those who I may dare to trust.

The fact that they were not 'published' meant that she could be harder both on her fellow-workers and on herself. But, 'above all I preserve for myself when writing this intense sense of nearness. I think they ought not to lose the directness and personal character the letters thus take. It had a struggle to survive the printing, it would be lost utterly if I could think of publishing.' With that she ended her explanation.

Octavia's letter was taking on the overwrought nature of much of her correspondence at this time, as the strains were building up in her personal and professional life. She did not want the preface to *The Homes of the London Poor* to talk of her own personal history, from where she had taken her ideas and what models she had followed. She hoped that Princess Alice would understand that she wanted to stand back – so that people would take up 'the work itself quite without any impression of *me*'.

Princess Alice had written of her children, and of her own institutions and foundations. Although Octavia had not been reading (a sure sign of bad health), her mother had been immersed in *The Life of the Prince Consort*. The dread of drunkenness over Christmas, Octavia said, was oppressing her, since 'my people . . . are so apt to drink to excess'. It was no use being impatient, however; 'the gradual increase of education, the refinement which is penetrating downwards will do much, and perhaps we may live to see a more deep and true sense of duty govern and transform the lives of many in all classes.'

On the day after Christmas Octavia added a postscript, ten days after she had written the main part of the letter. 'The refusal to meet fully and gladly your kind suggestion felt to me ungracious, but I do not see my way to send any other answer, I wish I had worded it better.' But she was unable to improve on it. The daughter of one of her best friends, and one of their dearest pupils, was with them – desperately ill. Although she was not nursing her, since the girl's mother was with her, she had to support the mother in her misery. It meant she had to assume 'and to keep a high calm brightness sustained and sustaining for all times and under all circumstances needs incessant effort, and thought of Him who alone inspires us.' Her own work had suffered; she could only snatch moments for it. 'Forgive me then for the delay in replying to your most kind, reassuring, and beautiful letter. Now I must wish you all best New Year's blessings, such as cannot fail or fade, and that they may abide continuously on you and yours.'[11]

The reply was obviously good-hearted. Octavia wrote again in early February, very glad that Princess Alice had not been disappointed with her response about the letters. A Miss Graves had been to see her, with news of the family in Darmstadt, and would take back a copy of the 1876 'Letter to Fellow-workers'. She was terribly busy, too busy, but was writing because she wanted Princess Alice to share the success of the plans at Whitechapel, which, of course, they had visited together.

We have actually arranged to purchase fifteen houses in St Jude's parish which are many of them let to the immoral poor and of which we are most anxious to obtain control. Among them – this is what I think will interest you – is that last common lodging house you saw, the one in Angel Alley, where there was the poor wizened little old-looking baby, and the degraded woman. We hope to have a model common lodging house there, where they may sing, and where young Oxford men or other gentlemen may go in and have a chat, or a discussion, and reach perhaps many a wild, undisciplined young man, or broken down old one; where too we may have pictures and colour, and flowers, and good order. Mr Barnett is so very happy in the thought, and I am very triumphantly glad only I am so overwhelmed with the arrangements about surveyor's reports, terms of lease, deciding which of our many friends waiting to purchase houses is to have this domain allotted to them that I have little time for other thoughts.

Edward Bond was, she told her, also hoping to buy a couple of houses adjoining, and there were two more East End courts in prospect. She described other ventures, such as Caroline Stephen's plans in Chelsea, and various open-space campaigns. There was continuing good progress at Barrett's Court; 'rebuilding goes on just now smoothly and does not require me.'

All these activities, including a visit to the pantomime with sixty Barrett's Court children paid for by members of the Revd Haweis' congregation, and the work for the COS, were keeping her mind 'perpetually strained to fullest effort, while my dear people, my fellow-workers and my house also take a good deal out of me so that I long often for a pause in the company of the few who rest me.' She recounted at great length one history of personal misfortune that involved the Stimpsons, the people from Manchester, whom Princess Alice had met.

Mr Stimpson, an habitual drinker, had had a job as a printer. That week his employer, who had money problems, departed by the back door, leaving the men unpaid. The following week they refused to work until they saw the money they were owed, and eventually their boss paid them up to the previous Saturday and dismissed them all. Mr Stimpson had been without work for a week, and had asked Octavia for help. She refused him money but found him a job. As she told Princess Alice: 'they seem small details to tell you of but somehow they seem to me to throw a strange light on the perverse alienation between master and men.'

She ended as usual, with an apology for the length of her letter. 'I hope this long letter may interest, not trouble you. I am believing that you do care to hear of English matters though it is difficult to estimate how far people and places and minor incidents . . . may fail to convey any living impression to you of what, were you face to face with it, I *know* you would care for.'[12]

There is a gap in the correspondence at this point, caused by the illness and death of Princess Alice's much-loved father-in-law, followed by that of his brother. As a result, in 1877 Prince Louis became Grand Duke. Princess Alice was herself in bad health and spent that summer in Normandy; when she returned it was as the Grand Duchess of Hesse-Darmstadt.

Ill health brought her back to England the following year, and she wrote to Octavia, hoping to meet her once more. Written on her behalf, the letter was unusually formal. 'Her Royal Highness hopes to see Miss Hill in town and should be especially pleased if Miss Hill could also come to Eastbourne on a few days' visit for the benefit of her health and enable Her Royal Highness to discuss some serious matters with her at ease.'[13]

This time Octavia could not oblige. By now she herself was prostrated by nervous illness and wrote back from the MacDonalds' villa at Nervi, full of regrets. Princess Alice's visit to England, a large part of which was a recuperative stay in Eastbourne paid for by Queen Victoria, was as usual spent in asking searching questions and meeting the poor and those who worked with them. Even in Eastbourne she was visiting poor cottages and wandering around the fishermen's quarter.

Octavia and Princess Alice did not meet again; she died, aged thirty-six, in December that year, of diphtheria contracted from her fatally ill youngest daughter, May.

At home in Germany she left behind an impressive network of institutions of many sorts. She had established the nursing profession, both active and auxiliary, advised by Florence Nightingale. She had also worked hard for women's education and left behind her all kinds of projects and achievements – including the provision of paid clerical work for women at the Central Statistics Office, and a mental hospital named after her. But the Princess normally sought anonymity in her work; the preface to the German edition of *The Homes of the London Poor* was simply signed 'A'.

Princess Alice had approached Octavia Hill very much as she had

Florence Nightingale – to gain the benefit of her experience. The result had been a friendship of real depth and warmth, and a correspondence from which we learn, in some ways more fully than from any other series of her letters, about the progress of Octavia's work at a given period.

In 1881 Octavia was asked to help provide material for a German memoir of Princess Alice, but little was ever recorded about her meetings with Octavia – the letters quoted above are the fullest record. Her younger sister, Princess Louise, preserved the contact with Octavia through her patronage of the Kyrle Society★ and, later on, as Vice-President and then President of the National Trust – which she took on particularly because of her high regard for Octavia.

★ See Chapter 11.

CHAPTER 11

Countryside matters

A ROMANTIC ideal of the countryside – a rural idyll in contrast with the distressing urban scene – was a consistent theme throughout Octavia's life and work. Observers have noted how the founders of the East End Settlements, Edward Denison and Samuel Barnett, feared the city and what it would bring in its train. Barnett had a 'fatalism about the chance for regeneration within an urban environment'.[1] Writing to his brother from Sevenoaks, he said he had just ventured up to London for a meeting: 'I confess that the sight of the people beat me. What is possible when houses are so close – the air so thick & when people love to have it so . . .'[2] Many social reformers shared an indirect anti-urban feeling, considering that the city posed a threat to ideals of home and family life. Window-boxes, a jam-jar of flowers on the window sill or a well-tended patch of open ground nearby, were all seen as inducements to the moral life.

Octavia would never have considered herself beaten by the problems of the city (although the properties she acquired in Deptford came very close to defeating even her spirit) but she personally retreated to the countryside at any opportunity, and in the later years of her life spent a considerable amount of time in a cottage near Edenbridge. She was at one with romantics such as C. R. Ashbee or, for that matter, William Morris, in her imagery of the countryside even if, in her scheme of things, open country was to be like a glorious back garden to city life and crowded conditions.

After she had brought back ninety bunches of flowers for the tenants from one of her own excursions to the countryside, she mused: 'I wish we could get the tenants more often into the country. Does it not seem that the quiet influence of nature is more restful to Londoners than anything else? But picnic parties carry London noise and vulgarity out into woods and fields, giving no sense of hush or rest.' It was an almost insoluble conundrum.

Her memories of the Loughton cottage and another in Finchley where the Hill family had lived after their father's breakdown, were combined with those of their grandfather's Highgate house, Hillside, looking on to the park just by Kenwood House. It had offered a 'life . . . like that of the country, and full of pleasure to a child. We had cows . . . a perfect orchard of wonderful apple-trees . . . in the summer came hay-making of our own, and all this so near London that half an hour's drive of our fast horse Ariel took us to its centre.'[3]

When the family had moved into London, Octavia was suddenly made aware that much of the population had no idea of the country-side – even those scenes that the family had taken for granted on the hillsides of Hampstead, just a few miles from the centre of the city. When Octavia one day had gone looking for 'Robin' (Amelia), one of her toymakers, she had found herself in a miserable court.

> A low archway led through a way, now half obstructed by a heap of dirt, to a wide paved court swarming from end to end with numberless children . . . a crowd of blighted lives . . . The gay spring fields, the village green, the bright brooks should have surrounded the young beings at that age when most subtle, endur-ing impressions are sealed on the soul. Oh, for power to cast away from them the misery around, to remove them from air poisoned and close, to give them God's free light . . .

The grim conditions of the 1850s merely worsened year by year.

As they never forgot the impact of city life and its visible poverty when they were exposed to it for the first time, so the Hill sisters never underestimated the delight that grass and trees could give city chil-dren, or for that matter, adults. Octavia always loved flowers and was very touched when the charwoman at the Working Women's College brought her a bunch of poppies one day to remind her of the country.

In the early years, Octavia loved going back from central London to see the Howitts in Highgate. On a June day, 'There were Mr Howitt and Charlton at work, early and late, at their beloved garden, talking about tame birds and pea-sticks as if there were no noise and bustle in London.'[4] A year or two later she planted a Virginia creeper from Mary Harris's home in Cumberland at Nottingham Place; 'it seems to bind me to that one against your house, looking towards the mountains. Oh, Spring is hard to bear in London.'[5] The countryside brought her close in spirit to her friends; on one occasion, enjoying the Harrisons' house, she wrote to Emily, wishing that Emma Cons were there. 'She would appreciate so much the beauty of everything. She would rejoice to look at the gigantic trees holding themselves so still, with, here and there, a branch all gold or copper coloured, and the brilliant berries; to trace the light wreaths of briony not yet transformed into streams of gold . . .' Emma, whose life and work in many ways closely mirrored Octavia's own, also had a country retreat in later years; a cottage called Chippens Bank at Hever, near Edenbridge.

Nature brought out a lyric strain in Octavia, less tortured when she expressed it in prose than, as sometimes, in bad verse. Writing to Florence in Italy, Octavia described a walk in the Buckinghamshire beech woods: 'acres and acres of beech woods, valleys and hills clothed and covered with them, and there are rounded hills with most beautiful slopes . . . and nearer hills covered with wood, and farmhouses with their great barns golden-roofed with lichen lying in a sheltered hollow . . .'[6] Many years later, she regarded the securing of Burnham Beeches for the public, bought by the City Corporation, as a major triumph for the Kyrle Society.[7]

On another occasion she wrote to Emily who had been to the sea. 'I long to hear from you about how it looked. It is many years since I saw it . . . I remember with particular joy a walk along the top of the high cliffs, at the edge of a cornfield, brilliant with poppies studded like stars among the ears of tall grain.' The cliffs were white, the sea and sky blue, with 'masses of torn clouds disappearing to the horizon.'[8] She loved the countryside, and the distant views from St George's Hill, near her grandfather's house at Weybridge. Even Parliament Hill Fields,[9] lashed by a thunderstorm and then brilliantly lit in the sun, filled her with admiration.

Discussion of the relative merits of city and country had been a regular topic between Octavia and Ruskin from the first days of their friendship. Knowing of Octavia's delight in gardens, he suggested that she should come regularly to his parents' house, with its large grounds and feel of the country.[10]

By 1874 the number of Octavia's tenants was such that to get each one into the countryside for one day a year involved fifteen excursions – at the least: 'No small tax on strength and time and money, yet giving the people a bright glimpse of fair and still places, not blackened or built over.' She was always looking for suitable destinations, and on more than one occasion they hired a river steamer for the event. However, she preferred using her fellow-workers' own places – in order to give 'that beautiful sense of personal hospitality'. In 1870 she had nervously taken some Barrett's Court tenants to Woodford, worried that if she took her eyes off them they would be drinking – 'we feared, all day, they would wander off to the public-house. All went beautifully but the responsibility was great.' Other destinations included Lady Ducie's house in Wimbledon and the MacDonalds' house, the Retreat, in Hammersmith.

The Hill sisters' half-brother Arthur frequently entertained dozens of tenants at his house outside Reading, and Octavia once told the fellow-workers of a treat for 'six or eight of our poor women, most of them widows' who had been taken 'from the East End to tea at a little cottage in Hampstead. They then took a country walk; journey and tea only cost 1s each; many of them had not seen country for years and their delight in the beauty and quiet was touching.' On another occasion, Gertrude and her family, now living at the old Southwood Smith house Hillside, entertained seventy tenants. They walked across the fields, 'the children ran and sang and made merry; the women enjoyed the bright air and quiet.' There was cricket for the boys, plenty of entertainment, tea for the older people, 'everyone was amused, and happy, and good. The arrangements were perfection. Two waggonettes took *all* the women and babies and toddling children back to the station.'[11] Blanche Lewes, one of Octavia's godchildren and an especial favourite, had made up bunches of flowers to give to every grown-up as they left.

The MacDonalds not only provided a pleasant garden setting for the outings, but laid on theatricals as well. One year the children performed *Snowdrop* in front of eighty-one tenants, with forty helpers. George Eliot heard about it all and wrote to Charles Lewes: 'it is so thoroughly satisfactory to see so many people concurring to help Octavia. That is just as it should be.' Another year *Blue Beard* was performed for the garden-party guests.

The consciousness of what a walk in open country could mean to a resident in one of the lightless tenements of Marylebone or Whitechapel lay behind Octavia's early dedication to the fight for the preservation of common land and open spaces in the city, whether these were the small breathing spaces between her blocks, or the great spaces of Swiss Cottage threatened by development in the early 1870s.

[175]

The Swiss Cottage Fields formed the steep slope to the west of the salubrious villages of Hampstead and Highgate and were the nearest available green space and open countryside to the lower levels, both physically and socially, of Marylebone and Paddington, some of the grimmest areas of Victorian London.

Characteristically Octavia set out to raise the money – £10,000 – to buy them. Edward Bond was her confidant in all this and together they decided 'that, for the moment, we would let the big-moneyed people alone . . . I believe (thank God!) more in nobodies than in "somebodies".' The Duke of Westminster and Baroness Rothschild had given £100 each 'which won't do to go on. Col. Gardiner will get some names among aristocrats who have little else to give.' She had high hopes of one famous philanthropist: 'I know Mr Mocatta *very* well, he consults me about many of his charities. I didn't know he was so great a gun!'[12] Gardiner, the Queen's Equerry, had returned from Windsor full of energy and determination. Later on Lord Shaftesbury agreed to give his name for the Committee, 'but won't work much or care much, already engrossed I fancy.'

Octavia set much store by the written word. 'Space for the People', the essay which she added to *The Homes of the London Poor* at the last moment, was her plea for the Swiss Cottage Fields, a moving entreaty for open ground which was used by people from the poor areas of Lisson Grove and Marylebone who 'spread over the green open space like a stream that has just escaped from between rocks'. It was a fine, campaigning piece. 'These fields may be bought now, or they may be built over: which is it to be?' she asked her readers.

She also believed in letters to the press; if published, they were a relatively easy and speedy way of drawing public attention to these appeals. Bond wrote to *The Times* on 9 July 1875. He mentioned that one gentleman had offered £1,000 if a cricket field would be provided. In his view, 'benevolent London' should be concerned to keep the open space 'for her multitudes', 'sanitary London' should favour the idea of 'air-holes for labouring lungs', whilst 'artistic London' should try to preserve 'remnants of rustic beauty'. Octavia, as she told Sydney Cockerell, sent a letter to *The Times* a few days later, but 'I never have believed in *my* succeeding in *The Times*, it isn't my line, they wouldn't like me, nor I them, we all incline to thinking the letter was too "emotional".'

Octavia's letter was published on 16 July in the *Daily News*. It was emotional, but effective.

Will the city merchants and bankers who, after the turmoil of the day is over, go out to country houses set on smooth lawns among bright flowers, think of people whose view from their window is only of the blank wall of area or backyard a few feet off, the same day after day, month after month, year after year, and whose walk, if they have the heart to walk at all, is through mile upon mile of ever lengthening streets?

The Leweses were busy on her behalf too, although they did not believe whole-heartedly in either the approach or in the feasibility of the scheme. George Lewes wrote to Charles that 'the Mutter' – George Eliot – had drafted a letter to Alfred Morrison,[13]

> but from all we have seen or heard, he is not at all a likely person to be moved in that direction (the names of the Duke of W and Lady Burdett Coutts would have more influence than any abstract idea of 'the people') and the Mutter feels so little personal sympathy with him that she cannot write to him more fully. No one else occurs to us. Indeed desirable as the proposed Park may be – especially to those who live near it – I fear that so large a sum could not be gained for a park so near Regent's Park and Hampstead Heath. But there is no knowing what ingenious advocacy may effect.[14]

August, in any case an unsuitable month for fund-raising, found Octavia resting with the Ducies at Tortworth. 'I feel like a war-horse out of the battle and hearing it far off.'[15] She was thinking of little else – 'I feel leaving my fields so that I could almost cry' – and writing many letters.

> How strange it seems to me (does it not to you?) that the momentary difficulty is to persuade the owners that there is a chance of anyone (any body of people in London or England) being in the least likely to be inclined to give the money for a place which must be a blessing to hundreds now, and hundreds yet to come . . . Fields reminding men and children long lost in the whirl of London, of child days and places near where they were born; fields where little children can see the wild flowers grow, as they are beginning to do once more on Hampstead Heath.

She had great faith in professional men, ladies with limited incomes 'who will make for once an effort and sacrifice to give £25 or £50 to save a bit of green hilly ground near a city, where fresh winds may blow, and where wild flowers still are found, and where happy people can still walk within reach of their homes.' This testament to the recuperative powers of countryside and open parkland was one she never improved upon and it was to be a guiding principle, quite as strong as any other, for the rest of her life. It took many of those small sums to raise £10,000. Yet in an astonishing three weeks, the fund stood at £8,150.

In mid-August the owners of the Swiss Cottage Fields withdrew their offer to sell, giving five days' notice. 'He confirms it, tells us we must consider the offer absolutely withdrawn, and refused even to receive a guarantee within a week for the full amount. I think the loss is very great. The spirit of many of the people who helped us was so beautiful. I shall never forget *that*.'[16] In the event Fitzjohn's Avenue was laid out as a prestigious and elegant development, complete with pink horse-chestnuts and houses designed by some of the best architects of the age.

Octavia learned an important lesson from the failure of the Swiss Cottage appeal. Sir Robert Hunter, in an appreciation of Octavia in *The Times* after her death noted: 'In all subsequent projects of the kind with which she was connected, a definite option of purchase for a specific time was obtained before public support was solicited.'[17]

Despite that disappointment, the flame was lit. It had been her first major open-space campaign and after it she honed her strategies to fight many other successful battles. Now she planned to approach a member of the Commons Preservation Society[18] to find out what they were doing and what their plans were. She wanted them to survey the open space currently available in London. 'If they won't do it, I will, or will get it done, and then bend my energies to whatever direction help is most needed.'*

She had already enthused the Barnetts with the idea that open space – for walking, sitting, playing – was a social necessity for those who passed their lives in one room. In 1875 the Barnetts began to lay out a garden behind the courts near St Jude's. 'In New Court a piece of void ground, long the receptacle of rubbish, is in process of being turned into a garden. An open railing has been substituted for the wall, soil has been spread, and a few trees planted. The people in the Court are

*See p. 183.

showing great interest in the work, and we look hopefully forward to the effect of one bright spot in this very dark neighbourhood.'

Octavia's contact at the Commons Preservation Society was Robert Hunter, who had been their Honorary Solicitor since 1868. In professional life a solicitor at the Post Office, Robert Hunter put his considerable abilities into securing open spaces – be they large or small – for the general good. By late 1875 Octavia was fully involved in Commons Preservation Society business. Mr Shaw-Lefevre, its Chairman (later Lord Eversley), whom she had met in discussion over the Artisans' Dwellings Bill that year, was to become a great ally as Octavia put her elbow to the wheel of the Society, with Edward Bond backing her up. When she asked her supporters, in the annual 'Letter to Fellow-workers', to give donations to 'causes or societies urgently needing liberal support', the two she proposed were the [Metropolitan] Society for Befriending Young Servants (Mrs Nassau Senior's organization) and the Commons Preservation Society.[19]

Octavia was now busy trying to lobby for a Burials Bill, which would allow the conversion of disused burial grounds into small public gardens. She told Gertrude in the summer of 1875 that Lord Wolmer had offered to talk to Sir William Harcourt, then Solicitor-General, about it. She had also been in touch with Sir Charles Dilke and Lord Salisbury.

In the same year Miranda proposed a 'Society for the Diffusion of Beauty', to improve, in modern parlance, the quality of life for the poor. It was set up later that year, as the 'Kyrle Society' after Pope's philanthropist, the Man of Ross, who had bequeathed to his birthplace a public park. Miranda's address to the National Health Society in December 1875 dealt with the question of burial grounds, which became a prime objective for the Society.

But the Kyrle Society, formally constituted in 1876, was dedicated to introducing colour and beauty in all respects to grim lives. For Octavia, it could be brightly furnished clubrooms or a proper choir; anything that improved the miserable lives of the very poor. 'Happy evenings' in Board Schools was another Kyrle Society initiative. Gradually the Kyrle Society grew to consist of a number of sub-committees: a Decorative Branch (chaired by Harrison Townsend, the architect, and enthusiastically promoted by, among others, William Morris), a Musical Branch and a Literature Distribution Branch. But the most active and influential, its Open Spaces Sub-Committee,[20] was formed in 1879, with Robert Hunter as honorary

[179]

legal adviser and Chairman. Treasurer of the Kyrle Society was Octavia.

There was soon a network of regional Kyrle Societies. The Liverpool branch was founded in 1877 by leading local philanthropists and carried out various picturesque missions, such as sending flowers from the country to city children. The Kyrle Society always ran the risk of appearing as merely offering suitable and safe charitable work for dilettante women. However the Liverpool branch supported a number of local social endeavours, such as Mrs Birt's Sheltering Homes.[21] The enthusiastic support of, for example, William Morris, who spoke in support of the Kyrle Society on a number of occasions,[22] rather disproves the suggestion of frivolity, whilst the Bishop of Bristol and Gloucester's inquiry into the condition of the poor reported that in Bristol in 1884 'there is not amongst all its benevolent associations any which has in view the Recreation of the People except a branch of the Kyrle Society which appears to be very slightly supported.'[23]

Octavia wanted to make it clear that the activities of the CPS and the new committee could be complementary. Robert Hunter's involvement in both emphasized the point. The work would help the wider movement for commons preservation, she told Emily: 'in fact there need be no difference in programme; but I think you ought at once to know that I see a wide difference in expectation. It is clear there is no large or zealous body to gather together . . . Take it very quietly; go on till it grows into more life . . . before all the commons are gone . . .'[24]

The differences between the two bodies, Octavia felt, were that the Kyrle encouraged 'gift and purchase and beautifying as well as "preservation", that you have to do with *private* land as well as *commons*, and that you have to do with Metropolitan as well as rural open spaces. A name never includes all objects; but a narrower one belonging to a somewhat analogous society would be very confusing.'[25] Put like this, the Kyrle Society's aims foreshadowed those of the future National Trust.

The original problem which had sparked off the Kyrle Society was the lack of accessible open space in the city, close to where people lived. Miranda had identified a solution. If people could not easily get out of the town, why not make the town itself more agreeable? 'I hardly know whether the increased hope of making places beautiful should count as extension or perfection, but distinct advance has been made in this direction.' Octavia's sister's small society was one step forward and she hoped that 'tiny plots, backyards and small fore-courts, may be fuller of trees or grass or creepers.'[26] Even a window-box or a vase of flowers at the window were something: later on, the Southwark flower show became a popular event for Octavia's tenants.

Years later Octavia characterized the aims of the campaign: 'These open spaces became more and more necessary as land rose in value and houses were built high and higher, and private gardens became rarer. They were no aristocratic luxury or exceptional superfluity but some faint reflex of what our modern civilization has taken away from the ordinary inheritance to which our citizens were born.' It was, too, a natural extension of the housing work; 'shall I call them two develop-ments of the same object, for to us in London, no less than to the dweller in the country, the house and the garden together form the home. We in London have to share our garden, perhaps England itself will learn to share some of its gardens.'[27]

Nevertheless the beginnings were not auspicious. The Kyrle Society had set its collective heart on obtaining:

> small open spaces for out-door sitting-rooms for the people in various parts of London – hitherto without one atom of success. I think I never spent so much heart, time, and thought on anything so utterly without apparent result. We tried for an East-end boulevard, with an avenue, and wider spaces of green and flowers – an East-end embankment, as it were, where the people might have strolled on summer evenings, and sat out of doors, and we failed. We tried to get a church-yard planted and opened in Drury Lane, and the matter has not progressed very far yet . . . We tried to get leave from one nobleman to plant trees along an East-end road [Mile End Road] where he is lord of the manor and he postpones the question. We tried to get the Board School playgrounds open, and so far without success. We tried – Oh! how we tried – to get the Quakers to devote to the service of the poor their disused burial grounds, and they, even they, have decided to build over by far the more precious of the two . . . They have one space left [Bunhill Fields] – the vicar, the guardians, we ourselves, are asking for it for the people, but their past action does not form much ground for hope.

Shaw-Lefevre of the Commons Preservation Society joined Octavia in the fight for Bunhill Fields. Lefevre was full of energy and interest in the scheme[28] and undertook to write to the Home Secretary about it.

Despite a long and impassioned letter to *The Friend*, it was one of Octavia's few lost campaigns.

Uncharacteristically Octavia was feeling defeated by the repeated failures in the open space campaign – so much so that the future outlook seemed bleak. 'Next year . . . will there be any spot saved from the waste of bricks and mortar or the hideousness of neglect to be devoted to the people?'

As she fought the battle for improvement in the city environment, her grandfather's shadow fell across her path. She cannily appealed to the self-interest of the upper classes: '. . . do you really think now, people who live in comfortable houses, that you do or can escape infection by any precautions if small-pox and fever rage in the back-courts of your city?' By ignoring the living conditions of the poor, they were jeopardizing their own futures: 'your best chance of escape is to make the places inhabited by the poor healthy, to let them have open spaces where the fresh wind may blow over them and their clothes.' People had not forgotten the idea that illness spread by miasma; Octavia recognized, even played upon, that fear.[29]

The Mile End Road never became the avenue she had dreamt of, but by the late 1870s (during Octavia's illness and prolonged absence abroad), the opening up of the burial grounds began to go on apace. St George's-in-the-East was the first, followed by Drury Lane churchyard which 'has been planted and opened as any outdoor sitting-room, so has St John's Waterloo Road.'[30] This Drury Lane scheme started with worries; there had been vandalism and it would take very little to turn the public against the idea of allowing the poor access to these places. Emma Cons, redoubtable lieutenant that she was, went to see the extent of the damage; it was merely an excess of enthusiasm, she reported. The ivy was trampled, the yuccas which had foolishly been planted unprotected on the gravel were the worse for wear but her impression was that no one intended any harm.[31]

St Giles' churchyard was

a capital bit of ground running down to Seven Dials, its wilderness of tall rank grass and shivering leafy trees would, even if untouched, be something green to look at if the great wall which hides them were but down, and should the untidy neglected graves and green damp paving stones be put in order, and bright beds of flowers be made in the grass, should the great gates be opened and a look of care and brightness given, what a possession the place would be to the residents near!

Bearing always in mind that it was the children to whom the most earnest efforts were being directed, Octavia also continued to lobby for playgrounds for the Board Schools. By 1880 she was reporting success.

In 1881 the Metropolitan Open Spaces Act became law, the culmination of the efforts of the CPS, of Octavia's various and persuasive campaigns (successful or unsuccessful, they still had propagandist value), and those of the Kyrle Society. It made the transfer of gardens and burial grounds to public authorities a relatively simple matter.

The weakness of the Kyrle Society was its lack of structure as an organization trying to set out on a mission of civic reform. It was not sophisticated enough for the task in hand; its membership was neither politically aware nor activist.[32] But the Kyrle Society's aims were entirely recognizable as those underlying the Garden City and later New Town developments, which were framed in terms suitable to more sophisticated times.

In fact, the Kyrle Society, like so much of Octavia's work, had mainly indirect effects. It caught the attention of people such as Patrick Geddes, the idealistic town planner. The vision that he and his contemporaries shared included the widening of cultural life of the city by providing open spaces, libraries and other amenities. He drew on the sort of initiatives that the Kyrle Society encouraged, but placed them within the framework of early twentieth-century town planning.

The obvious limitations of the Kyrle Society organization led to, for example, the Metropolitan Public Gardens Association, founded in 1882, which worked with the National Health Society thus promoting links with the sanitary reform movement. Lord Brabazon was Chairman, and his most active colleague was Ernest Hart – Octavia's supporter and Henrietta Barnett's brother-in-law. By the end of the 1880s the Metropolitan Public Gardens Association had laid out around 200 small city gardens. With the founding of the LCC, Brabazon, now Earl of Meath, became chairman of its open spaces committee and the Association handed over a number of its properties to the municipal authority.[33]

The Kyrle Society was to run into trouble in the early 1900s. A meeting was held to rally support and energies in 1903, but in 1906 Octavia was addressing an audience at the Mansion House with some desperation. 'We sorely want funds; our work is crippled for want of them.' In fact, as Octavia and Miranda grew old, the Kyrle Society would founder; it was essentially a Hill enterprise and had little substance without them.

It was Octavia's own invariable response to the countryside that guided her feeling that even one day in the open air could restore the spirits of her tenants. As the strains of her busy campaigning life built up, friends recognizing her own needs regularly tempted her out of London. She frequently joined the Barnetts for a walk at the weekend, and holidays with the MacDonald family in Cornwall and Scotland were often offered when her health was weak.

In 1877 she went back to Cornwall, ten years after her happy time there with the MacDonalds, but this time with the Barnetts. Samuel Barnett, who had himself been ill again, was standing in for the vicar of Wadebridge. They regarded the time as a holiday and set out to explore the coast from St Mawgan to Boscastle. Sometimes they went inland, to the woods near Bodmin, the moors or other favourite spots. Octavia, who had arrived ill and unhappy, joined in: 'in spite of our reverence for her we made her sit "bodkin" in the little chaise, and compelled her to join in our most frivolous pleasures.'[34] Inspired by the stay in Cornwall, the Barnetts helped to set up the Children's Country Holiday Fund which became a considerable organization with, around 1914, almost 3,000 helpers countrywide.

Octavia herself was an enthusiastic supporter of the boarding out of orphan children in the countryside and in memory of Mrs Nassau Senior five orphans were sent to 'happy country homes where child-life was a clear gain to foster-parents'. It was never a large-scale enterprise, but Octavia's love of children and the countryside and her veneration of the home were satisfactorily combined in the scheme, which spared children from institutional upbringing.'[35]

In 1877 Octavia published her collection of essays on open spaces, *Our Common Land*, and alerted the fellow-workers both to the growth and success of the movement to open the burial grounds, and the increase in the number of threats to common land. There were thirty-seven inclosures before the House in the coming year. She was also newly involved in a major campaign for landscape protection out of London. The plan to use Thirlmere as a reservoir for South Lancashire was arousing her to full action:

We ought not, as a nation, to bow to the greed of Manchester, and her dense incapacity for seeing or caring for beauty, but before we trust one of our loveliest lakes, and three valleys to her keeping, should know whether indeed there are not wells and collecting grounds in which she may build reservoirs without sullying one of the few peaceful and unspoiled spots in England, and monopolizing water to sell for profit to a whole county, without restrictions as to the way in which she mars the scenery.

This was the campaign of Hardwick Rawnsley, whom she had met when he was working in the parish of St Mary's Soho, helping at a lodging-house for vagrants. On the suggestion of Ruskin, one of whose student roadmakers he had been in 1874,[36] he made contact with Octavia, and soon found himself rent-collecting for Emma Cons, whose fiefdom Drury Lane then was. When he had a severe nervous collapse through overwork, Octavia arranged his convalescence with friends near Lake Windermere.[37]

On Rawnsley's recovery he was sent to Bristol, to take charge of a mission to the poor, the Agnes Mission, funded by Clifton College. 'There is a Mr Rawnsley, a young clergyman just going to work in Bristol, with splendid stuff in him and inclined to go the right way if he were shown it,' wrote Octavia to Samuel Barnett.[38] However, the rigours of Saturday football and Sunday walks with a group of excessively rough and unruly boys from the parish of St Barnabas ensured that Rawnsley hardly lasted the year.

Returning to his beloved Lake District in 1877, Rawnsley was fortunate enough to be entrusted with the tiny parish of St Margaret at Wray, on the edge of Windermere. He immediately began to campaign on a range of issues; the railways, public rights of way and the Thirlmere reservoir scheme.

It was somewhat ironic that Octavia's grandfather's campaign to bring clean water to the urban population should now be in conflict with her own activities to protect the beauty of the countryside. The issue was also complicated by the involvement of landowners, who only lent their voices to the campaign in order that the eventual level of compensation would be higher.[39] Robert Hunter, who had also been brought into the fight, saw the trap, and hastily bowed out. Manchester Corporation won the day, and the landowners received considerable sums in recompense.

Whatever the mistakes made, Octavia observed that, regardless of the outcome of the Thirlmere campaign, it had been an effective way of arousing public concern. 'Such an agitation as this is distinctly educational for the nation, and it may help to save other places.'[40]

CHAPTER 12

Crisis

THE first bad news of 1877 reached Octavia while she was
staying with Mary Harris in Cumberland. Her friend Jane
Nassau Senior was desperately ill. Octavia wrote to Henrietta:

I am quite stunned. I sit and listen for the telegram that shall tell me
news about Janey. I hear news, thank God, constantly, but the
hearing will soon be all over and the world hold one less who loves
me. None of you can know how specially awful her death is to me,
nor what the void she leaves, but you will know something of her
tenderness, the ardent generosity, the nobility of her standard . . .
[Octavia knew that some time she would understand it but] there
are times in life when we can only wait and wonder when the
inexpressible pain will be over and the peace begin to come, it must
some day.[1]

Jane, who had been appointed the first woman Poor Law Inspector,
had also founded the Metropolitan Association for Befriending Young
Servants which by the mid-1880s had some 800 visitors and was
placing 5,000 pauper girls in domestic service annually.[2]

Her Report for the Local Government Board on the conditions
which faced pauper girls in their places of work had been highly
critical of the role of the Guardians. After handing the paper in,
Jane Nassau Senior had resigned her post. Octavia had written to
Henrietta, referring to 'such a sad, but such a beautiful letter from Mrs
Nassau Senior who resigns her work tomorrow, broken down far
more . . . by the case of poor families than by public work.'[3] In fact she
was then already seriously ill.

She had always shown great spirit. Henrietta Rowland was struggling one evening with an unruly, fighting mob from one of Octavia's
night schools in a court – the children who had missed the benefits of
the 1870 Education Act and the establishment of the London School
Board – and recalled:

> Mrs Nassau Senior was in our school, when a specially noisy fight
> resulted in all the girls tearing out to watch or join in it. 'What shall
> we do?' I asked, as she and I stood alone in the deserted heavy-aired
> room. 'I will sing to them,' she replied, and standing on the raised
> step at the doorway, the shouting angry fighting crowd just below
> her, she lifted up her beautiful voice and sang, 'Angels ever bright
> and fair, Take, oh! take me to your care.' The people heard, found
> something more interesting than the fight, and gathered round her
> to listen and as she stood in the dark court with a background of
> flaring gas light which turned her flaxen hair into a halo, she seemed
> to some of us to be of the angels of whom she sang.[4]

Soon Jane Nassau Senior was dead and Octavia wrote to Henrietta
Barnett, eloquent in her grief.[5] By April she was in a highly precarious
state and had taken refuge with the Cockerells. 'I am I fear utterly unfit
for work, so I want to be and to be treated as out of town . . . I may
leave Beckenham [the Cockerells' home] and take flight much further
any day. I shall make a swoop when it seems really essential.'[6]

In fact, for a while Octavia seemed to rally; she went out to dinner
and attended meetings. Barrett's Court matters were occupying her
again and she was immersing herself in new projects in Lambeth. But
her frantic lists of engagements, the scored-out lines of her letters
(when in good health she wrote without any hesitations or deletions),
boded ill for the coming months.[7]

There was a startling event in store for Octavia's family and friends
in the summer. She announced her engagement to Edward Bond,[8]
wealthy barrister and tireless worker alongside Octavia and the
Barnetts. Bond had considerable private means, which in Beatrice
Webb's words allowed him 'to lead the life of unpaid public service'.
He also seems to have been remarkably good-looking. Beatrice
described him as a 'fine figure of a man with handsome features, large
soulful grey eyes, attractively set in dark pencilled brows and long
silken lashes, he alternated cultured comments with thrilling silences;

and was the beloved of the philanthropic set.' She even added the rumour that George Eliot had him in mind for Daniel Deronda.[9]

Octavia's own dependence upon his advice can be seen growing in the early 1870s but that she, almost forty, should contemplate marriage to a man six years younger than herself must have come as an enormous surprise to everyone. (Angela Burdett-Coutts' marriage at the age of sixty-five to her secretary thirty-five years her junior, took place in 1881 and set new standards for surprise in London society.)[10]

By 1873 Octavia was often in Edward Bond's company, which she enjoyed greatly – 'one easily gets on subjects with him, and seems to have much to say; there is a pleasant sense of friction and stimulus, though none of peace.'[11] Octavia and he often went walking together, the difference in their heights, for he was particularly tall and she unusually small, causing much amusement. He was closely involved both with the Barnetts' work in the East End and Octavia's at Barrett's Court. They discussed religion, and the various campaigns that they fought side by side took the friendship towards an easy intimacy. Two of those fights, Swiss Cottage Fields and Bunhill Fields, were to end in failure: perhaps Octavia turned to him for extra support in these major disappointments.

Any reference to Octavia's brief engagement was destroyed on her instructions. It is not even clear when it occurred, although there is a handwritten note referring to the destruction of some letters from early 1877, 'by Mrs Maurice's desire. September 30 1912'.[12] In his edition of Octavia's letters, Edmund Maurice dealt with the event by evasion and euphemism ('other troubles were already breaking down her strength'), whilst Emily's edition of her letters included none later than 1875. Miss Moberly Bell, whose account was prepared with considerable help from the family, was slightly more forthcoming.

According to Miss Moberly Bell, the schoolchildren at Nottingham Place were told one day of Octavia's engagement, and then 'were told the next day that it was a mistake and they were not to talk about it'. Everyone else in Octavia's circle preserved a discreet silence on the subject.

Mrs Bond – described as being of 'proud cold conventional reserve' – had intervened. The widowed mother of an only son is quite an adversary, even in the most conventional circumstances. The news that her son intended to leave home and marry Octavia had the predictable effect; she remonstrated, and he quickly capitulated to her wishes. When he told Octavia of the problem, she broke off the engagement herself. According to Miss Moberly Bell, they never met again.

Nor did Edward Bond ever marry. He had a distinguished career in local and national politics. An Oxford double first, he had been called to the Bar in 1871. He stood as a 'moderate' member on the LCC, representing Hampstead, and as Conservative MP for East Notting-hamshire from 1895 to 1906. Throughout, he continued his housing and social work, and was a prominent member of the COS. It must have been very difficult for Octavia to avoid him. In the 1880s he became heavily involved in the Commons Preservation Society.

Long after the ill-fated engagement, Beatrice Webb found herself talking to Mr Barnett about Octavia Hill. She recorded the conversation in her diary.

> I remember her well in the zenith of her fame; some 14 years ago. I remember her dining with us at Prince's Gate, I remember thinking her a sort of ideal of the attraction of woman's power. At that time she was constantly attended by Edward Bond. Alas! for we poor women! Even our strong minds do not save us from tender feelings. Companionship, which meant to him intellectual and moral en-lightenment, meant to her 'Love'. This, one fatal day, she told him. Let us draw the curtain tenderly before that scene and inquire no further.

Beatrice Webb seems to have allowed her own fantasies to intrude, or perhaps she was merely listening to the gossip which the event must have occasioned within her own circle. Undoubtedly the version of events in which Mrs Bond struck the blow for her son is the more likely. Lapsing into the style of bad romantic fiction, Beatrice Webb then extended the tale to the moment when Octavia left the country, broken-hearted by the rejection.

Few others mentioned the event at all, though, as Greville Mac-Donald put it, in prose purpler even than Beatrice Webb's, 'Of her own most secret cross little was known, and nothing may be told. As with other Saints, it lay between her and her God.'

It seems likely that the engagement was broken in July, for by August 1877 Octavia had collapsed once more, and was staying with Lady Ducie who stood by with constant support, hospitality and friendship, offering 'magnificent silent sympathy, and that exquisite depth of tenderness of hers'.

Henrietta Barnett too had been a tower of strength. 'Yetta dear, no one will ever know what the voices of my friends have been to me, they are, as you say, a tie to life . . .' The work was in good hands: 'I never had so strong a staff for the autumn.' The Barnetts had invited Octavia to join them on the coast, in the west country, and she was tempted. 'In some ways it would be easier than nearly anything.'[13]

She wrote also to Mrs Cockerell: 'I took courage and came here as I promised you all I would . . . the intense longing to be out of sight [of all her responsibilities] which haunts me took the ridiculous form of horror of writing to say where I was. It was very mad.' She continued: 'God is infinitely merciful to me and sends his Angels, be they only those of Time and Quiet, to vanquish for me the Demons who come to assault me.'[14]

Three weeks later Octavia was feeling better in some respects, although she had to lie down much of the time because of severe back pain. She was missing her work ('life is easier with the old duties') and no doubt she needed the distraction that occupation offers in times of misery. She had been persuaded not to return until the beginning of the next term, but Lady Ducie felt that she needed a complete year's rest.

Octavia's stay with Julia Ducie presented her with a taste of Victorian country-house living.[15] Tortworth Court was the first country house designed by S. S. Teulon, and had been built for the Earl's father between 1849 and 1852. A vast picturesque pile, sprouting turrets and a great central tower, it was nevertheless in the van of modernity. It boasted one of the earliest gas-lighting systems in the country, a heating system, luggage lift, and a railway to bring in the coal.[16] Despite the grandeur of the appointments, Octavia seems to have found Tortworth welcoming and a place in which she could find refuge in bad moments.

It was only at this time that she realized that Sydney Cockerell was seriously ill. Her letters to Mrs Cockerell alternate between optimism and pessimism, and she often apologizes for letting her own problems overshadow theirs – 'but I *do* feel it in so far as I can feel at all.'[17]

Writing to Henrietta from Tortworth, Octavia told her the latest terrible news: Cockerell had been in bed since early July, too weak even to write letters. When Mrs Cockerell wrote to give Sir William Jenner's diagnosis of the illness (Bright's disease) Octavia attempted to cheer her, whilst refusing to accept the gravity of her husband's condition. 'I cannot help hoping that some way the illness may really do good, it may bring others forward so as to relieve Mr Cockerell more in the future and the enforced holiday now may give him a long needed rest . . . Still I feel how sad, and difficult, and anxious it all is.' Jenner had prescribed up to three months' rest saying that a recurrence of the attack 'would probably be fatal'.

Octavia's troubles for the year were far from over. The next and perhaps worst hurt of all was provided by John Ruskin.

Octavia recognized Ruskin as a flawed hero, but he had been her friend and confidant for twenty-five years and was the means by which her work had begun. They had not always been of a mind: one of Octavia's visits to Herne Hill in 1870 had caused Ruskin to write petulantly in his diary that she had 'provoked' him.

Although there had only been intermittent contact between them for years, that was explained by Ruskin's precarious mental condition rather than by any cooling of the affection between them. Octavia might have been intrigued to read his diary entry for 4 September 1872. Ruskin had had a vivid dream of a party at the Working Men's College, 'where the people were well meaning, but ill behaved and radical' and where Ruskin had found himself deeply irritated 'by some vulgar decorations which Miss Hill had got done'. In 1873 Octavia visited Brantwood and Ruskin took her up to the cascade after dinner. He noted in his diary: 'quarrelled in the evening', but he did not specify whether it was with her.

In 1876 Octavia had taken on an unsuccessful teashop owned by Ruskin at 29, Paddington Street. The objective had been to run it on a non-profit-making basis, but the poor did not like best-quality tea. The enterprise had struggled on, staffed by two of Ruskin's mother's maids and managed by Joan Severn, since 1874. Ruskin refused at the outset to sell either sugar or coffee and would not compete in 'either gas or rhetoric'.[18] Octavia took it on with hesitation; the ground rent was high and she would 'be well satisfied if it is entirely self-supporting.'[19]

Ruskin's denunciation of her in print in late 1877 in *Fors Clavigera*, his monthly publication for working men, which he had begun in 1871, fell upon her like a bolt from the blue. (1877 was also the year that he unleashed his attack on Whistler, claiming that his painting flung 'a pot of paint in the public's face', which led to the famous libel action, and the payment to Whistler of a farthing's damages.)

[192]

Ruskin was provoked to lambast Octavia in public and in print by her doubts about his utopian scheme in Sheffield, the St George's Guild, founded in 1871. The first and most lasting reminder of this ambitious project was the St George's Museum in Sheffield, opened in 1875 for the education of the artisan. But Ruskin's plans went much further in order to put into action 'the rational organization of country life independent of that of cities'; he was planning to buy farmland and, to that end, was trying to attract financial support to the Guild.[20] It all must have reminded Octavia cruelly of the story of her father's futile attempts to set up an Owenite community in Wisbech.

There was something profoundly sadistic about the way that Ruskin constructed his accusations against Octavia in public, backing them by printing her pathetic answers in full. He was approaching his first major nervous breakdown, which occurred in 1878, and was deeply unbalanced. Octavia, however, was faced by statements in cold print, as was Ruskin's readership.

Ruskin began: 'For the last three or four years it has been a matter of continually increasing surprise to me that I never received the smallest contribution to St George's Fund from any friend or disciple of Miss Octavia Hill's.' Thinking that her satisfactory experiment in Marylebone which he had helped would encourage in her a measure of reciprocal support, he:

> was utterly disappointed; and to my more acute astonishment, because Miss Hill was wont to reply to any more or less direct inquiries on the subject, with epistles proclaiming my faith, charity, and patience, in language so laudatory, that, on the last occasion of my receiving such answer, to a request for a general sketch of the Marylebone work, it became impossible for me, in any human modesty, to print the reply.

Ruskin went on to claim that a month or two earlier the mystery had been cleared up by a woman supporter of St George's who recounted that 'a man of great kindness of disposition, who was well inclined to give aid to St George, had been diverted from such intention by hearing doubts expressed by Miss Hill of my ability to conduct any practical enterprise successfully.'[21]

Octavia began by denying the charge completely. She had never prevented anyone from supporting Ruskin's venture, whatever her own secret doubts about the practicalities of his attempt to set up his land colony and craft guild in Sheffield. Next she had to stoop to a correspondence with the woman in question – all of which was published in tedious detail in *Fors*.

> Madam – In justice to Mr Ruskin, I write to say that there has evidently been some misapprehension respecting my words. Excuse me if I add that beyond stating this fact I do not feel called upon to enter into correspondence with a stranger about my friend Mr Ruskin, or to explain a private conversation of my own.

At this point Ruskin utterly lost reason. He continued in his published account: 'I considered it her bounden duty to enter into correspondence with all strangers whom she could possibly reach, concerning her friend Mr Ruskin, and to say to *them*, what she was in the habit of saying to me.'

Bit between his teeth, Ruskin ploughed on. Another letter from Octavia, dated 7 October 1877, was published: 'if *you* like to know anything I ever said, or thought, about you for the twenty-four years I have known you, "most explicitly" shall you know; and you will find no trace of any thought, much less word, that was not utterly loyal, and even reverently tender towards you.' Carlyle, Octavia reminded him, had pointed out how faithful she was. She had always dealt levelly with him: 'I have not courted you by flattery; I have not feigned agreement where I differed or did not understand . . . I have not worried you with intrusive questions or letters.' At the same time, 'has there been thought or deed of mine uncoloured by the influence of the early, the abiding, and the continuous teaching you gave me? Have I not striven to carry out what you have taught . . . ?'

Ruskin annotated Octavia's replies but Octavia could only surmise that she had confused the issue by clumsy words, since she patently had no malicious intention. But the printed correspondence did not end with Octavia's conclusive denial of his accusations; on and on it went, and by early November Ruskin had provoked Octavia into retaliation.[22]

Finally, she could take no more goading – particularly from Ruskin's unassailable position on the printed page. Her letter, inevitably, appeared in *Fors*. 'I have spoken to you, I think, and certainly to others, of what appears to me an incapacity in you for management of great practical work . . . due . . . partly to an ideal standard of perfection . . . partly to a strange power of gathering round you, and trusting, the wrong people, which I never could understand in you, as it mingles so strangely with rare powers of perception of character.' She added, honestly but foolishly: 'I do think you most incapable of carrying out any great practical scheme. I do not the less think you have influenced, and will influence, action deeply and rightly.'

Now Ruskin was ready to fight; she had provided the ammunition. He lunged back, in print. 'I have never yet, to my own knowledge, "trusted" any one who has failed me, *except* yourself, and one other person.' In a postscript he added: 'Of all injuries you could have done – not me – but the cause I have in hand, the giving the slightest countenance to the vulgar mob's cry of "unpractical" was the fatallest.' On 5 November Octavia tried to curtail the pointless slanging match. 'My opinion of your power to judge character is, and must remain, a matter of opinion. Discussions about it would be useless and endless; besides after your letters to me, you will hardly be astonished that I decline to continue this corespondence.'

Now Ruskin rejoined by asking her to send a copy of her last letter – for publication. It had become a farce; Octavia objected strongly to the publication of her letters, but Ruskin took no notice and printed the whole unedifying correspondence.

The tragic aspect of it all is the insight it offers into Ruskin's unbalanced mind. Few subscribers to *Fors* could, surely, have taken Ruskin's position against Octavia's on the evidence provided.

The other explanation of the dispute probably lies in earlier issues of *Fors Clavigera* that year. Ruskin had published his intention to make over all the properties that had been bought with his money and were managed by Octavia to the St George's Company, 'under Miss Hill's superintendence always'.[23] Ruskin had been repaid £160 of the original £800 for Paradise Place and had invested it in the Temperance Building Society. The rest of the investment was paying a steady 5 per cent, which was more than the Building Society had paid 'for some years'. The largest asset was the property at Freshwater Place and the Marylebone Road, which was paying around £150 in interest.

But the prospect of becoming linked to the shaky finances of the Guild alarmed Octavia. If the St George's scheme were to fail, then Octavia would see her work wasted and the houses sold to cover debts. One explanation of his outburst is that Octavia had protested against his plan, preferring to remain directly answerable to Ruskin himself and that he, correctly, sensed her lack of faith in his cherished venture. Ruskin was in no mood to deal with those fears.

[195]

Whatever the root cause of the quarrel, Octavia was shattered by Ruskin's vindictiveness and spite. It was almost the last blow to her already delicate state. She wrote to Henrietta, who was greatly concerned for her, referring to a number of even crueller letters from Ruskin, which he had not published. 'I think just now I feel the publicity more than the unkindness. It increases the sense I have had for months of living sleepless in a world of uninterrupted sunlight and with no eyelids – not a pleasant one but this only increases – not causes – the feeling.' She added: 'You must all remember the thing is sadder for Ruskin than for me . . . even if it were all as he thinks it, and I were indeed all that he thinks, what good end *could* this publication serve, it can help on no work of his, it simply exposes me, to what end?' But, however quietly she was taking the hurt, Henrietta and those who knew her best would find 'the impression of the stabs all there, deep as today they are.'[24]

Sydney Cockerell's death in December was not unexpected, but no less shattering for that. Her letter to his widow is as moving as any letter of condolence she ever wrote:

> Words are but poor things at best, but let these just tell you I would say if I could how much I love you, and how I miss him now, and shall miss him on through whatever years are to come, and how largely this was due to that exquisite sympathy and goodness which all of us felt in some measure, – but you alone could know completely.[25]

It had been a terrible year. Octavia's health collapsed utterly; she had appalling headaches and violent back pain as well as chronic insomnia. Her doctor was amazed that she had kept going to this stage. The family found a dependable companion for her, Harriot Yorke, who seems to have joined the household by November.[26] Finally Octavia was ordered complete rest and it was decided that she, accompanied by Harriot, should go abroad for an indefinite period. She did not resume even the lightest of her housing work for four years.

When she came back, she was, Beatrice Webb noted, 'a changed woman.'[27]

CHAPTER 13

Absent

B Y January 1878 the benefits to Octavia of even prolonged visits to old and trusted friends were insufficient to relieve the effects of devastating nervous exhaustion. She wrote to Yetta, who had offered help, thanking her, but saying there was nothing to be done. 'I feel my way gradually in the darkness, it is a little difficult, and the steps must be taken one by one, each taking a day's, sometimes a week's strength . . .'[1]

George Eliot, writing to her old friend Barbara Bodichon, reported: 'On the other and gloomy side, poor Octavia Hill is peremptorily ordered away from her work by the doctor, and is going to start for Italy next Monday.'[2]

Octavia was able to leave so suddenly on a lengthy recuperative journey because her family and friends took the weight of all her work on their shoulders. Her sister Emily took charge of financial matters, collecting the donations, and disbursing the usual regular expenses. Octavia was to assure her supporters in the 1878 'Letter to Fellow-workers' that she had '*entire* confidence in her judgement . . . her greater leisure, and her utter sympathy, and quiet, and the fact that she is not dealing with quite such large things as I latterly did, made me extremely happy in the knowledge that she would make the fund *more* useful than I could in this way.'

Gertrude was to advise and help the volunteers, and direct the assistants 'as far as she can'. Given her family commitments she could not be expected to do more – 'the work cannot be her first duty.' Being directly responsible to the owners, Octavia felt, would make the volunteers more independent.[3]

Describing how she had organized her affairs prior to departure, Octavia told Yetta:

when I left England the volunteers who were collecting consented most kindly to accept more responsibility than of old. Several gentlemen were good enough to undertake to audit and supervise the accounts. My assistants, who used to work in a little company under my direction, were placed in direct communication with the volunteers and auditors, and these latter were asked to report direct to the owners of the courts, and obtain their decisions on all important matters. The work is thus entirely decentralized. The place I once filled – the place it was well for me to fill while the attempts were in their infancy, need be no longer filled.'

She wisely saw that it was all for the best.

The collector now had autonomy – 'She can act swiftly and securely, for she is certain that no decision of hers can possibly clash with any plan or thought of mine.' Equally the auditors were experienced business men: 'They easily do accounts which many ladies find difficult . . . Each has one, two, or three courts only to think of, and can think out the small financial problems.'

Harriot Yorke proved a perfect companion, a role which she fulfilled for the rest of Octavia's life. From Cannes at the outset of the trip, Octavia wrote to her mother that Harriot was 'kinder, brighter, and with subtler sympathy than I had imagined. She is an excellent manager, and prevents one's feeling forlorn in travelling. It is an immense comfort that all my work is so well started, and that I am anxious about nothing.'[4] Writing to Yetta she described how Miss Yorke 'takes away the feeling of desolation so far as can be done when all you love and all things you had to do are taken from you, and the things around have neither memories of the past, nor whispers of possible future.'[5] Octavia was in a deep depression but Harriot was already proving a bulwark against worries. 'She says little and does so much.'

To start with Octavia found it hard to let go entirely. She wrote from Cannes to Princess Alice, who had sent her a copy of *The Homes of the London Poor* which had been translated into German and published there through the efforts of the Princess.

Octavia told her that she had been sent abroad for complete rest; that the doctors had forbidden her to receive business letters, to deal with anything to do with the management of the houses. It was her first letter written in ink for some time, she told her. Although she had carried on for some months in ill health, 'able by will to seem and to do as usual when at work,' she had finally collapsed and 'the blow fell very suddenly.' The book had arrived at that moment – but her sisters had read her the preface and 'enough of the translation for me to realize how successfully it is done, before the doctor's verdict stunned me to all feeling.'

In fact, Octavia mused, her illness began to look like a blessing.

It seems that my leaving is going to turn out the best possible thing for the courts I have so long watched over. The various ladies who were working with me, the owners, and friends of mine, gentlemen skilled in business, instantly responded to my call, they have undertaken the work with an enthusiasm, an intelligence and an interest which went far beyond my hopes . . . the courts will be even better attended to, and they are so happy to be left in charge.

It was a revelation to her, and an invaluable lesson for the future: now she had a system into which she could feed new workers, upon which she could build, an established organization.

Octavia was going on from Cannes to join the MacDonalds at the Villa Cattaneo at Nervi. 'I shall find a kind of home with them and they look to me to help to uphold their hearts,' she told Princess Alice,[6] for the MacDonalds, for whom life had been consistently punishing, had a tragedy of their own to surmount.

In November George MacDonald, still in London and himself far from well, had written delightedly to his wife Louisa with the news that Queen Victoria had allotted him an annual payment of £100.[7] Friends were sure that the pension was Princess Alice's doing. George MacDonald, who had originally trained as a minister, had supported his ever-expanding family by a succession of teaching and lecturing posts, whilst writing the works of theology and the powerful children's stories by which he is known. Despite the publication of several of his best-known books, among them *Robert Falconer* and *The Princess and the Goblin*, in these years, financial security did not follow. The pension was a godsend, allowing George MacDonald to join the rest of the family in Italy for Christmas.

The whole object of the stay in Italy had been planned as a desperate last measure for the sake of Mary, the MacDonalds' second daughter, who had been weakened by a bout of scarlet fever and had then contracted tuberculosis. The mild winter climate of the Italian Riviera was Mary's last hope. By the time that Octavia arrived almost the whole family – ten out of the eleven children – was gathered there. Another visitor was Mary's fiancé of four years, Edward Hughes, nephew of the painter Arthur Hughes.

For Octavia, arrival in Nervi brought about another crisis in her own illness. In the first week of February she wrote to tell Yetta of 'a worse break down last evening than I had had before . . . I feel going among several people and into ordinary life sorely.'[8] She was shaky and giddy and could not move without pain.

Reunited in Italy, and despite the background of impending tragedy, the MacDonalds were to plunge into producing and performing their play, *Pilgrim's Progress*, for the expatriate community around Genoa and for local people. Although they had been doing performances of this adaptation of the second part of Bunyan's work since the early 1870s, Louisa had decided to turn the family into professionals (called, inevitably, The Pilgrims) – to earn desperately needed income. The first performance, at Christchurch in Hampshire, had been on George and Louisa's twenty-sixth wedding anniversary, in March 1877.

So dominated did they all become by the play that before long they were calling each other by the names of their parts; George played Greatheart, Lilia (Lily) Christiana. In fact Lilia was an accomplished actress and had hoped to take up a career on the stage but her role as eldest daughter, and surrogate mother, did not allow of such a step. Nor did it allow her to consider working for Octavia, as she also had wanted to do. Apart from Lilia, none of the others was more than an amateur but the odd spectacle of an entire family, including young children, acting as an ensemble, ensured appreciative audiences wherever they went – even non-English-speaking ones.

(Two years later, back in England, the MacDonalds were the agents of Octavia's one recorded performance on the stage. As her mother wrote to Emily, 'If you were to spend all your time from now till Christmas in guessing what Octavia was doing last Friday afternoon you would never guess aright, so I will tell you. She was acting to a Harrogate audience the part of Piety in the MacDonalds' *Pilgrim's Progress*.' Grace MacDonald had fallen ill, but the performance could not be postponed. Who should take her part? 'Octavia agreed and learned her part (eight pages) that night. I cannot tell you how beautiful she looked, and how lovely her voice sounded.'[9])

The MacDonalds had always given Octavia a home from home,

whether it was on holiday with them in Scotland or Cornwall, or at their house in Hastings. Now, together in Italy, they could help try to unravel the mystery of Ruskin's apparently inexplicable attack upon her.

Around this time, Octavia had had a letter from Ruskin. She replied that he should not think about her: 'If in anything you ever did or thought there is anything you would wish otherwise, forget it, as if it had never been . . . Be sure not to trouble, so far as I am concerned, about any painful thoughts of me, which remain to you, if such there be. They are either true and will abide, or false and will vanish – it can but be for a little time.'[10]

Octavia's health was soon sufficiently improved for her to be longing for news of 'the war', presumably the Afghan campaign, and to be missing the newspapers. Her mother wrote regularly, relieved that Octavia had been forced to rest, and hoping that the interval would be the beginning of an easier life. 'You have climbed the hill far enough to look back, and survey the road passed over . . . Accept this interval, as a precious time lent you for retrospect and prospect, and for renewing the bodily health that you have expended so unsparingly.'[11]

After leaving the MacDonalds, Octavia and Harriot visited Mazzini's tomb in Genoa's magnificent cemetery before pressing on. As Octavia and her sisters were among those who had subscribed towards the building of a new Italian villa for the MacDonalds (part of a list of familiar names headed by Princess Alice of Hesse, the Earl and Countess of Ducie, and the Maurices) it was appropriate that they should visit the area of Bordighera, where the Casa Coraggio (as the new house was called) was being built alongside the English church. After that they went south, to Rome.

Rome suited Octavia well, although she could only drive or sit out. She was seeing nothing of the city – no picture galleries, churches or museums. Dr Jackson's orders 'came back and back to lying down and doing nothing for many weeks.'[12] She wrote to the Barnetts: 'Yester-day was perhaps the best day I have had. I even walked for about ten minutes and I slept the entire night. I have not before had an entire night's rest for more than a year.' There was a suggestion that the Barnetts might come to join her; she hoped they would not mind if Harriot Yorke would be there too. 'You will find Miss Yorke very sweet in slipping out of sight, I noticed it at the MacDonalds and at home.' She was not sure if she would be much company for them.

'My head prevents me doing *anything* with you compatible with your bright and interesting holiday.'

Nevertheless, she and Harriot planned to press on via Assisi, Florence, Bologna and Venice, their destination the Italian lakes – moving north ahead of the hot weather.

Henrietta wrote back to say that they would not get so far south. Perhaps they could meet in the lakes, Octavia suggested? 'Minnie [Emily] said you said was I afraid of seeing you who are strong and well? Would you be like a March wind? There are moments Yetta and they are many when I am afraid of everything and everybody, but they are not my real self and I have never believed any good came of treating them as if they were.'[13] She wanted so much to see Henrietta, she told her, as 'a link for me with the old life'. In fact Harriot Yorke's brother joined them but the Barnetts never came.

Octavia's letters over the following weeks refer to a continuous blinding headache. She had begun to take medicine, having discovered that rest alone was not enough. The slight improvements, followed by relapses, continued for many months to come.

Ruskin's shadow had a tendency to fall across everything Octavia saw. 'Ruskin and Virgil made me feel more at home at Albano and Ostia.' She could detect an improvement in her condition by the pain the association of Venice with Ruskin caused her.

In June she wrote again to Princess Alice – again in pencil, a sign that she was bedridden – expressing deep regret that she was unable to meet her on the Princess's planned visit to Eastbourne. The translation of *The Homes of the London Poor* had been doing well in Germany, the Princess had told her, and Octavia thought this excellent news. It pleased her that her efforts could be of influence even whilst she was incapacitated.

'I hear of houses being bought in Huddersfield, Manchester, Liverpool and Dublin and many more blocks in London and my own workers go on so well.' If Princess Alice wanted to see any of Octavia's work, 'Mrs Charles Lewes [Gertrude] would tell or shew you anything about my work you wished, she knows most of my fellow-workers now and would gladly get from them any information which would be of value.'[14] She hoped the Princess's own work was also prospering: 'I am myself better, they say much better than I have been.'

In the mean time, Mary MacDonald had died at the end of April and Octavia sent on to the Princess the touching letter that Louisa

MacDonald had written about Mary's death. It had been an agonizing illness and there was now such a blank in existence, as she put it. 'At first I was glad – the Sunday that we laid her lovely body in the grave was a glorious resurrection morning and we rejoiced for her – we were really all so happy . . . but now, Octavia – without her – it is all so dull and dead. We can't bear it as we ought. Everything had been done *for* her – with her in view.' She was buried in the folds of the wedding dress and veil that she never wore, surrounded by white flowers.

Louisa longed to join Octavia in Switzerland but the family had decided to remain in Italy.[15] Octavia suggested to her own mother that she join them in Switzerland, but she did not come, either.

Octavia wrote again to Princess Alice from Vevey. She had been thinking of the Princess's visit to England often, with great regret that they had not met.

I felt your sympathy in my work so deeply. You cared, not for the name and noise and outside, but for the people, their hearts and their homes. You remembered the people themselves and cared for them. By the way do you remember that wretched lodging house where the little wizened baby was, it is bought now by Lady Pembroke and put under the care of one of my friends and is all put in order for families to live instead of passing through in that homeless way. Yes there is much I should like to have told and shown I should have been glad to see you again and I might have been of some little use too, about work in Germany, but it was not to be . . . I have thought more of my own regret in missing you – it might have put a little life into me but I hardly know, I am very tired. Anyway, it clearly was not to be so I must accept it faithfully.

It was the last letter between them; Princess Alice died in December 1878. However there were enduring memorials to that unusual friendship. Following the German translation of *The Homes of the London Poor*, an 'Octavia Hill Verein' was set up in Berlin – adding to the considerable network of groups following her ideas in Europe as well as in America.

As the weeks passed Harriot Yorke proved to be of sterling stuff.

At the inns and hotels Miss Y is perfectly at her ease, and makes every place at once like home. She is, too, up to all emergencies, like Mr Barnett or Miss Cons; so, if we have an adventure on the way, she knows what to do and all that is safe and right. She knows at a glance which carriages are large enough, what hotels are suitable, which drags are strong enough, at which places we may leave luggage unwatched, etc etc.[16]

Harriot was good at remembering people that they had met, a driver or a shopgirl, and in one place employed a man day after day who had won her heart by taking great care of his horse and correspondingly little of himself. He was the cut of man that they both liked; they had asked him to drive them again the following day, 'and I daresay he will carry home his 80 francs and spend or save it very providently,' Octavia told her mother.

In the Tyrol, Octavia and Miss Yorke met up with the Howitts, who had taken to spending every year from May to November near Bruneck, in an old house called Mayr-am-Hof.[17] They lived for the rest of the year in Rome. William Howitt passed his time in the Tyrol gardening, working on a field allotment and in the neglected kitchen-garden. He dug indefatigably with an English spade whilst his wife sat nearby, reading, knitting or (one year) making a vast net to keep the butterflies off the cabbages. The man from whom the Howitts rented the house 'began signalizing our arrival by a series of surprises, that on more than one occasion filled us with blank dismay. He replaced old hexagonal panes by modern square ones, stencilled the walls of the saloon to imitate a first-class waiting room in a Tyrolese railway station.' The Howitts watched these efforts to please in horror.

William observed the life of the peasants of the Tyrol and told Octavia of the laws of inheritance, which vested the ancestral home in the eldest child and left the others to work as labourers. It was no longer the tourist season and so they were seeing the country 'as it is and not in gala dress for tourists'. Miss Yorke was all seeing and all knowing – 'She knows the strength and power and time and chances of all things.'

Octavia wrote to little Blanche Lewes,[18] her six-year-old niece and god-daughter, about an exciting fifty-mile sledge ride they had taken over empty mountains; although they had not seen any, this had once been wolf country. She wrote vividly and interestingly for a small child; she was coming back to life, but slowly. In late November she told her mother to expect her home briefly and warned her she would be looking rather travel-soiled. 'I shall turn up in a very forlorn condition, as to dress fit for London . . .'

By February Octavia had embarked on a second journey abroad. She wrote another lively letter to Blanche, this time from the Spanish-French border. Although she was always attentive to her small nieces and friends, her numerous godchildren were the recipients of the most regular letters and birthday presents.

Sadly, when they reached Rome, in late March 1879, a shadow fell over the holiday. She wrote to Emily Shaen: 'Did you see Mr Howitt's death? We found him dying, when we came here. He was one of my oldest friends. I remember their house as one of the happiest and best I knew as a child . . . I was almost a daughter to her [Mrs Howitt] and her son who died in Australia one of my earliest companions.'[19] Octavia also wrote to Margaret Gillies, one of the Howitts' oldest friends, with the news of William's death.

Octavia and Harriot found somewhere to stay near Mary Howitt and her daughter Meggie, and a fortnight later Miranda came to join them. Despite the circumstances, the group of old friends enjoyed an evening together which provided a bright contrast to the sad business of mourning. Mrs Howitt described the occasion: 'They all seemed so happy and bright that we were drawn into their cheerful spirit, and told our bits of experience of Roman life; and everything seemed to take a comic turn.' By Victorian standards Mrs Howitt was robust and accepted her husband's death with the minimum of mawkishness.

Back in Britain again, Octavia was writing from Scotland in the autumn of 1879. In early 1880 she and Harriot embarked on their third journey. She went back to Rome, then via Brindisi and Corfu to Athens by boat. She was not doing much drawing and in any case 'this sea could not be attempted without emerald green'. Athens was more difficult; 'no hotels, no lodgings, no beds, hardly any food, no relays of horses, no posts, no accurate guide-books, no trustworthy people to give information.' Presumably Harriot coped with the problems. Soon introductions to the expatriate community had taken care of most of this, and there was even a cousin of Lady Ducie's to help them.

Their imperfect knowledge of Greek hindered their full understanding of the complexities of Greek politics but Octavia was following with interest a fiery Greek ministerial crisis. Miss Yorke had to restrain her from plunging into Greek grammar all at once. Not content with learning Greek she was mastering statistics; she told her mother that the Greek population had doubled since independence and the revenue of the country had increased by 500 per cent. The number of children being educated in school which had been no more than 7,000 was now estimated to be 81,000.

They had visited a girls' school, set up by a Dr and Mrs Hill (no relation) almost fifty years before. The Hills were very old now and a vigorous Scots schoolmistress, Miss Muir, carried on their work, 'animated with the true spirit of trust in the people, love for them, and desire, not to proselytise, but to work with all that is good and pure in what the people themselves believe – to strengthen that, instead of dwelling on differences,' as Octavia explained to Miranda.[20] Miss Muir was going to take them into the countryside – she rather reminded Octavia of Miss Cons. 'She always finds out all about the people and finds helpful things to do for them; and it makes one see all the gentle, helpful, friendly, hospitable side. It is *so* different from going about with guides.'

Octavia had not forgotten wider issues at home either. She was delighted with the election result, victory for the Liberals, but wondered whether they had the courage to increase taxes or 'to deal generously with the little struggling nationalities'. But she was confident that they would deal with the question of land.[21]

The Barnetts had come to join them in Athens, but Samuel Barnett's heart was at home and all he could talk about was the election. The party visited excavations at Olympia, where in a remote valley a handful of German archaeologists welcomed them. They were directing 500 Greek workmen in major works; digging, carting and shovelling. After Greece came Constantinople, and at Scutari they saw Miss Nightingale's hospital which looked 'so good, and solid, and in order'. Octavia preferred the Greek quarter of the capital to the Turkish areas, with their veiled women and rules of purdah. 'It was such a comfort to see the windows clean and bright, and without the dismal wooden lattice work, which shuts in the Turkish houses, and the women with bright, uncovered faces sitting at the windows sewing.'[22]

After this they took a steamer along the Danube, arriving in Nuremberg late in the month. It all looked reassuringly European. 'The town looks very comfortable and flourishing, as if the old things had been taken into use and would stay; – not like Italy and Constantinople.' It was a picture which Octavia longed to replicate at home. 'Trees grow among the houses, and children play around them, and clean industrious women knit at their doors; and comfortable little shops are opened in them; and you see "Burger Schule" put up over their doors; and yet they aren't all torn down and replaced with rows of houses, like Camden Town, and shops like Oxford St.' She and Harriot noted down the patterns of the windows, which she thought would add to the charm of housing in London and were, no doubt, the roots of the picturesque style in which Elijah Hoole designed her Southwark cottages a few years later.

Above all it was the generous public gardens everywhere that impressed Octavia and reminded her of the miserable state of affairs in England, 'our unconsumed smoke, and how it poisons our plants, and dims the colour of all things for us . . .' It was to this side of her work, encompassed in the already successful work of the Kyrle Society that Octavia, on the mend, was to turn.

CHAPTER 14

Back again

WHILE Octavia was away, her redoubtable team was busy. The sisters wrote to her regularly, and Caroline Hill conveyed a particular message from a tenant in the first scheme of all: 'Paradise Place is so quiet now; there are such nice respectable people. We are all so comfortable there. Will you tell Miss Octavia so.'

Things were far less cheerful at Barrett's Court. Gertrude had succeeded in collecting the rents but was disappointed on many other fronts. The Working Men's Club had foundered, with mounting debts, but she was putting it straight and the membership was growing again: forty-five teetotallers and twenty-four who were not total abstainers. The teetotallers had taken it on and had acquired the furniture in return for settling outstanding debts.

Although Octavia was not a hard-liner on temperance, she knew about the perils of drink. When, in the early 1870s, the public house next to the Sterling sisters' houses at Walmer Place, the Walmer Castle, had gone up for sale she had tried, and failed, to buy it. She then attempted to prevent it being re-licensed, attracting a great deal of opprobrium in the process. Her justification for doing so was the fact that there were thirty-two other public houses within a 300-yard radius.

Kate Potter, who shared Octavia's moderate views on the drink question, wrote to her fiancé: 'Would you mind seeing my name up over a beer shop in Whitechapel?' In her view the worst drunkenness and violence were provoked by adulterated beer. She wanted to persuade 'one of the great brewers who are so fond of subscribing to charities . . . to put me into one of their public-houses and see if I can't make it pay. The teetotallers are too narrow to take the whole world in.'[1]

In time the Walmer Castle did come into Octavia's hands and opened as a residential club for working men under the eagle eye of Emma Cons, who countenanced no half-measures in the matter of temperance. Emily wrote to Octavia, who was still abroad, about the opening. Rich and poor had been there and many old supporters such as Mr Hughes, Mr Hart, the Revd Llewelyn Davies, as well as Charles and Gertrude Lewes. Miss Cons had looked cheerful, and was busy talking to everybody. The guests had found good food, bright flowers and flags flying outside. Accommodation included a dining-room, smoking-room, and comfortable bedrooms for 'respectable men'. As Colonel Gardiner, Octavia's friend at Buckingham Palace, had put it: 'Some of us [would] have been glad of as good a bedroom as this at the University.'

Emily was concerned on one score: the rooms seemed too expensive. 'A shilling a night is not much to pay for so nice a little *furnished* room; but, if a working man has to pay seven shillings a week for his room, I fear he will think it too much.'[2] Miss Cons helped out there from three to eleven o'clock every other Sunday, to give the managers time off.

Such an establishment was exactly what Florence Nightingale had suggested in an article for S. C. Hall's *Social Notes*, published in 1878. She listed a number of ways in which the savagery of poverty (the root cause of which she considered to be drink) could be alleviated. 'Can a lesson be taken of Octavia Hill in London and others as regards improved dwellings, taking blocks of the present poor dwellings, letting them out, and collecting the rents and improving the dwellings and the dwellers by degrees?' To that she added the coffee public-house with decent lodgings for single men, co-operative stores and savings banks, and finally, the presence of a social worker, perhaps a trained nurse. 'Are not such the ways to help these, our own poor flesh and blood.'[3]

Octavia's ideas and writings had travelled on in her absence. In the 1881 edition of their *Economics of Industry*, Alfred and Mary Marshall quoted from *The Homes of the London Poor* to support the section on state and voluntary aid in poor relief. They cited Octavia's support for a 'free, yet systemized' system and for a 'united agency of corporate bodies and private individuals' – the COS, in short. But they also chose a passage in which the essential liberalism of her thought emerges: 'It is essential to remember that each man has his own view of his life and must be free to fulfill it; that in many ways he is a far better judge of it than we . . . Our work is more to bring him to the point of considering and to the spirit of judging rightly, than to consider or judge for him.'[4] On that point Octavia parted from the hard, dry men and women of the COS, with their case sheets and their judgements meted out from principle not observation. As always, her fundamental respect for the individual and the dignity of man was dominant. Friendship was what she saw herself offering and charity was in effect organized voluntary action.

The COS offered a strong, but paradoxical, view of the individual and the state, with its support for guild socialism, workers' co-operatives and yet its steadfast opposition to, for example, the pro-vision of free school meals, which they thought would destroy the role of the family. By strengthening the will of the individual, they held, the family unit would gain and, by that, society: Octavia was entirely in accord with this view. Responsibility and influence were what the COS and its adherents had to offer, rather than either financial or moral persuasion. The alleviation of poverty, the most debilitating of the ills of society, was all.[5]

The unveiling of the statue of St Christopher modelled on one of Octavia's favourite Dürers at the renamed St Christopher's Buildings (Barrett's Court), was one of those events (such as the May festival and the teas at Nottingham Place) that Octavia felt gave the tenants, and her work, a personal history. 'I think these common memories good for tenants and workers.' Nevertheless, the tenants could not be entirely relied upon. 'I don't much fear stone throwing; but one never *quite* knows how people will see things; *one* may throw a stone where *fifty* look with interest.'[6]

Freshwater Place was now in the capable hands of Emily Harrison who lived on the spot, and she gave a cheerful picture of it. On her return from holiday she found that her runner beans had been trained, her room had been left as it was, and the tenants told her that the place had seemed empty and dull without her. Before going away she had taken the children to Hampstead Heath.

The Open Spaces work had gone on in Octavia's absence, just as the housing work had. She was disappointed in the reception given to *Our Common Land*, 'which . . . does not speak quite as powerfully as the living voice would.'[7] In it she included essays on charity and open spaces; with *The Homes of the London Poor* it presented her views in a complete form. But there was no substitute for Octavia's dogged personal campaigning, the lobbying and speech-making that gave the fight for her causes its particular style.

When Octavia began to ease herself back to work in 1880, after an absence of almost two years, she started with light tasks such as her membership of the Kyrle Open Spaces Sub-Committee, of which Edmund Maurice was secretary. And she began a campaign for smoke abatement, also under Kyrle Society auspices, turning her attention to practical matters such as the development of domestic stoves which controlled the emission of smoke. 'The only work I have myself touched is the Open Spaces which not only interests me and needs help but is easily helped and very quietly and in proportion to my strength.'

During 1879 and 1880 Octavia did not work with the tenants at all, but she did keep in touch with them through a network of faithful correspondents. To Samuel Barnett she wrote reassuringly: 'I hope no one will ever feel wedded to old plans of mine, plans of course – the wisest ones – fit one place and time and not another and one has always to be looking out to see that plans are not blindly adopted, nor unintelligently carried out, else what should have suggested and enlightened becomes a burden and a snare.'[8] Family and friends, headed by Emily who took full responsibility for finances, kept Octavia away from the tensions and worries that had contributed to her collapse.

By 1881, however, she was returning to housing work. She had dropped her membership of the Council and committees of the COS, although she continued to support the organization. Robert Hunter was waging a Commons Preservation Society campaign in Sheffield and Octavia came to his assistance. He felt that the action should come from Sheffield people but Octavia was more understanding.

First, it seems . . . hard to punish the poor of Sheffield for the omissions of the rich; second, I think the subject still so new that a town may wake up too late, and bitterly regret what it has lost; third, these commons seem to me to be national treasures, and less and less to concern only the towns or villages nearest to which they happen to be.

If they could find a barrister who cared about the issue, the CPS should lend their support to the campaign.

Octavia was far-sighted in realizing that there was a need for national concerted action, and she also saw the difficulties that the CPS

[211]

had, without any powers of acquisition. 'Every acre kept is a certain possession for ever' and, despite Hunter's feeling that the case was not strong, she thought 'it is an important suit, as keeping the common till some plan for regulation can be arranged.'

On campaigning, Octavia's instincts were absolutely sure. A confrontation held the question in the public eye; 'causes are like stakes which are driven into a marsh and are buried, but carry the roadway.' Robert Hunter and Octavia Hill were already sure of what they wanted – statutory protection for the landscape – and there were many campaigns in the early 1880s.

From now on Octavia herself, for the first time since childhood, had a foothold of her own in the country. Gertrude and her family had fallen for the Warren, Crockham Hill in 1877, charmed by their first glimpse of the ancient cottage upon the roof of which stood a goat, munching the heather thatch. With growing knowledge of and fondness for the area, Harriot Yorke decided to build a cottage for herself and Octavia just a few hundred yards away, across an area of wooded common land. Gertrude reported: 'Octavia and Miss Yorke think the freehold may enable them to defend the common, if it is threatened by the Lord of the Manor'.[9] Octavia always took her work home with her.

Elijah Hoole was, of course, chosen to be Miss Yorke's architect, and designed a vernacular revival cottage, hung with soft red tiles and tucked into the slope. They took possession of it in 1884 and called it Larksfield. It was sited on high, lightly wooded ground, with a magnificent view over the Kent and Sussex countryside to the south. Both it and The Warren were a little way outside the village.

Octavia soon became an avid gardener. One summer, as she told her mother, she started gardening at 5.30 a.m. to stay cool, the cuckoo and larks keeping her company. One of the names frequently listed among the donors to her work was a Miss Jekyll; it is tempting to imagine that it was Gertrude Jekyll, the great gardener, a friend of both Barbara Bodichon and Ruskin.[10] She certainly would have approved of Octavia's eye for plants, and of the scene Octavia described to her mother:

> it is so delightful to watch what nature has done, now that she has taken possession of the ground, what lovely and various things she has set in it . . . There are wild roses in the hedges, and many more

foxgloves than last year; then there are great beds of white clover, and patches of golden lady's finger, and spaces of buttercup and potentilla, and tall large heads of crimson clover; the pink mallow is in bud; so is the sweet briar . . . one just steps out of this window and finds oneself on a sort of fraternal nearness with tall grass and stately and lovely flowers.[11]

Visitors to Larksfield were soon put to work wheeling barrows around, picking up stones, tearing up thistles and docks in the field that later became a much admired garden.

Crockham Hill instilled a love of the High Weald into all the Hill family – indeed direct descendants of theirs still live there. The Kent and Surrey Footpaths Committee was the first regional section of the CPS, and, as was typical with anything that Octavia touched, it was a notably dynamic and busy organization – despite its local remit. It also prefigured the structure of the National Trust, with its emphasis on strong regional organization.

The Open Spaces movement in both town and country was now gathering support. A meeting at Lambeth Palace to campaign for the use of the burial ground nearby brought further support from Florence Nightingale, this time in the form of a letter. Octavia believed that 'of all the people who have spoken or written on Open Spaces, F. Nightingale has got most to the heart of the matter.'[12]

In Octavia's absence, Emma Cons, encouraged by Octavia, had begun her work in Lambeth in earnest. Although entirely separate, it was an outpost of Octavia's work, and she often appealed on Emma's behalf for property and funds from the fellow-workers, 'that her own great power among the people may be effectual'.

Surrey Buildings,[13] Emma's block of model dwellings in Lambeth, was designed by Elijah Hoole[14] in the form of a quadrangle of tenement flats and two-storey cottages and shops for the South London Dwellings Company in 1879.[15] Viscount Hampden was chairman of the company and Emma Cons, the prime mover, was managing director. The Cons household, which consisted of Emma and her supportive sister Ellen, and included Caroline Martineau,[16] lived on the spot in a pair of the cottages knocked together.

The Buildings were grouped around open ground, with all the lavatories in one block, one per tenement with its own keys, and the wash-house and drying-ground on the roof. They followed the usual arrangement for model tenements, with outside stairs and balconies on to which the rooms opened.

Beatrice Webb noted that Emma seemed to have little interest in solving 'the general questions of the hour', her considerable energies being entirely devoted to practical matters. Sophia Lonsdale, who worked with her, remembered how:

> Miss Cons's courage and spirit and hopefulness never left her. I remember walking across Lambeth Bridge with her one day and we stopped in the middle to look down the river. She said to me: 'When one thinks of all the sin and misery there is in London, what's to prevent one's throwing oneself over there, except one's faith? I wish I were in Heaven with the gate shut.'[17]

When Beatrice Webb met her in 1885, Emma Cons had been managing the Royal Victoria Theatre (later the Old Vic) as a teetotal Coffee Tavern Music Hall for five years. Beatrice Webb noted that Emma spent much of her time 'in connection with the amusement and instruction of the people. In 1888 she bought the freehold of the music hall, raising £17,500 in three months – effective fund-raising was just one of many abilities that Octavia and Emma shared.[18]

In the East End, work was expanding under the energetic supervision of the Barnetts. Kate Potter had become friendly with them and joined them on holiday in Egypt.[19] On their return – 'warmer friends than ever, rather to my surprise' – they pressed her to superintend the Whitechapel houses.

In 1881 Kate met Leonard Courtney[20] who was soon impressed with her commitment to her work. 'You might have continued the indulgent life of a daughter of a man of fortune and fame and you preferred to put aside all this easy existence, to live in narrow lodgings and to give yourself up to work for the poorest, the most degraded of your fellow creatures,' he wrote to her.

Kate was indeed hard at work that summer.

> I have been spending most of my Sunday in doing something like office work which I hope is not wicked. At the end of the quarter in my Houses I always let the tenants pay up to Saturday night – so as to give them a chance of paying up any arrears before I send the accounts in . . . A morning spent like this always makes me feel as if

there were more machinery than real meaning or object in my work which apparently is something the same feeling that the National accounts give to the Secretary of the Treasury!

There was no escape from the scrupulous accounting system which Octavia had instituted.

Kate Potter had now been working for six years. Life in the city was wearing her down and made her feel 'like a bit of lifeless perpetually moving machinery'. In August Leonard Courtney asked her to marry him, agreeing to postpone the marriage to 'give you time to dispose carefully and well of a work in which you have been so successful and which for some years has formed so large a part of your life.' It was to be an unofficial engagement, a 'bond which is no bond' – respectful of the fact that she was in mourning after her mother's recent death.[21]

Throughout these years Kate Potter had worked closely with A. G. Crowder, whom she had earlier characterized for his earnestness and devotion to duty, with no care for his pleasures or comforts. He had approached Octavia in 1873, offering to help her work with his recent inheritance from his father. Octavia, while appreciating his offer, decided to hand him straight on to Samuel Barnett.[22] Kate, looking back, noted of Crowder: 'I did not then see that his somewhat narrow social sympathies and absence of much power of enjoyment make a life of work only easier to him than it would be to most of us.' It can have come as no surprise to her, then, to receive a rather dyspeptic note from him, having heard of her engagement. He wished her well but added, 'when you give up the tenants, which I may not tell you I always considered "fancy-work" I prognosticate that the plan will gradually fall through . . . I hope I may be wrong.' It was scarcely a generous testament to Kate Potter's considerable efforts and devotion to the cause.

In many ways Kate Potter and A. G. Crowder were typical of the kind of people attracted to Octavia's side and into her work – the able, frustrated, Victorian young women who wanted to bury themselves utterly in some kind of philanthropic work, and the earnest, often dull, young men of independent means who were also eager to offer their services in this cause. Crowder, like Edward Bond, remained active in housing reform all his life.[23]

On 15 March 1883 Kate Potter and Leonard Courtney were married at St Jude's, Whitechapel. Kate was delighted to find 'the church crowded with poor people to most of whom I was known and many of whom I know . . . Breakfast in St Jude's Schools with 100 of my poor people and about 40 others.'

By then Kate was working for the East End Dwellings Company which was set up in 1883 by Edward Bond and Crowder with the close support of the Barnetts. Octavia was no longer directly involved with this. An extension and formalization of the early work which Octavia had helped the Barnetts start up, it began with promised finance of £36,000 and was officially launched in 1884, with a dividend of 4 per cent, to

> build for the unskilled labourers, the day workers at the docks, and the many men and women who live by casual employment. For such there is as yet no provision by the Building Companies, and the rule of the Peabody Trustees is to admit no tenant who cannot give a reference to [sic] a regular employer. We shall have no such rule, we shall let in single rooms, and if possible carry out the plan of having lady rent-collectors.[24]

Their first venture for the 'poorest of the poor' opened in 1885 – Katherine Buildings named after Katherine Potter. The lady rent-collectors included her sister Beatrice and Ella Pycroft.[25] Beatrice started work there early in 1885, and wasted no time in telling the directors of the buildings ('amongst them stumbled on an old lover') her views on how any further buildings could be better planned. Samuel Barnett was at this time discussing with Octavia plans for an association of agencies for housing of the poor to set professional standards and help ensure a higher calibre of women housing managers. Beatrice thought such an organization an excellent idea. 'I think these strong women have a great future before them – in the solution of social questions. They *are not* just inferior men. They may have masculine faculty but they have the *woman's temperament* – and the stronger they are the more distinctively feminine they are in this.'[26]

Beatrice's brief period working in housing was part of a careful strategy, as well as a distraction from her woes – in particular her infatuation with Joseph Chamberlain. 'My special aim is to understand the conditions of the working class in the way of "housing", by digesting the evidence of others, testing and supplementing it by my own observation and actual effort in that direction.' She wanted to see how the state did or could intervene and whether it could feasibly replace the work of volunteers and individuals.[27]

Ella Pycroft, who was a highly experienced worker, guided
Beatrice in the mysteries of the work. Beatrice's diary records:

> Long trudges through Whitechapel after applicants and references,
> and tenants tumbling in anyhow. A drifting population . . . – a
> constantly decomposing mass of human beings, few rising out of it
> but many dropping down dead, pressed out of existence in the
> struggle . . . some light-hearted enough, in spite of misery and
> disease. More often feel envy than pity. Shall in the future, when
> other workers are found, and when once I am fairly started in the
> practical work, undertake less of the management and use the work
> more as an opening for observation.

The minutiae and the personal contact that had always appealed to
Octavia held little attraction for Beatrice. As a modern commentator
noted of their later work, the Webbs 'preferred to emphasize the duties
of citizenship and had no confidence in actual citizens'. Brunswick
Buildings in Goulston Street and Wentworth Buildings in Wentworth
Street were completed by the East End Dwellings Company in
1886 and Beatrice worked there as well, highly critical of the model
dwellings and increasingly revolted by the tenants. 'Even their careless, sensual laugh, the coarse jokes and unloving words depress one as
one presses through the crowd, and almost shudders to touch them.'[28]

Charles Booth, social investigator and Beatrice's cousin by marriage, estimated that in Tower Hamlets alone, 35 per cent of the
population – around 160,000 – was living at the lowest sustainable
level of life – types ranging from criminals and vagrants to a vast
floating population of casual workers and street vendors.[29] The
problem was growing inexorably, year by year.

When Beatrice and Octavia finally met in May 1886, at the Barnetts:

> We talked on [sic] Artisans' Dwellings. I asked her whether she
> thought it necessary to keep accurate descriptions of the tenants.
> No, she did not see the use of it. 'Surely it was wise to write down
> observations so as to be able to give true information?' I suggested.
> She objected that there was already too much 'windy' talk. What
> you wanted was action for men and women to go and work day by
> day among the less fortunate. And so there was a slight clash
> between us, and I felt penitent for my presumption, but *not
> convinced*.[30]

Nevertheless Beatrice was attracted to the idea of social work, if only in the privacy of her diary. 'Perhaps this last year of suffering will decrease my egotism, and instead of that cold observation and analysis, all done with the egotistical purpose of increasing knowledge, there will be the interest which comes from feeling, and from the desire humbly to serve those around me.' As it happened, that was not to be the path she followed, but a much more theoretical one, in company with Sidney Webb whom she married in 1892. Octavia would meet a very different woman when they later sat together on the Poor Law Commission.

A sometime friend of both Beatrice Webb and of Eleanor Marx (Aveling), Margaret Harkness was an observer of the world of philanthropy as it operated in the late-Victorian East End. Under the pseudonym of John Law she wrote a number of impressive and observant novels, and in *A City Girl* she offered a rather scathing account of the lady rent-collectors: 'Several times in the week ladies arrived in the Buildings armed with master-keys, ink-pots and rent books. A tap at the door was followed by the intrusion into a room of a neatly-clad female of masculine appearance.' Prompt payment assured their rapid exit, but otherwise 'they took stock of the room (or rooms), and said a few words about the broker.' The broker was the bailiff who would soon turn them out for non-payment. The tenants, according to Margaret Harkness, had little time or sympathy for the women visitors. '"I pity her husband" . . . "Females like 'er don't marry," mumbled a misanthropic old lady.'[31]

There were other views. One observer, but perhaps not a tenant, likened the arrival of the lady rent-collectors to the flowering of primroses in spring – an imaginative metaphor, to say the least. Miss Busk, six foot tall and 'as brave and buoyant as she was big', was one such bloom. Another young lady visitor attracted the attentions of a simple-minded boy who waylaid her with offerings, including a lark he had trapped for her.

Octavia's trained volunteers and workers were on the whole a generation older than the women who first took an active role in local government. But the experience they gained for them was invaluable. Local government was to be the beneficiary of all the energies captured by philanthropy, the idea of service and practical Christianity.[32] For the suffragists, more politically sophisticated, it also endorsed the role of women in a national administrative network. Work as Guardians, in the COS and in the wide range of philanthropic works available to thoughtful, active, mostly middle-class women prepared them for a wider role within State-assisted welfare. Women ratepayers had a local vote from 1869 and following the Married Women's Property Act of 1870 the local franchise widened further.

Among Octavia's own workers a number became prominent in politics. Eva Muller (later McClaren) was a Lambeth Guardian who founded the Women's Liberal Federation; Elizabeth Sturge, one of a Quaker family from Bristol, became a notable Guardian there; Emma Cons was the first woman Alderman on the LCC. The Women's University Settlement added to the supply of able, trained women from the 1890s onwards.

When Octavia returned to work in 1881, one chapter of her life closed. Ruskin, communicating with her through his cousin Joan Severn, announced that he wanted to sell Paradise Place and Freshwater Place. Octavia bought Paradise Place, the original property, herself. 'It has been the longest under my charge and I am thankful that the fact of ownership implies a continuous duty to the people there.'[33] Freshwater Place with its playground was too expensive for her but William Shaen and his wife stepped in. Octavia wrote, offering them joint ownership with herself. 'I couldn't throw myself into the personal work down there; I couldn't stand it; but, while I keep at all well, I would look into its affairs, choose and watch its workers, remove or guide them, and have its accounts regularly audited. There would then be an almost certainty of its paying 5 per cent.' The Shaens however wanted to be fully responsible, and bought it outright.

Following these transactions, a letter arrived from Ruskin at Brantwood.

> I have had great pleasure in hearing, thro' Mrs Severn, of the arrangements of Marylebone etc. and am entirely glad the thing should pass into your hands, and that you are still able to take interest in it, and encourage and advise your helpers. I trust, however, you will not be led back into any anxious or deliberative thought. I find it a very strict law of my present moral being – or being anyway – to be anxious about nothing![34]

Ruskin's involvement in Octavia's work was now formally over. The only outstanding matter remained the ill-fated teashop in Paddington

Street, which Ruskin still officially owned, as Octavia had to write and remind him some years later. The landlords wanted it painted and repointed, and she estimated it would cost £104. Apologizing profusely for troubling him, she said she would take silence as his agreement and proceed with this unless she heard to the contrary. However, 'you may be interested to know that the tenants have been very happy in the house.'[35] She received no answer.

CHAPTER 15

1884

B Y 1884 Octavia had become a figure of national and international standing. Her sisters, assistants and volunteers had
also taken on such a weight of responsibility that Octavia now
drew on an enormous fund of experience, not solely her own.
Inevitably, given the scale of the venture, she was now far less
personally involved with the tenants. Her almost obsessive involvement with them, and the inevitable crises and disappointments, had
been a major component of the stress that felled her in 1877. Now that
she had, of necessity, learned to delegate, she found people were
dependable and capable, even without her hand on every shoulder.

Interest in Octavia's work had grown in a number of other cities in
the 1870s. Octavia was extremely confident in her Leeds representative: 'they were wise enough to find a lady who was willing to come
up to London and work side by side with us and so gain an insight into
much which it is difficult to learn except practically.'[1] Miss Martin had
stayed at Nottingham Place during the spring of 1875 to learn the
work. As always, Octavia was active in the support of the Leeds
workers. She visited the city to explain her methods to a group of
business men.

The Revd Estlin Carpenter, a local supporter, reported on the
occasion.

> We arranged a meeting in the theatre of the Philosophical Hall, and
> some of the leading citizens were there. I well remember that
> surprise of some of them at the clearness – not only of her opening
> exposition – but of her spontaneous replies to questions concerning
> all sorts of matters affecting the treatment of house property,
> sanitation, repairs, bad debts.[2]

In Dublin, Miss Kennedy had taken on some property belonging to her father. Gertrude reported that 'she has adopted all your plans and books, and writes up for printed forms; and she seemed so interested.'

By 1879, although she was keeping on the sidelines because of her health, Octavia was in touch with schemes in Liverpool, Manchester, and Dublin. Dundee and Edinburgh followed. A few years later, as she told the Royal Commission on Housing, she also had personal experience of a scheme in Glasgow. The scale of the enterprise she inspired – despite its minute inroads on the national crisis – made it essential to have guidelines, for Octavia could not be everywhere in person, even when well. She therefore backed her work up with a stream of articles in leading periodicals, the annual 'Letter to Fellow-workers', and well-reported speeches.

In the early 1880s considerable interest was expressed from the Continent. Germany and Holland were the most fertile ground for her ideas in Europe, in the former because of the efforts of Princess Alice of Hesse-Darmstadt. Enquiries also came from Paris, and from Sweden and Denmark where good workers were established. Correspondence then poured in from all over the world. A Russian lady sent her the article she had written on *The Homes of the London Poor* from the *Journal de St. Petersbourg*. Inspired by the book, Octavia's correspondent took pride in the fact that the achievements were those of women.

There was sustained interest from the USA, too, the earliest coming from Henry Bowditch, Chairman of the Massachusetts Board of Health who had been highly enthusiastic about Octavia's approach as early as 1871, and had gone home to attempt to emulate her methods. He chose a disreputable Boston tenement and utterly failed to transform it.

An enthusiastic propagandist for Octavia's work was Louisa Lee Schuyler, the founder of the State Charities' Aid Association of New York; she published *The Homes of the London Poor*, for twenty-five cents, in the same year that it appeared in London – 1875. According to Octavia's brother-in-law Edmund Maurice, the American edition appeared before the British one. That was followed by an American edition of the essays from *Our Common Land*, published for the Associated Charities of Boston in 1880.[3] Octavia's ideas on charity, as well as those on housing, were becoming widely known in the USA, helped by the rapid spread of American branches of the COS: by 1883 there were twenty-five COS societies in cities along the East coast and in the Mid-west.[4]

In the 1880s two women, Ellen Collins and Alice Lincoln, respectively from New York and Boston, attempted to follow Octavia's approach to housing management more closely by taking on run-down properties and turning them into respectable dwellings. Yet despite their admiration in principle, the realities of the low financial return meant that any tenants who looked like trouble were summarily turned out. The housing was improved, but they operated a stern system without any of Octavia's attempts at moral regeneration.[5] A more direct link was through Ellen Chase, an American who worked for Octavia in Deptford for several years before returning to Boston. Her published account of those years must have greatly increased interest in Octavia's enterprise.

In 1896, the Octavia Hill Association of Philadelphia was set up. Two Philadelphia women who had worked for Octavia in the 1880s were behind it, Hannah Fox and Helen Parrish. Their stated objective was to 'refit old properties and small houses' and they firmly decided against building new tenements. When Hannah Fox wrote to Octavia to tell her of the naming of their Association Octavia replied:

Do believe me that I am touched and grateful for the kindness, and not unmindful of the honour of being thus associated with noble effort in America. The wonderful response which I have always received from America has been a cheer to me . . . [It is] one more link between your country and ours, and a bond between those of us who, with the ocean between us, are yet indissolubly one in our effort to make the lives of the poor better and happier.[6]

The Association managed its rehabilitated properties along staunchly Octavia-Hill lines, as well as mounting campaigns to institute a municipal housing code. It is still in existence, although over the years it began to add new housing to its holdings. In 1986 it echoed its founders' objectives with a 90th-anniversary resolution: 'The mission of the Association is to provide decent, affordable housing to families of low to moderate income in such a way as to preserve the dignity of the tenants and foster a sense of neighborhood and community.'[7]

Through the years Octavia's centre of operations was always in London. If visitors from the provinces, Europe or the USA wanted to be informed, they could read her publications, or come in person for training or a visit to one of the courts. Octavia's workers, too, were constantly approached by admiring observers of their achievements, but not all were as forthcoming as she; Emma Cons wrote to an American enquirer: 'I do *the work* but do *not* write about it. So if anyone would like to see what is being done in London, they can be taken around by one of my lady workers if your correspondents are coming to London.'[8]

Octavia's responsibilities were now mounting rapidly. She wrote to Emily from Penzance: 'I have a quite tremendous day on Monday, as I have to take over the Eccles Com. work, *and* to see to Deptford. Besides the necessary work at home, . . . Sir C. Dilke asks me if I can give evidence before the Royal Commission on Tuesday . . .'[9]

The Royal Commission appointed in 1884 to investigate the housing of the working classes was the outcome of the failure of earlier initiatives. The crisis in housing was pointed up in various ways; Andrew Mearns' *The Bitter Cry of Outcast London* was merely the most sensational publication in what had become a debate in print.[10] The fact that it recorded conditions without embellishment and still managed to be so profoundly shocking was a forceful argument for action.

The Marquess of Salisbury, Leader of the Conservative Party in 1883, had taken an unprecedented step for someone holding high office in the Tory party by writing a polemical article for the *National Review* on housing conditions of the poor. He touched on his own knowledge of rural problems from his Hatfield estate but, as he wrote, 'The housing of the poor in our great towns, especially in London, is a much more difficult and much more urgent question, for the increase of prosperity tends rather to aggravate the existing evil than to lighten it. It is, in fact, directly caused by our prosperity.' To the cost of building in the cities was added the high cost of land.

To give some illustration of the situation, Salisbury set out the findings of the London School Board, whose Chairman recorded that of 1,129 families surveyed, 871 lived in a single room. 'A more important subject of inquiry could hardly be suggested . . . it touches an evil that is not only grave, but continually growing.'

Salisbury discussed the efforts of bodies such as the Peabody Trust and suggested that the government might set an example by intervening and providing suitable housing for government employees. However, it was the achievements of Octavia Hill and her fellow-workers, active in the field for twenty years, that most impressed Salisbury. 'The benevolent ladies have solved the problem over which the great corporations have failed . . . they have reached the poorest class; and they have made the operation pay.' He outlined Octavia's method and her object, which he described as being 'to improve the tenants with the tenements'. Salisbury quoted Octavia: 'You can hunt the poor about from place to place, oust them out of one place and drive them to another; but you will never reach the poor except through people who care about them and watch over them.'

Salisbury's article was promptly answered in the *Fortnightly Review* by Joseph Chamberlain, who made a strong case for the reform of local bodies and introduction of efficient municipal authorities. Further voices joined the debate, and the argument, which soon reverberated through every room where housing reform was a topic, covered all points of view. Octavia Hill added her voice.[11] Inevitably she criticized the impersonal nature of the municipal body: 'Almost all public bodies do things expensively; neither do they seem fitted to supply the various wants of numbers of people in a perceptive and economical way.'[12] Lord Shaftesbury joined the debate, writing an article entitled 'The Mischief of State Aid'.

Early in 1884 Lord Salisbury had proposed setting up a Royal Commission on Housing, from the Opposition bench in the House of Lords. The Government followed up his suggestion swiftly. There was royal concern too. 'The Queen will be glad to hear Mr Gladstone's opinion . . . and to learn whether the Government contemplate the introduction of any measures, or propose to take any steps to obtain more precise information as to the *true* state of affairs in these overcrowded, unhealthy and squalid bodies.'[13]

Gladstone, having foreseen the request, asked Sir Charles Dilke to chair the Commission. Dilke had been preparing himself for such a role by visiting London slums (some of them owned by Salisbury himself) and his first candidate for membership of the Commission was Cardinal Manning. He accepted, as did Salisbury, the Prince of Wales, and a host of other distinguished figures.

The new publication *Justice*, organ of William Morris and Henry Hyndman's Social Democratic Federation, regarded the setting up of a Royal Commission as a 'favourite middle-class device for shirking responsibility and doing nothing'.[14] When the list of Commissioners was announced, the paper had more to say. An unsigned leader ran through the names: Dilke was a turncoat, describing himself as a Republican in public, a Socialist in private; the Prince of Wales was a 'voluptuary . . . [who] has never taken the slightest interest in the people'; Samuel Morley was a hypocritical capitalist; of the church

representatives, Cardinal Manning was able and the Bishop of Bed-
ford foolish; Salisbury, though able, was more interested in the rights
of the landlord than those of the people. It was a sham inquiry and 'it is
well no better are employed on such a useless task'.[15]

None of the views expressed in *Justice* was particularly surprising,
the Commission being hardly constituted to appeal to the radical
voice. However, shortly after, in one of its leaders entitled 'Women in
Politics', an energetic argument was put for the involvement of
women in public and political life. 'Women are wanted everywhere
. . . why was not Miss Octavia Hill on the Royal Commission is a
question which all of us women must ask continually.'[16]

Octavia had in fact been put forward by Dilke – with her unique
qualifications she was an ideal Commissioner. But Sir William Harcourt,
who as Home Secretary was the ultimate arbiter, refused to entertain
the unprecedented idea of a woman Commissioner. When the matter
went to Cabinet, however, his objection began to seem more personal. As it was reported to Octavia, 'Mr G [Gladstone] sided with
me . . . Hartington siding with Harcourt, and Lord G [Granville]
saying that he was with me on the principle, but against me on the
person.' It must have afforded her a measure of satisfaction to be the
subject of Cabinet discussion and to have the Prime Minister as her
champion.

Dilke's view was succinct: 'Completed by Royal Commission with
fewer fools on it than is usual on Royal Commissions.'[17]

The Commissioners included, both W. Torrens MP and
Sir Richard Cross MP, respectively the son of the begetter of
the 1868 Torrens Act, the first legislative action on the slums, and the
Chairman of the Commons Select Committee of 1881–82 which had
considered why the earlier measures (including two Acts bearing
Cross's own name) had been so notably ineffective.[18] Despite the level
of commitment to the question, and the expertise of several of its
members, Dilke's impression was that 'the Commission was dull,
although it produced a certain amount of valuable evidence.' He had
already been warned – Octavia Hill had written on 22 March 1884:
'You amongst all men realize most clearly that action is more needed
than words.'[19]

On Friday, 9 May Octavia Hill was called for examination by the
Commission. She was already familiar to Cross, having given
evidence to his Select Committee on two previous occasions. The
Commissioners, Dilke told her before the questions began, had her

evidence from that occasion before them. She told them, 'I have no knowledge of the country at all; all that I say will be confined entirely to London.'

The Commissioners were concerned to find out about her views on the efficacy of the Cross Act. Asked whether the provisions under Standing Orders to provide rehousing for those displaced by compulsory purchase orders was satisfactory, Octavia replied sharply, 'They seem to me to be practically almost a dead letter.' She pointed out that advance warning of railway works was habitually given to the landlords, who first evicted the tenants and then pocketed the compensation. 'The companies, therefore, can go before Parliament, and say, "We did not displace people; there is nobody there."'

Regarding the dispersal of the poor from the city, Dilke asked her whether 'removal to the suburbs is a satisfactory arrangement for them, having regard to the facilities afforded by workmen's trains?' Octavia replied that for some it was a satisfactory arrangement but 'utterly useless so far as others are concerned. When the head of a family is a man earning "good money," as they say, and is strong, and is the only member of the family at work, and has reasonable hours, those facilities work very well.' But, she continued, if several members of the family worked, or did casual labour, or mending or tailoring work which had to be done in the day, it was useless. 'I should say that they [the trains] are wholly useless to the entire class of people amongst whom I work.' The advantage was that it cleared a proportion of the population from the city, which thus had an indirect benefit. Octavia has often been held to be a propagandist for suburban development; she was not, except with major qualifications.

When she was asked for an example of a company building cheaply enough to benefit the poorest class, she nominated the East End Dwellings Company, run by 'former fellow-workers of my own, Mr Crowder, Mr Bond, Mr Martineau; Mr Barnett, of St Jude's, Whitechapel, who is really the heart and soul of the undertaking is not, however, a director.' She suggested the Commissioners call Mr Crowder as a witness.

Octavia then explained what she meant by 'greater simplicity', including the provision of water and drainage to each floor, but not to each room, and the letting of rooms *en suite*, so that they were entered as self-contained accommodation, not room by room off a common balcony. She emphasized the importance of the space around the buildings. 'The way in which people are building over back yards, and adding storeys to existing dwellings, diminishing air and light everywhere is, to me, dreadful.'

Asked about the provision of artisan housing, Octavia replied that the scale of building would before long be adequate for that class of tenant. With regard to housing for labourers – those with less certain and less well-paid employment – she felt that, 'if men are conscientious, economical and sensible, the thing [provision of housing] can be done: but it has not been done on any large scale yet . . . I am sure I could do it myself; but then, of course, one individual always has power that a large body cannot get; an individual can get a thing more cheaply done; but it wants immense care as to the details.' When the artisans and reliable casual labourers were accommodated, however, there would still be 'the large mass of the uneducated destructive poor left behind'.

How would she deal with them, Dilke asked? 'The difficulty with these people is not financial, but moral,' she answered. 'I know nothing for them but some individual power and watchfulness. They must be trained.' 'In short, what is commonly called your system?' Yes, she replied. To buy up the house in which the intractable tenant lives and make him 'profit by his own care' was not committee work, but depended on individual character judgement.

Questioned on her insistence on financial viability, Octavia countered that 'once you assume that it is your duty to provide houses for the poor at a price that they assume they can pay, it will just be a rate-in-aid of wages like the old poor law system . . . you will get people coming up to London, just throwing themselves as it were on your charity to provide houses for them . . .'

If the state were to lend building companies money at a low rate, would she consider that, Dilke queried? 'If such a loan is made quietly and they [the poor] know nothing about it, it does not do half the harm,' Octavia replied. To further questioning as to whether the state or the parish might be empowered to build, Octavia was firm. They would be unsuitable bodies for building and (her usual riposte) would 'paralyse effort on the part of the independent builders'.

The questioning turned to matters of sanitary standards, such as building over graveyards. Octavia was firm about the role of the sanitary inspector; without enlarging she told Dilke, 'I have a general dread of increased inspection; my experience of inspection is not happy.'

Cardinal Manning's questioning concentrated on the manner in

which Octavia obtained property, freehold or leasehold. She believed
that those who had bought on her behalf had never been asked to pay
too much; the houses in question were 'improvable'. She emphasized
that she had consciously operated by individual influence rather than
by forming a society – though in some respects the latter course would
have been far easier to administer.

To further questions about the class of tenant, she pointed out that
the building companies could not accept the 'destructive classes' as
tenants. 'But if I go down and purchase a street, I buy up a number of
houses inhabited by those people, and then I say to them, "You must
either do better or you must leave; which is it to be?" In short:
"Individuals can do what the companies can do, and the companies
cannot do what individuals can do."'

Manning doubted whether this approach could command sufficient
resources. Octavia countered: 'I do not see why individuals should not
have as much capital as companies, only that they have to take up a
number of small schemes instead of one huge one.'

The questioning continued into the role and responsibility of the
ground landlord, who received a peppercorn rent. Octavia was
customarily firm: 'I do not think that ground landlords can quite enter
into all the advantages of inheriting their ancestors' estates, and not
into the duties incumbent on them.' The Ecclesiastical Commissioners may have been in her mind as she spoke. Lord Salisbury took
up the point: 'You do not have much sympathy for the ground
landlord?' No, she answered, she had great sympathy for him, and had
'spent much of my life in getting people to become ground landlords'.
'You wish to multiply him, but to tax him?' 'Yes, and to see him tax
himself voluntarily.' Octavia was rarely at a loss for an answer, in
what must have been a most gruelling session.

Returning to the type of tenant, under Salisbury's questioning she
emphasized that, 'we cannot set up a perfect standard immediately,
but progress must be gradual.' They bought the rooms

> perfectly teeming with people, and for a few weeks we go on like
> that; and then we gradually get them to move into larger or to take
> additional rooms; and we deal with everything gradually in that
> way . . . I do not say that I will not have drunkards, I have quantities
> of drunkards; but everything depends upon whether I think the
> drunkard will be better for being sent away or not. It is a
> tremendous despotism, but it is exercised with a view of bringing

out the powers of the people, and treating them as responsible for themselves within certain limits.

There were no rigid rules? 'No rigid rules; we have not a rule, except that no lodgers are allowed.'

Regarding the quality of volunteers, Octavia admitted that they sometimes fell below the mark. Salisbury asked: 'Is there not a little danger in a very large system of volunteers that they are liable to crotchets, and caprices, and fashionable follies?' 'I think there is, but we get rid of the fashionable people pretty soon.' Mr Goschen asked her how many workers she had, but she could not calculate the number. Salisbury continued: 'Philanthropic instinct does not necessarily carry with it business aptitude?' 'It does not; but you have to get a combination of the two, and especially now that girls' education is so much better, the younger people are getting into it very easily.'

Many of the questions retraced the ground Octavia had already covered but she did not flag. She reiterated that she made a 5 per cent charge for rent-collection which went to a general fund for the training of paid workers. 'It is all paid to paid workers. It is the only common fund that we have; it comes from all the properties.' If the assistants were working directly for an owner, then she encouraged them to take the 5 per cent directly. When she was paying them, she began at £30 per annum, for two days a week. In one court, she knew that the 5 per cent paid to the collector amounted to £60 a year, 'not bad pay for a woman's work'.

Where arrears were concerned, Octavia told the Commissioners that she always began with a clean sheet. The owners had to agree to wipe off all arrears. Closely questioned on the finances, and the amount set aside for rates, repair and unlet properties, she admitted the figure could be between 30 per cent and 40 per cent of the gross rental. 'I have not made that calculation, though I could make it very easily.' There were immense variations in different parts of London, she added. The rent was calculated on 'what is the market rate in the neighbourhood'.[20] To a question as to whether the law of supply and demand led inexorably to a higher rent for smaller accommodation, Octavia assented, adding that 'the natural tendency of that would have been for wages to rise in proportion if the cost of living rises.' For once wishful thinking had skewed Octavia's grasp of economic reality.

The Commissioners were surprised to discover that she could not calculate the number or the value of properties under her management; when she went abroad they had been worth £70,000 but a great deal of growth had occurred since. Lyulph Stanley asked: 'You could not say whether it was, 3,000 or 4,000 or 5,000?' 'I am afraid I could not tell.'

She emphasized how economically the work was run. Without committees and boards to service, Octavia pointed out, 'We have next to no printing, and next to no stationery; we have no office, and we have no machinery that costs anything.'

By the end of her evidence Octavia had answered more than 400 questions, many in considerable detail. She concluded: 'I should like to say that I have been asked questions about things upon which I do not feel my opinions have any value; but I have answered them to the best of my power and knowledge.' It was an impressive performance. As she well knew, it would bring her work further into the public eye, thus gaining her more support and, inevitably, some detractors.

The Royal Commission Report was published in 1885 and it led to new legislation, the Housing of the Working Classes Act (1885). It largely consisted of amendments to earlier acts and was a generally unsatisfactory piece of legislation, tinkering around the edge of the housing problem without doing any justice to the wide-ranging and impressive work of the Commissioners. The Housing of the Working Classes Act (1890) was an altogether superior instrument, and with its powers the real reform of housing and sanitary conditions began.

Octavia's circle of contracts was constantly widening. It took in William Morris, who wholeheartedly shared her admiration for Ruskin. She had first met Morris a few years before. 'He took us all over the garden and into his study, and such an interesting carpet factory . . . It was just in his own garden. The tapestry he had been making himself in his study was beautiful!!'[21] The connection with Morris had been established through his support for the Kyrle Society and most directly through the Decorative branch.

In 1880 Morris addressed a meeting at the Kensington Vestry Hall as one of a distinguished list of speakers that included Prince Leopold, the Duke of Albany (President of the Society) and Lord Leighton (President of the Royal Academy). Morris's address was very warm: 'I feel that there is a difficulty in the way of my advocating before you the claims of the Kyrle Society to public support; its case is almost too good to bear much talking about it.' The Society could have no enemies, he continued; it was a cause which could not be questioned. This was unusual for him – most of the societies he belonged to 'count their foes by the thousand and their friends by the unit'. The Kyrle Society faced enemies called 'Carelessness, Ugliness and Squalor'. Morris was eager to emphasize the open-space element too, for 'it is idle to talk about popularizing art, if you are not prepared to popularize reverence for nature also, both among the poor and the rich.'[22]

Prompted by the Royal Commission on housing for the poor and by Octavia's own written account of her work in the *Pall Mall Gazette*, William Morris devoted a leader in *Justice* to her work and to his own prescription to the problem. Addressing a working-class readership, Morris began by criticizing Octavia's willingness to accept, albeit reluctantly, present conditions. 'She actually allows herself to say that after all it is not so bad as one might think for a whole family to live in one room; by a *room* of course meaning the ordinary twelve foot square hutch of an East-end house.'

But despite his reservations on detail, Morris defended Octavia on a wider front:

> I wish our friends to accept my assertion that Miss Hill is a well intentioned, disinterested and kindly person, for in that very fact lies the force of her words as an indictment of our present society; she, a good and eminently practical woman, with plenty of experience as to the extent to which it is possible to move the rich to help, and how far it is possible to use that help for the benefit of the 'poor', is forced to reduce her standard down to this point.

He felt, May Morris wrote in her biography of her father, 'It was an all-too-huge burthen for her [Octavia's] shoulders; the work to be done so tremendous that there were times when she implicitly professed herself content with certain conditions that were pitifully below any standard of decent life.' Yet Morris's own solution, given in the same leading article, was for 'vertical streets', alleviated by plenty of 'pure air and sunlight'. In true Kyrle Society style, he suggested 'cloisters or covered walking and playing spaces', attractive public rooms, and 'cheap ornaments such as fountains and conduits'. He was sure that 'co-operation among the men of diverse crafts who would inhabit these houses would make them not merely comfortable and pretty, but beautiful even.' He was, he admitted, puzzled by the solution to the housing problem: '. . . you [his working-class readers] can at the best only be housed as careful masters house their machines.

Alas! I fear that many of you will be housed as *careless* masters house them.'[23]

1884 was also the year in which the Ecclesiastical Commissioners entrusted Octavia with the first of their properties. In March, forty-eight Deptford houses were handed over by them to be managed by Octavia and her assistants, and more followed in Southwark later in the year. Despite her apparent return to health, she still had bad patches; when she wrote to Henrietta Barnett to tell her about the new properties, she added: 'I am so slow in all I do that I am like Napoleon who never opened his letters for a fortnight by which time half of them answered themselves.'[24]

The delegation of the Commissioners' responsibilities to an outsider, possibly intended only as a temporary stop-gap,[25] was caused by a major embarrassment that the Established Church of England faced. It had found itself accused of being one of the worst slum landlords in London. The church estates were largely ancient landholdings, the property of various bishoprics for several hundred years, which had subsequently become lost in a sea of leases and sub-leases. This was only curtailed under the Ecclesiastical Commissioners' Act of 1868. From then on, the Church made sure that none of these dubious leases was renewed and as many as possible reverted to the Commissioners directly the leases fell in.

Thus by the 1880s the Commissioners were faced with the realities of managing such estates as those in Paddington and Finsbury, inherited from the see and chapter of London, with the atrocious properties just behind Westminster Abbey which belonged to the Dean and chapter, as well as the Southwark estate, a black mark against the Bishops of Winchester.[26]

A committee in Brompton took on the task of investigating the connection between the Church and slum properties in Southwark and the results were published in *The Times* in January 1884, causing a sensation. The fact that it had based the article on properties which did not belong to the Church made little difference – the same charges were applicable just a few streets away.

The revelation of the condition of the Church's property holdings gave vent to public outrage, while the Temperance movement, in particular, gleefully pointed to the fact that the Church was frequently the leaseholder of public houses of the worst possible repute – and thus could be seen to be profiting from the sale of intoxicating liquor. The Church authorities found it was not a sustainable moral position to be linked to areas rife with poverty, drunkenness, prostitution and depravity. Something had to be done at considerable speed to salvage their reputation, and to make effective reforms and remedies in their estates.

In many instances the Church was beginning to rebuild its properties in the shape of model dwellings – not the ideal solution, in Octavia's view. It used as its agents the firm of Cluttons, who supervised the builders. At the same time as Octavia was asked to give her evidence to the Royal Commission, she was also approached by the Ecclesiastical Commissioners. Someone in her, by now, far-reaching network of contacts and supporters must have proposed her name to them and they invited her to meet them in 1883.

At first they wanted her to buy or lease their properties but she was adamant that she could only offer her services as a manager. By early 1884 she had persuaded them and, on a trial basis at first, she began rent-collection for a small number of Deptford properties. Gaining their confidence, she was soon able to propose a course of action for the large Southwark estate which was quite at variance with the Commissioners' current policy. If they were to build new blocks then, she suggested, these should be well-spaced out, broken by cottages and public open spaces.

Acting as sub-agents of Cluttons, Octavia and her workers began to prove that it was better to improve property rather than demolish it outright, and, more importantly, to show that direct contact with the tenants, through the medium of rent-collection, paid dividends. More important still, she persuaded the Commissioners to concern themselves with a poorer class than they had envisaged rehousing or helping. She demonstrated that property management involved more options than a simple choice between the building of model tenements for a fixed return or commercial development for maximum return.

Her work for the Ecclesiastical Commissioners, which began as a trickle in 1884, had become a flood by the 1900s, when they scarcely moved without consulting her on the nature of any developments in their London housing.

In 1884, Samuel and Henrietta Barnett embarked on a venture which in its early days owed much to Octavia's premises – the foundation of Toynbee Hall, the first of the Settlements. These Settlements were established in impoverished city areas to extend to local people amenities, education and guidance, which were offered by both resident and visiting volunteers. Many of the Settlements were directly linked to either the universities or public schools, and the majority were also missions in the religious sense. Edward Denison, a young man whose father was a bishop and who became for a short while a Member of Parliament, had established the idea by going to live in Stepney in 1867 – a kind of one-man Settlement. Although it was a short-lived exercise and although he died aged thirty in 1870, his example was widely known.

In 1883 Barnett, in an address to undergraduates, put his views:

Inquiries into social conditions lead generally to one conclusion. They show that little can be done *for*, which is not done *with* the people. It is the poverty of their own life which makes the poor content to inhabit 'uninhabitable' houses . . . Such poverty of life can best be removed by contact with those who possess the means of higher life . . . It is distance that makes friendships between classes almost impossible, and, therefore, residence among the poor is suggested as a simple way in which Oxford men may serve their generation. By sharing their fuller lives and riper thoughts with the poor they will destroy the worst evil of poverty . . . and they will do something to weld Classes into Society.[27]

The COS view of each poor family, as being made up of deserving or undeserving individuals whose fortune lay in their own hands, was, the Barnetts found from their experiences in the East End, simply a distortion of reality. It certainly was an inappropriate model for welfare workers to follow.

Samuel Barnett had been wanting to leave St Jude's as early as 1880. Henrietta had written to Octavia about her hopes for a transfer to Stepney, which seemed a quieter prospect. But Octavia had written back, in August 1880, with a sharp attack on Barnett's religious rather than his practical ministry. As she said, in the first of a series of letters which was sufficiently forthright, if not downright tactless enough, to strain the friendship near to breaking-point: 'If too the vast body of working men, now alienated from the Church and Christian world, are to be led back it must be, it seems to me, by someone who while entering with hearty sympathy into all the social questions they care for, tells them distinctly that he does so for Christ's sake.'[28]

Octavia admitted that Whitechapel was peculiarly unpromising territory for Anglican proselytizing, given that a large proportion of the population was either Roman Catholic or Jewish. Nevertheless:

> I suppose you have not succeeded – have you? – with the distinct question of faith among either your workers or parishioners . . . I am not myself sure . . . how far it is due to Yetta's own want of real affection for the Church and a certain uncertainty in her own grasp of the facts about God; how far – and this I believe it is largely – to your own intense desire not to separate yourself by criticizing . . . or dwelling on, differences between yourself and any single human soul you come in contact with.

He seemed, Octavia continued, to lack 'power – will – what is it?'; nevertheless she had recommended him for the Stepney living to 'both bishops'. It was a devastating letter, and a long one.

> I am not sure that the sick or the dying, the feeble or the old would turn to you for anything beyond practical help – Ask Yetta what she thinks – perhaps I'm not right, no one could owe you more than I do, no one could I think place more highly what you do, but just because of that I sometimes wonder . . . whether you will ever fill even a greater place than you now fill, just add that last touch of grace to your life to be able to lead people to see what God is, when they think of Him as a near person – I hope I shall not pain or discourage you.

She ended the letter with a further explanation:

> Will you think this letter foolish, or dogmatically and conceitedly in opposition, – I don't mean it as it costs me a good deal to say it especially now [she was still unwell]. I should like to stand very near you just now when the authorities don't seem to see all you and Yetta have done for the people, and I should like too for my own sake not to dwell on the difference there may be but on all we see and hold and do in common, but somehow I don't feel quite honest not to tell you all this – I do not myself feel it a separation but a vision of future things for you and a hope. If I am wrong forgive the presumption . . .

Few friendships could withstand such a dose of plain speaking and things were never the same between them again.[29]

When, a few years later, the Barnetts' plans for an East End Settlement had matured, Octavia was supportive, but only to an extent. Barnett had spoken at the Oxford Union in December 1883 on the motion that 'the condition of the dwellings of the poor in our large towns is a national disgrace and demands immediate action on the part of voluntary associations, municipal authorities and the legislature.' The debate encapsulated the concern of the intellectual middle classes with the condition of the poor and emphasized the impotence which both students and academics felt in the face of such misery. The motion was carried unanimously and immediately after the debate two meetings were held at Balliol to discuss the possibility of founding a Settlement as a way of harnessing that concern to practical ends.

Justice, from a politically radical standpoint, considered such meetings to be empty posturing. 'The social reformer is now played out and useful and constructive work can only be done by social revolutionists,' the writer thundered.[30]

Unlike the missions, which set out with a firm commitment to find converts, Settlements did not have proselytizing aims, and this suited Samuel Barnett's increasingly liberal views on religion in social work. Significantly, Octavia was present at another meeting in January 1884, at Keble College, which was held to counter the idea of secular Settlements. In principle, Octavia felt that Barnett's scheme was 'very hopeful and a very wise plan',[31] but the outcome of it all was that two Settlements were founded in 1884: Barnett's own Toynbee Hall, and Oxford House in Bethnal Green, which was both mission and Settlement. As one observer put it, the former was aesthetic, the latter ascetic; there was truth in the comment.

The Barnetts were deeply wounded by the suggestion that Oxford House fulfilled a function that Toynbee Hall, being avowedly secular, did not. The differences between the Barnetts and Octavia were further exacerbated when she addressed a meeting at Oxford House which represented what Henrietta Barnett termed 'the Church party'. In fact it was the failure of the Established Church, or any denomination, to reach the heart of the problems of the East End that had persuaded the Barnetts to leave the safer harbour of St Jude's, Whitechapel. They felt that to effect any changes, their efforts should be at social integration, using 'enlightened authority and hierarchy to achieve community'.[32] That Octavia seemed to put much of the blame for the failure of the Church in the East End upon Barnett's shoulders alone must have made the couple smart with indignation.

The reality was that neither church nor parochial organization, in an area of predominantly non-churchgoing people and, from the 1880s, accommodating a vast influx of Eastern European Jews, was appropriate or adequate for the appalling problems of the area. While the Revd Fremantle in Marylebone, years before, had been able to reach out across his parish, regardless of denomination or faith, there was a world of difference between St Mary's, Bryanston Square and St Jude's, Whitechapel which had no middle class with social or professional concerns touching the poor. The Barnetts, naïve in many respects, envisaged the personal influence and example of young Oxford and Cambridge graduates as helping to reach the urban poor of East London. It was a movement that became known as 'slumming'.

The young Oxford graduates who were attracted by these confused and confusing ideals were immediately insulated from their surroundings by the collegiate buildings of Toynbee Hall, which was designed (by the ubiquitous Elijah Hoole) with a saloon 'exactly like a West End drawing-room, erring, if at all, on the side of gorgeousness,' as Henrietta Barnett put it. This setting did little to integrate the young men with their environment. The Toynbee Hall settlers had to inveigle the community in their direction – there was no such pretext as the collection of rent with which to establish contact – and when the East Enders arrived they found a Gothic quadrangle, its rooms hung with paintings by Watts, and a rather daunting programme of educational and cultural activities. Watts was no doubt chosen since in Henrietta Barnett's words, he 'cares more than almost any man I know for art to be used to teach great lessons.'[33]

The Barnetts offered the East Enders instruction and entertainment of all kinds, but always in the form of 'vertical relationships' and with the uneasy background of what Beatrice Webb called 'the class consciousness of sin'.

A considerable distance had now opened up between Barnett's views on religion and those of his mentor, Octavia, as on the administration of charity along staunchly COS lines. The Barnetts were increasingly convinced by the environmental argument. Henrietta Barnett put Octavia's views thus: 'She expected the degraded people to live in disreputable conditions, *until* they proved themselves worthy of better one, whereas it can be argued that, for most folk, decent environment is essential to the promotion of decent life.'[34]

Finally, the Barnetts – who thought as one – were also moving towards recognition of the necessity of certain State-provided services. They came to see that the scale of social and economic problems was far beyond the grasp of any of the existing means of providing charitable support. State intervention and what they termed 'Pràcticable Socialism' (the title of their book, first published in 1888) was what they saw as the answer. They became pacifists and were strong advocates of the old age pension as early as 1883.

As Henry Nevinson said, Barnett was not afraid 'to lead a revolution against himself'. C. R. Ashbee, who stayed at Toynbee Hall in 1886, saw this as indecision, and later disguised him thinly as a character in his cultural polemic, 'A Few Chapters in Workshop Re-Construction and Citizenship', as the Revd Simeon Flux. What is certain is that the growing inflexibility of Octavia and the sometimes bewildering flexibility of Barnett was to lead to numerous misunderstandings between them, though always overlaid by long-standing affection.

Some years before, Barnett had become chairman of the Stepney Council of Public Welfare, which was, in his wife's words, 'an association born of disappointment at the settled determination of the COS to organize charity and not effort, and of the opportunity afforded by Toynbee Hall as the gathering place of innumerable social workers.'

After everything that both the Barnetts and Octavia had seen and done since the 1860s, the one area of agreement between them was a steadfast objection to municipal housing. Barnett wrote a pamphlet entitled 'The Ideal City'[35] with the aim of awakening the citizens of Bristol to a sense of pride in their city. Barnett's views presented there laid him open to Ashbee's charge of woolly-mindedness. 'The solution', he wrote, 'to the housing problem lies, as indeed lies the solution of every social problem, in the sense of fellowship founded, as I believe, on the sense of a divine relation. If English people deeply felt for their neighbours, they would have the will, and, having the will, they would find the way to prevent the evils which are destroying and degrading human beings.'

By comparison with Barnett's perorations, Octavia's approach, whatever its limitations, was much more intellectually specific and, above all, more practical.

CHAPTER 16

The established years: success and failure

OCTAVIA's work for the Ecclesiastical Commissioners in Southwark had been an enormous breakthrough. Some years later, when both Octavia and the Bishop of London were speaking in support of the COS at Fulham Palace,[1] Bishop Temple, later Archbishop of Canterbury, remembered how easily Octavia had managed in 1884 to convince him and his fellow Commissioners that she was right and they wrong. 'When she had talked to us for half an hour we were quite refuted. I never had such a beating in my life! Consequently I feel great respect for her. So fully did she convince us, that we not only did what she asked us on that estate, but proceeded to carry out similar plans on other estates.' Her eloquence on that earlier occasion[2] had led to various gifts of land, including the site for the Red Cross Hall which she persuaded the Commissioners to lease to a specially formed Trust for 999 years. Octavia was rather surprised to find how effective her pressuring had proved.[3]

The Red Cross Hall site was a burned-out paper factory in Southwark just east of Southwark Bridge Road, close to some of the Commissioners' improved dwellings, the home of around 500 families. Clearing the ground involved burning heaps of paper four or five feet deep, a job which took six weeks with fires alight day and night. However, in best Octavia fashion, everything had a purpose – the ashes turned out to be invaluable for the garden which was planned. A warehouse was demolished and the land was put into the hands of Trustees for public use.

Lady Jane Dundas gave money for the Hall and provided funds for the planned Red Cross Cottages, a project especially near to Octavia's heart, at a minimal return of 3 per cent. Elijah Hoole was the architect, in close consultation with Octavia. She had been much struck on her

travels with the generous external decoration of the houses; in particular, in the Tyrol she had admired 'the quaint irregularity of the
home-like oriel windows, set on at the corner of the tiny houses in the
village streets, with pretty little separate conical roofs, and I seemed to
see that this home-like irregularity, this prominence of roof, this
simplicity of brick ornament, could be at once applied to our people's
houses.'[4]

Southwark was hardly the Tyrol, but the gables and red hanging
tiles, the ornamental windows overlooking the garden, were in the
picturesque spirit of the houses which had charmed her.

In June 1888 the Archbishop of Canterbury opened the Hall and the
garden alongside. It was a perfect day, the Kyrle Society choir sang
and Hardwick Rawnsley sent one of his feebler poems – Octavia called
it a sonnet – to commemorate the occasion. Red Cross Hall itself
appeared in Hoole's drawings as a vast medieval space, with a fine
hammerbeam roof-structure – like a slightly reduced Westminster
Hall. The reality was a little humbler. Walter Crane designed a series
of panels for the Hall, depicting Heroic Deeds, including a recent local
tragedy in which a young girl, Alice Ayres, had lost her life rescuing
three children from a fire in Southwark. This had great poignancy,
since many of the local residents had known the victims and some had
witnessed the fire itself. Crane's busy life meant that the murals
arrived intermittently, but other episodes he commemorated included
the death of a group of navvies on the railway, and the rescue of a child
from a well near Basingstoke. The money for these was raised by an
appeal in *The Times*, since it was beyond the resources of the Kyrle
Society. In his autobiography Crane commented that the Hall was not
an ideal setting for such work and that the gas lighting had damaged
the panels.

Mrs Russell Barrington, in a pamphlet describing Crane's scheme
of murals (far from complete in 1890), referred to Octavia as 'the good
Squiress of the great village'. It was a rural imagery that the little Red
Cross scheme hankered after, with a scale to match. The success of the
six Red Cross cottages persuaded the Ecclesiastical Commissioners to
grant a lease on more land for a further six – the White Cross cottages.
The scheme, almost incongruous in an area of industrial premises and
industrial dwellings, was so popular that the cottages were let before
they had been completed.

Sydney Cockerell, her old friend's young son and namesake, who
had come to work for Octavia on the recommendation of Edward

Bond, described the garden in a letter to *The Times* sixty years after the project began. It had been laid out partly as a covered playground and partly as a pretty garden, with two plane trees with seats round them, a bandstand, a bridge and a little pond with goldfish. (Sir Robert Hunter had provided the latter.) Going back after the Second World War, he found it all gone, recently asphalted by Southwark Borough Council and bereft of flowers, shrubs or any other relics of the brave venture.

The Hall, designed to be the focus of community life, quickly attracted its own activities and, as at Barrett's Court, functioned as a Working Men's Club – Sydney Cockerell was its secretary from early 1887. Just as his father had once fielded a torrent of Octavia's letters relating to the detailed arrangements of the work at Barrett's Court, so for a few years young Sydney (who had at the age of five appeared on the stage at the Barrett's Court Club) became the recipient of an equally incessant stream. Octavia left no detail to chance: would he pursue the replacement of a defunct gas meter ('will you write very indignantly?'); could he call in to look at a collection of stuffed birds that had been offered to the tenants? She worried about the rent level that the Working Men's Club should pay and the kind of lease the members would like. Then there was the question of what sort of entertainment should be on offer. Octavia was 'a little afraid about getting an audience for lectures of the more interesting kind without magic lanterns or explosions.'

In Marylebone, at St Christopher's Hall, built by Harriot Yorke, an ambitious programme of activities had developed, with the emphasis on entertainment. From the late 1880s until 1911 there were regular annual productions of Gilbert and Sullivan operettas, the cast made up of workers and tenants. The organizers here were the Hamers, Sam and William, their sisters – one of whom worked for Octavia there on leaving school – and their friends. The illustrator Arthur Rackham painted scenery for at least one production and also took part. Roles had to be distributed with considerable tact, lest the tenants felt that they were being excluded. The Hamers remembered Octavia at some of the evenings, in particular her energetic enjoyment of the Sir Roger de Coverley which ended the evening. The events were free, everyone coming as Harriot Yorke's guests.[5]

At the Red Cross Hall, Sydney handed over his secretarial duties to Miss Bartlett in the summer of 1889 but carried on his general duties at the Club and Committee. He was also becoming involved in the

Society for the Protection of Ancient Buildings (SPAB), William Morris's society. Octavia wrote to him: 'I am delighted you are getting some congenial society among the Anti-Scrape'– the Society had been founded to check the over-zealous restoration of medieval buildings, hence its nickname. Before long he was on the SPAB Committee, and he also spent time at Toynbee Hall. His regular work, in the office of his family's coal firm, was disagreeable to him but Octavia encouraged him to take a partnership there, probably to give him financial stability. In 1892, however, he gave up the unequal struggle and began to work for William Morris at the Kelmscott Press.

Morris was generally an admirer of Octavia's work, even if he questioned the detail. In much the same spirit, Octavia read his work and found it stimulating. As far back as 1868 she reread the poem, *The Life and Death of Jason* – 'It is marvellous to me how any one can so throw himself into so noble a time without Christianity; the hint of deeper meaning is so telling, and goes so home, because it is only suggested and kept subservient to the intense realism of the scenes and incidents . . . It is true poetry.'[6] Five years later she found it 'so old-world as to be a refreshment to those mixed up with nineteenth-century things. The images are lovely . . . but the sustained melancholy of the whole poem is very terrible.' She had been looking forward to see how he would treat a Christian subject, and was disappointed that he did not write his promised *St Dorothea*.

Octavia and young Sydney remained good friends, exchanging letters about Olive, his sister and her god-daughter,[7] who caused them both a great deal of worry, and drawn together by the memory of Sydney Cockerell senior[8] and perhaps, in the shadows, the connection forged through Edward Bond. Sydney continued to keep Octavia informed about his employer, including some surprising, and intimate, snippets of Morris's personal history. 'I had no idea that William Morris had ever thought of the church! It is very evident that he saw his way clearly. I hope his mother responded,' Octavia wrote in 1897.

On Sydney's engagement to Florence Kingsford both Miranda and Octavia sent warm letters ('I am prepared to love any one you love, and who makes you happy,' Octavia wrote). The following year, 1908, he became the Director of the Fitzwilliam Museum in Cambridge and before long was the father of an expanding family, Octavia welcoming them one by one.

As at St Christopher's Buildings, life in and around the Red Cross Hall was the focus of the community. A visitor remembered:

the slim, springy, fighting figure of Mrs Julian Marshall conducting her orchestra for the entertainment of Miss Octavia's Southwark tenants. And there is Miss Octavia herself, benignly surveying the scene from the uttermost back of the Hall, not that she may hear the better, but because, as she says, she likes to watch their faces – the faces of her poor whom she is slowly but surely civilizing.[9]

The Trustees decided to invite working men on to the Managing Committee of the Red Cross Hall, and people respected and enjoyed these new amenities to an extent which surprised Octavia, though the unruly minority sometimes caused her to lose faith in 'her people'. Over the years the Committee included representatives of various supportive organizations, notably the Women's University Settlement and the Borough Polytechnic. Maud Lewes, one of Octavia's nieces, was on the committee for some time. Each year there was a Report, with the usual scrupulous accounts presented by Octavia as Treasurer.

As at the Barrett's Court Club, the Red Cross Hall band was well supported and prospered, and Octavia also had plans for a cadet corps, following the example of Samuel Barnett who had organized the first such corps in 1885, reporting that the Whitechapel Corps had been the making of many a lad. In May 1889 the inaugural meeting of the Southwark Corps was held, presided over by Viscount Wolseley.[10] Octavia could have hardly found a more distinguished soldier but it was typical of her to aim high. For once she did not have the support of all her family in one of her ventures. Her mother seemed to have made her views clear, for Octavia wrote in reply:

> Of course I realize all you say about war; but I do not feel any doubts about the Volunteer Cadet Corps; for at least three reasons. First, I do feel defensive war right . . . Secondly, because the volunteer movement seems to me a helpful form of preparation to take . . . Thirdly, because I do so clearly see that exercise, discipline, obedience, *esprit-de-corps*, camping out, manly companionship . . . will be to our Southwark lads the very best possible education.

Emily, with her husband a life-long pacifist, shared her mother's doubts.

The Corps attracted 160 cadets, with many more refused. Cadet drill was held at Red Cross Hall, rent free. In 1890 the Corps and the band took part in the Lord Mayor's Procession, which helped encourage and increase its membership. Octavia was having trouble persuading the War Office to pay for brighter uniforms than the dull green that the parent unit wore. Ingenious to the last, she wrote to Eton College, suggesting a link between their Hackney Wick Mission Corps and that in Southwark; they accepted and helped pay for a smart red uniform which Octavia felt would do much to cheer the dull Southwark streets.[11]

Other missions and Settlements also promoted the cadet movement. It had clear objectives: 'The provision of interesting occupation for the evening hours of London working boys, especially for those of an enterprising and active character, and the inculcation of habits of order, discipline, cleanliness, punctuality & good conduct, thus developing self-respect at an age (13 to 18) when most susceptible to good or evil influences, and when character is forming.' It had provided large numbers of recruits into all the services but 'takes into its ranks only genuine working boys . . . to allow grown-up sons of comparatively well-to-do people in the ranks, would be to miss the object of the existence of the corps.'

Armed with Maritini-Metford Artillery carbine and bayonet, the Southwark Corps became the Senior Cadet Battalion in the country,[12] soon numbering almost 400. Colonel Albert Salmond commanded the company and Octavia was nominated as an Honorary Colonel; eventually it became the 1st Cadet Battalion of the Royal West Surrey Regiment. Henry Nevinson,[13] who had commanded the Whitechapel Corps, became involved once the six London cadet corps were amalgamated into a battalion. (It was, Nevinson was sure, Octavia's name that gained them War Office recognition and funds; he said that when she chaired the meetings at which six or eight officers were present, she reminded him of Queen Elizabeth, with her admirals and explorers.[14])

The Corps was to suffer numerous fatalities in the Boer War, including the death of their commander Colonel Salmond. In the 1903 'Letter to Fellow-workers' Octavia discussed a memorial to these dead in the shape of rebuilding the meeting-house in Union Street. A fund-raising meeting was held at the Admiralty, arranged by Lady Selborne whose husband was First Lord of the Admiralty and who was one of Octavia's staunchest supporters, both in building houses in Southwark and in helping with the work. Lord Methuen was chairman, the Bishop of Stepney spoke, and the Hill family were there in force. The work had already begun and, as Octavia wrote in the annual Letter, there was £200 left to find.

Octavia's concerns in the 1880s were so many that she could not engross herself in the problem areas with the same intensity as before. Another major fight on open spaces had begun; this time it was a renewed threat to Parliament Hill Fields which had first given cause for worry in 1875. Petitions to save it from development included one from the co-operative movement who sent in 2,000 working men's signatures and another from fifty East End clergymen.

During October and November of 1885 Octavia was back in the fray on this account. It was an issue which crossed all the divisions; class, wealth and position were immaterial in the battle to keep development at bay. A Hampstead Heath Committee, 'a large strong, determined one', was aiming to get a parliamentary Bill passed. Lord Mansfield, the owner of Kenwood House, met Shaw-Lefevre and Robert Hunter from the Commons Preservation Society. Elizabeth Sturge, one of Octavia's helpers in 1886, was sent to collect signatures for the petition for Parliament Hill from Oxford Street shopkeepers, all of whom were signally uninterested in the campaign.[15]

Despite that, the campaigners could soon sound a note of triumph. Miranda sent a telegram to Octavia in Scotland, telling her that the Heath Bill was passed. Octavia declared, 'I do really think that makes it nearly sure that we shall have 50 acres saved and every acre saved makes the saving of other more likely.'[16] Money had to be raised to buy Parliament Hill Fields from the Metropolitan Board of Works and two private landowners, and so successful did the fund-raising prove that there was a surplus.

The Ecclesiastical Commissioners, under Octavia's encouragement, had now begun to build cottages themselves; first nine in Southwark, rising to fourteen on that site, then more in Westminster – all under the care of Octavia and her workers. In the spring of 1889 she was talking to Elijah Hoole about yet more cottages; 'he was so nice. He is just going to Wells, where you know he is building some cottages for the Bishop. I am so glad to have given him the introduction.'

Another new venture concerned nine recently completed blocks called Ossington Buildings, very close to Nottingham Place and overlooking one of Octavia's recently acquired open spaces. It included a laundry, for which Octavia was not responsible, and the repairs remained the responsibility of the company who had built them. After two years the company gave up the arrangement with Octavia, since dual management did not work. Octavia found the tenants remarkably respectable, so that perhaps her degree of close stewardship was unnecessary.[17] The owners gave Octavia charge of some other, less amenable, tenants.

Octavia was beginning to plan ahead. In middle age, she realized that the work might soon have to continue without her. One expedient was to set up a number of trusts, whose trustees would be family and long-term supporters, sympathetic to and familiar with her aims. They would sustain her schemes in her lifetime or after it. The first had in fact been the Red Cross Trust, the second was the Horace Street Trust. When Mrs Russell Gurney, a friend whom she had lost touch with many years before, the wife of the Recorder of London, wrote to tell her that she had left her a block of model dwellings, Westbourne Buildings in Paddington, Octavia combined these with the Horace Street properties and over the years added other property to them. It continued to grow after her death and in 1921 the Red and White Cross cottages were included. Eventually this became the Octavia Hill and Rowe Housing Trust.

In Edinburgh, there was considerable interest in Octavia's activities in the 1880s. As so often seems to have been the case, this interest was aroused by a young woman who knew of Octavia's work. Patrick Geddes's[18] fiancée, Anna Morton, suggested that he spend some time in London looking at philanthropic activities and in particular Octavia's work. He and a Mr Oliphant duly went to London to meet her.

The Edinburgh Social Union, which was set up along COS lines in 1885, was initially the outcome of Geddes's observations of Octavia's work. In 1886 Anna Morton founded a girls' club and from 1887 to 1894 the Geddes lived in a rundown tenement building in considerable discomfort, in order to witness conditions at first hand.[19] Geddes became distracted from the Edinburgh Social Union by other activities which were to lead to the Outlook Tower venture, set up in 1895.[20] From this basis he pursued various ventures including an Open Spaces Scheme, begun in 1907, which owed much to the Kyrle Society. His sister went to Dublin in 1911 to continue the work there.[21]

R. B. Haldane's sister Elizabeth was another Edinburgh girl who came to work with Octavia in 1884, and was the driving force behind the Edinburgh Social Union – which for a short period was the first such body called upon to co-operate with a municipal authority. She explained how it had been inspired:

> Green at Oxford and Toynbee in the East End were bringing home our responsibilities . . . We were red-hot with the idea of social service – the idea that forced us to look out for methods not of simply doing good to others, but of identifying our lives with theirs . . . it seemed to us that this social spirit was being in great measure realized in the particular system of ownership which had been worked out by Miss Hill. I don't think on looking back that Miss Hill's view was quite ours. She belonged to the earlier generation – to the broad-minded, large-hearted school of Frederick Denison Maurice and Charles Kingsley. But the result was the same though the road taken might have been a little different.

One difference to which she was perhaps referring was the lack of professionalism which Octavia's generation exhibited – despite their efficiency.

Elizabeth Haldane, who served on the MacDonnell Royal Commission on the Civil Service in 1913, one of only two women on it, had gone to work for Octavia when she was twenty. She had helped in one of the playgrounds and also at the annual Maypole Festival. She noted that 'its quaint picturesqueness, set in the midst of the dreary surroundings of a London slum, was clearly the result of Ruskin's teaching.' Later on she went to learn more about the technicalities of the housing management work, in preparation for the establishment of the Edinburgh Union.[22]

By 1900 they were managing the entire housing stock owned by the City Council, but the conflict between tenants and their vote caught the lady managers in the middle. The situation was so difficult that they handed back their responsibilities to the Council. Octavia kept in close touch with the work in Edinburgh, and went there to address their annual meeting a number of times. The problems they encountered reinforced her prejudice against municipal intervention in housing.

On her travels abroad, which were now a regular part of Octavia's routine to ensure that there would be no further collapses from strain and overwork, she was always observant. These breaks allowed her to think about the work in a broader context; she had little aptitude or inclination towards a theoretical or analytical approach but certain issues puzzled her. A holiday in Switzerland in 1885 prompted some thoughts about owner–occupation, which she shared with her mother. 'I wonder if we shall live to see a larger number of English owners?. . . I doubt the tenants caring to buy *much* for occupation. . . few, I fancy, desire to bind themselves to one spot and way of life. They like the freedom and the change of hiring.' Even young married couples, who might be expected to settle, will move with a change of job or a larger house. 'Some little sense of individuality would be quickly stamped, even on London houses, if they were owned by occupiers.'[23]

Later in the year Octavia spent her birthday with the MacDonalds in their new house, Casa Coraggio, and enjoyed the company of little Octavia, her god-daughter and namesake, whose grandmother was looking after her following her mother Grace's death. On 10 December, George MacDonald's birthday, they played charades.

The peace of the Genoan Riviera was shattered one day when seven men-of-war appeared off the coast, having a practice fight. 'We could see them all confused in the smoke, and the great heaving mass of water somehow caused by the firing.'[24] As usual, the MacDonalds were getting up some Christmas tableaux which they performed for local peasants, apparently to their delight.

From there Octavia went on to join Lady Ducie at Menton and Nice, where her old friend had herself been recovering from an illness. She was now much better, and they drove in a little basket carriage, drawn by a pair of small ponies, along the Mediterranean coast, enjoying the olives and cypresses, vivid blue sea and craggy promontories.

Her journey home was comfortable: she travelled from Marseilles to Dijon in a carriage with six ladies – a reassuring crowd, she told Emily. Her sister was herself setting out for Italy, to stay with the MacDonalds and then venture further south; Octavia gave her some tips. Siena was quite the most lovely and interesting city she knew, and 'as to Assisi, it is just a vision of angels; it is like having looked thro' the gates of heaven for a season.'[25]

Return to London brought a rude awakening from these golden memories. Soon after Octavia came back, London was rocked by the unemployment riots of 1886, culminating in Bloody Sunday, 13 November 1887.[26] For the first time the comfortable citizens of the West End and the suburbs were being made aware of the desperation of the urban poor. Octavia did not distrust political action *per se* – she was sure that working men could organize perfectly orderly gatherings – but was deeply suspicious of the part played by the Social Democratic Federation, Henry Hyndman's socialist organization, in these riots. She convinced herself that outside agitators had stirred up the ferment. The riots had not aggravated the state of affairs in Deptford but there were always lurking worries; the properties and tenants that Octavia took on in Queen Street, Deptford caused her more constant worry than any she had yet encountered, even in the frightening early days at Barrett's Court.

In the dreadful winter of 1885/6 the Deptford houses had suffered from blocked and frozen gutters which had then flooded the houses and meant that the internal repairs had to be done all over again. The tenants had not been angry, merely listless.[27] A year or two before that, she had been prepared to consider Queen Street a defeat; the tenants were immune to calls upon their sense of responsibility and care. 'I am bound to record this street as a failure up to now.'

In the early months of 1886, however, Queen Street seemed to be calm and relatively untouched by the political and social turmoil. It all proved the efficacy of her approach to the tenants. She wrote to Emily:

> Of course, after such a breakdown of police administration, one feels as if one *might* meet violence *any*where; but I think of all places I should feel . . . safest in Deptford. That this is so marks progress that I had hardly realized till your post-card recalled the old state of things. The people are gentle, responsive, and tractable there, if sometimes a little ill-tempered – that is the worst. At least I know they would stand by us.'[28]

One result of the riots was a panicky outpouring of money from London's well-to-do. The Mansion House relief fund, for instance, reached £20,000 in almost no time. Octavia was desperately concerned about this. 'It is a dreadful calamity, this fund being formed.' By late February the fund had swelled to £70,000. 'This miserable huge fund, which can be used for nothing radical, won't help.' The COS also saw this fund, and its implications of indiscriminate, untargeted charity, as a disaster: 'The Mansion House Fund, its terrible mistakes and failures, have occupied us a great deal.'

Nevertheless something had to be done with the money. Octavia reported: 'the most utter confusion prevails; and the crowd of regular roughs awes some into giving soup tickets!' Working men were getting relief, falsified vouchers were being handed out: 'the City Missionary at Deptford says that, if the money had been thrown into the sea, it would have been better.'

It is difficult for us to grasp the horror that Octavia and those like her felt for a crisis appeal which was overwhelmingly successful. But their feelings must be seen against a lifetime's work of trying to raise money, alleviate conditions and campaign for a wide range of amenities where none existed. Suddenly a tidal wave of money had appeared, and it was disappearing, without account or justification, at alarming speed.

But for Octavia the daily work of patiently chipping away at the foundations of poverty continued, and became no easier. It was a relief, she wrote, to come home and plant her hyacinth bulbs after a wearing day in Deptford. At dinner with Lord Hobhouse she had met a Mr Ghose, an Indian, whose brother was standing for Deptford. 'Lord H says he would not have a chance with a middle-class or rich constituency; but that there is a strong feeling among the working men that he ought to get in.'[29]

The situation at Deptford improved considerably with the arrival in 1886 of Ellen Chase, an American worker who seemed to find no problem insurmountable. She worked there for six years and her published account, *Tenant Friends in Old Deptford*, gives considerable insight into the work, and Octavia's 'method', as it was to become known. From the beginning Ellen saw that the work was a two-way process. 'The insight into human nature and the knowledge of what is really essential that these full happy years of work brought to me personally has been one of the richest gains of my whole life.' Because of the pressure of work, Ellen Chase had a baptism of fire. Instead of being trained in a well-equipped and established property in Marylebone, a receiving-ship for new workers, Ellen was immediately 'on the firing-line, so to say, in the South-East'.

Queen Street was already established as a problem property, yet 'it was not the bareness of living, but the richness of life that struck me most in Green [her disguise for Queen] Street, since what really matters was there, as everywhere else, within the reach of all.' While the object of improving character was uppermost in the workers' minds, 'the business relation, upon which the whole rests, is a most real one.' There were accounts, repairs to be decided on, organized and checked, references for incoming tenants to be followed up – the first reference to any such system in Octavia's properties – and notices to be served if rents were in arrears.

Then there was the matter of tactfully dealing with all the personalities. Utterly resilient, Ellen reported the worst of it: one tenant had wrecked his garden and would not show himself; another tenant offered no payment and so she was given notice. But she was reducing the unlet properties. Perhaps as an American she was less easily classified as a 'lady' or 'not a lady' and was treated with more confidence by the tenants. Octavia referred to her after one difficult patch as 'bright as a sunbeam'.

Ellen pointed out the challenge of 'the actual meeting and solving of successive problems, just as in the private life of a family. Indeed, in time the property with which one is connected comes to hold almost the place of an enlarged family, tied together by mutual affection and service.'

The forty-eight houses in Queen Street belonged to a City gentleman who had taken an eighteen-year lease, believing that a tram-line was due to be cut through the street, which would secure him ample compensation. Finding that this was not the case, he had approached Octavia Hill to act as agent, supervising three volunteer workers – Mrs Lord, Anna Hogg from Dublin (another particularly trusted helper) and Ellen herself.

> Out of consideration for the neglected state of the property, the owner, in addition to the usual 5 per cent commission to the agent, made the further liberal allowance of three shillings in the pound for current repairs. In return, he expected to have the houses kept in a habitable condition, the rents collected, and a repair list sent in accompanied by vouchers, when his quarterly cheques were forwarded to him at Lady Day, Midsummer, Michaelmas and Christmas.

Octavia was always unsure of the gentleman's commitment, whether he would sell or fulfil his promise to spend some money on the houses 'with a view to raising the property' and she added, the people. As agents, they had:

a right to deal . . . with the outward surroundings of the people . . .
Moreover having to do with the family as a whole, and constantly
seeing the people in their home-life before a crisis as well as in the
stress of trouble, we had unusual advantages for arriving at something like a true appreciation of their difficulties, failings, and
triumphs. The details of management were left wholly in our
hands. We were allowed to govern our little domain as we liked and
make of it what we could.

The women decided amongst applicants for the rooms, who should be
neighbours to whom, who had to leave for persistent non-payment of
rent, and 'who were ready for added comforts, and who must show
greater care of what they had, before they were entitled to more.' It
was a curious mixture of clear-headed housing management, recognizable as such today, and moral guardianship – the hidden agenda to
the social concern.

Octavia fluctuated in mood over Deptford. In 1892 it was a 'black
sheep' but in 1893 there was a chink of light: 'under a firm, a vigilant
and a wise rule even the Deptford poor people are beginning to feel the
blessings of government. There is a marked improvement.' In 1894
pressure of work, and her continued optimism, allowed her to hand
over Deptford to the principal worker there, Ellen Chase having
returned to the USA in 1893.

Octavia observed that her workers were all the better for a spot of
difficulty and resistance; 'it tests them, and draws them together . . .
All my workers have stood to their guns splendidly, and have been so
helpful too.' The old grit was still part of Octavia's character even in
these years of achievement and support for her work and campaigns.
But in Deptford unprecedented and continuous trouble with tenants
and the poor condition of the houses finally persuaded her that they
should be demolished; a few years later their site became a main road.
Presumably the landlord received his compensation, as intended.

Deptford was to be Octavia's major failure. Houses that she took on
in Notting Hill from 1886 onwards, in Horace Street and later
elsewhere in the neighbourhood, were to be a worry, but they 'came
round' eventually, whilst Queen Street proved finally insoluble. The
cause lay in the fact that the tenants did not have a secure prospect, and
thus had no commitment to the place. Morale must have been affected
by the landlord's attitude and the fact that the houses were, in modern
terminology, 'short-life'. All the cajoling of their conscientious

managers was ineffective against these harsh realities. Fifteen years earlier, Octavia had remarked on the problem of some houses which were known to be earmarked for demolition – 'the knowledge that they were coming down made all the bad tenants cease to pay.'

Nor, despite money spent on repairs, could the cottages be said to be well built or in good structural condition. Deptford was far from the other centres of work and its staff therefore changed more than usual. Added to these problems was the rapid rise of domestic rates in the early 1890s (ironically, in order to pay for those legislative and sanitary improvements that Octavia had fought for so tenaciously). Octavia insisted that her tenants should pay these rates themselves, in order that they should be more aware of and politically involved with expenditure on municipal projects.

In many of Octavia's properties, the passage of years produced a stable group of tenants, who in turn attracted those who appreciated the sound management offered. Tenancies in Octavia's houses were much sought after. Good tenants produced stability, stability produced good tenants. If Octavia was unable to offer the Deptford tenants the prospect of housing in the long term, then there was little inducement to prompt payment of rent, and so the incremental work upon the fabric of the houses and the moral fibre of the tenants was wasted effort.

CHAPTER 17

The established years: recognition and new directions

O CTAVIA turned fifty in 1888. The occasion seems to have passed uneventfully. She told Henrietta Barnett, 'The day is one on which the words of old friends seem to bear a special value – I see few indeed of them now as I spend what of the day is not needed for work quietly with my mother.'[1]

Octavia's correspondence in her middle years is full of the names of the famous and influential. She was unimpressed by her grand connections, her only purpose being to interest people in the work and persuade them to contribute money or, better still, time and effort. At a big party at the Red Cross Hall, early in 1886, 'Lord S. [the Earl of Stamford, a Trustee] came looking *very* clean and prim. I set him soon to bring some very dusty chairs and so broke the formality; and he was soon waltzing away with one of the tenants.'

Octavia's regular visits to the Ducies brought her into contact with a range of interesting and influential people slightly outside the philanthropic and charitable circles in which she moved. She met and liked Lord Aberdare, Gladstone's Home Secretary in 1868, and enjoyed her talks with him. James Russell Lowell, poet and US minister to Britain gave her an opportunity to discuss poetry, especially the merits of the Brownings. She was continually broadening her range of contacts. One suspects that many of them received letters drawing their attention to a particular cause or appeal in the weeks and months after they made Octavia's acquaintance. Occasionally the roles were reversed. C. R. Ashbee wrote to Octavia in 1888 asking her to support his Technical and Art School for East London (to become the Guild of Handicraft), but she replied courteously that she had too many commitments already.[2]

In 1887 Octavia received an invitation to join the distinguished people who were offered seats in Westminster Abbey for the Service of Thanksgiving for the Queen's Golden Jubilee. With Josephine Butler, the social reformer who fought against the abuses of the white slave trade and prostitution, and Florence Nightingale, Octavia was invited as one of the three women who had most influenced the course of Victorian Britain. She was probably the only person in her circle taken by surprise: to everyone but herself she was a famous figure by now.

21 June was a public holiday. The Abbey had been transformed to squeeze as many seats as possible into its area and according to the *Annual Register* it was an extraordinary scene – enlivened by exotic figures such as a bevy of Indian princes bejewelled from head to foot and the Queen of Hawaii, decked out in 'a large number of Hawaiian orders'. The Abbey was full by 10 a.m., foreign royalty arrived at midday and the Queen at 12.30. An hour later it was all over.

In 1890 Octavia sent a hurried note to Gertrude, 'to ask whether you could *absolutely* easily lend me the carriage to go to Marlborough House tomorrow afternoon.' She had been invited to meet the Queen, 'weather permitting'. Typically unselfconscious, 'I don't care a straw for going queerly if I get in all right but I wonder whether a Hansom would be admitted.'

In the same year the Prince of Wales opened Vauxhall Park, or 'The Lawn' as Octavia called it. Her contact with royalty had survived Princess Alice's death. Princess Louise was patron of the Kyrle Society and letters still came from Darmstadt, from Princess Victoria who was carrying on her mother's work. She applied to Octavia concerning the care of abandoned illegitimate children. 'My mother entirely agreed with your opinion of the superiority of home education and there exists no large orphanage in Hesse. The ladies of the Alice Society see that the children are in the charge of respectable people and properly cared for.' However, at the age of six these children passed from the supervision of the police (with which the Alice Society helped) to that of school officials. If the children were classed as paupers, these individuals had sole charge and the Society could do no more for them. England was a richer country than Germany and 'knowing how far in advance England is in most charitable branches I offered to try and get some information.' She was hesitant to trouble Octavia, knowing how busy she was, but 'I know of no one else in England who can give me the necessary information.' Octavia was becoming a resort for all who wanted advice on social and welfare issues.

Queen Victoria with Princess Alice (left) and Princess Louise – both the Princesses took an interest in Octavia's work.

George MacDonald as Evangelist in the family
production of *Pilgrim's Progress* (see page 200):
photograph by Robert F. MacDonald.

The MacDonald women at Portofino, c.1878 – daughters Irene, Lilia, Grace, and Winifred,
and Mrs MacDonald (right).

Left: Emma Cons: 'Such marvellous loyalty, such sweetness of temper,' Octavia wrote of her. Right: Harriot Yorke, Octavia's dependable companion from 1878 onwards: 'She says little and does so much.'

Casa Corragio at Bordighera – the Italian villa built for the MacDonald family through the generosity of their friends, Octavia and her sisters included.

Miranda, in later years – the friendship and collaboration between her and Octavia was remarkable, even in a family of close loyalties.

The Red Cross Cottages, designed by Octavia and Elijah Hoole and built in Southwark in 1888. The Red and White Cross Cottages are now in Ayres St.

Larksfield at Crockham Hill: a vernacular revival cottage, hung with soft red tiles.

The Warren, Crockham Hill, owned by Gertrude Lewes.

The seat on Mariner's Hill dedicated by the family in memory of Caroline Southwood Hill (see page 317).

Long Crendon Court House, Buckinghamshire, c.1895: one of the earliest properties that Octavia helped acquire for the National Trust (see page 306).

Octavia towards the end of her life: 'wonderful brown eyes and a deep voice'.

Octavia's marble effigy, now in Crockham Hill Church: it was begun by Miss Abbott and finished by Edmund Burton.

The christening party in 1908 of Elinor and Carrington Ouvry's son Norman, at The Warren. Harriot Yorke is second from left, back row; Octavia is fifth from left, back row, with Miranda, half-hidden, next to her. Elinor is seated third from right, with Romilly Ouvry on her lap; Emily is seated second from right and Gertrude (Lewes) next to her.

In 1887 an event occurred that gave Octavia enormous pleasure: the healing, at last, of her rift with Ruskin. It came about through the good offices of Sydney Cockerell who was going to visit Ruskin and offered his services. Octavia did not want him to precipitate a discussion on the subject but: 'If you felt as if any mention of me, or the work you help me in, comes under this head, I should be greatly delighted.'[3]

On Cockerell's second visit to the old man of Brantwood, this time with his sister, Octavia's god-daughter Olive, 'I felt so much emboldened to allude to his lamentable quarrel with Octavia Hill, which had kept them apart for ten years.' Ruskin did not respond well. Cockerell was nineteen, Ruskin almost seventy. And Ruskin had many grievances in addition to the central quarrel with Octavia about the St George's Guild. 'He did not like the way she dressed – her mother fretted him, and so on. "Will you not now forgive Miss Hill," I urged, though in my heart I felt that forgiveness was at least as much due from her as from him. "I never forgive," he answered firmly: "it was too great an injury. And yet I *can* forgive," he added after a pause.'[4]

Later on, this time in London, Cockerell decided to return to the subject. Again Octavia urged caution: 'think *only* of what is best for Mr Ruskin.' But now feeling more loyal to Octavia, 'under whose guidance I was then diligently sowing my philanthropic wild oats,' Cockerell felt:

> I must needs do it, even if it cost me his inestimable friendship. I returned to the charge that I abandoned at Brantwood, first gently, and then vehemently. I took him to task and . . . insisted on his forgiving her and cancelling the peccant leaves in *Fors*. At first he appeared obdurate but Olive . . . seconded me bravely and we continued the attack until finally he could but surrender to our alternative demands and entreaties. Quite vanquished, he owned that he had misjudged her, promised to do whatever we asked of him . . . kissed us both, joined our hands, gave us an affectionate blessing and bade us farewell, we being touched to the heart and in tears.[5]

The letter that Ruskin wrote to Olive is deeply moving in its contrition; some months later Sydney sent it to Octavia. Ruskin was bewildered and cast down after their meeting, but closing the rift meant asking forgiveness:

[257]

nor that for error merely but for total wrongness in all one's thought – in all one's angers – in all one's pride. And while I see the disease now clearly, I am not yet the least convinced that my thoughts of city and country work were wrong. This is what I have to think out, in whatever I write to explain my abolishing those wild numbers.[6]

He referred, of course, to the injurious issues of *Fors Clavigera*.

As Walter de la Mare wrote to Sydney Cockerell in 1935, after reading those letters: 'I hardly know which astonishes me more – the boy's intrepidity in suggesting the reconciliation with Octavia Hill or John Ruskin's magnanimity in welcoming it and even confessing himself to have been wholly in the wrong.'[7] The rapprochement had the advantage of re-establishing the link between them before Ruskin died, in 1900.

Octavia was more forgiving than Ruskin deserved. In the spring of 1889 she wrote to Cockerell that the 'difficulties' with Ruskin in the past were 'mists and clouds which will be one day cleared away'. More important, 'all that Mr Ruskin is and has always been of good and great is quite independent of such things.'[8] After reading Collingwood's *Life of Ruskin*, which Cockerell had sent her, she admitted that some of it was 'exquisitely painful' but held that silence was the only path. 'Time is needed, Time and to be let alone. Nothing is all I can do, but that I will do if I may.'[9]

By the time of Ruskin's death, Octavia was confident enough to be his champion, and to uphold his ideals when the question of his memorial arose. 'To place anything in Westminster Abbey to the memory of one whose teaching was against anything modern tampering with ancient buildings seems to me a strange anomaly.'[10]

It was Cockerell, too, who reinforced the link between William Morris and Octavia. He kept her constantly supplied with Morris's works. He sent *A Dream of John Ball* (in 1890) about the Peasant Uprising of 1381, and the following summer a 'pamphlet' (probably *News from Nowhere*). Octavia thought:

the miseries of the middle ages [were] slurred over in a marvellous manner! . . . it gives the sense of a crooked way of looking at things. On the other hand I felt heartily one with the author in his longing to better things, and tried hard to see if he threw any fresh light. In fact I thought the *aim* of the book helpful, but nothing else.[11]

From this time on, Morris's books were beautifully produced on his own press, the Kelmscott Press. The first volume produced was an elegant reprint of Ruskin's chapter on the Gothic from *The Stones of Venice*, with a preface by Morris himself. Octavia supported his idea of the craftsman, 'the home joy which glorifies and gladdens the daily work'. She did not want to explain away the misery and unhealthy conditions of much modern work, but she thought Morris unduly emphasized it.[12]

By 1894 Cockerell had become William Morris's 'right hand', as May Morris, his daughter, termed it. In 1892 he had been given the job of cataloguing Morris's library in his new house in Hammersmith – a house which Octavia knew well for it was the Retreat which Morris had bought from the MacDonald family in 1878, renaming it Kelmscott House.[13]

Octavia was greatly interested in the moves to set up a Women's University Settlement in Southwark, and joined the Committee in 1889, although initially she had some doubts about women living without family ties. It was the first Settlement dependent on women volunteers, and was headed by Miss Margaret Sewell, a staunch advocate of COS principles. Following the opening in 1891, the Settlement asked to be allowed to use the Red Cross Hall for some lectures. Octavia felt this was an ideal arrangement, since it would bring together a large group of like-minded people.

> The members interest me much. They are all very refined, highly cultivated (all, I fancy, having been at one of the Universities) and *very* young. I feel quite a veteran among them; and they are so sweet and humble and keen to learn about the things out of their old line of experience. I much delight in thinking one may link their young life with the houses, and hall, and garden in Southwark.[14]

Writing to Margaret Shaen, who had been ill, Octavia suggested that she stand for election to the Women's University Settlement Committee. It met once a month and was well conducted by Miss Sewell. 'Through her one comes into touch with that second stage of life – the one of helping others – which opens out to so many Girton, Newnham and other girls in this age of service.' It was also, as Sir Frederick Maurice in his autobiography pointed out, part of a line descending from his father's original foundation, the Working Men's College.

Toynbee Hall, the Oxford House, the Working Women's College and many like efforts, of which the name is legion, including in some measure 'slumming' – though of course that often takes a vulgar form from its period of fashionability – and all Miss Hill's work, are the true brothers, sisters and cousins of the Working Men's College, and most of them acknowledge the family connection.[15]

The Women's University Settlement supplied women for a wide range of social work – much as its male counterparts did. It provided many of Octavia's best workers in the 1890s and 1900s and she gave an account of its progress, year to year, in her 'Letter to Fellow-workers'. One of Octavia's schemes, with the WUS, was to enrol district visitors who would work with a small group of families. It would be the same kind of work as in housing management, but since the actual housing would not be their responsibility, the contact would be made by means of a savings collection. 'We shall gradually add . . . such work for the various legal and voluntary bodies' and 'unite the human sympathy of the old-fashioned district visitor with the wise methods of action now better understood.'[16]

Unlike Toynbee Hall and other Settlements for men, which became 'informal social laboratories where future civil servants, social investigators and established politicians could informally work out new principles of social policy',[17] the women were working towards professional standards in the areas of work to which they knew they would be admitted. The limitations of their role dictated the way in which they operated, learning their work 'in the field'.

But the climate of opinion was changing, as Octavia recognized. In an article written in 1889 she described those changes, as they affected women's work.

Long ago hardly a woman I knew had any opportunity of devoting time to any grave or kindly work beyond her own household or small social circle. Now there are thousands who achieve it . . . With the different ideal of life, customs have altered in a marked manner; it used to be difficult for a girl to walk alone and it was considered almost impossible for her to travel in omnibuses or third-class trains. The changes in custom with regard to such matters have opened out fresh possibilities of work.[18]

[260]

By 1892, as Octavia told the fellow-workers, she was more closely involved with the WUS than ever. She and Miss Sewell were considering setting up a one- or two-year training course, for both volunteers and paid workers; and two scholarships worth £50 a year would be offered. By the following year, they had been secured. The WUS was granted £3,000 by the Pfeiffer Trustees to endow the scholarships on a permanent basis. Octavia believed that trained women would be immensely valuable 'in these critical times of social change'. A few years later students from the School of Sociology (soon to become the London School of Economics) were seconded to women working in housing management, despite the fact that few of them were considering a career in the field.

The WUS was well known in the USA and attracted some distinguished visitors. One was Jane Addams, the founder of Hull House, the Chicago Settlement. On her third visit to London in 1896 she and her companion talked to Sir John Gorst at the House of Commons, listened to Keir Hardie's plan for the new Labour Party, and attended a reception given by Mrs Aveling (Eleanor Marx) to bid farewell to Liebknecht, the German radical politician, who was going back to serve a gaol sentence – 'a glimpse of the old-fashioned orthodox Socialist who had not yet begun to yield to the biting ridicule of Bernard Shaw although he flamed in their midst that evening'.

Jane Addams had specially requested to meet Octavia, and Henrietta Barnett had written to both Octavia and Emma Cons to ask if they could receive her. Octavia replied directly to Jane Addams regretting that 'the great pressure of work will prevent my having the pleasure of calling on you' but hoped that they would meet, perhaps at the WUS Annual General Meeting or the Red Cross Hall flower show on Saturday 27 June.[19]

Jane chose the former – at which she was asked to speak but declined – and afterwards Octavia conducted her around the Red Cross Hall and gardens. Although 'Miss Hill was very nice and took me around the outside of the cottages and a big block . . . she said it was quite impossible to go in unless it were collecting day.'[20] For Octavia, the tenants' privacy was far more important than a visitor's desire to see the interiors of the cottages, however prestigious that visitor.

As Jane Addams recalled in her memoirs, Octavia

kindly demonstrated to us the principles upon which her well-founded business of rent-collecting was established, and with pardonable pride showed us the Red Cross Square with its cottages marvellously picturesque and comfortable, on two sides, and on the third a public hall and common drawing-room for the use of all the tenants; the interior of the latter had been decorated by pupils of Walter Crane with mural frescoes portraying the heroism in the life of the modern workingman. While all this was warmly human, we also had opportunities to see something of a group of men and women who were approaching the social problem from the study of economics; among others Mr and Mrs Sidney Webb . . .[21]

After that they travelled on to Russia, being taken by Mr and Mrs Aylmer Maude to visit Count Tolstoy who appeared to take exception to Jane Addams' garb. (Much more politically aware than Octavia, Jane Addams later became a pacifist and was involved in labour disputes such as the infamous lockout at Pullman, Illinois.)

The transatlantic traffic went both ways. Helen Gow,[22] who had been involved in Settlement work since 1891, and knew Octavia from there as well as from family connections, went to the USA in the autumn of 1896. In her regular letters home to her sister Kate Mann[23] she described her visits to a number of American Settlements. At the beginning of November she was at Denison House in Boston and noted that, 'I *must* collect some facts of our Settlement work at home – in which they are all hungrily interested – for I am enquired of on all hands.'

The College Settlement in New York, Helen Gow's next port of call, included a surprising number of well-heeled young ladies including one who 'had never made a bed in her life till she came here three weeks ago and as for waiting at table –!' Slumming had taken on a specifically American tinge. Helen was also given an introduction to the Theological Seminary Settlement. There she gained more insight into the appalling educational and housing problems in the city. 'And tenements! No one can form any idea of the stacks and stacks of dark homes in New York and yet Miss Octavia Hill's work is not attempted . . .'

In Philadelphia, at 617 Carver Street, another settlement, the links with home were even more direct. She met Miss Susan Wharton: 'She is dissatisfied with the aims of the Settlement, knows the Misses Hill in London (her cousin Miss Helen Parish [sic] lived in Miss Hill's house and worked with her for six months) and understands the aims of our Settlement . . . her respect for our London work being the sweetest flattery to this stranger.' (Susan Wharton visited the WUS the follow-ing July where Octavia and Helen Gow gave her 'a delightful time'.)

In the summer of 1896, Helen Parrish and Hannah Fox, another of Octavia's American workers, were busily setting up the Octavia Hill Association, an attempt to tackle the housing conditions of the poor in Philadelphia by the rehabilitation of old properties, although Helen Gow did not mention their initiative which by the time of her visit was formally established. [24]

Despite the society girls in New York, Helen Gow's impression was that in the USA 'personal philanthropy seems very largely confined to working women (who *must* earn) . . . I do not think I met the elite of the nation in the Settlements.' Everywhere she went the Americans repeated their high regard for the state of social work in Britain and Helen was frequently asked to send messages back to Octavia. She was a little timorous about writing to the esteemed figure but, 'I feel I might take the liberty of writing for it need not take her long to read, and it eases my mind to have the messages delivered.' In return, Octavia sent various enclosures for Helen to distribute.

In March 1897, Helen Gow was thrilled to receive a personal letter from Jane Addams, whom she had met the previous summer in London, offering her a ten-day stay at Hull House – the aristocrat of the American Settlements. In early April she was duly in Chicago. The visit fully lived up to her hopes, although she was horrified to find her hostess, 'so awfully ill and tired looking. I shall feel obliged to speak to her about it, if she does not do something herself: I know if a poor woman looked as she does she would relieve her of all necessity of work and insist on her getting into hospital.'

Helen reported to Kate: 'Miss Addams is a most saintly and exquisite personality and a pleasure and an inspiration to be beside.' She had invited Helen back next fall, 'to organize the charities of the city'. Trying to describe Jane Addams, Helen was struck by the similarity of her character to that of Miranda Hill. Jane clearly did not resemble Octavia in any way, beyond her lack of consideration for her own health.

Despite the considerable prestige of the WUS, its physical sur-roundings were unsatisfactory and Octavia flung herself into provid-ing decent living accommodation for the WUS residents and a centre for the outworkers. To this end some freeholds in Nelson Square,

Southwark, were obtained; finances being tight, one was bought by Harriot Yorke. In later years a terrace backing on to these houses was also acquired and partially rebuilt. By the mid-1890s the WUS had a firm base in Southwark. Miss Sewell's successor was Miss Helen Gladstone, also a friend of Octavia's.

On 5 March 1898 Octavia addressed the students of Newnham College, Cambridge on the subject of work with the poor. She wanted the young women to realize the change in conditions since her arrival in London in 1851. 'In Seven Dials when I was a child the water was turned on in the centre of a court for an hour in the day only . . .' There had been major advances, especially for trained women: 'there is nothing in which this age is more distinguished from that of my youth than the standard of work, and specially of women's work.' Good will, intelligence and sympathy were not, alone, enough qualification to become a teacher or a nurse. 'Nor is this higher standard, which implies training, less needed in the many other branches of work for the poor. It has not yet been so clearly *recognized* . . . but every year now you will find it more recognized that to do helpful work in parish or institution, technical knowledge is wanted, careful training is essential.' The Women's University Settlement was a centre for such training and she encouraged the Cambridge students to consider the possibilities it offered.

At the beginning there had been a suggestion that the Hill family might move to the Settlement, but Octavia thought they should delay moving until the following winter. 'I cannot tell whether dear old Marylebone or Southwark will seem the most natural working centre, nor how far such a body as the Settlement would leave you and me enough sense of home,' she wrote to Miranda.[25]

In the end, the Hill family decided to move round the corner to 190, Marylebone Road in March 1891. The school was closed; Miranda at last had earned a rest. Astonishingly, old Caroline Southwood Hill was alive and in good heart; Octavia set aside a peaceful room for her regular visits to Larksfield, knowing that she liked to be alone, or just the two of them together. In her mellower middle years Octavia often expressed her gratitude to her mother.

Octavia threw herself into making the new house attractive, just as thirty years earlier she had done at Nottingham Place. She described the house to her mother.

My room has turned out so pretty; and I am so astonished because it was the room where all the leavings naturally gravitated. But you know it has a pretty bow like the back drawing-room; and my one extravagance has been a very nice brass curtain rod . . . we have hung the curtains which Minnie [Emily] gave, – crimson – and they look so bright in the western sun, and so snug when drawn at night. Then I have my writing-table in the bow, and my pretty dark bookcase, and the old drawing-room carpet from Nottingham Place, which looks quite handsome, as good things do. *My* photographs group themselves prettily on the walls; and altogether it is very nice.[26]

Miranda described the house just before they moved in. It was smaller than Nottingham Place, with correspondingly smaller rooms, and it was quiet, light and cheerful, the main rooms having a southerly aspect. It was cheap – the sisters had to think economically, now that the school was closed – and they had decided to take it on an annual basis, at least until they were certain that it suited them. There was a front garden and a backyard; 'a little light space and *quiet* being our chief requirements'. Although the Marylebone Road had been noisy, a wooden pavement had recently been put down – a great boon, Miranda thought. The house was big enough for Miranda, Octavia, Harriot Yorke and two fellow-workers who lived with them, Miss Pearson[27] and Miss Sim. They did not want to break up the household and so it was satisfactory to find a house which could accommodate everyone.

Although Miranda had decided to stop teaching there was plenty for her to do. 'Octavia's work is so wide and many-sided, and she is so large-hearted and wise in giving all her fellow-workers leave to work in their own way, that she often hands a little domain over to me to work in my own way.'[28] Not only was Miranda good at the accounts, she had decided to stand for election as a Guardian, a post which if she were successful would allow her first-hand experience of Poor Law administration. 'I do hope she will get in. She is so much interested in the schools and the children,' Octavia wrote to Mary Booth.

Christmas 1891 brought the family together; Mrs Hill, Emily and Maurice, Florence as well as Margy Whelpdale their half-sister, were all there. Miranda and she, Octavia wrote to Mary Harris, were becoming very fond of their new home. For that matter Mary should come to visit Larksfield, which had more space now since Elijah Hoole had carried out some extensions for them. In 1894 Mary did so, and told Miranda that she found Octavia 'life giving' and was very struck by her combination of the poetical and the practical.

In 1895 one of Octavia's closest friends died. News of Lady Ducie's death came to her as she stayed at Erleigh Court, with her brother. She wrote to Sydney Cockerell: 'I can hardly yet realize what the void in my life will be from the loss of the friend of some thirty years, and of such a friend. She was quite unique, the majesty of intellect being only equalled by the depths of her affection, and the greatness of her spirit. The intercourse has been unclouded for all these years . . . Still all this is a great possession, and one to be thankful for.'[29] Octavia was good at friendship; she both inspired and reciprocated it. A little later, the Earl of Ducie wrote to tell her that his wife had left her a bureau – she also left her the freehold of Sarsden Buildings, one of the Barrett's Court properties which Octavia had managed for so many years.

Octavia spent frequent weekends at Larksfield. In 1897 Crockham Hill organized its Diamond Jubilee celebrations, lighting a vast bonfire to form one of a chain all along the rim of the Weald. There was a greasy pole, and plenty of village matrons trying to catch a pig by its tail, reported David Garnett whose mother Constance had just built a house nearby. The Garnetts often entertained Russian visitors, including Prince Kropotkin, the Russian anarchist.[30]

In later years famously dowdy, Octavia seemed determined to play upon the image of herself that others had presented to her. Some people were repelled by her lack of style, notably Ruskin. Others, such as C. R. Ashbee, found it rather touching. One day Octavia went over to Aldworth in Sussex to meet the Tennysons, a meeting engineered by Robert Hunter. It was not a success. 'Lord Tennyson and I had some talk before luncheon, but nothing of any real interest.'[31] She never lost her interest in art; she found time to go to exhibitions, and was bowled over by Burne-Jones's *Wheel of Fortune* on show at the Guildhall.

In the late 1890s it was decided by a group of admirers, headed by Lady Pollock and Mary Booth, to mark Octavia's sixtieth birthday with a portrait, to be painted by John Singer Sargent. He carried out the commission in August and September of 1898. Sargent was a curious choice; his slick technique, polished on countless society ladies, made Octavia look slightly coy, glancing sideways, and somehow elongated her posture to overcome her short neck, and a head which seemed to sit more directly than is usual on her shoulders.

A lavish oil by a society portraitist was not to Octavia's taste. She wrote to C. S. Loch about the proposed portrait in some dismay. It was, she said, 'almost impossible . . . to prevent memorials, presentations and testimonials . . . from becoming a real oppression and pain to contributors.' She felt it was an unsuitable use for money, especially when contributed by those who had little or by those with more serious claims on their funds, whilst her close circle had already given help and friendship. She did not want more. 'Giving is too good a thing when it is spontaneous, to be spoiled by the slightest pressure or unwilling sense of not liking to be left out.' A chalk sketch by a good artist would be adequate, if there must be a portrait.

In the event, sitter and artist grew to admire each other. Mary Booth heard that things had got off to an awkward start, for Octavia 'retained a certain personal shyness with strangers, putting down a veil, as it were, between her own personality and theirs and hardly allowing a glimpse of herself to shine through.' But Sargent was too experienced with sitters to find her impenetrable. 'He engaged her in conversation and had the happy instinct to differ from her categorically on a point where she felt strongly . . . Her face lit with all its characteristic force and fire. Our modern Velasquez seized his chance and he succeeded in transferring to his canvas . . . something of the inward spirit which we have reverenced.'[32]

Although Mary Booth was impressed by the physical likeness, Harriot Yorke commented that Octavia never looked sideways and certainly almost all accounts refer to her enormous dark eyes and penetratingly direct gaze.[33]

On 1 December 1898 the portrait was presented to Octavia at Grosvenor House. The occasion was a moving testimonial to her achievements and the esteem in which she was held. Although it was attended by many eminent figures, it was essentially a private and personal tribute.

Since the Duke of Westminster was unable to be there, the Duchess presided over the event. C. S. Loch addressed the gathering. 'Her face was engraved on their minds and her character on their hearts, but they were anxious that those who should come after, and who had never had the privilege of knowing her, should be able to realize something of what she had been and how she had looked.' Her power of giving hope and strength was what her friends admired; she was not, as Loch put it, a 'public woman' and hated notoriety. 'The home and family were the centre from which to work, and she was always dwelling on the importance of quiet individual effort.'[34]

The Revd Fremantle, now the Dean of Ripon, next recalled meeting Octavia, who had soon begun to help him organize the administration of charity in the St Mary's parish. He remembered the 'happy, hard-working home in Nottingham Place which . . . has furnished a great novelist with some of her prettiest domestic scenes.' (There can be little doubt that he had in mind George Eliot.) At the outset, Fremantle said, he had known nothing of Miss Octavia Hill, but he was immediately persuaded by the strength of her views. It was her determination and perseverance that seemed to him the outstanding characteristics of her personality. He recalled their fight against the granting of a licence to the Walmer Castle public house – three years running the Marylebone Magistrates had granted it, and the Middlesex Magistrates had then cancelled it. Someone, he said, had once referred to Octavia as the best 'man of business' he knew.[35]

Another speaker, the Revd Alford, vicar of St Luke's,[36] was much struck when reading her grandfather's memoir by how much both Octavia and Miranda had inherited from him. He referred to the 'apostolic succession of workers' and praised Octavia's work in rescuing the countryside from encroachment, which he appreciated every time he walked outside London. Charles Booth was equally eloquent: 'It has been our privilege to know and love a very great and good woman. These things cannot be said often, but they may be said today.' Mrs Booth then thanked Sargent and Loch presented the portrait to Octavia.

Loch gave Octavia the option of remaining silent; but she gave an address, emphasizing that she did not want to be remembered for a 'system' but for her ideals.[37] She thanked her friends, and remembered those who had died; especially Mrs Nassau Senior, Mr Shaen, Professor Maurice, Mrs Russell Gurney and Mr Cockerell senior.

The list of subscribers to the portrait, set out at the end of the printed account of the proceedings, was almost 200 names long and included many from the USA. The Duke of Westminster, Leslie Stephen, C. R. Ashbee, F. D. Mocatta and colleagues from every branch of her activities were listed. Even Ruskin's name was there. Sargent gave the frame, his own contribution to the celebration of a life of such extraordinary achievement.

The occasion had something of the feel of a memorial service, although Octavia had another fourteen years to live and much more still to do. But her physical health was becoming less robust. She was in the early stages of a long battle with lung cancer.

CHAPTER 18

Theory: housing management

Octavia was an enlightened advocate of what we should now term rehabilitation. She knew, from her sure personal instinct, that the familiar streets and cottages were where people wanted to stay – provided they were in habitable condition. On the other hand, her tussles with the authorities over the condition of the first acquisitions at Barrett's Court had made her sensitive to charges that certain of her property was substandard. At Barrett's Court, which was by 1877 one of the jewels in her crown, 'clean, fresh wholesome work now replaces the decayed and rotten.' Yet, 'if we ever rebuild the rest of the court it may be well to try to rebuild it as separate houses, not as a block; it is not good to concentrate too large a population on a small area.'

She has been much misrepresented on this issue, being depicted as a sturdy defender of model or block dwellings. The 1900 account *No room to live*, written by George Haw, a journalist on the *Daily News*, was one example of how confused the record became. His indictment of a housing policy which had led to 400,000 Londoners living in one-roomed accommodation – with 9,000 living seven to a room and 3,000, living eight or more – was passionate and graphic. The remedy that was widely proposed was the block dwelling: 'This,' he wrote, 'has been the cure urged by good and excellent men and women like Miss Octavia Hill, Mr Peabody, Sir Sydney Waterlow and Lord Shaftesbury.'

Haw was wrong, however. Octavia managed a number of model dwellings for others, but her policy to build them was short-lived, ending in the '70s. As she wrote in her contribution to Charles Booth's massive publication, *The Life and Labour of the People of London*,[1] the third volume of which was published in 1892: 'I have built very few blocks but I have been consulted about some.' Her delight in Red and White Cross Streets and the Ecclesiastical Commissioners' pursuit of cottage-building was evidence of where her true emphasis lay.

Although the Ecclesiastical Commissioners were the largest land-owners to engage the services of Octavia's trained workers, the Northampton estate in Clerkenwell had also used one of her workers for many years. At the outset, Octavia strenuously objected to the estate's plans to demolish existing buildings – and won the argument.

An early report of her work for the Ecclesiastical Commissioners described how she argued such cases.

Miss Hill addressed her observations to various matters connected with the management both of the ancient small tenements now under her control and of the two new model dwellings containing numerous families and single tenants in what are known as Stanhope Buildings and Mowbray Buildings – recently erected in Red Cross Road. There appeared, from Miss Hill's statements, to be many drawbacks and inconveniences inseparable from the housing in a single large building of numerous families and in particular that the nuisance which would be produced by allowing children to play in the internal courts comprised within Stanhope and Mowbray Buildings would be intolerable by reason chiefly of the great noise and reverberation inseparable from their so playing in confined spaces within very great height. And she contended that the indisposition of families to occupy rooms in buildings of that character was, in a considerable degree, caused by the impossibility of their children finding any place but the streets to play in or take exercise.

The Commissioners assured Octavia of their co-operation and compliance with her management, and after she had left the room, discussed the matter of providing a playground in the area. They earmarked Henry's Place and its adjacent buildings. It was these deliberations which led to the setting up of the Red Cross playground.[2] When the Commissioners baulked at the length of lease Octavia was requesting she reminded them 'that the need for the garden arises from the permanent alteration of the character of the neighbourhood owing to the recent destruction of a number of cottages with their separate little yards or gardens.'[3]

Octavia reiterated these points in her article for Charles Booth's book. First she accepted the inevitable, as she saw it: 'It is pretty clear that the working population of London is likely to be more and more housed in "blocks", and it is not very profitable to spend time in considering whether this is a fact to rejoice in or to deplore . . .'

She ran through the supposed advantages and disadvantages of this form of housing; the former included better sanitary arrangements, and the fact that inspection and regulation – on which modern legislation was based – would prove easier. The system might be equally faulty in a block, but it would be easier to locate and check. But she was not sure about economy; block dwellings were not invariably cheaper than small houses. 'I do not think we can permanently congratulate and pride ourselves upon, hardly that we can permit, a form of construction which admits so very little sunlight into lower floors.' Yet to improve matters would increase the ground rent per room. Losing a storey often gave distinct advantages but 'with our increased means of cheap transit we should try to scatter rather than to concentrate our population, especially if the concentration has to be secured by dark lower rooms.'

There was a moral argument, too. The problem with block dwellings was that they concentrated 'a huge community of those who are undisciplined and untrained'. The block often became a disgrace. 'Sinks and drains are stopped; yards provided for exercise must be closed because of misbehaviour; boys bathe in drinking water cisterns; wash-houses on staircase – or staircases themselves – become the nightly haunt of the vicious, the Sunday gambling places of boys . . . the life of any decent hard-working family becomes intolerable.'

> I would implore well-meaning landlords to pause before they clear away small houses and erect blocks with any idea of benefiting the poorer class of people . . . Let them either ask tidy working people . . . or learn for themselves, whether I am not right in saying that in the shabbiest little two-, four-, six- or eight-roomed house, with all the water to carry upstairs, with one little w.c. in a tiny back yard, with perhaps one dust-bin at the end of the court, and even perhaps with a dark little twisted staircase, there are not far happier, better, yes and *healthier* homes than in the blocks where lower-class people share and do *not* keep in order far better appliances.

With 'civilization', as Octavia quaintly put it, respectable working-class families form clean and orderly groups in 'well-ordered quiet little homes, behind their neat little doors with bright knockers, nicely supplied with well-chosen appliances.' It was a law-abiding life, 'regular, a little monotonous . . . consistent with happy home-life.' It was, above all, the life that Octavia had had in mind for her tenants from the earliest days in Paradise Place.

What should be done for the irresponsible, then? Octavia was prepared to believe that 'the gradual progress of educational and other influences may permeate their ranks . . . (but of this I am not hopeful if they are herded together in blocks); it may be that some form of self-government, some committee of the tenants, may be arranged to organize and bring to bear the standard and rule of the better men and women.' She wanted to be optimistic but found it difficult to imagine such organization where it was most needed, in the poorest blocks.

Another objection was the 'painful ugliness and uninterestingness in external look' – for 'let us hope that when we have secured our drainage, our cubic space of air, our water on every floor, we may have time to live in our homes, to think how to make them pretty, each in our own way . . . because all human work and life were surely meant to be like all Divine creations, lovely as well as good.'

But above all, her objection to blocks was a more general one, the lack of individuality of the family home. 'The creepers in the back yard, the rabbits the boys feed, the canary the sickly child listens to, the shed for the man's tools, the washing arrangements, or the arbour, are all arranged to suit individual tastes and for all these the separate house, or the small house, gives scope.' Octavia clearly understood the concept of what today would be called defensible space.

Octavia's contribution to Charles Booth's volume was a credo and unambiguously stated her views on housing. Only wilful misrepresentation, or carelessness, could suggest that she supported the standard model dwelling; her every instinct was against the anonymity and the inhumanity of such a solution. But neither could she see the suburbs as an answer. Despite her liking for the individual cottage and garden, life at the end of a railway line was not appropriate, Octavia knew, for the poor people that she was housing whose work was either casual or had to be done and delivered quickly, as in the case of those employed in the garment trade. Neither fares nor timetables were tailored to their needs. The Cheap Trains Act 1883 had proved ineffective.

She considered 'that there should be some deliberation before compulsory powers of purchase are granted by which large bodies of the poor shall be forced *en masse* to migrate to suburbs where they will form necessarily new and numerous districts like the East End – that is, where acres and acres of houses are occupied exclusively by the poor.'[4] On another occasion she emphasized the importance of mixing the classes within an area; this provided employment and, by inference, ensured a scattering of the socially concerned middle classes – which was not the case in the East End.

Octavia's solution was, as ever, small-scale. Some of her modern critics suggest that her argument against industrial blocks and in favour of cottages implicitly promoted dispersal to the suburbs, given the value of building land. Octavia did not see it that way, any more than she saw mass emigration as a solution, despite her half-brother Arthur's position acting for the British Government facilitating free emigration to Australia.[5]

Discussing the latest cottages to be built for the Church Commissioners in Southwark, she admitted that they had as many rooms

> as we can hope a Londoner of the kind who resides in Southwark will need. Of course one looks for more in the country, but the rents in London have altered the habits of tenants, they do not expect *and would only sub-let* additional rooms if they were built. It will be long before such tenants as need houses [in London] will learn to occupy more than four rooms – I wish most of them had as many. We have to remember with regard to bedrooms that our Londoners sleep down-stairs often, and do not keep the nice sense of absolute distinction of parlour which country people do. It is not that I wish to plead a low standard, but, while half the families around live in two rooms, not too healthy, I think we may feel thankful if we can supply them with three or four good ones . . . the very point of these cottages is that they should be separate homes.[6]

A few years later, in the 1897 'Letter to Fellow-workers', Octavia referred to a new type of house which had been built in her Lisson Grove district: 'compound houses, each of which comes to be practically two distinct cottages one on the top of another.' A single front door and passage led to a five-roomed cottage, containing three ground-floor rooms and two rooms below with coal cellar, washhouse and small backyard. Above it, entered by a separate stair, was a seven-roomed cottage, with three first-floor rooms and four above. Octavia felt that this arrangement, common in the north country and familiar in Scotland, solved a number of problems, 'diminishing ground rent, without resorting to high blocks, or to so much life in public as many buildings necessitate'.

Another new initiative, this time in the realm of ownership, appealed greatly to Octavia. This was Henry Vivian's co-partnership movement, a co-operative housing venture which encouraged tenants to become both 'owners and managers' of their own housing. It also encouraged mobility, since they could exchange their houses with other co-partnership schemes elsewhere in the country.[7]

The rates discussion and how to organize rates payment occupied Octavia a great deal in the mid-1890s. The rates were rising at an alarming pace and with it 'the gigantic accumulation of municipal indebtedness'.

With the increasing domestic rate burden, the costs of rented housing were also rising inexorably. While rates for the blocks had to be paid by the company or owner (known as compounding), in the cottages Octavia was adamant that the tenants should pay their own rates. By fixing a lower rent, she ensured that they did not suffer financially, but her motive was a political one – and a familiar one. Paying their own rates, 'our tenants are keenly alive to many of the facts about the rates that they, and they only can alter.' It was difficult to manage, since her tenants were paying weekly, and the rate demand, made in advance, was payable quarterly or twice a year. She wanted her tenants to share her dread of 'these large loans lightly voted by thousands who little know what they mean in the future . . .'

Octavia had a political sense, but it was, as in all things she touched, a pragmatic one. Some years before this she had had a long talk with the young Sydney Cockerell who wanted to involve himself in social work. Edward Bond, who readily dismissed socialism as a solution, had advised Cockerell to contact Octavia. Their discussion lasted two hours. 'She was wholly opposed to sweeping State remedies and placed her reliance on individual example and influence,' he reported.[8] He was convinced by her arguments, being himself no socialist, and then began to work with her in Southwark. Many others who shied away from socialism also turned to Octavia to offer them a practical outlet for their unease over social conditions. She was not a theorist, nor was she remotely politically inclined. She had, however, a gift for putting into words what she thought, what she did, and what she observed. It was based on purely practical experience, moulded by the climate of Victorian opinion and shared with others through a ceaseless stream of articles and publications throughout the years – always remaining remarkably consistent in their viewpoint.

While Octavia Hill's message was spreading nationally and internationally, Octavia herself was learning from experience. 'I would earnestly commend to everyone concerned the absolute necessity of training future collectors. Let those of you who have charge of courts introduce, side by side with yourselves, promising fellow-workers, who may see and learn what is being done and may, in the future, be ready to fill vacant places . . . Beware of well-meant failures.'[9] The work at the Women's University Settlement fulfilled this objective to train workers, who would in their turn train others. Octavia's housing management operated on an effective cell system that any revolutionary political group would admire.

She insisted that women of the highest calibre should be trained for the work. The opportunities were widening all the time and the scholarships at the Women's University Settlement were an important step in broadening the social catchment for candidates.

In 1899 she gave a talk on the management of houses, which stressed her emphasis on the practical. She emphasized how any aspiring housing manager must understand the complicated London rating and assessment system as well as the law affecting weekly and quarterly tenancies.

> . . . if any of you think of extending this work you must set yourselves under a good leader and get a steady training in all branches of the business as if you were learning a profession. When the technical matters are mastered there will be scope for all your spiritual powers of sympathy, judgement, observation, gentleness and firmness . . . your kindliness is worth nothing . . . if your sinks are dirty, your yards uninspected, your tenants overcrowded or in arrears, for as a manager such matters are your first care.[10]

Octavia was now training a steady supply of workers on both voluntary and professional bases. By 1900 she realized, as she put it in the 'Letter to Fellow-workers',

> my best plan would be . . . to train more than we could use ourselves, and as occasion offers, to introduce them to owners

wishing to retain small tenements in their own hands and to be represented by a kind of manager not hitherto existing. The ordinary collector is not a man of education having time to spare, nor estimating his duties as comprising much beyond a call at the doors for rent brought down to him, and a certain supervision of repairs asked for.

Considering the payment of social workers, in an address to Newnham students in 1898, Octavia admitted, 'I have myself done a good deal of paid work in both teaching and drawing in my life . . .', but she had never received direct payment for the housing work, favouring the idea of time as a gift, and she was offended by the idea of donations being spent on salaries. On the other hand, the students should avoid the idea that 'paid work for the poor is any nobler, or more self-sacrificing than any other paid work . . .' She noted the 'modern young ladies whose parents have enough to support them, and are ready and glad to do so, [who] have a sort of preference for paid work because they think it proves their capability. It does so, to a certain extent.'

In the early 1900s Octavia's problem lay not in the supply of houses, but the supply of trained workers, those who would work with the volunteers. When she scented that someone was suitable, she was very tenacious. Paula Schuster was a supporter who in 1900 had given some funds for open spaces projects, but was open to other suggestions. Octavia gradually pointed her towards housing, in particular the tricky areas of Notting Hill that had recently begun to engage her attention – almost as difficult as Barrett's Court had been in the early days. She wrote to Miss Schuster that the *Daily Mail* had pronounced the area 'irreclaimable'; but, she continued, although 'such words look very sensational . . . with love, and sympathy, and firmness one comes face to face with individuals, one learns to know how men and women in all places are like ourselves with infinite capacity for reception of influence, and for rising or falling, and how false all such generalizations are.'[11]

In 1907 she wrote to Miss Schuster who had offered to buy another group of houses. Her parents ('our ever faithful friends', as Octavia called them) had already bought sixteen 'old-fashioned cottages' in Notting Hill that year. The problem, she told Miss Schuster, was now to find a worker. Although she was always training people, her own work was growing constantly and always absorbed them. She had some advice about a caretaker: 'a nice motherly woman of the right character, encouraged by the owner, and backed up by a husband in good work would be by far the best. We never employ a man, except for an area with 200 or 300 families.' A woman caretaker was more dependable for matters such as 'the cleaning of stairs, shewing rooms, and all the numerous household matters on which good management depends.'[12]

Soon afterwards she was writing again. She had a lady, who wanted to be trained in housing work, 'of whom I hear an excellent account and of whom I got a very favourable impression the only time I saw her.' She could board with the Miss Josephs, next door to 190, Marylebone Road, 'but she is dependent on earning and I do not feel sure that she will really, when it comes to the point, face the cost of sufficient training. I wonder whether you would care at all to help, with the understanding that, if she proved successful, when you got houses, she should undertake them . . . it *might* be a means of enabling you to start work more satisfactorily.'[13]

A few days later Miss Schuster had replied and duly given a 'magnificent offer of help'. Miss Mackintosh, the woman Octavia had in mind, could, she suggested,

enter upon a course of training . . . in October, *strictly on trial only*, and giving, if you really see your way to do so, at the rate of £40, so long as she continues training and till work begins. I certainly should not give more. Sacrifice is a good test of zeal and interest in the career, and it will be more encouraging for salary to increase markedly when work begins.

Octavia liked the way in which Miss Mackintosh spoke of the work and her approach to people, but did not know 'to what religious body she belongs'. Interestingly, that was not a question that usually entered into her choice of workers; perhaps it was a requirement set by Miss Schuster.

Octavia was very sensitive on the matter of her workers keeping their opinions on matters religious or political to themselves. She wrote to one applicant on the subject:

I forgot to mention that as we work among a large group holding different religious and political views we have all to be careful to be silent one to another and among the tenants on questions on which

[278]

we may differ, and that I should regret if any of my staff took public or very pronounced part in political questions. Our work is practical and individual, and best done in silence.[14]

So eager did Miss Schuster seem that Octavia turned to her a few weeks later; she had just learned that five more houses in the street 'we are so keen about reforming, in Notting Hill' were coming on the market. 'They are right in the midst of those we have struggled so hard to improve and we know that two of the worst landlords will try to get them to let in furnished lodgings. You can imagine how eager I am to secure control of them if it be possible, were it only to preserve our people from harm.' She had found a buyer for two, but three remained. Would Miss Schuster consider them or 'are you set on, and limited to, the East End?' As far as management was concerned there would be no problem; Miss Yorke and two of her best workers were already working in the street. She estimated the houses would go for a maximum of £300 each.[15] Miss Schuster obliged, buying two at auction in December.[16] Sadly three others adjacent, according to Octavia, 'were purchased by a man who will turn out all the tenants and let in furnished rooms.' She had felt that she could not justify spending the sums required, even though supporters had offered to do so.

When one realizes that Octavia was keeping up this kind of correspondence with dozens of new and old supporters constantly, whilst balancing and organizing the supply of housing workers throughout her properties, her continued tenacity and resolve have to be admired.

One can gain a vivid impression of what joining Octavia's team was like from Janet Upcott's account. She was trained at the School of Sociology at Denison House and at the London School of Economics. After an unsuccessful application to the Ecclesiastical Commissioners to work on their Walworth Estate, she was referred to Octavia. Her interview took place under inauspicious conditions: she was seated on a chair which she was given to understand was hallowed, since it had belonged to George Eliot, but which was nevertheless uncomfortably low and put her at an immediate disadvantage. Then she was grilled by Octavia and Emily, and taken on.

She remembered Octavia as an impressive but very dominant woman.

She sat facing the window with her portrait by Sargent behind her. I was set to copy the rent sheets. At first she was rather cautious about my ability saying, 'What is Miss Upcott doing? Isn't that rather a responsible job for her?' but when it came to the next quarter, and having satisfied herself about me, – 'Isn't that rather a waste of her time?'[17]

She was impressed by Octavia's minute attention to detail, particularly financial detail, and her immensely high standards. 'She would sweep into the office every morning – a small, stocky figure laden with account books – and work with a diligence expected of everyone . . . Her large brown eyes missed nothing, and could flash devastating disapproval. But the slow, deep voice could commend warmly, and her greatness was manifest when she welcomed a correction where some mistake had been discovered by a timid beginner.' Janet Upcott remembered the various district managers bringing in their books weekly and discussing their problems. By then Octavia had no personal dealing with the tenants. She gave her workers sound advice: 'Remember you have no right to cross the tenant's threshold.'

Octavia's old problem of personal relations continued, though now more often with her new workers. She had, she told another trainee, Miss Jeffery, at this time, 'the faculty of always saying the wrong thing'.[18] In later years, Miss Yorke seems to have often acted as a kind of buffer between Octavia's peremptory abrasiveness and the sentivities of her greener recruits.[19]

Octavia's views on the newly constituted LCC, given in a speech in 1898 or 1899, supported them in their wish for abundant and cheap housing but not as the providers of such accommodation. She abhorred subsidy of any sort – a heresy, to the COS way of thinking – and held that to provide housing supported by the domestic rate would stop all other bodies building for the poor and deter those who willingly put their money in for 'a small percentage'.

The effect of the LCC housing programme would, in her opinion, be to 'force all buildings up to an ideal . . . of structural perfection, rather than to steadily raise the minimum standard and to give free play to the ever resourceful labour of myriads of persons conversant with the needs of the poor.' In short, 'rate-supported dwellings paralysed independent effort.' Her argument, in fact, had inbuilt inconsistencies, for elsewhere she acknowledged with pleasure that in later years there had been less work improving standards of housing since 'companies and sanitary authorities, private builders and public building Acts have helped us in this great object'. The two positions did not tally.

Octavia, late in her life, was unable to contemplate the housing solution that stared her in the face. Her opinions had been formed and set in the strict school of individualism and a distrust of State intervention in any form. The COS guidelines were her lexicon, always. Miss Upcott remembered Octavia's curious hostility to local authorities and thought that it stemmed from long experience with inefficient and corrupt vestries. Perhaps she did not know the history of Octavia's lengthy battles with the Medical Officer of Health over Barrett's Court, almost thirty years before. Whatever the cause of this suspicion, the result was that, 'We were not allowed to pay the half-yearly rate too promptly, as she [Octavia] did not see why the local authority should have the use of owners' money before it was actually required.'[20]

That hostility extended to all forms of municipal building. 'I see no hope of large well-considered schemes for building till municipal building is abandoned. The municipality cannot, in my opinion, be good landlords to its own constituents; it cannot supply the huge requirements of London.' She thought that local authorities should limit themselves to appropriate regulation and 'instead of messing with building and managing, help with approaches and areas of locomotion and regulating traffic.'[21]

In 1902 she addressed the Edinburgh Social Union at their Annual Meeting. Corporations were being driven, she said, 'to all manner of ill-considered and, to my mind, ill-judged schemes for housing. Such schemes are most unlikely to be financially sound . . .'; it was the spectre of unwarranted subsidy that haunted Octavia. If that should prove to be the case then no doubt those subsidies would come from the rates, 'open or concealed by clever balance-sheets. This means rating the *really* poor, the steadily industrious, to meet part of the rent of their demoralised neighbours.' Nor would the municipality be a 'strong or wise landlord'; the tenants would be their constituents 'and firm, quiet, beneficent rule, which alone can help the undisciplined to grow, will be relaxed at recurring elections.' It would be better, in her view, if the municipality took a supervisory function which would be easier to exercise if it were not the landlord. The Edinburgh Social Union had in fact undertaken the management of the Corporation's own housing stock, but ran into just the problems Octavia described and gave up the task.

State provision was increasing everywhere she looked, but Octavia stood firm. Writing a few years later, she summed up everything she abhorred:

> the rise of rates, the unsound competition of rate-supported bodies, and the ignorance of trustees of large new charities. The LCC is feeding nearly 100,000 children, the Chelsea Borough Council is arranging for rebuilding on a large scale, and the Sutton Charity, which surely should have been devoted to pioneer work in rural building, is arranging schemes for overbuilt London.[22]

Yet some boroughs were eager to involve Octavia in their work. Kensington approached her to engage her co-operation; 'they are disappointed, and rather angry, at my refusal to manage for them what they have got. They have no right to be so, I have always opposed municipal building and it would ill become me to accept office!'[23] The Borough was trying to buy the freehold of some of Octavia's properties for its own expansion plans, which involved taking over part of backyards and leaving the existing leases intact. Octavia was quite agreeable but could not contemplate weakening her anti-municipal stand. Though without her direct collaboration, both Kensington and Camberwell in fact followed Octavia's line in their housing management from early days.[24]

What Octavia could not or would not see was that without political muscle the huge requirements for rented housing could not be met even in the tiniest degree. Boundary Road in Shoreditch, the earliest of the LCC housing estates, provided more housing at a single stroke than she managed in the accumulation of a lifetime's work. On the other hand, quality was always her aim, not quantity.

As always, it was the scale of Octavia's influence, rather than that of the actual number of properties she or her assistants managed, that was the key to her operation.

In 1899, entirely prompted by her admiration for Octavia's system, Amy Hayne, who was working for the Harrow Mission, set up the Improved Tenements Association. Octavia, like Miss Hayne's cousin Reginald Rowe, was at the founding meeting in South Kensington and the first houses were in Walmer Road, bought for a few hundred pounds. It grew from there to be a sizeable organization which in 1938 owned streets of houses. It was merely one association of the many private initiatives that took their inspiration from Octavia, but on such a limited scale that they made no impact whatsoever on what had become a housing crisis.

However, the profession of housing management was now quietly becoming established, and it was a professional breakthrough for women. In 1900 George Haw commented on the Health Missioners of Manchester who acted as women welfare visitors. They were so useful as a source of information on overcrowding and discovering insanitary conditions that the Corporation undertook to pay half their salaries. Haw argued that Octavia Hill's workers had performed the same function, voluntarily, for many years, and that to ensure its continuation they too should be supported by the municipality.

The training programme for the housing managers strengthened international connections and those in other cities. In Manchester the schemes under Miss Hankinson, 'the life and soul of the movement', were growing apace. In 1909 Octavia had been in correspondence with men and women interested in houses in, amongst many towns, Birmingham, Tunbridge Wells, Oxford, Nottingham, Torquay.

The Dutch had been interested from early days and had a 'wonderful "School of Sociology" with far more practical experiences in managing houses than ours gives.' Miss Ter Meulen from Amsterdam had been the first arrival and had been drafted into Queen Street, Deptford in 1893. To Ellen Chase, now back in America, Octavia sent a glowing account of Miss Ter Meulen's abilities, as well as a touching account of the recent vicissitudes in the lives of some of the Deptford tenants. [25] From then on there was constant stream of Dutch workers. In the 1900s various students arrived, including one who came for six months and who, living at the Talbot Settlement, 'sees much of general social undertakings in South London on her off days and is most kindly helping me at Red Cross Hall.' [26] More 'capable Dutch ladies' followed, as did a Swedish worker in 1911, in the footsteps of Miss Lagerstadt, 'who came to us for training some twenty or thirty years ago and has been carrying on work there ever since.' [27]

The Americans were also, as we have seen, watching closely; not only did they imbibe Octavia's housing theories, though with relatively few practical applications, but her speeches on limiting charity were circulated into many parts of the USA via the numerous COS branches which had sprung up there. In many ways, America with its individualist ethos was a more fertile ground for Octavia's anti-municipal stand than Britain, where the emphasis swung increasingly towards official intervention. Central and local government action merely institutionalized and built upon trends that had been developing since the 1880s.

Octavia had now been left far behind.

CHAPTER 19

Poor Law

OCTAVIA'S status had now become so considerable that she was asked for her views on almost any social question of national concern. In 1889 she told her mother that she had turned down a 'post' on a Commission – perhaps the forthcoming Royal Commission on Labour, which reported between 1892 and 1894. In April 1892 she gave evidence to the House of Commons on the Manchester and Southern Railway proposals, and in 1893 to the Royal Commission on Pensions for the Aged Poor.

She had just completed her contribution to Charles Booth's vast undertaking (eventually to comprise seventeen volumes), *The Life and Labour of the People of London*,[1] which *The Times* had described as 'the grimmest book of our generation'. It was a curious undertaking for a businessman; he approached the organization of a dismal catalogue of facts with a mixture of detachment and moralistic judgement. Like Octavia, he was imprisoned by the conventions of his time which allowed a dispassionate stance that seems hard to reconcile with social concern.

Booth was a believer in the character-building nature of economic cycles and their attendant unemployment for the nation. He divided the population into categories, A to E. Category A ('loafers and criminals') and Category B ('degraded casual workers', some 8.4 per cent of the total) should be sent to labour colonies. The groups C and D, the working poor, who amounted to 22.3 per cent, were those for whom he was concerned.

Nevertheless Booth was an ardent campaigner for old age pensions, which he justified on the basis that they gave 'security of position which will stimulate . . . play of individuality on which progress and prosperity depend'. Charles Booth's 'startling suggestion of

[285]

pensioning everybody without distinction, over sixty-five' was a highly contentious issue.

It was an issue on which Octavia had iron-clad views. In November 1891 Charles Booth took her into his confidence and discussed the subject with her at length. She was utterly opposed to it. Rigidly following the COS line, she was adamant that a pension as of right was just more State charity. She and C. S. Loch were as one with the *COS Review* which called Charles Booth's proposals 'the most outrageous and absurd scheme yet promulgated'. It was another major difference of opinion between herself and the Barnetts, too.

In 1893 Lord Aberdare chaired the Royal Commission on Pensions for the Aged Poor, which reported in 1895. In her evidence Octavia put her views on the official record. She did not mince her words.

I should describe it shortly as the most gigantic scheme of inadequate relief ever devised by any human being. It seems to me to have almost every flaw in it. It would not be adequate. I cannot believe that it would promote thrift. It seems to me that it would do a great deal to destroy what one is of all things the most desirous to cultivate – the sense of responsibility of relatives; and I also should object very much indeed to the idea of its being applied to all classes of people.[2]

On the other hand, in her argumentative evidence on the subject Octavia had proved herself to be a good match for Joseph Chamberlain who had, Aberdare said, 'acknowledged himself vanquished'. At the end of the year she was giving evidence to a Committee on the Unemployed; it took an hour and a quarter to give and, wrote Miranda, nearly six hours to correct the proofs of her evidence. A lighter task fell to her in the summer of 1905: she was asked to judge the Letchworth Garden City model-cottage exhibition. There were 120 to consider, but, she wrote to Emily, 'it won't be so tiring as an ordinary day.'

In November 1905 she received a letter from Arthur Balfour inviting her to join the Royal Commission on the Poor Law. It was a fair, if belated, recompense for the rebuff she had received over her membership of the 1884 Housing Commission. She wrote to Canon Barnett about it: 'I do feel this Royal Commission a very solemn matter, it is a great departure from my hitherto approved kind of work, but life changes and one must be quick to perceive new calls of duty.'[3] The new Commission was a legacy of the outgoing Conservative administration. Balfour confided to Beatrice Webb, in the carriage on the way to the first performance of Shaw's *Major Barbara*, that he had had great problems keeping politicians out of the Commission and in finding a chairman. He had chosen Lord George Hamilton, who, he explained to her, 'is not the fool he looks'.[4]

The Poor Law, last amended in 1834, was proving utterly unsuitable for the social-welfare needs of the twentieth century. The Poor Law Guardians, often lamentably out of touch with reality and sometimes corrupt, struggled with albatrosses such as the workhouses (which were in any case physically crumbling), and suffered from their isolation from both central and local government. The Commission was sitting too late, for the reforms were long overdue and the functions of the Boards of Guardians would shortly be carried out elsewhere as comprehensive social security was introduced.

As a Commissioner, Octavia joined a widely disparate group of old friends and colleagues – Charles Booth, Helen Bosanquet and C. S. Loch from the COS, and Beatrice Webb herself. George Lansbury was the representative working man. There were at least six strong proponents of the COS line among the Commissioners.

In a preliminary investigation Beatrice Webb thought she had ascertained the object of the Commission as set by the Local Government Board. The objective was to reform radically the structure of the Poor Law but also to clarify the policy, inherited from the 1834 Amendment. Beatrice, ever the sceptic, detected that they were to be spoon-fed with selective evidence, and witnesses: 'above all we were to be given *opinions* and not *facts.*' More expert witnesses were essential, concluded Beatrice and Charles Booth, who had discussed the matter together, but at least the high COS membership would ensure that many Commissioners would be personally experienced at social investigation.

Beatrice who was much more self-aware than she appeared to be, set herself some goals as a Commissioner. 'Beware of "showing off" superior knowledge of irrelevant details. To be single-minded in pursuit of truth, courteous in manner and kind in feeling, and yet not to betray one's trust for the sake of popularity and be modestly persistent in my aim must be my prayer.' Not many of her fellow Commissioners thought she kept to these standards, and certainly not her old friend and cousin-in-law Charles Booth who found her

[287]

increasingly exasperating. In turn she thought Charles 'too well-bred and feeble in health to be much good'.

However, in these early days Beatrice saw Helen Bosanquet and possibly Octavia as potential allies in some issues affecting working women. As the meetings progressed there were more clashes. Lord George Hamilton, the Chairman, had imposed a procedure; there was to be no agenda, merely a 'cut-and-dried scheme was laid before us, and we were not asked to vote on it, only to express our opinion on half-a-dozen points.' Beatrice lobbied Mr Duff, the secretary, 'an attractive and sensible young civil servant' who implied that he also thought Hamilton had acted in a high-handed way.

The Commissioners' remit was countrywide and in the following three years they travelled a great deal. For Octavia it interrupted the habits of many years; she had to forgo the Monday and Tuesday tenants' meetings – which she had attended for forty years – and she had little time for much else. Though her physical health was beginning to fail she threw herself into the Commission work.

In her 1907 'Letter to the Fellow-workers' she described how the Commission had occupied a great deal of her days and would do so for some time. She was finding it very interesting; they had visited Lancashire, Yorkshire, the Midlands, South Wales, the eastern counties, the western counties and Scotland. The only visits that she missed had been that to Shrewsbury and another to Northumberland. Next year it was proposed they should visit Ireland. It was too early to draw any conclusions but

> it is deeply interesting, partly by the great and important questions it suggests, partly by the large number of individuals of whose life-work we get some idea . . . the righteous manufacturer, the devoted leader of the Friendly Society, the generous founder of some out-of-sight charity, the faithful nurse, the energetic matron or teacher, the self-sacrificing wise Guardian, the humble and gentle pauper . . . Or course there is the other side; and the problem appears to me the more puzzling, the more the solution of it depends, not on machinery which Commissions may recommend and Parliaments set up, but on the number of faithful men and women whom England can secure and inspire as faithful servants in their manifold duties.

Early in 1907 the Commissioners visited both Bradford and Hull on successive days. Octavia read Emerson in the train, she told Emily, and found him very refreshing. Nevertheless she was longing to set off home. It was arduous business for a woman in her sixty-ninth year.

Charles Booth, who was also suffering intermittent bad health, pressed on too. In his letters to his wife he recounted the ups and downs of the Commission, its journeys and its personalities.[5] In June 1907 the Commissioners turned their attention to Scotland. Writing from the Princes Street Station Hotel, where despite the Scottish summer chill the heating had been turned off, he noted that 'Commissioners all very warm and pleasant will hot up the hotel nicely I hope.' The procedure was to take witnesses one day and do the visiting the next. Charles was defining his views: 'I get firmer and firmer on my own position – but I don't believe the Commission will follow. Some weak sort of middle term will come I fear – but who can say?'

On 6 June, 'We had another long – but quite pleasant day at Glasgow and saw a good deal of interest. Miss Octavia and I with Mr Jeffery accompanied by Professor Smart in the morning and Mr Loch in the afternoon we got in a good deal of talk and it all goes well.' The following day, the mood of the group had changed:

I had a conversation with Loch on our way back by train yesterday from Glasgow – Miss Hill joining in a little. He is in a very impossible blocking sort of position, pure COS the only medicine – I wonder whether he and his lot will sheer off entirely. I think the rest (exculding Beatrice) tend a little to converge – but of course B. may get some support and a weak division into three be the result.

A week later, Booth spent a day with Helen Bosanquet at Kirkcaldy and Dunfermline, visiting boarded-out lunatics and recipients of out-relief. Despite bad rheumatism he was keeping up with the travelling. However by 14 June he was happy to report that the Commissioners had scattered, and 'I am not sorry to have Edinburgh to myself for the weekend,' he wrote to Mary, 'lots of nice walks offer as an alternative to Linlithgow and Poor Law literature.'

Octavia wrote to Emily about a typically gruelling day. They had been to visit an orphan school for 1,300 children on a large estate; 'it is one of those institutions where they make a point of having no capital invested, or funded income; they say all depends on prayer. There is a sanatorium for phthisis and a farm for sane epileptics close by.' They were told that business in Paisley provided unlimited employment for factory girls, paying around £1 and £2 per week. 'Some manufacturers have a very high standard of duty. The Coatses have built beautiful lodging houses and clubs for the girls who work there. They would teach girls work, which is readily learnt.' Then there was a visit to a poor-house and lunatic asylum, and they attended a parish relief committee. 'I am longing to be home.'[6]

Despite the attractions of the scenery of the Highlands and Islands, it had been decided, Booth reported to Mary, to drop that part of the itinerary since there was 'nothing in it except the good fellowship and prospective *pleasure* of the trip – nothing of Poor Law value I mean.'

The Commissioners tended to split up and travel in parties. By 10 July they were in Taunton and then moved north to Shrewsbury and Leominster, via Birmingham. Travel arrangements could be unpredictable. 'Bentham came from Bradford in his motor and got all right to Oswestry on Monday morning where he met other Commissioners – but after that one puncture after another happened – and he did not reach us here till nine o'clock.'

In October of that year, Booth collapsed with a skin condition and continued in bad health which forced him to resign from the Commission in the spring. By then the atmosphere between the Booths and Beatrice Webb had further deteriorated; Beatrice heard that the Booths felt aggrieved, 'saying that somehow or other I "drove Charles Booth off the Commission". This is the most annoying story.'[7]

Octavia, on the other hand, valued her old friend Charles's company and good sense. She wrote to Mary Booth: 'I have not written before to tell you how very much I miss Mr Booth at the Commission. His earnest and generous work, his energy, his single-minded interest in the subject, were a continual strength and help to us all, and I personally miss him much.'[8]

Octavia was keen that as many of the Commissioners as possible should reach a unanimous decision and so she wrote to Hamilton in November, 1908. She was worried that the current draft for the Commission Report did not take into account the overtaxing of county councillors and the fact that the nominees might be untrustworthy.

I hear all round of the impossibility of County Councillors doing the work entrusted to them; of the duties devolving necessarily on officials; and of their being put on committees, other than those for which they have aptitude and experience. The *minor* Committees are those that really do the work, face to face with the poor; and I see no provision that they shall be composed of the right people.

Still, she admitted, she was too ignorant about statutory committees to object absolutely. She was not in favour of any sort of public works schemes (she had heard of one such in Leeds for which, it was said, the labour could not be found) and supported the idea of 'country work-houses with space for real work (called Labour Colonies if the world likes)' – properly supervised, there was nothing wrong with out-relief.

Booth, though no longer a Commissioner, still kept abreast of developments and in February 1909 he received a letter from Lord George Hamilton, who was trying to promote unanimity amongst the Commissioners, without success. There would be a Majority and a Minority Report. 'He has secured 14 out of 18 signatures and had assumed that Beatrice Webb had secured Russell Wakefield in addition to Lansbury and Chandler, and that is so.' He was pleased that Hamilton had asked for two sections and some maps from his own *magnum opus*, *The Life and Labour of the People of London*, to be published as an Appendix to the report.

When the Majority Report was published in 1909 Octavia was among the signatories, although she added a memorandum of her own. The Report listed twelve defects of the present Poor Law system. It criticized the existing administrative boundaries of the designated Poor Law areas, the excessive size of the Boards of Guardians, and the distance the system now stood from local government. It also attacked the lack of uniform standards and principles, the lack of investigation given to applicants, the giving of outdoor relief 'without plan or purpose', the poor state of the workhouses and their inappropriateness to the problems, the lack of co-operation between the Guardians and other charitable bodies, the tendency of candidates to buy votes with lavish promises, the failure to attract workers of the right calibre or 'leading citizens', the rise in expenditure without commensurate rise in efficiency, and the want of control and interest from central government. Much of this was pure COS ideology; but the Commissioners had also addressed the fact that the system was increasingly ineffective and inoperable.

Octavia's own dissension was encapsulated in 'a brief but emphatic memorandum' to the Majority Report. She objected to medical relief 'because it opens the door too widely to free medical relief'; she demurred at extending the voting power to those dependent on public funds; and 'emphatically dissented from the recommendations as to special work at times of depression'. For 'artificial work provided by State or municipality has never yet been successful, whether financially industrially or in its influence on character.' People must be trusted 'to provide against times of crisis by foresight, insurance and savings; we must not buoy them up by visions of State, or municipal employment . . .'[9]

Beatrice Webb's Minority Report endorsed a complete change. Tinkering at the edges was an ineffective path to reform. She and her fellow signatories proposed the abolition of the Poor Law Authority and the Boards of Guardians, the continuation of its remaining functions by new specialized authorities building upon those that already existed, and the separation of provision for the able-bodied and the 'non-able-bodied'. They agreed that assistance should be registered and co-ordinated, which would ensure that the obligation 'of able-bodied persons to support themselves and their families' be enforced. Under the aegis of county and county borough councils, a series of committees should be set up to deal with education, health, asylums and pensions. Finally the Minority Report recommended the introduction of a system of labour exchanges and the introduction of some kind of unemployment benefit, as well as public works schemes to take the stress of periods of high unemployment.

While the Minority Report was to have a far-reaching effect, the Majority Report was, in effect, treading water and signing the death-warrant of the Poor Law system – albeit unintentionally. The Guardians lingered on until 1929, by which time they had long been bypassed in many important areas of social welfare.

Octavia's contribution to the debate showed her to be out of step even with her own COS colleagues. There is little doubt that Octavia's dogmatism and age were telling against her; she had taken her stand and was unable to envisage change. Her health had been deteriorating in the four long years that the Commission toiled, and she was far from being its most vociferous or dominant member – as she might once have been. She was in no state of health or mind to be persuaded, by either what she had seen or heard.

Octavia's inability to grasp the wider implications of the issues illuminated the inherent deficiencies of her thinking and of her own 'system'. The weakness of her small-scale, individualist approach when applied to problems perceived and investigated on the national

scale was cruelly revealed. Never a theoretician, Octavia utterly failed
to grasp the responsibility incumbent on a wealthy State to assist its
weakest members. Yet if she had looked overseas, she would have
found that in Germany between 1883 and 1889 Bismarck had introduced a series of measures that included sickness insurance, accident
insurance and finally old age and invalidity pensions, with State
contributions. Denmark had followed in the 1890s, providing old age
pensions and health insurance. Octavia's thinking was anachronistic in
the 1900s and by the year of her death, 1912, the National Insurance
Act had been on the statute book for a year.

Yet while there were enormous changes in attitude to State intervention over social welfare, there was still the intractable problem
of the 'residuum', the poorest of the poor. This bottom layer of society
did not go away, but was viewed through a succession of different
lenses. In the 1880s the fear had been of social discontent, even of
revolution, and palliatives had ranged from the use of emigration and
labour colonies to the individualist approach – in particular the
carefully targeted charity provided by the COS.

In the 1890s the focus changed from the deficiencies of the individual to those of the environment. The Dock Strike of 1889 had
thrown new light on the poor and illustrated the fact that the residuum
was 'no longer a vast horde capable of holding the capital to ransom,
but a small and hopeless remnant, a nuisance to administrators rather
than a threat to civilization.'[10] Trade unionism was seen as a way in
which labour organization would 'be a lesson to these men in self-
restraint and fellowship.'[11]

Darwinian thinking envisaged urban life as survival of the fittest and
it was a short step from there to eugenics, prompted by the outcry
about a nation unfit to fight. The Fabians had little time for the 'idle
and incompetent; those who are a tax on the community for which
they have never done a fair share of work and never will.' Beveridge,
the future father of the Welfare State, contemplating unemployment
from Toynbee Hall, was eager to promote the organization of labour
and the setting up of labour exchanges. In 1906, the year of the Liberal
landslide, he considered that those recognized as unemployable 'must
become the acknowledged dependents of the state, removed from free
industry and maintained adequately in public institutions, but with a
complete and permanent loss of all citizen rights including not only the
franchise, but civil freedom and fatherhood.'

Octavia's dogged objection to unemployment benefits or old age pensions may seem strange to us, but she also evidenced a sense of personal obligation (based as always on her religious belief in duty towards one's fellows) which neither socialists nor welfare-minded liberals had yet approached. In many ways the arguments about the shape of society remained oddly apolitical. As Stedman Jones comments, Cardinal Manning was a far more influential voice where the largely Irish Catholic casual labour force was concerned than the Social Democratic Federation. Octavia, schooled in Owenite and Christian Socialist co-operative beliefs, essentially operating on a small scale, may justifiably be accused of parochialism and lack of vision, but never of adherence to specific political dogma.

Ironically enough, while Octavia was engrossed in the work of the Commission and signally failing to respond to the wider challenge, her workers were engaged in putting her principles of housing management into practice on the largest scale yet. As many of the long leases on their properties fell in, the Ecclesiastical Commissioners had to confront the problem of large areas of desperately substandard housing in some of the poorest areas of London. As they reclaimed these estates they had to put forward a strategy for the future, frequently involving large-scale rebuilding, to provide fit housing. The church would no longer be seen as a slum landlord.

Earlier the Commissioners had favoured offering leases to individuals, such as Miss Townshend and the Countess of Selborne, or to proven trusts or housing companies (including Miss Cons's) to carry out the work. But in the 1900s the Commissioners began to build cottages and tenements on their own behalf, and to depend on the services of Octavia's managers in whom, by now, they had complete confidence. To these managers fell 'besides the collection of the rents, the selection of tenants, the ordering of necessary tenants' repairs, the general watchfulness over the maintenance of good order, and against abuse of privileges and joint rights among the tenants.'[12]

In 1901 a major rebuilding scheme by the Ecclesiastical Commissioners on their land near Waterloo provided housing for 250 families, and in 1903 another, larger development at Walworth provided 800 tenancies by 1906. Further cottages were built in Southwark and in Westminster. Octavia, unable to deal with the work personally, was content to hand it over to one of her most trusted assistants,

Mary Lumsden. In 1906 a booklet was published, chronicling those achievements.

Octavia's influence can be seen in every point. Her suggestions went far beyond basic management to the detail and form of the new development. She persuaded the Commissioners to concentrate on the provision of cottages with private backyards and to ensure that the tenement houses did not exceed three floors in height. The intention was not to exceed two tenements per floor, 'the greatest care having been taken to obtain the maximum amount of sunlight and the freest circulation of air having regard to the surroundings.' Lobbied by Octavia and following the example of the Red Cross garden and playground, the Commissioners allocated land for recreation grounds in each of their sites.

The Walworth scheme was a sizeable venture. Twenty-two acres of land owned by the Dean and Chapter of Canterbury became available on the expiry of a 200-year lease. The site was covered with small houses and shops but in such a condition that rehabilitation would have been out of the question. At an estimated cost of £200,000 the Commissioners took the decision to rebuild the estate. The Commissioners' own stipulation, as on all their estates, was that there would be no public-houses.

Octavia described the 'great day' when she and her workers took over the Walworth Estate in October 1903. Fourteen of them prepared to collect rent from five or six hundred unknown tenants. 'We organized it all thoughtfully; we had fifteen collecting books and all the tenants' books prepared, had opened a bank account, had found a room as office, and divided the area among our workers. Our first duty was to get the tenants to recognize our authority and pay us. I think we were very successful.'

The next priority was repairs, and over 1,000 orders came in during the first weeks, despite the fact that the area was to be shortly rebuilt. The tenants had to be moved into existing empty houses in order to carry out a phased decanting, ahead of the rebuilding. It took much thought and effort to organize but the first two streets were emptied in the early months. Over the next three years the tenants were moved ahead of the demolition gangs and then back into their spanking new homes.

The plan for the Estate included a new parish school, an acre set aside for recreation, improved and widened roads, and 'accommodation for 790 families in four-roomed and three-roomed cottages, cottage flats [on the lines of those Octavia had built off Lisson Grove earlier], and flats of three- and two-roomed tenements in houses in no case higher than three storeys.' In the event there were also five-roomed cottages.

Almost three years later Miss Lumsden reported on the changes. The costermongers' donkeys, ducks and chickens had been cleared away and the place no longer looked like 'some out-of-the-way country district'. New gardens were flourishing behind the cottages (though the shared tenement gardens were less harmoniously ordered) and the Commissioners had taken care to preserve the old trees and shrubs on the site where possible. The combined rent and rates ranged from a weekly 5s 6d for two-roomed tenements to 14s for the five-roomed cottages. Miss Lumsden described the facilities, shared in the tenements, and the fittings which included cupboards, Larbert ranges and a gas supply. As she summed it up: 'The neighbourhood had undergone a transformation, and the improvement cannot be measured in words.'

The Walworth Estate, which came into being as Octavia travelled the country with the Poor Law Commissioners, was in many ways the embodiment of Octavia's ideas upon housing for the poor. She had never touched anything on this scale and its success suggested that her approach could have been applied on a far larger scale. But for Octavia, approaching seventy, it was too late.

CHAPTER 20

The National Trust

OCTAVIA and Hardwick Rawnsley had originally met through Ruskin, who had commended Octavia to Rawnsley as 'the best lady abbess you can have for London work'. At much the same time, Octavia had met Robert Hunter through her interest in the Commons Preservation Society for which he had been Honorary Solicitor since shortly after its formation in 1865. Hunter's sister Dorothy had helped found the Kyrle Society and was a friend of Octavia's. 'They . . . had the same passionate love of natural beauty and believed in its power to help the workers of the world.'[1]

Earlier CPS campaigns had been one-off affairs, reacting in the heat of the moment to the proposed depredations of an avaricious owner or developer, and constantly limited by the fact that the organization was unable to acquire and manage land in any quantity. With their combined experience, Rawnsley, Hunter and Octavia saw that there was a need for an organization which could combine both roles – a campaigning body with powers of acquisition.

Octavia looked back on those aims in a speech in Oxford, the notes for which are undated. 'We wanted a body to hold in perpetuity such lands [open spaces] and that it should consist of men and women who should be free from the tendency to sacrifice such treasures to mercenary considerations, or to vulgarizing them in accordance with popular cries.'[2]

In 1884 W. J. Evelyn, the aged descendant of John Evelyn, wrote to Octavia over the fate of his family house, Sayes Court in Deptford, which he had hoped to offer to the Metropolitan Board of Works to ensure public access to the historic site. But the Board was not so constituted as to be able to take the house and land, or to fund its maintenance from the public purse. Given Evelyn's advanced age, a trust seemed risky. The proposed gift fell through.

Octavia and Robert Hunter, whom she had consulted over the future of Sayes Court, now concluded that the need for some kind of public holding trust for land was urgent. Hunter suggested a Company constituted for this purpose; Octavia felt sure that 'at any moment some other important scheme may present itself and our body ought to be ready.'[3] In a speech to the National Association of Social Science in Birmingham that year, Hunter outlined his idea for a joint stock company 'which shall administer its property with a view to the protection of the public interests in open spaces.'

Octavia preferred the idea of a trust, rather than a company, for 'you will do better, I believe, to bring forward its benevolent than its commercial character. People don't like unsuccessful business, but do like charity where a little money goes a long way because of good commercial management.' The name she suggested to Hunter was: '"The Commons and Gardens Trust" – and then printing in small letters – "for accepting, holding and purchasing open spaces for the people in town and country".' Above this on the letter Hunter scribbled: '?*National Trust. RH*'[4]

In 1885 a memorandum of association for the Open Spaces Preservation and Land Development Society was drawn up and printed. Many of its objects were remarkably close to those of the Kyrle Society – such as the use of buildings as museums, galleries or 'for the purposes of recreation or instruction', and the securing of burial grounds as open spaces. Its inclusive aims, dealing both with the 'promotion of preservation' and the acquisition of a wide range of properties, from graveyards to smallholdings, suggest that Octavia may have drafted the document. The Society proposed to issue £20,000 in £1 shares. Nothing became of the Society in this form.[5]

The long interval between Octavia's letter to Hunter in February 1885 and the inaugural meeting of the National Trust in July 1894 was caused by the pressure of other business but more particularly by a lobby which felt that the overlap with the CPS might lead to the CPS's being submerged. But in her own accounts of the formation of the National Trust, Octavia always cited the importance of the Kyrle Society as well as that of the CPS – the Open Space Sub-Committee was a testing ground for her aims and objectives.

In 1888 the CPS meeting at Grosvenor House, the Duke of Westminster's town house, was addressed with some force by both Octavia and Hardwick Rawnsley. Octavia's platform was the duty of the society to support the footpath protection societies, who were fighting to defend 'one of the great common inheritances to which as English citizens they are born – the footpaths of their native country.' These battles were being lost in the courts because the poor dared not object and the rich were *parti pris*. The footpaths were being eroded by neglect or 'judicious planting . . . so that the stranger is unconscious of his right', and once lost, these tracks were irrecoverable. 'You are asked today to sanction the Commons Preservation Society becoming a distinctly recognized centre for the preservation of footpaths.'

The issue which had brought all this to a head was access to the Latrigg footpath skirting Skiddaw, in the Lake District. The case was due to be heard in court in July 1888. The guarantee fund required was £2,000, of which £400 had been raised (only £100 from Londoners). Rawnsley, who was fighting the matter on the spot from his Crosthwaite parish, thought it was a matter of principle. 'Living as he did in a country which year by year was more visited by people in need of rest, in search of thought and inspiration . . . he could not help knowing that the love of scenery was becoming yearly more and more the possession of many.' A settlement out of court secured public access to the path and was a triumph for Rawnsley's campaign.

To avoid the problems of interfering local interests, Rawnsley proposed setting up 'a great impersonal limited liability company, after the manner of the Scottish Rights of Way Society . . . such a society by its very existence would deter much of the illegal closing of rights of way.' He was the third of the founders to propose a model for the new body. There were still worries about an overlap with the CPS, so much so that Octavia wrote to Hunter in October 1889: 'Mr Shaw Lefevre does not rise to the idea of the new society. Failing him would Mr Briscoe Eyre be our head man?'

Octavia turned to her American contacts for help. Ellen Chase, back in America, was asked to get hold of the latest reports of the Open Spaces movement in the USA – the Boston Metropolitan Park Commission and the Trustees of Public Reservations. Robert Hunter had asked for them in order to compare the statutory protection afforded to landscape in the USA against its British equivalent. Since one of the Trustees of Public Reservations was called Philip Chase, Ellen presumably was well placed to provide the information and quickly sent over a copy of the Trustees' Report.

Thus it was an American Act of 1891, establishing the Trustees of

Public Reservations, Massachusetts, that suggested the constitution for the new British trust.[6] An inaugural meeting was held on 16 November 1893 in the offices of the Commons Preservation Society.

Whatever his doubts, Shaw-Lefevre was there, as were G. F. Watts and Holman Hunt, Professor Huxley and Walter Besant, among others. The new association would be 'general trustee for all property intended for the use and enjoyment of the nation at large'. It was set up as a joint stock company and would apply for a Board of Trade licence to give it non-profit-making status. *The Times* ran a leader the following day, welcoming the nascent association; it ended:

> the memorandum of association ought to contain a clause excluding oranges and sandwich papers from any bit of beautiful scenery that may come under its control. Perhaps the greatest of all national benefits it could confer would be the education of the sight-seeing public up to the point at which it could regard leisure as tolerable for fifteen minutes without these accessories.

A meeting at Grosvenor House on July 1894 agreed Octavia's formal resolution (seconded by Edmund Maurice) which provided the means of setting up a corporate body capable of holding land. Octavia reminded her audience, *The Times* of 17 July reported, that 'The same spirit which had saved Parliament Hill would save many a lovely view or old ruin or manor-house from destruction and for the everlasting delight of thousands of the people of these islands [Cheers]' Sir Frederick Pollock moved that they should try to obtain exemption from death duties for those who left land or historic monuments to the new body, in the same way that works of art and antiquities currently were exempted.

The Memorandum and Articles of Association, dated 12 December 1894, clearly drafted by Robert Hunter and witnessed by nine signatories (Octavia included) were registered on 12 January 1895.

The first executive meeting was held shortly afterwards at the Trust's offices (shared with the Kent and Surrey Footpaths Society) at 1, Great College Street in Westminster. Octavia had earlier written to Sydney Cockerell to ask if he knew of a secretary for the National Trust. In looking for the right candidate, she said,

> I fear we want a great deal, and give next to nothing. Of course, it might grow, but then it might not. The work would be delightful to

one who cared for it: all the good results of the Commons and Footpaths work, with little or no fighting. On the contrary, calling on the generous and good people. But then we want interest in the cause, and accurate habits of business . . .

Lawrence Chubb was appointed, although Hardwick Rawnsley shadowed him as Honorary Secretary.

The twelve-member Executive Committee included both Harriot Yorke and Edmund Maurice. At its first meeting it discussed the Trust's first acquisition – Dinas Oleu, land at Barmouth which Mrs Fanny Talbot wanted to present as the first gift to the new Trust. Mrs Talbot had been a close friend of Ruskin's from 1874 and a staunch supporter of the Guild of St George (to which she had also presented land and cottages at Barmouth). Dinas Oleu was a rocky fell, a tiny pocket of four and a half acres above Barmouth, looking out over Cardigan Bay. Rawnsley was the key figure in securing the gift but it must have delighted Octavia. Tiny as it was, it had enormous significance to her both as the Trust's first acquisition of open space and as a spot well known to Ruskin, who had visited Mrs Talbot at Barmouth in 1876. At the meeting there was also discussion about raising funds to buy Carlyle's house in Chelsea.

Octavia's status at the National Trust was always unspecific; she was on the Provisional Council and, adept at the task of asking people to give, she became responsible for appeals. A number of the early appeal leaflets are obviously her work. She thus had a central position in the expansion of the organization and, above all, in the direction it took. Sir Robert Hunter was Chairman. The Honorary Secretary was Rawnsley (since 1893 a Canon of Carlisle cathedral), who frequently deferred to her when drafting letters of appeal. In one case she wrote to him apologizing for amending his draft, but, 'I thought perhaps it would be well to dwell a little on the breeze and beauty of the space as well as on its historical and poetical side, and so I have . . . added to it . . . All my friends seem keener about beautiful open space . . . we don't seem to reach the antiquaries and artists.' A few years after its foundation, Octavia acknowledged that the new National Trust 'has not so much to fight as to ask men to give'.

The original Council was a large body, the co-founders joining Lord Eversley, Lord Bryce, Lord Rosebery (first Chairman of the LCC), and the ubiquitous Harriot Yorke. The Duke of Westminster was President. Harriot became Treasurer in 1896, reporting a credit of £52 17s 4d to the August Council meeting. Two years later she threatened to resign 'if the work of the Trust was to include more house property'. But she did not carry out her threat, and remained Honorary Treasurer until 1925, continuing on the Executive Committee until her death in 1930. In later years Lord Chorley described her representing 'so to speak, the Octavia Hill point of view, but she seldom intervened in the discussions and was noteworthy more for her appearance and her impression of personality than for anything she said.'[7]

A number of the members of the National Trust Council and the Executive in the early years had long-standing connections with Octavia. Professor Patrick Geddes was one, F. D. Mocatta another. Edmund Maurice was a member of the Executive until his resignation in 1899. Despite its many august supporters, it was a small organization. Annual subscriptions came to less than £300 in 1902.

A royal patron for the new body was easily secured. In 1902 Princess Louise, Duchess of Argyll, accepted the Presidency. As Nigel Bond, by then Secretary, wrote: 'from its earliest days, the Princess took a sympathetic and encouraging interest in the aims and work of the Trust . . . I believe HRH's interest in the Trust was first aroused by her admiration of the work of Miss Octavia Hill.'[8]

Octavia's mother, now well into her nineties, watched her daughter's work expand, and wrote to an old family friend, Miss Schuyler: 'Octavia's work grows and grows, and according to its wont flourishes. Her heart is chiefly interested just now in saving *beautiful* spots in England, securing them in their beauty for future generations.'[9] The subscription list for Brandlehow includes Mrs Southwood Hill, who gave one guinea.

Brandlehow consisted of 108 acres on the west shore of Derwentwater. Again it was high among Octavia's priorities because of its connection with Ruskin. The appeal document was directed to 'lovers of Ruskin, who once said, "If there is one thing I can boast of, it is that I can be a guide to all the beauty of Derwentwater".' Clearly Octavia penned the pamphlet. £6,500 was raised to secure Brandlehow, including £100 from the Guild of St George.

Octavia described the site to an audience in Oxford.

I should like you all to see it. It comprises about a mile of the lake shore, it commands views of Skiddaw in one direction and Borrowdale in the other, from its slope you can see the whole space of the lake set with its islands, it has crag and meadow and wood, on it the sun shines, over it the wind blows, it will be preserved in its present loveliness and it belongs to you all and to every landless man, woman and child in England.

She no doubt remembered the drive around Derwentwater searching for a house for Ruskin, more than thirty years before.

Octavia wrote to her mother vividly, describing the opening ceremony at Brandlehow in 1902, at which Princess Louise presided.

I have just come back from the great opening, and want to tell you about it. It was very successful, very simple, and real and unconventional. The place was looking very lovely, I never saw the light more beautiful . . . The wind was high and tore the tent to ribbons when it was being put up, but I think it really did better, because the simple little red dais was under the free sky, with the great lake lying below . . . It was very funny and primitive and the nice north country people were quite near and saw and heard all. The Princess was most friendly and kind, and really did show deep and intelligent interest in the National Trust work. She asked me whom we were going to make President and added, 'I hoped you would ask me, I should like really to do more for the work, and I should like Lord Carlisle as Vice President.'

Octavia was delighted, she told her mother, as Lord Carlisle was her preferred candidate. Princess Louise then told her about some beautiful old houses that she wanted the Trust to campaign for; 'she really does care and know, I think.' It had been a thoroughly cheerful stay, for Octavia had taken Gertrude's daughter Elinor, her niece and assistant, and another young helper, and their high spirits had brightened up the elderly group, which also included Harriot and Miranda. They had stayed on Derwent Island and the successful event must have brought back memories of the many happy visits to Mary Harris, stretching over almost fifty years. She ended: 'I feel almost overcome by the extreme beauty of everything here, so bountiful in making and giving is the great Creator, and a song of thankfulness seems to be singing on in my heart for having been given power to have some hand in devoting some of the lovely places to people for ever.'[10]

Octavia and Sir Robert, as he became in 1894, treated one another as equals. Canon Rawnsley, on the other hand, seems always to have deferred to Octavia, sending her drafts of his speeches to comment upon and when he was offered the Bishopric of Madagascar, writing to her for advice. Although, as she pointed out, she was hardly qualified to offer advice on Madagascar as such, she knew Rawnsley's work intimately. Was it really his duty to break with everything he had so successfully pursued and 'to lose so much of training, of association, of knowledge of fellow-workers'? What is more, Madagascar was French, which did not make it a particularly 'hopeful sphere'. She continued:

> And what a work you have here in England. It almost seems to me unique. I am sure that the National Trust owes, and must owe, much of its special character to your influence. If it is to gather in the givers, if it is to seize on the important opportunities for good, if it is to retain some element of poetry and of hope, it seems to me as if it must depend on you. There is no one among us who has so wide and appreciative an outlook, who brings in so many harmoniously or who can show the poetry of a place so vividly. I really should feel *most* discouraged about the Trust if you were to leave us.[11]

She used her eloquence to such effect that she persuaded Rawnsley, and he remained in England.

Janet Upcott, who started work with Octavia as a housing manager in 1910, was also brought in to help with Trust work and accompanied Miss Yorke to meetings of the Finance and Estates Committee. Miss Upcott had to keep a ledger of all Trust properties, since 'Miss Hill's practice had been, as far as possible, to have each property self-supporting. The ledger was posted each month from accounts sent up by the Trust offices. "Figures", Miss Hill used to say, "mean to us the happiness of the people".'

When the Trust was offered an entire village Octavia, sensitive to the tensions between landlord and tenant, was not eager to take it on. 'Imagine the Committee faced with the prospect of turning out a poor widow!' Janet Upcott remembered her saying. She also remembered Octavia's constant reference to Sir Robert Hunter's example – although Hunter was no longer active in the organization by the time Janet began work at the National Trust. After Octavia's death, Janet Upcott, then only twenty-three years old, took Octavia's place on the Finance and General Purposes Committee and also became a member of the Estates Committee, on which she remained for fifty-six years. Her other position was Honorary Adviser on Housing.[12] She, as much as anyone, remained the living link between the founders and the expanding organization into the late 1960s.

Constituted so as to save both landscape and buildings of historic interest, the National Trust now began to acquire various properties. One of the earliest was another stretch that Octavia knew very well, Barras Head – eighteen acres looking across to the Tintagel headland, where she had spent holidays with the MacDonalds and the Barnetts. She described it: 'the black rock feet . . . are for ever deep in the breaking waves of the Atlantic, a heather-covered height on which the sheep browse, the whole scene haunted by thoughts of Merlin and King Arthur.' It proved easy to raise funds for so well-loved a spot – of the purchase price, £505, there remained just £23 to be found.

There was much active discussion about the Clergy House, Alfriston, in Sussex, which was the first building that the Trust acquired. Octavia loved the house, the site as much as the building itself, 'tiny but beautiful, with orchard and a sweep of lowland river behind it'.[13] From the early days Octavia often made the analogy of the National Trust with the National Gallery. On that reckoning, Alfriston was a tiny Cranach.

The small vernacular buildings of the countryside had a special place in Octavia's affections. She described them:

> our small houses, steep in roof and gable, mellowed with the colour of ages, picturesque in outline, rich in memories of England as our ancestors knew it. Alfriston, pre-Reformation clergy house, nestled below the Sussex downs; Long Crendon Court House, used since the time of Henry V, standing at the end of the long street of a needle-making village of Oxfordshire; the old post office at Tintagel, a picturesque 14th century cottage . . .

They were all of a piece. There was 'nothing great about them, nothing very striking, only quaint picturesque out-of-the-world places . . . greeting the eye with a sense of repose.'

Perhaps assisted by Octavia's good offices at the Ecclesiastical Commissioners, the National Trust acquired the Clergy House, Alfriston in the winter of 1896 for £10; funds were needed for repairs, and the Trust had to find £350. Alfriston was in very poor shape, Octavia wrote to the Revd Alford who had sent a donation; to let it deteriorate further would be 'a sort of breach of trust . . . because it is ours now, given in the expectation we could preserve it. Besides all this hope is a great factor in inspiring people to work and gift, and if our National Trust failed in these small schemes in this the opening of its work, it would throw back the future work.'[14]

The Alfriston campaign brought Octavia into contact with William Morris's own campaigning body, the Society for the Protection of Ancient Buildings, which had been founded in 1877 with enthusiastic support from Ruskin. The connections between the SPAB and the National Trust were close. Octavia was given honorary membership of the SPAB in 1897 and the Society introduced her to a group of architects, particularly Thackeray Turner and C. R. Ashbee, with whom she had protracted dealings. Sydney Cockerell was another link between them. She knew the doctrines of Morris and Ruskin and was aware of the distinction between repair and restoration. She wrote to Cockerell, of Alfriston: 'We should very naturally be asked to "restore" it, in so far as that odious word means preservation from decay.'[15]

At the Annual General Meeting of the SPAB in 1898 H. E. Luxmoore commented on the sense of fellowship and common purpose between the various groups and societies which would, in contemporary terms, be classed as conservation bodies.

> I shall not be wrong in claiming my society as kindred which has for its object to make or keep this country of ours either interesting or beautiful: and on the committees of many of these societies appear names which are also prominent on our roll . . . let me mention, as an instance only, the Kyrle Society, and join with it the name of Miss Octavia Hill who is not only one of our members, but one of the best of all ringleaders in all plots for making our country not only beautiful and interesting, but also, if it may be, good.[16]

The Court House, Long Crendon was another building which the SPAB brought to the attention of the Trust. Typically, Octavia was not just concerned about the architectural features and fabric of the building, which needed some £300 spent upon it. She was also planning how it could be used.

> The top room, a large one, will be used as a Sunday School . . . A member of our Committee will rent the rest of the house partly for

his wife and himself . . . partly to use as a holiday home for London boys connected with his Art Classes. They will go in groups through the summer, fortnight by fortnight. It is a great blessing to get these lovely old buildings into the hands of the National Trust.[17]

The 'member of the committee' she referred to was Ashbee and the understanding that he could use Long Crendon soon led to a major disagreement between them. Ashbee's insistence on filling the house with Guild of Handicraft furniture and inscribing its emblem over the fireplace in the upper room was among the things that caused her to change her mind. Octavia concluded that Ashbee's boys' hostel was an inappropriate use for a vulnerable old building. She intervened, bringing about Ashbee's resignation from the Council of the Trust in the summer of 1901 and 'practically a quarrel with Octavia Hill', as he wrote. He was sorry because the boys had grown to love the house 'and would have given it such a soul as no dead museum in the Trust's charge can . . . possibly have.'[18] It was an early instance of a familiar criticism.

Yet it was only a temporary setback to their friendship. On his American lecture tour in 1900 to gain support for the National Trust, Ashbee was struck by the affluence of his American audience in contrast to the poverty of the organization at home, including, 'Miss Yorke with the money bag and the last 2s 6d duly noted and that most lovable of great little women Octavia Hill . . .'[19]

Ashbee's memories of Octavia after her death were equally fond, although he remained critical of her style in committee.

She was too tough an individualist for me. I worked with her for some years and watched her work often with wonder, but admiration was tempered with awe and – shall I say malaise. She was of the women whose function in life it is to manage – keep you in order – see that you work on set lines, and with a hard stern power of regulating her own life she expected other folk to do likewise. She belonged I think to that early and mid Victorian mould out of which the Unitarians and the positivists are made and those others whose God is an abstraction, but like many of them her enthusiasm was a very noble quality. Did it embody itself? I've no doubt it did but to one who like myself only met Octavia Hill on committees and once had to fight her on a question of principle she was just a moral force that could take curious and tremendous forms and was certainly dangerous to wrestle with:- better to let it go its way and to realize that it had its own purpose to fulfil. Moral forces are apt to fight in the air like flames and they burn.

Thinking about the particular case, 'I suppose we were both of us rather too high-handed in our methods of procedure and perhaps mine was too American and swift into the bargain, but the dear old Lady's way of ordering things grew to be intolerable – something akin to an English Government Department and a seaside lodging-house land-lady – and as one must leave a woman in command of the field under certain conditions, there was no other way out.' He felt that the decision against his tenancy of the Court House had been taken 'by very magnificent subcommittees hidden in the ample skirt pockets of a venerable old lady'. Ashbee saw that a collective mentality had already descended on the Trust: 'the pretence of doing things through the collective wisdom of a number of individuals when the real work is being done by the energy [illegible] . . . Here it was the old lady and I who were doing the work.' The outcome was that the

> beautiful Court House is for the present at least to remain a mere dead lumber house with no humanity in it but just to be looked at by Tourists. No more singing by the Ingle, no more buzz of life and living links with the past but dead grey walls and weeds all over our garden. For it is ours in the spiritual sense – we made it . . . I wish that punctilious old lady could have seen the faces of the boys when they heard the news, their looks would have given the lie to all her petty peccadilloes.

In contrast with Ashbee's view, John Bailey, a barrister and literary critic who taught at both Toynbee Hall and the Working Men's College, found Octavia surprisingly deferential yet somewhat relent-less. He had joined the Council and Executive Committee in 1898, becoming Vice-Chairman in 1913 and later Chairman.

In 1902 he wrote to his wife from the Lake District where he was on a walking holiday. Octavia had tracked him down. 'I have had to write a long letter to Octavia Hill in reply to one I had from her this morning about various matters. I enclose it that you may see her curious modesty and ridiculous deference to your superior husband! It is very odd she is so polite. But the result of it is bad – for I had to give her my views on all these subjects and it is now ten o'clock.'[20] It was not much of a holiday.

For Octavia, as for Rawnsley, the Lake District was Ruskin's country. Among the various memorials that the Trust acquired was 'one which the years will we believe render always more valuable, the simple stone erected to John Ruskin on Friar's Crag at Derwent Water, where first he learned the beauty of that nature that he was to love so much and describe so eloquently.' From his love of this part of England had sprung Octavia's own, and it made the Lake District, where he had spent the final years of his life, hallowed ground.

As a small organization the National Trust had to choose its objects carefully, and there were so many deserving causes. It fought campaigns for the preservation of footpaths and commons, against gravel digging and encroachment, and had the added responsibility of the repair and consolidation of the buildings in its care, which were often handed over to it in poor condition.

In 1904 the National Trust acquired its first sizeable country house, Barrington Court in Somerset, which turned out to be a financial nightmare. Nigel Bond was very reluctant to take on other such houses as a result, and there was little call for the Trust to do so. It was not until the Country Houses Scheme in the late 1930s that the National Trust became associated with that scale and kind of building. The awkward problem of using the houses fittingly so as to avoid the mummification of their contents remains as hard to solve today as it was when Octavia and Ashbee argued the point.

Like Nigel Bond, Octavia was not enthusiastic about the acquisition of houses. Perhaps Harriot's threatened resignation as Treasurer in 1898 was a muted protest against any threat of undue expansion of the Trust in that direction. Octavia told her niece Elinor that it was a mistake, and she always regarded the acquisition of buildings as an adjunct to the saving of the countryside for the benefit of the public.[21] She often quoted a remark which confirmed to her the enormous importance, and potential, of the National Trust: 'When collecting money for securing a bit of the Lake country, I received 2s 6d from a factory worker in Sheffield, she said "all my life I have longed to see the Lakes. I shall never see them now, but I should like to help to keep them for others."'

That poignant comment encapsulated Octavia's wish to preserve the best of the countryside for the common good. Whether it was the Lake District, the unspectacular River Wandle (another of Ruskin's favourite places) or any other quiet undeveloped spot, ordinary men and women could enjoy 'the holiday [which] to so many landless

[309]

families who have no deer park, yacht or country house becomes year by year more important.'

Years before Octavia had written a powerful article, 'More Air for London'.[22] She had argued eloquently for the preservation of open spaces in the city, in phrases which she had frequently rehearsed in connection with her many campaigns, but she also added a valuable analysis of the open space ('not . . . the spaces unbuilt upon, but those really secured to the people') available to Londoners. She suggested a network of paths, a 'green belt' as she termed it, linking the various open spaces already secured, and backed this appeal with some statistics. She had calculated that the population of the western section of the city had one acre of 'preserved open space' to every 682 people, whilst that of the eastern half had one acre to every 7,481 people. 'There are indeed many good things in life which may be unequally apportioned and no such serious loss arise; but the need of quiet, the need of air, the need of exercise, and, I believe, the sight of sky and of things growing, seem human needs, common to all men.'

The achievements of the infant National Trust, anticipating the later achievements of Town and Country Planning legislation, suggested the possibility of more ambitious green belts of protected countryside stretching around the perimeter of the ever-expanding metropolitan areas, providing a breathing space and a check on development.

The objectives of the Trust in the early days united the three founders, all middle-class social reformers[23] who were dedicated to giving people without regular access to the countryside a hint of its beauties. In other hands, with other priorities, the Trust changed its nature dramatically.

A constant question was how far the Trust could expand. Hunter became nervous over the Gowbarrow appeal for a site of 700 acres, costing £12,000. But Octavia was a fighter. She was, after all, the woman who had raised £52,500 to secure Parliament Hill for the public. No National Trust appeal failed in her lifetime. Her eloquence on the platform for these causes ensured their success. Speaking in Oxford to raise the Gowbarrow funds she invoked both Turner and Wordsworth. The site comprised:

a mile of lake shore, not to be cut off from the visitor by enclosure or garden but by which he can wander at will and hear the ripples breaking on the pebbles . . . valley, lake, mountain peaks, slopes of russet fern or heather, wood and stream and rocks, when spring sets the primroses in thousands on the banks of the stream, or autumn turns the wild cherry trees crimson, and the birches gold, when the storm sweeps over the mountains, or the summer sun streams among the trees . . . . Is it all to be ours for our rest, refreshment and inspiration and handed on by us in all its beauty in perpetuity for the England that is to be?

As a friend of the organization observed: 'It would be easy, no doubt, to throw ridicule on the present achievements of their ambitious scheme . . .' – but Octavia, more than anyone involved, knew that from tiny acorns large oaks often grew.

In the early years of the National Trust Octavia's hand, and often purse, could be seen behind most of the acquisitions. A considerable number were places that she personally knew and loved. She encouraged the idea of leaving land *in memoriam*, and the Hill family set the example. Miranda Hill presented the Trust with the first land on Ide Hill. Dr and Mrs Jamieson Hurry presented thirty-four acres at One Tree Hill, near Sevenoaks in Kent in memory of Arthur Hill, Octavia's half-brother, whilst a list of housing workers, friends and supporters later gave forty-three guineas towards the Borrowdale appeal in memory of Miranda.

The names of donors to appeals in the early Annual Reports are familiar from their support for Octavia's other projects. Life membership was £20, and annual membership ten shillings, so that the £25 that Octavia and the £10 that Harriot gave to the Alfriston appeal in 1897 were considerable sums. The Maurices, Mrs Hill, Miranda, Miss Schuster, Miss Sim, Miss Baumgartner were all listed in the Reports each year, as well as regular joint contributions from the fellow-workers – even Herman Southwood Smith, Octavia's uncle, had joined before his death in 1897.

Year by year Octavia extended the family donations of land around Crockham Hill. In 1904 another parcel of land at Crockham Hill was added to those already in Trust ownership at Ide Hill, Toys Hill and Mariner's Hill – all high points on that stretch of countryside along the rim of the High Weald which was virtually Octavia's own backyard. The Annual Report of 1904 recorded the latest gift:

Like the terrace owned by the Trust on Toys Hill, it thus carries out the suggestion made by the Council some years ago that the presentation of such spots to a body which is pledged to retain their

[311]

natural beauty as far as possible, is a fitting mode of perpetuating the memory of those who in their lives have shewn at once an appreciation of Nature and a desire to make a permanent gift to those who have no beautiful parks or gardens of their own, and whose lives are spent in the gloomier and more sordid surroundings of a great city.[24]

In 1903 Octavia had begun to buy Mariner's Hill on her own behalf, although she feared she might have to build one or two houses to finance the purchase, but her hopes were that the National Trust would take it on, which it soon agreed to do. She was able to reassure her solicitor Carrington Ouvry, who had recently become her niece Elinor's husband, that clauses restricting the uses of the land, as to 'institutions, holiday homes etc.' were perfectly acceptable. After all, the Trust 'by no means plan to give access to the tramp, the London rough, the noisy beanfeaster, or the shouting crowds of children, they offer no attractions for them, but plan to preserve the land in its natural beauty for the artist, the professional man, and such of the public as appreciate and respect natural beauty.'[25] It is an interesting insight into Octavia's aims for the Trust and bears more than a trace of Ruskin about it.

All went well, and she sent the deposit for £130 to Ouvry ten days later. A month afterwards the vendor died suddenly, so Octavia hoped the contract would be binding on the heirs; one disappointment was that the ancient common rights had been lost and, it seemed, could not be reclaimed. The sale was completed by Christmas. Carrington Ouvry had also been elected to both the Executive and the Estates Committee of the Trust; Octavia hoped that he was 'pleased to have had so large a hand in providing a spot which will be a joy to many in the years to come.'[26] She wanted him to come down and see to the planting and placing of seats, but the weather had not been kind.

Octavia particularly favoured acquisitions in her home area because it was so easily accessible by train to 'the Londoner who takes a Saturday afternoon from gas-lighted city office or many storied London street. There he can rest on the grassy or wooded slopes, and feast his eyes on the marvellous blue of the hill before him.' Achieving Trust ownership of the three most prominent headlands around Crockham Hill delighted her. 'Each forms a vantage ground for looking over (what Rudyard Kipling calls) "the blue goodness of the

Weald".' Octavia 'constantly stressed . . . that every effort should be made to keep open the tops of hills round London and other big towns.'[27] She knew and loved 'the blue of the Ashdown Forest range . . . seen across the near slopes of wild hyacinths or meadow grass, the sight of sunset or moon rise.'

In the summer of 1908 Octavia planned an open day on Mariner's Hill, on 25 June. Miss Yorke was in charge of catering – beef and lamb (ham was rejected) and no sweets. A brake would meet guests at Oxted station, and the only question was how much to fit into the day. Her appetite for detail had not diminished. Carrington Ouvry threw a damper on the plans by pointing out that it was hayfever season but Sir Robert Hunter was already invited and it was decided to go ahead. Despite fears that not many of the invitees were coming, Octavia energetically informed the newspapers of the event and of her gift to the Trust.

Thirty miles to the west, near Hindhead where he lived, Robert Hunter was securing large areas of the same south facing scarp of the North Downs, including the Devil's Punchbowl. The Trust was already encouraging a decentralized approach. 'It is proposed that the land, though vested in the Trust, which will of course be ultimately responsible, shall be managed by a local committee mainly composed of residents.'

The sums needed to purchase Mariner's Hill and other properties, however, paled into insignificance beside the astonishing £300,000 that Andrew Carnegie had left his native town, Dunfermline. The Trust was asked to advise the recipients on what Octavia termed 'the beauty side', and Canon Rawnsley produced a report. The Trust founders must have felt envious at Dunfermline's good fortune as they mounted countless appeals for hundreds, or sometimes thousands of pounds.

In the early days, the National Trust was busy lobbying on important issues such as the statutory protection of ancient monuments – scheduled monuments were not protected unless they were officially under the care of the Office of Works. This was the branch of the Trust's work which Robert Hunter untiringly pursued – both in print and in public speeches. The National Trust Act of 1907 gave the body its unique power to hold property on an inalienable basis, so that government departments, local authorities or other agencies could never intervene without parliamentary permission. It was Hunter who drafted the 1907 Act and it was his unmatched legislative know-how that helped give the tiny, newly established body its cutting edge.

In his speech to the Women House Property Managers' Association meeting at the occasion of Octavia's centenary, Nigel Bond characterized the contribution of the three founders. They were a well balanced triumvirate. Hunter

> was a man of very wide vision, very long-sighted, an idealist, and in addition (a rare combination) an extremely able lawyer . . . Canon Rawnsley was different. He did not claim to be a business man, but he was a great enthusiast who did not know the meaning of the word 'No' and it would have been his way to have said, 'There is no obstacle there; go on' and he would have given a leap and nine times out of ten would have landed safely on the other side. Miss Hill, like Sir Robert Hunter, would see the obstacle; she would not bother to find a way round, but she would say, 'This is an obstacle we have got to face, and we will build a ladder and we will start on a sound foundation, climb up, get over, and go down the other side.'

It was a shrewd assessment of how the three oddly assorted founders consistently pulled together.

Bond also emphasized the importance of Octavia's prestige. If there was a cause for which the National Trust wanted publicity, a newspaper editor would happily publish an article by Octavia Hill, or the mayor of some northern town would agree to arrange a meeting on condition that she address it – 'so great was her influence'.

Another speaker at Octavia's centenary dinner, Lionel Curtis, remembered how her convictions gave all the causes that she backed a sense of certainty. 'It was more than a question of that vague factor personality.' It was, he felt, the product of absolute clarity of vision: 'No one ever suggested or thought for one moment that Miss Hill in any of her projects had any personal or ulterior motive. Her aim was to better the conditions of the working classes, to which end she put the whole strength of her personality, clear sightedness, singleness of purpose, unbounded enthusiasm, and above all her great attention to detail.'

To an extraordinary extent the infant National Trust bore the imprint of Octavia's interest. The early committee members, the first acquisitions, the wider policy issues were more often than not a direct reflection of her views, her personal network and her very particular way of achieving her aims. The fact that she had no official role beyond that of committee member somehow conveys how pervasive, yet self-effacing, she remained within the early organization of the National Trust.

CHAPTER 21

The last years

IN 1902 Caroline Hill died, aged ninety-four. Until the end of her life she remained mentally acute and the lynch-pin of her family. She had been a formidable matriarch. Ruskin had found her irritating, and small children were intimidated by her great age, but many people had delighted in her continued active mind. Up to the age of ninety, she was still contributing articles to the magazine *Nineteenth Century*.[1]

At the age of eighty Caroline discussed Tolstoy's polemical pamphlet *What shall we do then?* with the young Sydney Cockerell.

> Probably I could reckon up a thousand passages in this book in which I agree. There would be the passage in which the author depicts the 'iniquity' – inequality – which marks the state of the civilized world at this date. But yet I doubt if the remedy he proposes is the right one. I do not see that . . . it would do any good for the generality of mankind to set to work to dig and to eat sour cabbage and black bread and wear coarse garments. I rather think we cannot go back to the primitive state of society.

Caroline Hill believed in the advances of science and that 'machinery could be a boon to all if all shared its products equally' for 'why *should* a man plough if steam can plough better?'

Caroline felt that Tolstoy and his followers would do better to follow the example of Sir Moses Montefiore and philanthropists in his mould, and '*use* their advantages for the good of mankind instead of *renouncing* them'. She concluded that, if it were in her power, 'I would have society so constituted that each individual should grow to his full capacity and live the highest life he is capable of, so that in time if not all equal yet all shall be excellent.' (Perhaps Caroline's interest in Tolstoy was intensified by the fact that his English translator, Constance Garnett, lived with her husband Edward as near neighbours at Crockham Hill.)

Caroline Hill's existence was rather surprising to those who did not know the family well. Miss Boord, later Mrs Bowen, was trained and worked with Octavia from 1893 to 1900, when she went to New Zealand.[2] On hearing a radio broadcast by Miss Upcott in the late 1940s, she wrote with her own recollections of the Hill household. She referred to 'dear old Miss Miranda, the Power behind the Throne', always on hand and 'better at accounts than her more celebrated sister'. She had had, like Miss Upcott, the impression that they were both old ladies and she had thus been taken aback when, 'one Thursday, the drawing-room door opened and Miss Octavia entering, informed her sister that she had left "Mama" much better.'[3]

Octavia wrote a special postscript to the 1902 'Letter to Fellow-workers', telling them of her mother's death. 'No more on this earth we can carry to her our completed work for her approval, nor turn to her for sympathy in its progress. But that inspiration which has been for all our long lives drawn from her love, from her lofty nature and utter devotion to duty, will not cease because she has passed before us into light, and we have to trust our hearts to hear what she would teach us.'

In 1907 the family dedicated a seat in Caroline's memory on the first patch of Mariner's Hill that Octavia had secured. Miranda wrote to Emily about the ceremony: Octavia had placed the first stone and Florence had been there, having walked over from Chartbrow, a cottage which Octavia owned and which first her mother and then Florence frequently used.[4] (Soon afterwards Octavia gave the cottage to her youngest sister.) Her niece Elinor and Elinor's little son Arthur in a red cap and a long golf cape 'that made him look like a little gnome', were of the party. Arthur had helped spread the mortar and then helped plant an oak tree, as the eldest great-grandchild – his part in the ceremony had been Octavia's idea.[5] Then Octavia, just back from a journey to Scotland with the Poor Law Commissioners, had read from James Russell Lowell's 'Commemoration Ode', a line of which formed the inscription. The stone and the lettering were admired. It was, once again, the work of the old family friend and architect, Elijah Hoole.

History does not relate the views Caroline Hill held on women's suffrage, but Octavia was quietly but doggedly against votes for women, despite her active support for women's rights in connection with property, education and the work of elected Poor Law Guardians. Octavia did not adapt her views on the subject to face the new century or the issues raised, ironically enough, by her own efforts to extend professional training to women.

Octavia, in common with many women who had achieved immense advances for their sex in the Victorian era, had what to us is a confused perspective on the subject. She felt that now that women had found an avenue for their energies and abilities through social work with the poor and in education, the business of the vote was 'a sort of red herring drawn across the path of her fellow-workers, which hindered them from taking an adequate interest in those subjects with which she considered them specially fitted to deal.'[6]

It is doubly ironic that, holding these views as she did, when she enthusiastically canvassed for Tom Hughes as a Liberal candidate in 1874 she was thought to have done his cause a disservice because it was imagined that she was covertly campaigning for women's votes.[7] The cause of women's suffrage was disapproved of by many, and that was another reason why active philanthropists such as Octavia Hill and Angela Burdett-Coutts were convinced anti-suffragists,[8] who considered that it might endanger the success of their work. In a letter to the *Standard* in August 1910 Octavia explained the difference of opinion between herself and 'some of my earnest young fellow-workers': the sexes were quite different, and women with a parliamentary vote would be lost to good works. It was near the end of Octavia's life and not a very illuminating exposition of her views. Why the vote would prevent women from continuing their welfare work she did not explain.

Octavia could have called upon a wide range of women to join her opposition to women's suffrage. From Queen Victoria, who had objected to the 'mad, wicked folly of "Women's Rights"' to Beatrice Webb in her youth, large numbers of active and otherwise enlightened women were adamantly against it. It was in part a reflection of the political culture of the period – in which a disaffection with mainstream politics was widespread. Nevertheless, Octavia's letter to the *Standard* in 1910, which put her views in their most reactionary light, was the measure of her opposition to the cause – partly, no doubt, intensified by her deep distaste for the activities of the Militant Suffragettes.

That year Lord Cromer, the leading figure in the anti-suffragist movement, asked for Octavia's support, but he received a swift refusal. 'The very thing which makes me feel how fatal it would be for women to be drawn into the political arena precludes my signing the letter and joining in what must be a political campaign.' She was all for unobtrusive action. An irony of the anti-suffrage movement, as Cromer himself acknowledged, was that 'in combating the views of the Suffragists, they are obliged . . . to enter into all the hurly-burly of political strife.'

Octavia's faith in the individual, the home and the family was supreme. 'I feel deeply that home life prepares one for other work . . . I believe it to be in itself full of the deepest blessing. It is for the sake of the homes that we are all working and it is in our own that what we are and do tells most deeply.'[9] Yet her own life and achievements, in common with almost all the women that she knew and worked with, were distinctly at variance with such a confined role. Elinor, her niece, worked for Octavia for some years as her secretary and was fully trained in property management. 'I do really feel as if *at last* there was someone who *could* help me with the papers . . . Please thank your Mother for lending you to me thus!!'[10] To have a member of the family working with her, Octavia said, 'was like a breath of spring'. When Elinor married Carrington Ouvry and gave up her work, Octavia was rather disgruntled. (In fact Elinor returned again until she started her own family.) Emily, who, though married, never had children, always continued to work.

Octavia drew a distinction between the working-class family, in need of a stable background against which to deal with adversity, and the middle-class family, in which financial security and correct moral values might be taken for granted. Octavia delighted in the domestic virtues which families such as the Howitts, the MacDonalds, and that of her own brother Arthur seemed to embody[11] and she clung to her own family, romanticizing others and curiously reluctant, despite the example of her own mother, to grant the possibility of a life fulfilled on both levels.

Much of Octavia's achievement came from an effortless physical and mental dominance. Despite her small stature, her striking speaking voice (described as a rich contralto) and her definite views ensured that she was always heard. Many of those who worked with her, however, found her too dominant. According to Elizabeth Sturge, who knew and worked with her in the late 1880s, she did not leave 'much room for smaller people.'[12] Elizabeth noticed that 'older workers generally left after a time to take up independent work.' She also felt that Miranda was 'a woman of much charm and talent whose gifts were somewhat overshadowed by those of her more powerful sister.'

Yet Octavia's brusqueness hid, as always, a considerable sensitivity. Miss Jeffery, who joined Octavia in 1907, was one of Octavia's most trusted housing workers. Writing to thank her for the gift of a plant at Christmas one year, Octavia showed her softer side. 'Somehow the mere abundance of work seems to necessitate such an engrossed tone of mind, that I seem so seldom to see anything of you all with whom I am working. I do not know if it is my fault . . . I often feel as if I must seem to you all a sort of inhuman machine. So when you step out of the rank and greet me thus it is a real kindness and believe me I am really grateful.'[13] It was that humility that could disarm even Octavia's strongest critics.

Octavia held a rather low opinion of central government – which in her field had proved remarkably unefficacious. She held that social-welfare concerns were better dealt with at the local level. She was adamant that her brother Arthur would be doing more important work as a municipal councillor than standing as a Member of Parliament. Central government did not engage the interest of women, partly because it excluded them from the vote, partly because it was seen as a masculine organization – dealing with international affairs, defence, the national budget, but with no remit in any area of social policy, welfare, housing, education or health. Women were only just beginning to sit on Royal Commissions, an area where Octavia had personally encountered prejudice.

But for Octavia, ever the pragmatist, it was not just a matter of women's roles, as her advice to Arthur proved. So, if a woman were to busy herself in politics it was appropriate that she should do so at local authority level, where the issues that concerned women most were discussed.[14]

After the Nottingham Place school closed Miranda stood for election as a Guardian and, succeeding, became engrossed in the work. All Miranda's humanity and sweetness seems to have been called for in her new role, late though it came to her in life. Octavia shared her pleasure in its satisfactions: 'This room is gay with daffodils sent as a present to [Miranda], with such a nice letter – from a pauper boy she started in the

Scilly Isles who is learning to cultivate bulbs and such cheering incidents are frequent.'[15] Miranda had known him as a sickly boy, visiting him once a fortnight in the workhouse infirmary until she found a place for mother and eight-year-old son. After Miranda died his widowed mother wrote that she owed her son's life to Miranda.

Another election was held in March 1904 and Miranda's seat was contested. Octavia was all set to canvass, she told Gertrude, although it had to be done from Larksfield. But Miranda sailed home, at the head of the poll.

Octavia had also been active in support of her brother-in-law, Charles Lewes, when he had stood as a candidate for the LCC years earlier.[16] Gertrude had proved a great ally; in particular in her powers of organization, which was a notable Hill attribute. Octavia spoke at one meeting, and Mrs Hill noticed that she no longer seemed to dread public speaking.[17]

After her veneration for the family, friendship came very high on Octavia's list of priorities. Of all those who had shared her early aspirations and difficulties, Emma Cons was one of the most steadfast. Having known the family for almost forty years, her achievements were greeted as if she were one of them. Old Mrs Hill had a soft spot for her; and despite their divergent views on some matters Octavia and Emma's friendship rose above any differences of opinion. Emma's enthusiastic activities for women's suffrage (she became Vice-President of the London Society for Women's Suffrage) did not prevent Octavia whole-heartedly supporting her candidature for the London County Council.

Octavia had been approached in 1888 by the Society for Promoting Women County Councillors – shortly to be renamed the Women's Local Government Society – to stand as an LCC councillor herself, but had refused – not on principle but because of pressure of work.[18] In the event Jane Cobden, elected in Bow, and Margaret Sandhurst, in Brixton, joined Emma Cons, who had been nominated as an alderman for her housing and social work.

They took their places on various committees – Emma following the cause of women asylum patients until she was challenged by the extreme anti-suffragist Beresford-Hope, whose court action proved that they did not hold their seats in law. Emma Cons battled on, resigning from committee work, rejoining six committees (including housing, parks and sanitation), until she and Jane Cobden (Margaret Sandhurst had lost her seat) reached a stage when they could attend meetings, but not participate in official business. By the time the first LCC dissolved they had, temporarily, lost the fight.[19] Emma Cons settled for her place on the LCC School Board, 'inspiring everyone, and keeping herself in the shade'.

The Barnetts were also friends with whom Octavia was able to agree to differ. Writing to Henrietta Barnett she acknowledged the strains but celebrated the friendship. Thanking her for a book by Stevenson, probably a fiftieth birthday gift:

> We do indeed seem to see little of one another now, and it is doubly good of you thus faithfully to keep memory of the old days – I suppose these outward separations, and even differences of view, if not of ideal are appointed in life, but it always seems to me as if the love, and knowledge of what old friends are at the heart, went so much deeper than these small outside separations.[20]

Ten years later, the Barnetts called on the Hills, to celebrate Octavia's sixtieth birthday. Canon Barnett (as he had become around 1893) described the scene: 'We found the old group in the old surroundings, aged and not altered. She was very glad to see Jetta [Barnett's spelling of Yetta] and we had some talk on the moral backwater. She fought for the goodness of their lives but as Jetta shrewdly says her satisfaction is another sign of the present stagnation.'[21] A few months later they met again on another social occasion; this time at the Maurices'. 'Met the Octavia Hill gang – good folk – dowdy in appearance but pure in soul – I understood when I was with them how easily they might arouse anger and how their dress was worn almost as a monk's habit, something separating them from the world. It is hard to be in this world – to identify oneself with its spirit.'[22]

The Barnetts had by now changed their views on most things; on the COS, on State intervention, even on the role of religion. Octavia, most markedly, had not. After telling his brother of a meeting with the Webbs ('you will like them both – I think') Canon Barnett mentioned that Octavia had spent the day with them. 'She is more and more dogmatic . . . more convinced of her power of law. She is for war and speaks of the Boers as tyrants and hypocrites – what power that imperial spirit has got.'[23] Octavia, fired by her contact with military men such as General Maurice and the activities of the cadet troop in Southwark, was sternly patriotic.

A few years on, the atmosphere had mellowed between them: 'We spent Wednesday with Miss Hill,' wrote Samuel Barnett. 'She is very well – very active and very kind. She made much of our visit and Jetta was a comfort to her as she took her away from her letters and made her live in other things. She is a beautiful character with an ideal of conduct which dominates (?) even trifles.' Barnett adds, surprisingly, that Octavia was thinking of going to Australia to see some cousins.[24]

In 1904 the Barnetts, now deep in the planning of Hampstead Garden Suburb, sent Octavia a birthday telegram: 'seldom as we meet and far apart as our several duties lie, it is sweet to think how real and deep the old links are, rooted deep in the long ago years.'[25] A few weeks later Henrietta approached Octavia for advice over the Suburb and received a courteous refusal: 'I fear I must not think of looking at "Garden Suburb" questions. I have more than I should do to follow the work before me, and I dare not turn to other problems and ideals.' She wished Yetta would come and see her 'just to talk over old times and that we may see one another'. She signed herself, 'Your affectionate old friend'.[26]

Portraits of Octavia are more numerous in these later years; the generation that had known her when they were young trainees were those who continued and wrote about her work. Miss Joan Sunderland was one such: 'I want to give, if I can, some idea of her individuality. My first interview with her was in February 1901, and my first impression was of someone utterly unlike anyone else, with wonderful brown eyes and a deep voice.' On starting work, for the Ecclesiastical Commissioners' estates, Miss Sunderland became one of the group of workers who were invited down to Crockham Hill on occasion.

Those were wonderful days – the drive from Oxted in the old wagonette, the glorious walks, and the readings in the evening. Miss Hill read beautifully, and we often had Browning – 'Saul' and 'Rabbi Ben Ezra' I remember best – and Lowell's 'Vision of Sir Launfal'. One will never forget the way she somehow lit up things by the fact of her personality coming into contact with them.

She also recalled Octavia's love of beauty, especially of colour. She had sung well in her youth, Joan Sunderland had heard. 'The story of her walking home when she was a girl, singing the *Magnificat* because Ruskin had praised some of her drawings, is absolutely characteristic

[323]

of her . . . she was perfectly natural, and if she felt like singing, she would sing.'[27]

A great pleasure in beauty was something that Octavia kept all her life. Her pleasure in painting particularly was an enduring one – from the days with Ruskin, on into those of the Kyrle Society and her friendly contacts with Watts, Walter Crane, Holman Hunt and de Morgan. In 1897 she addressed the Annual Meeting of the Manchester Art Museum: 'We cannot all go to Barmouth or Tintagel[28] . . . We want some beautiful things for our daily enjoyment, and near us. Now these are what your Museum is providing, not on rare holidays, not for those who have money, but day by day as their surroundings for the poorest of your Manchester children, the most toil-worn of your Manchester men.'

She remembered many years ago taking some of her girl tenants on holiday, when they had begun to talk about what they had on their minds. 'Such a ghastly record it was, corpse of suicide, drunken row, gossip of low life. I felt sickened, and from that day I have always felt that to present beautiful and good images was as great a gift as any could be.'[29]

Another visitor, Mary Brinton, later Baroness Stocks, remembered visits to the house in the Marylebone Road in her teens. By then Miss Pearson had left and Mrs Hill had died, but the household was otherwise unchanged. 'I think that among the pleasantest of my Edwardian memories were visits to Miss Octavia's house. Periodically I would walk through a narrow London garden, up a short flight of white steps, and nervously ring a bell – with just a shadow of an impulse to run away.' The four hostesses would be in a small L-shaped drawing room; Miss Sim, 'large and mild, yet strangely shadowy in my memory, and Miss Harriot Yorke, the youngest member of the elderly household, with her deep voice and reassuring vivacity. Miss Sim would pour out tea. Miss Yorke would keep the ball of conversation rolling. And always there would come a moment when to each visitor in turn would be said the words: now you must come and talk to Miss Octavia.' Mary's connection with, as she termed it, 'the enervating social services which Miss Octavia so distrusted' imparted a nervous thrill to this part of the afternoon. 'To talk to Miss Octavia was an adventure. To talk to Miss Miranda was a benediction.' While she remembered Octavia as 'wise and just and firm', Miranda was 'gentle, beautiful and gracious'. It was a common view.

Mary was struck with Octavia's remarkable appearance.

She looked unquestionably significant. It was not simply that she looked so very different from other people. She did, of course, but anyone could have done that, given the thick figure and the brown silk dress with wide sleeves and white ruffles which must have been specially made to some ancient and peculiar pattern of her own. But on the top of that dumpy, oddly-dressed figure there was a head of such massiveness, with so broad a brow, and a glance so steady, as only greatness fortified by some consciousness of greatness could have produced.

She also sensed the iron in the character. 'She might survey her tenants benignly on a Sunday afternoon, but on Monday morning they had to pay the rent.' She did not remotely agree with Octavia's views on charitable assistance, since she herself was involved in an LCC initiative to provide school meals for deprived children, which the COS considered pauperizing, but she had great affection for the household, and above all for Miranda.[30]

Octavia's immediate family circle was shrinking. Arthur's wife died in 1901 and Arthur in 1909. Octavia had taken some tenants on a visit to Erleigh Court, which now had to be remembered as 'the last there can ever be'.

The early years of the century were busy ones for the Hill aunts. Gertrude, the only sister to have children, was now seeing her three daughters marry and start families of their own. Inevitably, given the closeness of the Hill family, the younger generation also became involved in their eminent aunt's work.

Elinor was the first to become engaged, to Carrington Ouvry, the solicitor. Then Gertrude's second daughter and Octavia's god-daughter Blanche married Edward Hanson, the celebrations being held at North End, Miss Johnston's house, one of the regular destinations for the tenants' summer outings. Maud, the third daughter, became Mrs Hopwood.

Carrington (Octavia always wrote the name in inverted commas, as if it were not quite proper) was the favourite nephew-in-law. The couple sent her a birthday gift from Tintagel in 1904 which touched her as 'a sort of gathering together of the places we have worked for, and the workers who are devoted to similar objects'. Elinor continued as a Horace Street Trustee after the arrival of children prevented her working for Octavia on a regular basis. Carrington joined the Estates Committee of the National Trust, having been 'elected last Thursday with acclamation', as Octavia reported, just a few months after his marriage.[31] In the last years of her life he became an invaluable helper; constantly receiving letters from her, just as in the past William Shaen, the Cockerells father and son, and certain other favoured and patient male friends had done. By the time of her death, his firm was dealing with all her affairs relating to the properties and the Horace Street Trust, as well as all personal matters.

Despite all the other activities in her life, Octavia continued to look in on Gertrude, as her daughters married and left home, to make sure she was not feeling lonely. There had been a support meeting for the cadet corps at the Admiralty, with Lord Methuen in the chair; Arthur Conan Doyle was there ('he looks exactly like a typical British workman') and 'it was a very interesting meeting and "Aunt Octavia" spoke splendidly though I think she was really rather nervous,' a cousin, Geraldine, reported.[32]

One day Octavia and Miss Yorke came over to enlist Gertrude and Mica,[33] her companion:

to go down and help at Southwark on Saturday afternoon the 23rd, the Maypole day, when she is asking a good many people, (some influential) to come down and see the Maypole and the Cadet head-quarters and the new houses. They are to have tea, and to be personally conducted by herself and others. It is a sort of reception to follow up the Admiralty meeting. Miss Ironside has to attend to the children and flowers and band and Octavia to the dignified people. Mica and I . . . to the tea for the guests. Mica offers to pour out or do anything else and offered my services in the same cause.[34]

Elinor, who knew her aunt's powers of persuasion at first hand, must have been amused by this account.

Before long Elinor started a family. Octavia was delighted as the children arrived; she wrote to Miranda about 'the glad news that Elinor has a little son'. The eldest, Arthur, was born in March 1904 in the midst of all the excitement about Miranda's contested election to the Board of Guardians. The second son, Romilly, was Octavia's godson as well as her great-nephew. He received a letter from her from Switzerland on his first birthday; she had sent a present which 'comes with much love from your godmother and is sent to shew how much she hopes that good and happy thoughts may be with you directly you can begin to understand them, and help you to grow into a good and useful man.'[35] She was travelling with Miss Yorke and Miss Martelli and had been exploring, both by vehicle and on foot, with the old spirit.

Other letters followed, on each of his birthdays. The presents were usually for the future – in 1909 it was something 'which you will hardly care about now, but Mother will take charge of it for you till you are a little older . . .' In 1910 the letter was addressed to 'my dear little Godson' and enclosed a present 'though it is no use to you now, some day you will find it helpful. Many good things are like that. They come and we hardly notice them, and years afterwards we find that they were blessings.' In 1911 the present was a book, telling him 'about all that happened in years long ago in England. I got it for you because I thought it would interest you.' However, if his mother thought it unsuitable, he was to return it and she would try to find something else. Octavia had always had trouble entering into a small child's mind and enthusiasms; she was happier at instruction and making a moral point.

Romilly Ouvry remembers Octavia as one among a number of aunts, all very small and dressed drably. Although he was small himself they still seemed tiny, 'but my mother said they towered above their mother. My mother was only 5'3", she in turn towered over the others.' Harriot Yorke, known as the 'Keeper' to Octavia's 'Lion', was kind but had an alarmingly deep voice. Aunt Florence was Romilly's favourite aunt – perhaps she was more like the kindly Miranda, whom the younger Ouvry children scarcely knew.

Larksfield, Miss Yorke's house which Octavia had shared for many years, Arthur Ouvry[36] remembered as being extraordinarily spartan; straight-backed chairs, rush mats rather than rugs, no carpet on the stairs, and beds, his father commented, which were harder than the High Veldt. It was the garden which engrossed the ladies.

There were frequent excursions from Larksfield, for Octavia was drawing up a survey of the footpaths, commons and rights of way in Kent and Surrey. Information came from all quarters. 'Gertrude's coachman is very helpful about Chartwell . . . He knows another path better, but recognizes this and will look and see how far his own evidence will go. He will speak to several working people there.'[37] Octavia's practical application to detail was still evident. Without accurate information, the local fight could not be effective.

[327]

When they came down to visit, the fellow-workers were encouraged to go walking, armed with 'at least a pair of secateurs, probably an old sword, and a pair of old pliers'. Each took different paths and cut the farmers' wire where it blocked rights of way. Romilly remembers them as 'amazing walkers' despite their very cumbersome clothes, usually voluminous gowns of strong thick tweed.

Octavia's dress sense, veering from the dingy to the eccentric, caused much comment. Romilly remembers it as 'absolutely terrible'. One of Octavia's staunchest admirers, Greville MacDonald, who considered her 'one of the noblest women ever sent upon earth', could not exonerate her on the charge of dowdiness. 'Much as she depended upon Beauty, she never thought of adorning her person, and well I recall my boyish regret that it must be so.'[38]

For obvious reasons, Octavia made a point of wearing old clothes going to collect rents from the very poor. Romilly remembered an incident which showed her as being very far from humourless.

One time she was visiting one of her contacts, the Earl of this or Lady that. It was pouring with rain, she suddenly realized she was wearing all her rent-collecting clothes, probably the 'pen-wiper' hat (a particularly shabby and frightful old hat), the door opened, she very quickly held out her foot and said, please remove my galoshes, in a very high and mighty tone.

In August 1909, John Bailey wrote to Nigel Bond, 'Have you heard how Miss Hill is? I dread to think it but I am afraid that she will not be with us very much longer. Do not quote me as saying she is seriously ill as I hear she objects to it being known.'

In fact it was Miranda who now fell gravely ill. The illness took its long course during the summer and she was conveyed to Larksfield, where she had a far more peaceful sickroom than that in the house on the Marylebone Road. By the end Miranda needed both day and night nurses, as well as the attention of Octavia herself, Florence, Miss Yorke and Miss Sim. Octavia recorded: 'I think no one was ever more supported and blest.'[39] Miranda died in May 1910.

Octavia was deeply saddened by Miranda's death; the friendship and the collaboration between the two sisters was special, even within that family of close loyalties. The funeral was held at St Luke's, Nutford Place, close to the very first properties, and the service was conducted by the Revd Alford, another old friend and (in the view of the Hills) a worthy successor to F. D. Maurice.[40] Letters and wreaths poured in from teachers, children and Guardians. 'I hear the scene when the Board passed the vote of condolence was most impressive, all standing through the speeches and deep feeling shown. Her gentleness, her high ideal and her love and care for the children and her faithful work for 15 years had impressed them.'[41] For Henrietta Barnett, Miranda 'still lives in my memory as the most beautiful of human characters'.[42]

For a committed Christian like Octavia, there were consolations in death. 'She [Miranda] lived so near to God at every moment of her life and her nature was so pure and so true that the going seemed for her only a step on,' Octavia wrote. 'There is nothing anywhere to put to rights, or to regret, or to forget. Her life was all love and thought and service. It had been a very happy and a very full one and I have so much to be thankful for.'[43] When Octavia herself was dying, she told her companions that the prospect of joining Miranda was cheering her on.

After Miranda's death Octavia turned as usual to patient Carrington Ouvry for help. Her letters show her grasp of business was as clear as ever; she did not let a detail go unconsidered. Investments had to be sold to meet liabilities and she suggested that the Marylebone Association or Waterlow shares, both building companies, could be sold. 'We have so much in houses, one way or other.' They brought a 5 per cent return after tax, as well as regular bonuses.

Octavia was now drawing up a new will, but she decided to make Florence (who was then holidaying in Transylvania!) a gift of her cottage at Toys Hill, Chartbrow, before her own death. Looking at her own assets she computed them at around £20,000 and reassured Carrington, 'it certainly can't reach £40,000!!' She was also much concerned about the design of 'our grave', to be designed of course by Elijah Hoole. She asked Carrington for advice over who should be residuary legatee, 'should Miss Yorke die with me, we are usually together and anything might happen.' There had been some confusion over the ownership of the Horace Street Trust properties; she did not wish to be taxed on these or others in trust, and she asked him to confer with Mr Johnson, solicitor to the Trust.[44]

The correspondence continued, letters coming from Glastonbury and Dunster as Octavia took a late summer holiday, which she was revelling in, with 'unbroken sunlight . . . a beautiful visit to Wells and a quite enchanting time at Cheddar'.

Octavia seems at this time to have had the classic symptoms of cancer, with lengthy remissions. On this journey they spent a lot of time walking, including all day from Minehead to Porlock over the moors and in sight of the sea. She had also pursued some National Trust business while in the west country. Early in 1911 she was travelling in Wales, and in May she was at Como, but she found time to write a lively letter to Carrington about open space and National Trust matters.

In the spring of 1912 she learned that her illness was terminal. For the first time some of her letters were dictated, though she still added her signature. She was still worrying about details of the will: she wanted the legatees to pay their own duty, rather than it being chargeable to the estate. Even to the last her belief in individual responsibility extended to all spheres. On 30 July she dictated a letter, telling Carrington about progress with an appeal and other business. She died peacefully, and in the last hours unconscious, aged seventy-five, on 13 August 1912.

CHAPTER 22

Afterwards

OCTAVIA'S funeral at Crockham Hill was a private affair for family, close friends and fellow-workers. Two old friends were absent: both Emma Cons[1] and Elijah Hoole had died that year and, ironically enough, Sophia Jex-Blake too. Carrington Ouvry made all the funeral arrangements, as he had done for Miranda. The workers from the courts caught the midday train down to Kent, so that the routine was not unduly affected. The faithful Miss Ter Meulen was there from Amsterdam. Octavia's nephew, the Revd F. C. Hill, assisted the vicar of Crockham Hill with the service. It was followed two days later by a well-attended memorial service at Southwark Cathedral.[2]

'So the little old lady in the mushroom hat is dead,' wrote C. R. Ashbee. 'She was a great little lady and I admired her.' He went on: 'I find I have now met or come across in life most of the great women of Octavia Hill's type – Mrs Fawcett, Emily Davis [sic], Mrs Garrett Anderson, Miss Beale, Miss Buss, Miss Cons. Life is a fuller and larger thing for having done so.'[3]

A little later a man who knew Octavia much better than C. R. Ashbee made a similar comparison between outstanding women. Sydney Cockerell wrote to Emily Guest:

You have set me pondering over the little group of women I have been privileged to know who have combined profound knowledge and understanding with the ripe wisdom of which charity is so large a part. Octavia Hill and Lady Burne-Jones – both blessed women and women of genius – contest the place with you. But about the one there was a touch of sentimentality and about the other there is more than a touch of puritanism, of which you are wholly free.

However it is an impertinence to criticize any of you. The only reasonable attitude, as Morris said of Chartres Cathedral, is one of gratitude and admiration.[4]

Henrietta Barnett thought the fulsome obituary notices, from Italy and the USA as well as national and local newspapers, failed to catch Octavia's particular qualities, and herself summed up Octavia's character with great shrewdness.

When I read obituary notices of her, crediting her with the commonplace virtues of kindness and unselfishness and gentleness, it annoyed me because those were not her virtues, and enumerating them gave the wrong impression of her character. She was strong-willed – some thought self-willed – but the strong will was never used for self. She was impatient in little things, persistent with long-suffering in big ones; often dictatorial in manner but humble to self-effacement before those she loved or admired. She had high standards for everyone, for herself ruthlessly exalted ones, and she dealt out disapprobation and often scorn to those who fell below her standards for them, but she somewhat erred in sympathy by urging them to attain her standards for them, instead of their own for themselves.

Another person who had worked closely with Octavia for over thirty years was Sir Robert Hunter. He recalled, in *The Times*, her performance on committees and in business affairs, her 'scrupulous pecuniary accuracy, her business ability, and her sobriety of judgement'. Her support for any project was enough to persuade donors and people often gave her money to spend at her own discretion.[5]

At the Annual General Meeting of the Commons and Footpaths Preservation Society on 7 May 1913, Sir Robert, who had seen Octavia in action on two committees he had chaired, the Kyrle and National Trust, remembered her.

I had exceptional opportunities of realizing the strength which she brought to any movement which she supported. Her power of brushing aside all subsidiary details and piercing to the heart of any question, her careful choice of methods and her scrupulous regard for the rights and wishes of those who supplied her with funds, and her courage and boldness in carrying through any enterprise of

[332]

which she approved, were as valuable a moral and intellectual stimulus to those Societies . . . as her remarkable power of raising money was an invaluable means of supplying the means of action.

Many among Octavia's old friends and colleagues wrote memorials to her, whilst the annual reports of the bodies with which she had been associated all paid their tributes. Lucy Harrison, who had rowed Octavia's toymakers round the lake at Romford sixty years earlier and who was now headmistress of the Quaker girls' school, The Mount, in York, remembered her in *The Friend*.[6] There was a lengthy article in the *Boston Evening Transcript*[7] by Raymond Fuller and the author of another long obituary in *La Cultura Popolare* (the Italian journal of popular education) remembered visiting her in her '*piccola stanza artisticamenta severa*' (her artistically severe small room), watched over by a portrait of Ruskin.

But the revision of Octavia Hill began the moment she died. On the one hand family and supporters presented an unflawed character, with a sweetness which as Henrietta pointed out, was certainly not her own.[8] At the other extreme, there were plenty who wanted to destroy her achievements, by any means. They began with Octavia's will.

The will was published in *The Times* on 5 November 1912. She left £20,280 gross, £8,315 net. She bequeathed the Sargent portrait to the National Portrait Gallery; £400 to Miss Yorke's nephew Philip; £1,000 to Emily Maurice, £1,000, the freeholds of 188–190 Marylebone Road and the contents of her residence to Harriot Yorke. The residue of the estate went to her sister, Emily Maurice.

Probably the last letter Octavia wrote was to her beloved niece and secretary Elinor. She explained that she had not been able to hand on as a cash gift the £400 each that Miranda had left to the sisters, but that she was leaving them property worth considerably more. Hereford Buildings, built for £4,000, went to Blanche; the freehold of Sarsden Buildings – part of St Christopher's Place – which had cost £7,000, went to Elinor Ouvry and Maud Hopwood. Elinor, she felt, would 'know enough about them to secure that they are rightly managed as a great trust – they will pay for a lady worker who should report to you.' They had been bringing in a 4 per cent return. She had arranged for Emily to give Romilly a gift of money; the other children would have suitable objects. 'Give my love to your sisters and to them. That they may all grow up happy and noble men and women, and that all your lives may be blessed and full of joy is the prayer of Your affectionate aunt, Octavia.'[9] It was, she knew, a farewell, and with its unsteady hand was eloquent proof of her spirit in the face of fatal illness.

Many professed to be surprised by the amount Octavia left. Rumours began to circulate that she had profited out of her charitable endeavours. The family was concerned. Gertrude wrote to her son-in-law, Carrington Ouvry, conceding that the figures in the will were 'startling to many who knew her simple life – and are making others (especially amongst the tenants) think that she and Miss Yorke had made a good thing out of the rents and that they have been picking up leaseholds and freeholds out of rents for their own advantage!!' If Carrington thought it wise, perhaps they should write to the press to put the record straight? They could emphasize that the houses had been left to her by their owners in order that she could carry on the work. In the end, they decided to stay quiet.

In fact much of the value of Octavia's estate was the outcome of a quite remarkable frugality and the fact that the wealthy Miss Yorke had borne the day-to-day expenses of their life.

The family had decided to prepare a published edition of Octavia's life and letters by the end of August 1912. Edmund and Emily Maurice kept in touch with Sydney Cockerell through it all. She wrote to him early the next year that Edmund

has had to read more than a thousand letters and the selection has been very difficult . . . We have had a rather unpleasant correspondence with Mr Wedderburn[10] but Mrs Severn has been *most* kind and helpful . . . so he [Ruskin] will fill, as he ought, a very prominent position in the book. I hope you will like the way my husband has dealt with the question of *Fors*. I am sure Octavia would have wished the matter passed over as lightly as possible . . .'[11]

The completed volume, interesting and full as it was, in fact passed lightly over many matters, in particular the unhappy episodes of engagement and illnesses.

Deciding that the Sargent portrait had not conveyed Octavia's spiritual qualities fully, Margaret Shaen, the daughter of Octavia's legal adviser and old friend, commissioned a marble effigy from Miss Abbott, an American sculptress who lived with her friend Miss Fergusson on Mariner's Hill. It turned into a protracted business. Miss Abbott's health was very poor and the clay model was not produced until 1922. A local girl never forgot her uncomfortable spell lying on a slab as a model for the recumbent figure, to which the head was added.[12]

Miss Yorke regularly took visitors to see the work in progress. Miss Abbott, now in her seventies, was finding the likeness a problem since she had only seen her subject four times and so had to rely on photographs. Nevertheless, Miss Yorke felt it was beautiful and dignified, "and a speaking likeness almost sometimes as if it were alive. It will be a great thing if it is placed in Southwark cathedral.'

After Miss Fergusson died it became clear that Miss Abbott would never either carry out the work herself or superintend anyone else to do so. In 1925 Margaret Shaen persuaded Mr Hope Pinker to carry on the work, but the day he was to take the figure to his studio he too died. Miss Abbott then recommended Edmund Burton; he completed the work and designed the substructure entirely.

In 1928 an appeal was mounted, through a letter in the *Spectator*, to meet the cost of the effigy, which had vastly increased since 1913. This was met, and the monument was installed, not in Southwark Cathedral but in Crockham Hill church, on 3 December 1928.[13] The marble recumbent figure, technically competent though it is, remains an icon to Saint Octavia, a worthy but unmoving commemoration.

Harriot lived to the age of eighty-seven, dying on 1 October 1930. In an obituary note in *The Times*, it was recorded that 'Miss Yorke's was the practical mind; it was she who saw that Miss Hill kept her appointments, attended the various committees, was furnished with the necessary information and was relieved of all tiresome details.' Octavia had owed her an immense debt – and thirty-five years of almost unbroken good health.

In 1928 Emily Maurice followed her husband's book with the publication of Octavia's letters to Mary Harris and John Ruskin.

Emily and Edmund, who had a long and happy marriage but no children, had actively supported Octavia in almost all her schemes, but as convinced pacifists, they drew the line at the cadets.[14] In 1918 the Maurices were intending to vote for their Hampstead Labour candidate, Mr Mackay, a past student of Ruskin College. 'We are supporting him altho' there is much in the programme of the Party that we disapprove. But there is no Liberal in the field, and we want to keep out the Conservative; besides thoughtful and moderate working men will help much, and it will probably be long before they will be in a position to carry out their extreme views.' Emily adds, touchingly

[335]

for someone approaching eighty, 'it seems strange and appropriate that my first vote should be given for a working man seeing that I have been interested in all progressive measures for the working people since I was eleven years old, and read *Cheap Clothes and Nasty* and other Christian Socialist tracts, and heard the Christian Socialist leaders speak in the Hall of Association.'[15] As Octavia had done, so Emily continued to cherish those early memories.

Although Emily was rather circumspect, she was not a Hill for nothing. Age did not sap the Hill spirit. Romilly Ouvry remembers in the 1920s someone mentioning a good cause. 'Aunt Minnie [Emily] woke up like a little war horse and began planning all her campaigns, must get Lord So and So into this . . . can't we have an appeal. It all sort of sprang to life.' He remembers the Maurices as a devoted couple, Minnie with an odd quavery voice and Edmund, a 'fussy little man'.

In Stepney, Florence lived simply, completely dedicated 'in a Hill sort of way', conducting Sunday School classes and remaining a pillar of the Unitarian Chapel until her death in 1935.[16] Gertrude played her part in fanning the family flame, beginning in 1898 with her biography of her grandfather, Dr Southwood Smith, and twenty years later corresponding busily over a planned selection of Octavia's writings.

The National Trust recorded its debt to Octavia in the form of a resolution, printed in the 18th Annual Report. It concluded:

> Alike by the wisdom of her counsels, and by her energy and eloquence in commending the work of the Trust to the public, Miss Hill has, in the opinion of the Council, contributed to a degree it would be impossible to overestimate to the success of the Trust, and the Council deeply laments that she has not be spared to continue her invaluable aid.

An assiduous attendance record at Council meetings was noted, and also her legacy of £200. Happily, before her death the extension of National Trust ownership of Mariner's Hill had been achieved – some 25½ acres were now secured, to benefit 'the dwellers in crowded streets who seek a restful and inspiring spot within easy reach of town'. The last £500 for it was received from the Misses Davenport Hill the day before Octavia died.

An appeal was mounted for Hydon Heath and Hydon's Ball near

Godalming specifically in Octavia's memory, but the timing was unfortunate – it was hit by the crisis of the outbreak of the First World War. An area of some 92 acres, it was on the market for £5,000, although an extra £500 was required for a caretaker's cottage and other expenses. £1,600 was immediately pledged by the memorial committee. Ironically, the appeal for funds to commemorate the National Trust's queen of appeals looked as if it might fail, for the first time in Trust history, to raise the money. At the last moment, the owner agreed to reduce the price, Miss Yorke and Mrs Maurice stepped in to advance the necessary money.

In the 1920s, with all three founders now dead,[17] the Trust continued to acquire land. A major success was Dovedale, whilst in the Lake District gifts of land rolled in; by 1930 there were sixty-three separate properties in the area. Nearer to London, the sale of the Ashridge estate at Berkhamsted in 1925 and the threat of development prompted the National Trust to secure at least part of it. Where historic buildings were concerned, the Trust confined its attentions to small, vernacular houses, several of them cases brought to its attention by the SPAB. Essentially the organization continued very much as the founders had left it into the early 1930s.[18]

That decade saw an influx of new personalities at the head of the organization, as well as members of staff and benefactors. The new direction was signalled by the Marquess of Lothian's speech at the 1934 AGM. Country houses were 'under sentence of death, and the axe which is destroying them is taxation . . .' Death duties had risen from 4 per cent in 1904 to 50 per cent in 1930. In 1936 the Country House Scheme was launched and the National Trust changed direction. One of the first properties that it took on under the Scheme was Lothian's own estate, Blickling Hall in Norfolk, following his death in 1942.

Initially, the idea was that the country houses would be dealt with by an affiliated body, 'a Country Houses Association as a Branch of the National Trust'. Implicit in that proposal is the acknowledgement that the protection of large numbers of country houses was a deviation from the original purposes of the Trust. In the event, the complexity of the new responsibility, involving changes to the legislation and to taxation, threatened to overwhelm the organization and more important, to distract it from the objectives which the three founders had so unanimously espoused. It is not surprising that their names were seldom mentioned in those years.

But in the housing movement, Octavia's name was still on many lips. Her example had led to the entry of dozens, if not hundreds, of young women into a new field – that of housing management.[19] The Association of Women House Property Managers was founded in 1916 to give muscle to women in the profession.[20] Until the incentive offered by the Sex Disqualification Removal Act (1919), the 'technical' professions, such as architecture[21] and surveying[22] were considered quirky choices for a woman, but housing management was viewed (for all the reasons that Octavia gave) as a 'natural' career for them.

The earliest major opportunity offered to the women housing managers was their appointment in 1916 by the Commissioners of Woods and Forests (later to become the Crown Estate Commissioners) to assist in the planned major redevelopment of Marylebone Farm (Cumberland Market) north-east of Regent's Park. Even before the redevelopment began Miss Jeffery[23] was installed in an office on site to liaise with tenants on relocation.

Miss Jeffery and her colleagues, including Irene Barclay who was to become the first woman chartered surveyor, busied themselves providing much-needed amenities, such as playgrounds, and saw that urgently needed repairs on the rundown properties were speedily and punctiliously carried out. They also encouraged the formation of a Tenants' Association. One of its first requests was for a working men's club, to be housed well apart from a public house. Miss Jeffery and her helpers also persuaded the Office of Woods to reduce the number of public houses and improve the quality of those remaining. By the time the estate was completed, Miss Jeffery had 1,267 tenancies, 563 houses and four helpers. The experiment showed that Octavia's concerns could be integrated within the framework of a large new estate, so long as adequate staff were provided. Its contemporary touches – the neighbourhood housing office, the Tenants' Association and the concern for tenants' views – point much further forward, and demonstrate that, shorn of the Victorian moral overlay, much of Octavia's theory was timeless common sense.[24]

The war years, 1914–18, offered an unprecedented range of openings to women trained in housing management. The Director of Housing at the Ministry of Munitions, George Duckworth (Leslie Stephen's stepson) was through his family a long-standing supporter of Octavia Hill's work,[25] and consistently appointed women housing managers 'not only during the War but in the difficult and unpopular time afterwards,' energetically pleading their cause. Miss Lumsden who was appointed to a war-time advisory role within the Ministry itself, devised a training scheme to ensure the continuance of women housing managers for the munitions estates.

Despite this promising start, the women in government departments stood down at the end of the war to give the returning soldiers their jobs, out of a sense of duty which they felt showed proper respect for service personnel returning to civilian life. Yet the industrial depression emphasized the importance of organization, in housing as elsewhere.

Miss Jeffery justified the projected publication of some of Octavia's writings on housing management by outlining the expanding work of women housing managers.[26] By 1919 they sat on numerous committees; the Ministry of Munitions were employing two women at Barrow[27] and three or four at Dudley; they looked after 1,800 properties belonging to the Ecclesiastical Commissioners; and the Women's Municipal Party recommended such work for women. New estates were likely to follow the Rowntree Trust Estate at New Earswick, outside York, and employ women managers. 'So I do not think our work can be said to be dead, and I am sure our experience and training will be needed in the future.'[28]

Opportunities were opening up in local government, too. Amersham Rural District Council appointed the first woman housing manager, simply because she was the best candidate. Nine local authorities employed women housing managers in the 1920s, including Manchester, Birmingham, Leeds and Rotherham.[29]

Edith Neville of the Mary Ward Settlement, who with Miss Jeffery co-edited *House Property and its Management*, the eventual title of the anthology of Octavia's writings on the subject, published in 1921, pointed out that although many of Octavia's workers had disagreed with her anti-municipal stand, 'there can be no doubt as to the soundness of her method . . . now being successfully employed by Municipal Authorities in Holland, and by Public Utility Associations in the United States.' Reading the essays reminded Elizabeth Haldane, one of Octavia's more critical admirers, of the 'awful conditions of slum life, and how one had to kilt one (sic) petticoats (no knee lengths those days!) going through the rooms. Municipal action has helped, despite all the sins it has to answer for. How interesting it all is.'[30]

In 1924 Janet Upcott's book, *Women House Property Managers*, followed, making a powerful case for a professional career in housing management. 'The insight such work would give into working-class

[339]

life, wages, health and housing, would be an invaluable training for a Member of Parliament.' Nancy Astor wrote the foreword.[31]

Janet Upcott, who died in 1985, three years short of her century, was a typical twentieth-century housing professional, a new breed Octavia would have recognized in all but name. She was a graduate of Somerville and had begun to work for Octavia in 1910. After war work and a stint on the editorial staff of the *Economist* (Janet Upcott had a succinct and vivid writing style) she was appointed Superintendent of the Ministry of Munitions' 'temporary' Housing scheme in Dudley.[32] She resigned in 1921, giving way to men back from the war. She used the time to write her book and then, armed with a glowing reference from Captain Street of the Office of Works, referring to her 'tact, ability and constant attention to the problems', she joined Miss Jeffery at the Cumberland Market estate. Her work there commended her to Parker Morris, who appointed her as Property Manager to Chesterfield Town Council.[33]

The LCC was never favourably disposed towards Octavia's approach – perhaps largely because of her outspoken opposition to its role in housing provision. From as early as 1893 the LCC had chosen resident male superintendents appointed by the Valuers' Department, while rent-collection remained the responsibility of the Finance Department. Overall management was at County Hall. It was not until 1930 that the LCC changed, in a handful of cases, to an estate-based management approach, but it was very timid about appointing women. A few years later an LCC report confirmed its doubts, and in so doing helped to preserve the centralized status quo that had been in place for forty-five years. 'We cannot subscribe to the view that it is essential in every case for one officer to maintain contact with a tenant for all purposes. We do not accept the theory that women are, by reason of their sex, more suitable than men for this work.'[34]

Until the Addison Act of 1919, housing built for rent was not subsidized and thus the LCC could not afford to house the very poor. Their tenants were hand-picked. In the post-war years they built better-class housing, designed to attract a self-selected class of tenants who would thus vacate the cheaper properties for the poor. The 'sink estates' had arrived. The irony is that responsive, careful management – backed up by properly targeted expenditure – is now recognized as the most helpful approach to such problem estates – in fact, the last resort.[35]

The preferred, centralized, system of the LCC set a precedent for a distant and dislocated housing management style which is still providing its own problems.[36] In the early 1980s several Labour councils were to attempt an energetic decentralized policy, which took housing management (alongside other social services) to Neighbourhood Offices. Their approach – estate-based works teams and local housing offices – has now been widely adopted. The fact that there were massive rent arrears was a strong incentive to improve contact with the tenants. Octavia might have been amused.[37]

The high hopes of the immediate post-war period had foundered. By the mid-1930s there were still only forty-six women housing managers in local authorities. In 1932 the Association became the Society of Women Housing Estate Managers.[38] Five years later it dropped 'Estate' from its title and in 1948, significantly enough, it dropped 'Women' to become the Society of Housing Managers. Men had broken into the stronghold. There was increasing tension between the Society of Women Housing Estate Managers and the new Institute of Housing, formed in 1932 with an almost entirely male membership from local authority departments.[39] It institutionalized the already yawning divide in approach and served to lower standards by requiring less intensive training and a simpler examination.

Octavia Hill's followers in the 1930s were under siege. They struggled to keep her principles afloat, with the emphasis on the personal approach, often working in the growing housing association field.[40] They faced the facts of life – increasing politicization of housing and a rising public-housing sector, which accounted for around one million of the four million houses built in the inter-war period – but found themselves largely excluded. Nevertheless, when a decision was taken to appoint a housing management adviser to the Minister of Health, the first two appointees were women.[41]

On 1 December 1938 an Octavia Hill centenary dinner was held by the Society of Women Housing Managers at Claridge's. A distinguished guest list included Princess Alice, Countess of Athlone, the Earl of Athlone and Lord Balfour.

In his speech Sir Parker Morris wished the Society well: 'I hope that the banquet will be a new kicking-off point for further progress and further employment of trained women property managers by local authorities.'[42] He was an appropriate speaker, for in his capacity as Town Clerk of Chesterfield he had appointed the first woman Municipal Housing Manager, Janet Upcott, who had worked for him from 1927 until 1929.[43]

The centenary sparked off a number of events including a well-attended exhibition held at the Housing Centre, which ran for six weeks. More lasting was a memorial fund which set up an annual studentship.

The Second World War again drew on the expertise of the trained women housing managers, before the war numbering around 200. Some specially formed departments, such as the Administration for Married Quarters and the Ministry of Aircraft Production, put trained women in charge of property management.

The studentship set up at the time of the centenary had been running successfully for twenty years when a group calling itself The Friends of Octavia Hill announced its foundation with a letter to *The Times* in 1958. The fur began to fly. The Society of Housing Managers objected to an attempt to raise funds in Octavia's memory which seemed to duplicate their own assiduous and continuing effort. Under closer observation, The Friends of Octavia Hill were not quite what they seemed. Prime mover was William Thomson Hill, who claimed to represent her family – without any reference to the Ouvrys – backed by his literary agent, an ancient journalist, Mr Toye Vise. It so happened that W. T. Hill's biography of Octavia had been published that year and it soon became apparent that the two initiatives were not unconnected. Several organizations held back from any involvement – notably the National Trust. The most solid result of the Friends was a commemorative seat in St Bride's, Fleet Street; a memorial to Octavia and Mr Hill himself, who died in 1959. Mr Vise died in 1961. There, it seems, the matter rested.

With various trusted workers at the helm the Horace Street Trust had expanded in Octavia's lifetime to take on the twelve houses in St Katherine's Road and Westbourne Buildings. Horace Street became Cato Street, St Katherine's Road became Wilsham Street,[44] original Trustees retired or died. After her death it continued, amalgamating with other small trusts and associations and expanded to become the Octavia Hill and Rowe[45] Housing Trust, providing 1,230 houses and flats.[46] In 1989 it merged with the Latimer Housing Society to become the Octavia Hill, Latimer and Rowe Housing Trust.

One suspects that the modern housing association movement, more carefully structured to respond to its tenants' needs and (nominally) less politically controlled would have appealed to Octavia. She would, perhaps, have been particularly enthusiastic over late-twentieth-century 'self-help' in housing, over self-build, and the sporadic efforts of community architects and tenant co-operatives. Yet even housing associations now find themselves somewhat in the position of the early Peabody Trustees, who could not afford to house the genuinely needy.

Some of the properties which Octavia owned personally at her death, and left to members of the family, reverted to Horace Street Trust ownership. Among these were the Red and White Cross Cottages in Southwark. Visiting them today, one is at first surprised at the tiny scale of the scheme on which Octavia lavished such energy and commitment. They are stranded in a corner of Southwark where extensive bomb-damage and the subsequent rebuilding has left a more than usually random scene: a 1960s school, some 1930s municipal flats, various Victorian institutional and industrial buildings – and then, innocently and inappropriately nostalgic, twelve little Tudor-revival cottages. Beside them the garden is a fly-blown patch of grass, and the Red Cross Hall is a nondescript building only partially used. Back in Marylebone, Garbutt Place (once Paradise Place, where it all began) is a neat little cul-de-sac of early-nineteenth-century artisan cottages. They give nothing away, except respectability.

Other areas where Octavia struggled to improve the quality of life have sunk back to levels of misery approaching those she first encountered. Walmer Place is now a stinking alley, strewn with mattresses and beer cans, with a large resident population of homeless drunks although a blue plaque to Emma Cons ornaments the corner building, once the old Walmer Castle. St John's churchyard by Waterloo is little better, though it still boasts grass and rose bushes. By some malevolent irony, St Christopher's Place, where St Christopher is still lodged in his niche above the shoppers' heads, is now a monument to conspicuous spending – a parade of jewellers, expensive dress shops and exclusive restaurants.

It seems appropriate that Octavia should have the last word in this book. On the occasion of the presentation of her portrait in 1898 she gave a glimpse of her aims, against which her achievements may be measured. 'When I am gone, I hope my friends will not try to carry out any special system, or to follow blindly in the track which I have trodden. New circumstances require various efforts, and it is the spirit, not the dead form that should be perpetuated.' What would her workers inherit?

Not a system, not an association, not dead formulas. We shall leave them a few houses, purified and improved, a few new and better ones built, a certain record of thoughtful and loving management, a few open spaces, some of which will be more beautiful than they would have been, but what we care most to leave them is not any tangible thing however great, not any memory, however good, but the quick eye to see, the true soul to measure, the large hope to grasp the mighty issues of the new and better days to come – greater ideals, greater hope and patience to realize both.

Notes

The abbreviations CEM and ESM refer to the editions of Octavia's letters edited by her brother-in-law C. Edmund Maurice and by her sister Emily Southwood Maurice (see Bibliography). Books referred to by author and title only appear in full in the Bibliography. When I have transcribed directly from Octavia's letters I have written out her personal abbreviations in full. Major manuscript collections referred to are: the University of London Library MS.797/1/4908 etc. and MS 797/II/67/1 etc. (for Booth and Hill material); the British Library of Political and Economic Science at the LSE (the Courtney Collection, Passfield Papers and letters from Octavia to Henrietta Barnett, Coll. Misc 512); the Greater London Record Office (Barnett papers F/BAR etc.); and the Marylebone Public Library, the most comprehensive accessible collection of Octavia Hill material, including letters between Octavia and both Cockerells, father and son (D: Misc 84/1–5/1 etc.).

I: BEGINNINGS

1. Extracts from the Baptist College Reports (Ouvry papers).
2. The *Christian Life*, 5 March 1921 (Ouvry papers).
3. Lewes, *Dr Southwood Smith*.
4. Also the home of Dr Guthrie's Ragged School. Scottish Unitarians were also called Universalists.
5. The *Christian Life*, 10 May 1913 (Ouvry papers).
6. Mary Howitt described them in her autobiography: 'the one an embodiment of peace and an admirable writer but whose talent, like the violet, kept in the shade: the other, the warm-hearted painter.' According to Gertrude their father was 'a city merchant of refined literary tastes', but another account refers to his lack of success and the fact that their uncle brought them up. Mary (d. 1870) and Margaret (1803–87) became respectively a writer (using the name Harriet Myrtle) and miniature painter. Margaret studied in Paris and London, and was invited to paint Wordsworth, for which he wrote her a sonnet.
7. Letter to the Hon. D. G. Hallyberton in Rome, quoted in Lewes, op. cit.
8. Herman is a shadowy figure but he appears in the autumn of 1841 travelling with William and Mary Howitt in Germany; they heard spirited piano playing in the next railway carriage, and discovered

Meyerbeer, trying out passages of *Le Prophète*. Herman died in 1897.

9. R. H. Horne, *New Spirit of the Age*. Bentham is still lodged in central London; his cabinet, with its doors sometimes open, is on a landing in University College, London.

10. Johann Heinrich Pestalozzi (1746–1827). His theories were published in *How Gertrude Educates her Children* (1801) and the Pestalozzian method achieved wide fame. His own efforts at setting up schools were less successful.

11. These were Julia and Louisa, Hill's daughters by his first wife, Margaret, Ida, Kate and Arthur by his second wife.

12. Information on the house and town from N. Scarfe, *The Shell Guide to Cambridgeshire* (1983, London). The house, Nos. 7 and 8 combined, is now in use as commercial premises.

13. From her unpublished MS, entitled 'Early Life & Influences of training on Octavia Hill' (Romilly Ouvry, family papers.)

14. Bills announcing the failure of the Wisbech Bank, and the repayments to creditors, Wisbech Museum collection. Hill's own account of the affair said that the Yorkshire bank of Wentworth stopped payment, leaving him liable for £14,000. This was compounded by the failure of five London banks, including Hill's own agents: see letter in the *Star*, 2 July 1837. He was replying to slanders, which suggested that his subsequent wealth was suspect in view of his penniless state in 1826.

15. From a biographical account of Arthur Hill, *Reading Standard*, 23 February 1907.

16. See Minute Book of the Wisbech Museum Society, now at the Wisbech Museum.

17. Owen's was the first infant school opened in the country: see J. W. Adamson, *English Education 1789–1902*, London 1964. James Hill's only son Arthur was educated at a Pestalozzian school in Worksop.

18. For example on 17 June and 8 July 1837, the piece earlier published in the *Monthly Repository* was run as a two-part article.

19. *Star in the East*, 20 January 1838.

20. References from *Star in the East*, (Wisbech Museum); also N. Mansfield, *James Hill and the Wisbech Owenites*, Wisbech Society, 46th Annual Report, 1985.

21. Notice in the *Stamford Mercury*, 29 May 1840.

22. In 1856, see MS notes by Margaret Howitt (Ouvry papers).

23. It transferred from Birmingham in July 1839 and continued sporadically until the early 1840s.

24. Malcolm Chase, *People's Farm, English Radical Agrarianism 1775–1840*, Oxford, 1988. Chase discusses the various Owenite land experiments, those preceding Hill's as well as his own. Dennis Hardy, *Alternative*

Communities in Nineteenth-Century England, London and New York, 1979 expands on the Chartist venture, begun in 1945 and claiming 70,000 members at its short-lived peak.

25. James Hill remains in the shadows after this, living with a daughter Mrs Whelpdale for many years. He died on 20 July 1871.
26. Romilly Ouvry remembers how angry his mother Elinor, Octavia's niece and helper, became at this process (conversation with the author).
27. Hill, unpublished MS (Ouvry papers)
28. The house was rebuilt in 1876 and in 1882 Gertrude Lewes moved back there with her husband Charles. It was demolished in 1950.
29. Poor Law Commission, 4th Annual Report, 1838: Appendix A, No. 1, Supplements 2 & 3.
30. Parliamentary Papers, 1833. Vol. XX: it proposed that no child under nine should be employed in mills or factory, and that until 14 they should work a maximum 8 hours, never at night. They could use the time gained for education; it would also, he pointed out, ensure that a child was not employed 'in two different factories on the same day'.
31. She also drew the portrait of Smith in Horne's *New Spirit*, of which Elizabeth Barrett noted: 'The power, the serenity, and sweetness of the whole expression have exceedingly impressed me.'
32. Mary Howitt (née Botham), 1799–1888; William Howitt, 1792–1879.
33. See Caroline Southwood Hill, *Notes on Education*.
34. MS notes by Caroline Southwood Hill (Ouvry papers).
35. Ibid.
36. CEM, p. 7.
37. The Sanatorium opened in 1842 for clerks, governesses and middle-class men and women if they became ill away from home. It was available for those who paid an annual subscription. It was decided to build a purpose-built hospital, but despite the patronage of Prince Albert and a mass of fund-raising events, including theatrical performances organized by Dickens, it failed to raise the necessary money.
38. Letter reproduced in Lewes, *Dr Southwood Smith*.
39. *Letters of Charles Dickens*, Madeline House and Graham Storey (ed.), Vol. 2, Oxford, 1969.
40. See M. Howitt, *An Autobiography*.
41. See Amice Lee, 'Recollections'.
42. Evidence to the 1840 Select Committee.

2: GUILD WORK

1. CEM, p. 6.
2. December 1844, the inaugural meeting of the Health of Towns

Association. It was a weighty membership; among the peers were Lords Normanby, Ashley, Morpeth, Grosvenor and Ebrington.

3. See Lewis, *Edwin Chadwick.*

4. S. E. Finer, *The Life and Times of Sir Edwin Chadwick,* London, 1952.

5. Written from the Ladies' Guild, 11 June 1854 (Ouvry papers).

6. Margaret Hill ran the school with her sisters, probably in Norwich. Later she became Mrs Whelpdale. After she was widowed she seems to have assumed responsibility for her father. She also seems to have been the half-sister who remained closest to the later family; she constantly offered support for Octavia's work, and as late as 1891 shared a Hill family Christmas.

7. *Household Words,* 17 May 1856. See also A. Lohrli, *Notes on Contributors to Household Words,* Ohio, 1973.

8. 'The invention of a lady [Mrs Wallace] and may be remembered by some as furnishing the Tudor Villa, a model contributed by her to the Great Exhibition.'

9. CEM, p. 17. Robin was traced, sent to an Industrial School and eventually emigrated to Australia where she married. See also ESM, p. 46; letter from Octavia to Mary Harris describes her return in November 1857, to ask for employment. Robin was a nickname; she was called Amelia.

10. For example, those published as *Two Little Folks' Plays* in 1903.

11. CEM, p. 78, to Mary Harris, 29 March 1856.

12. F. D. Maurice (1805–1872). In his time at Oxford he was responsible, with John Sterling, for turning the Apostles into a very influential and secret University society, moving its centre to Trinity. The Apostles of the 1820s had little in common with the more notorious Apostles of the 1920s.

13. An observation from Edward C. Mack and W. H. G. Armytage, *Thomas Hughes,* London, 1952. He was not in the charismatic emotive class of Dr Spurgeon or the matinée idol style of the Revd Haweis.

14. Mary Hughes (1860–1941), from R. Hobhouse, *Mary Hughes,* London, 1949.

15. A letter to Susanna Winkworth, discussing the differences between the Unitarian and Anglican standpoint is typically impenetrable (p. 149–53, Shaen, *Memorials of two sisters*).

16. Julia Wedgwood, author of *The Moral Ideal,* a book which Octavia and her mother read with interest, to Emelia Russell Gurney, wife of the Recorder of London. *Letters of Emelia Russell Gurney,* edited by Ellen Mary Gurney, London, 1902, p. 61.

17. John Ludlow (1821–1911) had lived in France which had influenced his thinking and attitudes. He brought to the group French experience in co-operative enterprise and was sympathetic to the ideas of Fourier.

18. Charles Kingsley (1819–1875) was a complex man. According to Norman, 'enthusiasm for improving the conditions of the working classes was held in balance with a profound belief in the general unsuitability of those classes for government or for social influence.' He was much influenced by Mayhew's articles, published from 1849, in the *Morning Chronicle* and which were published as *London Labour and the London Poor* (1851–2, revised 1861–2).

19. See Ch. 4, Colloms, *Victorian Visionaries*.

20. F. J. Furnivall (1825–1910). For an entertaining account of Furnivall the philologist, see K. M. Elizabeth Murray, *Caught in the Web of Words* London, 1977, a biography of James Murray, editor of the *Oxford English Dictionary*, a close colleague of Furnivall's for many years.

21. Thomas Hughes (1822–1896), author of *Tom Brown's Schooldays* (1856) and in 1882 made a County Court judge in Chester.

22. Unfortunately Cooper, some years later, appropriated the funds of his association – a sad end for the only successful co-operative enterprise at this time.

23. John Ludlow, *The Autobiography of a Christian Socialist*, ed. A. D. Murray, London, 1981.

24. In fact sanitary reform began to interest the Christian Socialists. They decided to form a National Health League to campaign for fresh drinking water and efficient disposal of sewage. Maurice was not keen, owing to his dislike of formal organizations.

25. Octavia Hill wrote to her sister Miranda in 1852 (CEM, p. 23) about two of Kingsley's publications about the condition of the poor, '*Cheap Clothes and Nasty* and *Labour and the Poor* are some of the most dreadful things I have ever read. They have made a deep impression on me.' Later on she recommended Miranda to read *Yeast*.

26. Edward Vansittart Neale (1810–1892). Philip N. Backstrom's *Christian Socialism and Co-operation in Victorian England*, London, 1974, gives the fullest account of Neale.

27. Despite the passing of the 1852 Industrial and Provident Societies Act, Neale's attempt to achieve a Union of Societies was unsuccessful. There were a number of conferences, but the Leeds one, held in 1854, was the last.

28. Ludlow, *Autobiography*, op.cit.

29. ESM, p. 28, to Mary Harris, June 1856.

30. See Prochaska, *Women and Philanthropy*.

31. Archibald Tait, then Bishop of London; he became Archbishop of Canterbury in 1869.

32. Ludlow, *Autobiography*, op.cit.

33. Rogers was described as 'woodcarver to the Queen'. His daughter Mary went to Palestine and worked with Moslem Arab women.

34. For example, in her sister Emily's introduction to *Early Ideals*: 'even at that early age she was pondering over deep and serious subjects, and keenly interested in a variety of questions, while dominated by a sense of duty and a strong love of home and family life.'
35. CEM, p. 49, 16 July 1855.
36. 'A sedate yet captivating girl, twelve years older than myself . . . Lucy Harrison, with her blue eyes, gold-brown hair,' was greatly admired by Greville MacDonald. In later life she became headmistress of the Mount School, York. One of her accomplishments was that she was a skilled carpenter. She died in 1916.
37. From Caroline Hill's MS account (Ouvry papers).
38. CEM, p. 63, to Mary Harris, 3 December 1855.
39. Vol. I was published in 1843 (anonymously), Vol. II in 1846. *Modern Painters* III and IV were published in 1856. Vol. V, to which Octavia contributed, was the final volume, in 1860. According to Emily, she knew Volume I well by the age of twelve.
40. CEM, p. 30, letter to Gertrude, 5 December 1853.
41. Emma Cons, as well as Octavia, was one of the putative members. He also had a number of students from the Working Men's College in mind. Henry Swan, an engraver who joined the College in the 1850s, and who became the first curator of Ruskin's St George Museum in Sheffield in 1875, spent time copying illuminated manuscripts in the British Museum (information from Barnes, *Ruskin in Sheffield*). In the published letters to William Webb, another College student, he often referred to the Convent Plan. It seems to have been subsumed within the St George's Guild.
42. ESM, p. 116, nd.
43. CEM, pp. 36–9, 16 March 1855.
44. ESM, p. 117, 20 October 1855.
45. CEM, pp. 73–4, letter to Emily, 18 February 1856.
46. Emma Cons, following a visit to Switzerland and after her unsatisfactory stint working for Ruskin, hit upon the idea of engraving watch-backs. She and a group of friends took an apprenticeship to a Clerkenwell watchmaker and hired a room. It was a pioneering step for a group of women in the 1850s. Men in the watch business resented them and on one occasion beat up a messenger who was delivering some of their watches. After that she turned to designing and repainting stained glass, the first woman at Powell's glass factory in Whitefriars, again enduring much opposition from the male work-force and soon joined by her sister and other friends in a workroom of their own (see Baylis).

3: CLASSES

1. See Barnes, *Ruskin in Sheffield*.
2. Quoted William Benzie, *Dr. F. J. Furnivall: Victorian Scholar, adventurer*, Oklahoma, 1983. The eccentric spellings were part of Furnivall's campaign for phonetic spelling.
3. See Ludlow, *Autobiography*.
4. CEM, pp. 116–24, Emily to Florence, 12 December 1858.
5. Shaen, *Memorials of Two Sisters*: letters to Catherine Winkworth, dated May 1855, 23 January 1856, pp. 128–9.
6. He had 'adopted' a girl much younger than he, and after the birth of many children he left her.
7. For Furnivall's account see, *The Working Men's College 1854–1904*, ed. the Revd J. Llewelyn Davies.
8. John Llewelyn Davies (1826–1916) became principal of the Working Men's College for two periods in the 1870s. His sister Emily Davies was the founder of Girton College, Cambridge and his daughter Margaret became Secretary to the Women's Co-operative Guild in its successful reincarnation.
9. It was her favourite brother's successful passage through Cambridge, becoming President of the Union, that helped form Emily's resolve to open up a similar path to women. See Manton, *Elizabeth Garrett Anderson*.
10. He took Maurice's funeral service, years later.
11. From Harrison, *History of the Working Men's College*.
12. Working Men's College Library; the cost was 6d a week for the full course, 3d for any two.
13. Barbara Leigh Smith (Bodichon) (1827–1891) was one of the illegitimate daughters of Benjamin Leigh Smith, a Radical Unitarian Member of Parliament – another member of the Highgate circle around Dr Southwood Smith.
14. Lee Holcombe, *Wives and Property*, Oxford, 1983.
15. CEM, p. 270, letter to Miss Mayo, 26 September 1871.
16. 23 November 1857 (Ouvry papers).
17. Letter to Emily in Italy, from 10 Pall Mall East, 4 June 1856 (Ouvry papers).
18. The Arundel Society, founded in 1848, had a special fund for the copying of Old Masters. From 1853 to 1860, Ruskin helped to supply them.
19. ESM, p. 142, 16 December 1858.
20. CEM, p. 102, 22 November 1857.
21. ESM, p. 28, letter to Mary Harris, June 1856.
22. ESM, p. 43, 28 July 1857.
23. ESM, p. 36–7, to Mary Harris, 30 May 1857.

24. CEM, p. 100–1, Mrs Hill to Emily, 22 September 1857.

25. 24 April 1848, (Ouvry papers).

26. CEM, p. 127, 4 January 1859.

27. *Charles Kingsley, letters and memories* (Vol. 2) ed. his wife, London, 1877.

28. CEM, pp. 95–6, to Mary Harris, 19 March 1857.

29. In 1857 Ruskin had told her that 'six hours a day is as much as you can possibly work at painting.' By 1859 she could only manage four or five hours.

30. 'Can you fancy me at work by a large window opening above the wide gravel and smooth grass and purple brown network of trees . . . A gold frame with eight Turner sketches hung on the shutter before me, all my working things on a nice wide window ledge, and my little book on my knee.' Ruskin was at work there too, though not in the same room. ESM, p. 129, to Mary Harris, 11 December 1857.

31. Morley dates it 1859; the reference to the painting in ESM gives it as 1864.

32. CEM, p. 134, to Miranda, 3 April 1859.

33. CEM, p. 136, 16 April 1859.

34. 12 May 1859, from Milton Street (Ouvry papers).

35. Anna Blunden (1829–1915) was a solitary figure, living in Islington, and painting. She exhibited each year at the Suffolk Street Gallery and at the Royal Academy.

36. She did so; just before Christmas he wrote: 'I like what you have done exceedingly. Both filberts and sunset.'

37. *Sublime and Instructive; letters from John Ruskin to Louisa Marchioness of Waterford, Anna Blunden and Ellen Heaton*, ed. Virginia Surtees, London, 1975, pp. 118 *et seq.*

38. ESM, p. 147, to Mary Harris, 1 July 1860.

39. CEM, p. 146, to Florence, 26 June 1859.

40. CEM, p. 215, to Emma Baumgartner, 11 December 1864.

41. Respectively, a toymaker and the daughter of a former nurse, possibly Amelia Wilson, from Wisbech days.

42. Fuller version of letter, Greater London Record Office F/BAR/460.

43. CEM, p. 152, 20 August 1859.

44. Elizabeth Whitehead (1828–1916) married Frank Malleson in 1857, excluding the word 'obey' from the marriage vows. Later she became instrumental in the Working Men's College, extending its classes to women and was Hon. Sec. of the provisional committee which had support from J. S. Mill, Barbara Bodichon, George Eliot, Harriet Martineau and others. Her efforts led to the Working Women's College which opened in October 1864 at 29 Queen Square, of which she was Secretary. She was related to the Courtauld family, one of the great

Unitarian philanthropic dynasties. Derek Hudson, *Munby, Man of two Worlds*, London, 1974.

45. p. 108, see Harrison, *A History of the Working Men's College*.
46. CEM, pp. 182–3, 16 August 1860.
47. CEM, p. 183–5, 19 August 1860.
48. CEM, p. 186, 15 November 1860.
49. ESM, p. 26; 3 August 1856.
50. CEM, p. 91, letter to Mary Harris, 27 October 1856.
51. Emily Maurice in a footnote points out that the wearing of the white surplice was considered ritualistic, against the traditional black.
52. ESM, pp. 58–9, 24 June 1859.
53. CEM, pp. 163–5, letter to Miranda, 23 October 1859.
54. CEM, p. 178, 26 February 1860.
55. The author was Ellen Ranyard herself.
56. CEM, pp. 173–4, Christmas, 1859.
57. See Hilton, *Ruskin, the Early Years*.
58. Marian Evans (George Eliot), reviewing it in the *Westminster Review* in April 1856, praised his emphasis on realism – 'the doctrine that all truth and beauty are to be attained by a humble and faithful study of nature . . . the thorough acceptance of this doctrine would remould our life; and he who teaches its application . . . is a prophet for his generation.' (Haight, *Eliot*, p. 182).
59. Miss Wedgwood to Emelia Russell Gurney, from Brighton, *Letters of Emelia Russell Gurney*, op. cit.
60. CEM, p. 204, 25 July 1863.
61. CEM, pp. 175–7, 29 January 1860.
62. See Hilton, *Ruskin*.
63. George Allen (1832–1907) worked closely with Ruskin, and married one of the maids from Denmark Hill.
64. ESM, p. 133, 18 April 1858; Ruskin encouraged her to follow any path 'which enables you to make your way in the world and be of use. As soon as you can do without help from me in money (help in all other ways I shall always be ready and happy when I can give) you can tell me . . . as long as you need work I can always find you what will be useful to me, so don't worry yourself.'
65. ESM, p. 131, to Mary Harris, 29 January 1858.

4: NOTTINGHAM PLACE

1. Sophia Jex-Blake, 1840–1912: all quotes, unless otherwise noted, are from Todd, *The Life of Sophia Jex-Blake*.
2. Probably *The Scapegoat*, exhibited at the Royal Academy in 1856 and widely shown thereafter.

3. George Eliot, a most feminine and heterosexual woman, was pursued by a number of young women admirers. Haight quotes Edith Simcox, the most emotional of them all, whose reports of her meetings with her 'darling', seem highly suggestive despite the fact they took place in George Lewes's presence. Haight argued that with Freudian insights it is now difficult to accept the idea of pure but passionate friendship between members of the same sex. For an alternative view see Jeffries, *The spinster and her enemies*, who argues that distinctions between lesbianism and passionate friendship are difficult to draw.

4. Manton, *Elizabeth Garrett Anderson*, pp. 121–22.

5. *The Letters of William Morris* (ed. Philip Henderson), London, 1950 –letter to Jane Morris, February/March 1887.

6. Edwin Hodder, *The Life and Work of the Seventh Earl of Shaftesbury*, London, 1886.

7. Copy of 1862 accounts with the Residuary Legatees (Ouvry papers).

8. Ouvry papers.

9. CEM, p. 200, to Gertrude, 1862.

10. CEM, pp. 203–4, 4 February 1863.

11. ESM, pp. 68–70, letter to Mary Harris, 1863.

12. CEM, pp. 202–3, to Emma Baumgartner, 18 January 1863.

13. CEM, p. 205, letter to Emma Baumgartner, July 1863.

14. See Hobhouse, *Mary Hughes* (see Note 36, p. 360).

15. They were drowned on the *Titanic* in 1915.

16. B. Stephen, *Emily Davies and Girton*, London, 1927.

17. CEM, pp. 209–11, 18 February 1864.

18. L. Holcombe, *Victorian Ladies at Work*, Newton Abbot, 1973.

19. See Burton, *Barbara Bodichon*.

20. Stephen, op. cit., letter to Emily Davies.

21. Arthur Munby noted that they hoped to attract 'teachers, shopgirls, and even servant girls' (p. 177, Derek Hudson, *Munby: Man of Two Worlds*, London, 1972). He taught Latin at the College for some years.

22. Copy of part of letter to Miss Tyrell, dated 9 August 1870 (Ouvry papers).

23. These qualifications were not copied into the section of the letter given.

24. This was unusual; physical education did not feature in girls' education at the time.

25. Caroline Southwood Hill, MS notes (Ouvry papers).

26. Moberly Bell (p. 179) states that the school closed in 1884, but I can find no evidence for this.

27. Marylebone Records Office: Letter to librarian, dated 3 December 1961.

5: RUSKIN: PRACTICAL HELP

1. See Tarn, *Five Per Cent Philanthropy*, pp. 15–22.
2. Chadwick commented that such a low return would ensure all funds were essentially charitable. Effectively it removed the speculative element from the return on capital. Angela Burdett-Coutts's Columbia Market development reduced the return to 2.2%. John Burnett, *Social History of Housing 1815–1970*, Newton Abbot, 1978.
3. Rent levels were between 4s and 7s per week. The first Peabody Dwellings of 1864 ranged from 2s 6d for a single room to 5s for a set of three: see Tarn, *Five Per Cent Philanthropy*.
4. Mrs Shaen was a Winkworth, whose sisters Susannah and Catherine were reformers in education, housing and welfare fields in Bristol. She was a workhouse visitor, manager of five Board Schools and of a number of refuges for unmarried mothers. Later she became a Westminster Guardian, holding strong COS views. See Hollis, *Ladies Elect*.
5. From 1879 the Howard de Walden estate, in whose hands it remains.
6. In Ruskin's *Fors Clavigera* (April 1877), Octavia gave the figure of Ruskin's investment as £800.
7. She began to hold sewing classes for the mothers and sisters of the toymakers immediately they moved to Nottingham Place.
8. See Miranda's handwritten notes, Ouvry papers.
9. ESM, p. 161–3, to Mary Harris, 11 September 1864.
10. ESM, p. 163–4, to Mary Harris, 29 July 1865.
11. In 1857 George Eliot was giving Bessie Parkes, editor of the *Waverley Journal*, some advice. 'For my own taste . . . the more business you can get into the journal – the more statements of philanthropic movements and social facts and the *less literature*, the better. Not because I like philanthropy and hate literature, but because I want to *know* about philanthropy and don't care for second-rate literature.' (Haight, *Eliot*, p. 205).
12. Letter to Francois d'Albert Durade, 24 June 1864, and to Sara Sophia Hennell, 25 June 1864, both published in *The George Eliot Letters*, Vol. IV ed. by Gordon Haight.
13. ESM, p. 79, 1 January 1865; George Eliot and Barbara had met in the early 1850s but the deep friendship between them, and between George Lewes and Barbara (she had 'quite revised' her view of him), dated from a holiday in Tenby, in July 1856 (Haight, *Eliot*, p. 205).
14. One poem they both admired was Mrs Browning's *Aurora Leigh*, which George Eliot had reviewed favourably in the *Westminster Review* in January 1857, while pointing out the similarities of the story to *Jane Eyre* (Haight, *Eliot*, p. 185).
15. ESM, p. 80, 8 January 1865.

16. Gertrude seems to have stayed within the Unitarian congregation, as did Florence. The others had all joined the Church of England.

17. See Haight, *George Eliot*, p. 381.

18. *Adam Bede* had been published in 1859 to enormous acclaim, followed by the *Mill on the Floss* (1860), *Silas Marner* (1861) and *Romola* (1863). By then, George Eliot was known to be Marian Lewes (or, strictly, Evans). She was working on *Felix Holt* in 1865.

19. Ruskin and MacDonald had a common friend in Mrs La Touche, mother of the tragic Rose.

20. ESM, p. 78–9, n.d., but probably 1864; letter to Mary Harris.

21. CEM, pp. 214–5, from Egerton House, Beckenham, 11 July 1864.

22. ESM, p. 87–8, to Mary Harris from Godmanchester, 3 September 1865.

23. William Holman Hunt, pre-Raphaelite painter (1827–1910). CEM, p. 212, letter to Miss Baumgartner, 11 March 1864: 'Will you be interested to know that I have got to know Holman Hunt very well, through the Hughes's . . . ?'

24. G. F. Watts (1817–1904) became a great supporter of the Kyrle Society (see Ch. 11), lending pictures and welcoming parties of working people. Similarly he supported the Barnetts, lending many pictures to Whitechapel exhibitions. In the 1890s Watts provided a series of plaques commemorating the heroic deeds of the common people at Postman's Park, at St Botolph's, Aldersgate (see catalogue notes to G. F. Watts exhibition, Whitechapel Art Gallery, 1974). When Octavia first met Watts at dinner, she commented: 'He is transparently, deeply good, a quiet sympathetic man, with large childlike heart . . . There is nothing pathetic about Watts as there is about Ruskin.' ESM, January 1866. In fact Watts' non-consummated marriage to Ellen Terry was somewhat comparable to Ruskin's own marriage to Effie Gray.

6: FRESHWATER PLACE ONWARDS

1. Freshwater Place was slightly further west, off Homer Street, not far from the Edgware Road.

2. Some accounts refer to Ruskin's having inherited the properties; this was not the case. He used the money from his inheritance to buy leaseholds (Paradise Place) and freeholds (Freshwater Place) for Octavia to manage.

3. *Macmillan's Magazine*, July 1869.

4. From the *Fortnightly Review* article.

5. ESM, p. 188, notes.

6. See a conflicting story, Ch. 8, p. 134.

7. ESM, pp. 189 *et seq.*, letters to Mary Harris, all undated.

8. MS in Ouvry papers.

9. ESM, p. 165, 10 March 1866.

10. Burne-Jones was much less impressed: 'Edward was repelled by the old lady's sharp decisive manner . . . At dinner, if anything her son said . . . did not reach her ear, she demanded to have it repeated and from her end of the table came a clear thread of voice, "John, John Ruskin what was that you said?"' P. Fitzgerald, *Edward Burne-Jones*, London, 1975.

11. In 1871 she married Arthur Severn, but she looked after Ruskin until the end of his life.

12. The accepted rate of return on rented working-class housing was calculated at around 10%, a higher rate than for more substantial houses, which yielded between 4 and 7% because of their longer life-expectancy. See S. Muthesius, *The English Terraced House*, New Haven and London, 1982.

13. See Tarn, *Five Per Cent Philanthropy*, pp. 34–5.

14. The account in ESM rather conflicts. Emily suggested that Ruskin purchased another property on the Marylebone Road with a cottage behind it, and used a large room there for night classes and a women's workroom in the day, while letting off the tenements.

15. The new citizens of Letchworth Garden City, which came into being in 1903, promptly organized May Day events which became a regular point in the calendar for many years.

16. Mary Booth (1847–1939) was a first cousin of the Potter sisters, and a niece of Charles Macaulay. She later married Charles Booth.

17. The Harrison family (numbering 12 brothers and sisters) lived in Romford. Mary Howitt was their aunt. In 1869 the sisters founded the Harrison Homes for the Aged Poor, which are still in existence.

18. Mary Booth, unpublished draft of memoir, University of London, II 67/1.

19. CEM, p. 224: Florence wrote to Emily from Wales, informing her that a cholera outbreak was expected. She and Gertrude had been compiling information, 'from the cholera reports and sent . . . the lecture on epidemics'. Presumably these were their grandfather's notes. Octavia saw a good deal of Ruskin that year; he noted in his diary two occasions on which Octavia had called, on 19 July and 12 October. On the latter occasion she came with her sister.

20. ESM, p. 170, 15 September 1866.

21. Mrs Maclagan refers to paid workers in 1871, although Octavia included the reference in her article, since those who followed her example might need to employ paid helpers.

22. She claimed to have joined the COS, or its predecessor, in 1867. In 1869 she addressed the Social Science Association in Bristol on 'The importance of aiding the poor without almsgiving' (see Chapter 8).

23. In 1895 she lent it to Margaret Sewell for the Women's University Settlement.

24. See Raeper, *George MacDonald*, Ch. 23, note 10.

25. ESM, p. 83, 11 August 1867.

26. Greville MacDonald became an eminent ear, nose and throat consultant at King's College Hospital, later becoming a Fellow and Emeritus Professor there.

27. See MacDonald, *Reminiscences of a Specialist*, p. 34. He also remembered her 'indescribable charm of voice'.

28. Ibid., p. 95, letter dated 16 June 1901.

29. CEM, pp. 241–2, to Emily, 1 March 1868.

30. Loaned by Mrs Ross, one of the Sterling sisters. The Hill net was already spread wide.

31. CEM, p. 241, letter from Emily, 1 March 1868.

32. CEM, pp. 242–4, to Miss Mayo 5 April 1868.

33. Wife of Col. Gillum, founder of the Industrial Boys' Home.

34. CEM, pp. 244–5, letter from her mother, probably May 1868.

35. Marylebone PL, 5 September 1871.

36. From 'District Visiting' published in Hill, *Our Common Land*. See Summers 'A Home from Home. Women's philanthropic work in the nineteenth century', in *Fit work for Women*, ed. S. Burman, London, 1979. The author argues persuasively that voluntary visiting was 'an engagement of the self which involved the sacrifice of leisure and the development of expertise . . . [which] created an informal interest group among them'. Despite the domestic allusions and its voluntary nature, it was not wholly reactionary.

37. CEM, p. 248, to Emma Baumgartner, 29 November 1868.

38. ESM, p. 100, to Mary Harris, 12 November 1868. '. . . so keenly clear, definite, and far-reaching. Compulsory Education, Disestablishment of the English Church, Separation of Married People in workhouses, the right of landlords over tenants, all were dealt with so distinctly. You know that Mill would never win my heart, but he is decidedly an able man . . .'

39. *The Amberley Papers* ed. Bertrand and Patricia Russell, London, 1937: 1 March 1869.

40. Ibid., letter to her mother, 14 January 1869.

41. See p. 264 (address to Newnham students).

42. ESM, pp. 103–4, 17 July 1869.

43. Mrs Duckworth became Mrs Leslie Stephen.

44. *Victorian Studies*, autumn 1985, pp. 97–124. H. L. Malchow, 'Public Gardens and Social Action in late Victorian London'.

45. This and subsequent quotes from *Canon Barnett*, by his wife (Vol. 1).

46. Another view on the same subject came from Henry Nevinson: 'Knowledge makes it all the harder for me to explain the secret of his power . . .

He had none of the attraction that the jolly, jolly Christian of Chesterton's ideal appears to possess for some, and neither to rich nor poor was he ever hail-fellow-well-met. Nor was he in the least eloquent. In speaking and writing his style was unmistakable, but unattractive.' See Nevinson, *Changes and Chances*, pp. 87–90.

7: CHARITY ORGANIZATION SOCIETY

1. An argument being repeated today, regarding aid to third world countries.
2. See Owen, *English Philanthropy*, p. 220 *et seq.*
3. Octavia's Bristol speech, see below, cites one such example.
4. See Prochaska, *Women and Philanthropy*, p. 4; in the 1820s women sat hidden behind the organ at a meeting of the Society for the Propagation of the Gospel. However, the National Association for the Promotion of Social Science was an organization in which women played a major role.
5. Printed pamphlet of Bristol speech, 'The Importance of aiding the Poor without Almsgiving'. By the early 1870s she had slightly modified her view – 'if gifts *must* reach them from various sources, that there should at least be concert amongst those who give' (draft of speech given in Marylebone). Both from Ouvry papers.
6. ESM, p. 107, to Mary Harris, 3 October 1869.
7. See Owen, op. cit.
8. See C. Loch Mowat, *The Charity Organization Society*, Ch. I.
9. In particular, in her 'Report on the work in Marylebone', printed as the Appendix to the 3rd Annual Report of the Local Government Board, 1874. 'The important difference between the Elberfeld and Marylebone systems is that, whereas in Elberfeld the volunteers themselves decide on the parochial relief, our volunteers have no such authority committed to them.' In Marylebone 'the Visitor brings information and the Guardians vote relief.'
10. By 1867 they numbered 234 women working in poor parts of London; they had raised over £133,000. From the beginning it was paid work; by 1867 Mrs Ranyard was paying salaries of £32 per annum. In 1868 she widened the scope of the work to include nursing care. See Prochaska, pp. 126–30.
11. Owen, op. cit., refers to Edward Denison (1840–1870) as 'the John the Baptist of the COS'. Sir B. Leighton (ed.) *Letters and Other Writings of the late Edwardian Denison*, London, 1875.
12. Charles Trevelyan (1807–1886) was also Macaulay's brother-in-law, Indian Finance Minister (1862–5), and was created Baronet in 1874.
13. See Loch Mowat, op. cit.

14. For example, a pamphlet produced in 1874 giving the history of the COS provoked considerable argument, Loch Mowat, p. 14.
15. CEM, p. 276, letter to Mrs Shaen, 3 September 1872. His father, F. D. Maurice, died at Easter 1872 while staying in London with Julia and Hester Sterling.
16. 27 October 1876, letter to Cockerell in Marylebone PL – not published by Edmund Maurice! ('I do not think his presence *would* be helpful, much as he cares for the subject. He has too little power of understanding how other people see things.').
17. The first successful candidate was Miss Martha Merrington. Twenty years on there were over 800 women Guardians, see Hollis, *Ladies Elect*, p. 8 etc.
18. Later to be Dean of Ripon.
19. Letter to Florence Davenport Hill, CEM, pp. 253–4, 7 June 1869. Florence's field of charitable work was juvenile paupers; before long she was involved in the COS too.
20. *Recollections Chiefly by Himself*, ed. W. H. Draper, London, 1921, pp. 82 *et seq.*
21. Also published as a pamphlet, 'Employment or Almsgiving'.
22. They were bought by Julia Sterling.
23. *Canon Barnett*, by his wife, Vol. 1.
24. *George Eliot Letters*, Vol. V, 2 December 1870. Haight notes that Octavia probably discussed the Walmer Street Industrial Experiment with the Leweses when, as Lewes noted in his diary, she spent the evening with them, 21 November 1870.
25. O. Hill, 'Further Account of the Walmer Street Industrial Experiment', 1872.
26. 'Letter to Fellow-workers', 1872.
27. *Canon Barnett*, Vol I, p. 28.
28. Ibid., p. 31.
29. Ibid.
30. She was also a friend of George Eliot who wrote to congratulate her, saying the news was a New Year's gift (*George Eliot Letters*, Vol. V). 'You have only got to be a good faithful woman such as you have always been, and then the very thought of you will help to mend things.'
31. J. & L. B. Hammond, *James Stansfield*, London, 1932, pp. 112–4.
32. Her report is published in M. Smedley, *Boarding out and Pauper Schools*, 1875.
33. See Gauldie, *Cruel Habitations*.
34. Letter to S. Barnett, LSE Coll. Misc. 512, 1 November, 1874.
35. 'Letter to Fellow-workers', 1876.
36. For a typical critical account see Rosa Hobhouse, *Mary Hughes* London, 1949, p. 28, in which she recounts how, despite strong testimonials from

employers, one small slip in a man's life was held against him, and reiterated thereafter.

37. In his obituary in *The Nation*, H. W. Nevinson said that the harshness of the COS 'can only have arisen in so far as it has departed from her [Octavia's] principle of personal service and hardened into a machinery'.
38. LSE Coll. Misc. 512, 16 February, 1873.
39. See Loch Mowat, pp. 55 onwards.
40. CEM, p. 323, Lord Shuttleworth to Mr Edmund Maurice, nd.
41. See Lumsden, *Edinburgh Review*.
42. CEM, pp. 319, on 14 February, 1875.
43. Marylebone PL, letter to Cockerell, 3 October 1875.
44. For a discussion of how Booth diverged (like Barnett) from the COS 'solutions' of poverty, see Stedman Jones, *Outcast London*, p. 306.
45. CEM, pp. 278–9, nd., Mrs Hill to Mrs E. Maurice (Emily).

8: BARRETT'S COURT

1. *George Eliot Letters*, Vol VIII, p. 477, 2 June 1870. The Married Women's Property Act 1870 gave women the right to keep their earnings. The 1882 Act extended it to cover property owned before marriage, or acquired after. Octavia had joined the earlier campaign (see p. 58) so she must have been sympathetic to parts of Lady Amberley's paper.
2. Emma was also in charge of a Working Girls' Home in Drury Lane which eventually became a modern girls' hostel.
3. CEM, p. 295, to Cockerell, 26 October 1873. (The MS letter in Marylebone PL gives Emma's name; Maurice left it blank.)
4. The shops were let to a grocer, two upholsterers, a French polisher, a cobbler and two old-clothes men.
5. All quotes from handwritten memoir of the Hon. Mrs Maclagan (Ouvry papers).
6. 'Letter to Fellow-workers', 1873.
7. Elijah Hoole (?–1912) began to practise in 1863 and his first recorded building was the Chubb's Safe factory in the Old Kent Road. In addition to a large volume of work for Octavia, in later years his practice was almost exclusively the design of model dwellings and other housing for the various philanthropists to whom Octavia introduced him. See RIBA biography file.
8. CEM, p. 287, 25 May 1873.
9. Cook, *The Life of Florence Nightingale*, Vol. I, pp. 97–8. Cook was quoting from an article FN wrote for *Fraser's Magazine* in May 1873. She again extolled Octavia's example in S. C. Hall's magazine, *Social Notes*, Vol. I. No. 10, 11 May 1878.

10. From an account in *The Workmen's Club Journal*, 23 October 1875, included in Princess Alice's papers in the Hesse Archives, Darmstadt (D 24 29/7).
11. Cockerell papers, Marylebone PL, 21 December 1873.
12. CEM, p. 287, 25 May 1873.
13. Raeper, *George MacDonald*, p. 265.
14. CEM, p. 267, to Matthew Davenport Hill, 24 April 1871.
15. CEM, p. 311, 23 November 1874.
16. CEM, p. 262, notes to Ch. VI.
17. CEM, pp. 311–12, Miranda to Emily, 27 November 1874.
18. Letter to Cockerell, 28 April 1875; portion not used by CEM (p. 326) Marylebone PL.
19. Marylebone PL 3 October 1875.
20. Marylebone PL, 17 November 1874.
21. Marylebone PL, 27 June 1876.
22. CEM, p. 319, 14 February 1875.
23. Emma's pioneering teetotal club was supported by Tom Hughes and his friends and was called the 'Cat and Comfort'. She expanded it to provide a club for women, on the same premises.
24. CEM, p. 310, letter to Mary Harris, 1 November 1874.
25. Marylebone PL, 5 July 1876.

9: EASTWARDS

1. CEM, pp, 295–7, 26 October 1873.
2. ESM, p. 186, 24 July 1874.
3. CEM, p. 312, Edmund quotes Ruskin's report of Carlyle's comments.
4. CEM, p. 313, 20 December 1874.
5. CEM, p. 313, 26 December 1874.
6. This letter, dated 3 October 1875 was, ironically enough, published by Ruskin at the end of his *Fors Clavigera* diatribe against Octavia (see p. 192) to prove that she had once valued his example.
7. LSE Coll. Misc. 512, 25 October 1874.
8. *George Eliot Letters* (journal entry), Vol. VI, p. 31.
9. CEM, p. 298, 11 November 1873.
10. See Moberly Bell, p. 126.
11. 'Letter to Fellow-workers', 1876.
12. LSE Coll. Misc. 512; postscript to letter to Henrietta Barnett, dated 25 October 1874.
13. Webb, *Diary*, Vol. I, 12 August 1885.
14. LSE Coll. Misc. 512, to Samuel Barnett, 27 December 1875.
15. Marylebone PL, 6 March 1877.

16. LSE Coll. Misc. 512, letter to Henrietta Barnett, 26 December 1873.
17. Ibid., letter 11 March 1876.
18. Ibid., letter 29 March 1876.
19. 'Letter to Fellow-workers', 1874.
20. Ibid.
21. *Canon Barnett*, Vol. I, p. 130.
22. Henrietta Rowland was very wealthy; the heiress to a fortune made in macassar oil. However her money was held in trust, under the existing legislation which prevented a married woman from owning property.
23. CEM, p. 324, from Derwent Bank, 28 March 1875.
24. Stedman Jones, *Outcast London*, p. 195.
25. LSE Coll. Misc. 512, letter dated 10 July 1876.
26. *Canon Barnett* Vol. I, pp. 134–5, and Tarn, *Five Per Cent Philanthropy*, pp. 100–3.
27. Marylebone PL, 3 October 1875.
28. Caroline Stephen (1834–1909) – see Robert Tod, *Caroline Stephen 1834–1909*, privately printed, 1978. She was immortalized by her niece, Virginia Woolf, as Aunt Lucy in *The Voyage Out*. She was known in the family as 'The Nun'.
29. Hereford Buildings still stand on Old Church Street, Chelsea. They are still the property of the Octavia Hill, Latimer & Rowe Housing Trust, having been incorporated into the Horace Street Trust.
30. Noel Annan, *Leslie Stephen*, London, 1984, p. 120.
31. She married Jack Hills a few months before her death.
32. CEM, p. 338–9, letter to Mary Harris, 21 November 1875.
33. Webb, *My Apprenticeship*, entry for December.
34. LSE Courtney Collection 21.R(S.R.) 1003 – and subsequent quotations.
35. There were always workers living at Nottingham Place. Elizabeth Sturge, a member of a noted Bristol philanthropic family, and who had worked with Mary Carpenter at the Red Lodge Reformatory, came to work for Octavia in 1886 and lived there for eighteen months. She replaced Anna Hogg, from Dublin. Before her there had been Miss Janet Johnson who died in 1955, aged ninety-seven. Her father, Manuel Johnson, Radcliffe Observer, was closely associated with the Oxford Movement. In 1888 she became the first woman Guardian in Southwark. Her obituary mentions her delight in travel, with holidays in 'the form of complicated bicycle tours, having the dual object of looking up boys [from workhouses] in country situations and of visiting properties of the National Trust of which she had become a trustee in succession to Miss Octavia Hill.'
36. LSE Coll. Misc. 512, 22 January, 1877.
37. Later their father 'began to take an interest in the experiences . . . of his daughter Kate, and in the conversations of such co-workers, thus

introduced into the family circle, as Octavia Hill and Samuel and Henrietta Barnett.' (Webb, *My Apprenticeship*, p. 175.)

38. LSE Coll. Misc. 512, 20 November 1875. It was one of the courts visited by Princess Alice the following year.
39. In 1888 Jack the Ripper found one of his victims here (Fishman, *East End 1888*).
40. A very fashionable pursuit; even Ruskin was embroiled with the Cowper-Temples at Broadlands.
41. See Shaen, *Memorials of Two Sisters*, pp. 306–7.
42. CEM, pp. 330–1, dated about 12 June 1875.
43. Marylebone PL, to Cockerell, 11 May 1876.
44. Marylebone PL, 3 October 1876.
45. CEM, p. 346–8, to Mrs Gillum, 7 February 1877, plus paragraph not published (Marylebone PL MSS).

10: A ROYAL SUPPORTER

1. See letters quoted in Gerard Noel, *Princess Alice*, London, 1974, pp. 223 to 228.
2. See letters from Catherine, giving a lively account of the occasion, Shaen, *Memorials of Two Sisters*, pp. 288–92.
3. *Letters to HM the Queen from Alice, Grand Duchess of Hesse*, London, 1885, p. 252. Letter dated 13 October 1872.
4. Jo Manton, *Mary Carpenter and the Children of the Streets*, London, 1976.
5. ESM, p. 93, incorrectly dated to 1866; 5 November 18(7)6.
6. Letter from Princess Alice to her daughter Victoria, quoted Noel, op.cit., p. 221.
7. Incomplete, so addressee is not given, Hesse archives, Darmstadt (D 24 29/7).
8. Letter, 10 November 1876, Hesse archives, Darmstadt, ibid.
9. Letter dated 25 November 1876, Shaen, *Memorial of Two Sisters*, p. 324.
10. Letter 29 November 1876, Hesse archives, Darmstadt, ibid.
11. Letter dated 26 December 1876 (Hesse archives, Darmstadt, ibid.)
12. Letter dated 11 February 1877 (Hesse archives, Darmstadt, ibid.)
13. The same letter reported the success of the book, 'and the numerous improvements it gave to the care of the poor. A great and valuable part of the German Press approved the contents of the book in the highest terms.' (Darmstadt, 3 June 1878). Ouvry papers.

11: COUNTRYSIDE MATTERS

1. See Meacham, *Toynbee Hall and Social Reform*.
2. GLRO, F/BAR/173, 12 June 1897.

3. See Lewes, *Dr Southwood Smith*.
4. ESM, p. 58, 24 June 1859.
5. ESM, p. 63, to Mary Harris, 27 April 1862.
6. CEM, p. 97, to Florence, 8 July 1857 (from 45 Great Ormond Street).
7. 'Letter to Fellow-workers', 1879. The Kyrle Open Spaces Sub-committee worked closely with the CPS to achieve this outcome.
8. ESM, p. 31, 12 September 1856.
9. Which she referred to as Traitor's Hill.
10. CEM, p. 36, to Emily, 16 March 1855.
11. CEM, p. 447, letter to her mother, 19 July 1883.
12. CEM, p. 331, letter to Cockerell, 19 July 1875. The two latter excerpts were not published; see Marylebone PL MS.
13. Alfred Morrison (1821–1897) was an art collector and bibliophile.
14. *George Eliot Letters*, Vol. VI; George Lewes to Charles Lewes; 24 June 1875.
15. Marylebone PL, to SJC, 3 August 1875.
16. CEM, p. 334, letter to Mrs Nassau Senior from Church Row, Hampstead, 19 August 1875.
17. *The Times*, 17 August 1912.
18. Founded in 1865 to fight threats to enclose Epping Forest and many other commons and public spaces.
19. 'Letter to Fellow-workers', 1876.
20. In 1878 there was a meeting to discuss whether the Open Spaces Sub-committee could be funded independently of the main committee. It was decided not.
21. See Simey, *Charitable effort in Liverpool*.
22. *Morris*, Vol. I, pp. 192–205, extract from his speech to the Nottingham branch in 1884.
23. H. Meller, *Leisure and the Changing City 1870–1914*, Leicester, 1976.
24. CEM, p. 384, letter to Emily, from Bagnières de Bigorre, 5 February 1879.
25. CEM, p. 387, to Emily, from Verona, 9 May 1879.
26. 'Letter to Fellow-workers', 1875.
27. Address to Newnham College students, March 1898 (Ouvry papers).
28. LSE Coll. Misc. 512, 20 November 1875.
29. Hill, *Our Common Land*.
30. Now a sad space, much frequented by the homeless to which the church offers a day centre. Along the wall of the church overlooking the garden is a mosaic inscription: 'All may have if they dare try a glorious life or grave.' Unlike the Freshwater Place inscription, it was fixed to last.
31. Hill, op. cit.
32. *Victorian Studies*, 29, 1985–6, p. 109. H. L. Malchow, 'Public Gardens and Social Action in late Victorian London'.

33. Ibid.
34. *Canon Barnett*, Vol. I, p. 177.
35. 'Letter to Fellow-workers', 1877.
36. Another of the Oxford student roadmakers was Oscar Wilde. Ruskin
    wrote: 'It is, I know, the fashion to sneer at those Hinksey digging days
    . . . it will be found that many of the diggers who have helped their time
    in social movements, in the improvement of dwellings of the poor, in
    university settlements in big towns, in home industries for the people,
    and the like, probably owe all their interest in such matters to the spirit
    gained . . . in old Hinksey days.'
37. See Murphy, *Founders of the National Trust*, p. 75.
38. LSE, Coll. Misc. 512, 3 January 1875.
39. Murphy, pp. 80–1.
40. 'Letter to Fellow-workers', 1877.

12: CRISIS

1. LSE Coll. Misc. 512, 22 March 1877.
2. See Prochaska, *Women and Philanthropy*.
3. LSE, Coll. Misc. 512, 30 October 1874.
4. *Canon Barnett*, Vol. I, p. 43.
5. She also wrote to Cockerell, CEM, p. 349, 21 March, 1877. Edmund,
   however, omitted the most poignant message; 'the thought that I can
   never again in human words receive any message from her shakes me
   with passionate sobbing.' (Marylebone PL).
6. LSE Coll. Misc. 512, 6 April 1877.
7. Marylebone PL, 28 April 1877.
8. Edward Bond (1844–1920).
9. Webb, *My Apprenticeship*, note 2, p. 263. Beatrice knew him a few years
   later, during her time working at Katherine Buildings, he being a
   director of the East End Building Company.
10. In *The Diary of Lady Frederick Cavendish*, ed. John Bailey, 2 Vols,
    London, 1927, she commented: 'the disgusting Burdett-Coutts marriage
    . . . has actually come off . . . the bride wore orange-flowers and
    cream-coloured satin and had her veil off her poor old face!' (27 February
    1881).
11. Moberly Bell, p. 157.
12. Marylebone PL, Cockerell papers.
13. LSE Coll. Misc. 512, 19 August 1877.
14. Marylebone PL, 13 August 1877.
15. Born Julia Langston, in 1849 she married her first cousin, Lord Lieuten-
    ant of the county, Member for Stroud in 1852–3, and a member of the

Council to the Prince of Wales from 1888 until 1908. Earl of Ducie, 1827–1921; Lady Ducie died 1895.

16. Mark Girouard, *The Victorian Country House*, Oxford, 1971.
17. Marylebone PL, 7 August 1877.
18. *The Professor; Arthur Severn's Memoir of John Ruskin*, ed. J. Dearden, London, 1967.
19. *Fors Clavigera* 77.
20. See Barnes, *Ruskin in Sheffield*.
21. The subsequent history of the Guild proved Octavia all too right.
22. Ruskin made no entries in his diary between mid-July and mid-November 1877.
23. *Fors Clavigera* 76.
24. LSE Coll. Misc. 512, nd.
25. Marylebone PL, letter dated 23 December 1877.
26. Harriot Yorke was the eldest daughter of the Revd Charles Isaac Yorke, vicar of Shenfield, Essex, and a descendant of an ancient family, the Yorkes of Hardwick. She had considerable private means.
27. Webb, *Diary*, Vol. I, May 1886.

13: ABSENT

1. LSE Coll. Misc. 512, 7 January 1878.
2. *George Eliot Letters*, Vol. VII, 17 January 1878.
3. CEM, p. 356, Miranda to Mary Harris, 10 January 1878.
4. CEM, p. 356, to her mother, 24 January 1878.
5. LSE, Coll. Misc. 512, 28 January 1878.
6. Letter dated 29 January 1878 (Hesse archives, Darmstadt, op.cit.).
7. The Queen was a great admirer of MacDonald and gave a copy of *Robert Falconer* to each of her grandsons: see Raeper, *George MacDonald*.
8. LSE Coll. Misc. 512, 5 February 1878.
9. CEM, p. 438, 4 September 1880.
10. CEM, p. 383, around 1878.
11. CEM, p. 358, 27 January 1878.
12. LSE Coll. Misc. 512, 23 March 1878.
13. LSE Coll. Misc. 512, 26 March 1878.
14. Letter dated 7 June 1878, from Vevey (Hesse archives, op.cit.).
15. Letter from Louisa MacDonald, 3 May 1878 (Hesse archives, op.cit.).
16. CEM, pp. 368–9, to Miranda from Thun, 5 August 1878.
17. Howitt, *Autobiography*, Ch. XV.
18. Later Hanson.
19. CEM, p. 387, 27 March 1879.
20. CEM, pp. 408–11, 20 March 1880.

21. CEM, pp. 416–7, to her mother, 8 April 1880.
22. CEM, p. 432, to her mother, 6 May 1880.

14: BACK AGAIN

1. 7 June 1882: G. P. Gooch, *Life of Lord Courtney*, London, 1920, p. 186.
2. CEM, p. 394, 3 November 1879 or 80.
3. *Social Notes* No. I, 11 May 1878.
4. Alfred and Mary Marshall, *Economics of Industry*, London, 1879; 1881 edition, pp. 34–5.
5. Vincent and Plant, *Philosophy, Politics and Citizenship*. The authors draw a distinction between the personal solution to poverty (COS) and the community-based solution (Settlement movement) – which does not reflect the more active role of the WUS (see p. 260) and its practical training within a broadly COS approach.
6. CEM, p. 413, letter to Miranda from Athens, 26 March 1880.
7. 'Letter to Fellow-workers', 1878.
8. LSE Coll. Misc. 512, 7 January 1879.
9. See Moberly Bell, p. 181.
10. Jane Brown, *Gardens of a Golden Afternoon*, London, 1982.
11. CEM, p. 495, 23 June 1889.
12. CEM, p. 484, Miranda Hill to Ellen Chase, 16 December 1888.
13. Beatrice Webb noted in *My Apprenticeship*: 'South London Building Company, cost £20,887, pays 4 per cent, no depreciation fund.' See also Tarn, *Five Per Cent Philanthropy*, p. 95.
14. Elijah Hoole also carried out work for Emma Cons on the Royal Victoria Theatre in the early 1890s.
15. Evidence to the Royal Commission in 1884 described it as three-quarters let.
16. She became the first principal of Morley College, Lambeth in 1889. For more on Surrey Buildings, see *Recollections of Sophia Lonsdale*, ed. V. Martineau, London, 1936. A cousin of Caroline Martineau, Sophia went to help at Surrey Buildings, and began by answering correspondence for Emma Cons – 'one of the most remarkable women it has ever been my good fortune to meet'.
17. Ibid. Later on, Sophia returned home to Lichfield and became a Poor Law Guardian, holding staunch COS views.
18. See Baylis, *The Old Vic*.
19. Another sister, Theresa, took on her work when she was away. B. Caine, *Destined to be Wives, the sisters of Beatrice Webb*, Oxford, 1988. She incorrectly states that Katherine worked directly for the COS.
20. Leonard Courtney (1832–1918) became Deputy Speaker of the House of Commons, later Baron Courtney of Penwith.

21. LSE, Courtney Papers, Vol. III, folio 8: midnight, 18 May 1882.
22. She introduced him to the COS and he became a Guardian and Magistrate at St Georges-in-the-East.
23. Edward Bond was to be involved in raising funds for Hampstead Garden Suburb in the early 1900s, on behalf of Henrietta Barnett.
24. *Canon Barnett*, Vol. I, diary entry, 1883. See also various references, Fishman, *East End 1888*.
25. Ella Pycroft later became the Chief Organizer of Domestic Economy subjects for the Technical Education Board of the LCC.
26. *Diary*, Vol. I, p. 127 and p. 142.
27. Ibid., 6 October 1885, p. 141.
28. Ibid., undated entry for 1886, pp. 185–6. She noted: 'Practical work does not satisfy me; it seems like walking on shifting sand, with the forlorn hope that the impress of your steps will be lasting to guide others across the desert . . . These buildings too are to my mind an utter failure. In spite of Ella Pycroft's heroic efforts, they are not an influence for good.'
29. In 'The Inhabitants of the Tower Hamlets'; see Fishman, *East End 1888* p. 11 etc.
30. *My Apprenticeship*, pp. 278–9.
31. Fishman, *East End 1888*, p. 31.
32. Hollis, *Ladies Elect*, p. 7.
33. 'Letter to Fellow-workers', 1881.
34. CEM, 5 May 1881, p. 445.
35. Marylebone PL, letter 9 November 1885.

15: 1884

1. 'Letter to Fellow-workers', 1879.
2. CEM, p. 314, to Emily Maurice, nd. Leeds, with a population which had more than tripled between 1801 and 1851, had a particularly desperate housing situation. The Leeds Social Improvement Society held a meeting in 1874 to plead with the council to improve sanitary conditions. The 1875 Act gave powers to the city authorities to close the 500 remaining cellar dwellings. The Guardians noted in this year that there was very little philanthropic action in the town. See Tarn, *Five Per Cent Philanthropy*, pp. 34–5.
3. Pamphlet No. 8 (Ouvry papers).
4. See Loch Mowat, *The Charity Organization Society*, pp. 94–5.
5. *Social Service Review* II (Chicago), 1965: R. Bremner, 'Iron scepter twined with roses'.
6. 11 December 1897: letter reproduced in the supplement to the 75th Annual Report of the Octavia Hill Association Inc., 1971.

7. See Annual Report for 1986 (kindly forwarded to the author by Robert Kaufman, President of the Octavia Hill Association).

8. Fawcett Society Library; letter to Miss Somerville (of the State Charities' Aid Association, New York), 31 January 1898.

9. CEM, p. 450, to Emily, 25 April 1884.

10. The author was W. C. Preston, working from Mearns' notes.

11. To the debate, which was published in December 1883, *Nineteenth Century*.

12. Tarn, *Five Per Cent Philanthropy*, Ch. 7, p. 112.

13. Quoted in Roy Jenkins, *Sir Charles Dilke*, London, 1958.

14. *Justice*, Vol. I, 26 January 1884.

15. *Justice*, Vol, I. 24 May 1884.

16. *Justice* Vol. I, 21 June 1884.

17. Ibid.

18. See detailed discussion in Tarn, op.cit.

19. S. Gwynn and G. Tuckwell, *Life of the Rt Hon Sir Charles Wentworth Dilke* Vol. II, London, 1917.

20. Rent for a single room in London in the 1850s was 2s 6d and had jumped to 4s 9d by 1884. The increase was not matched by a commensurate rise in wages. By the 1880s rents were soaring, and wages were static. See Burnett, *A Social History of Housing (1815–1970)*, Newton Abbot, 1978.

21. CEM, p. 446, to Mrs Shaen, 3 June 1881.

22. *Morris* Vol. I, pp. 192–5.

23. *Justice*, Vol. I, 19 July 1884.

24. LSE Coll. Misc. 512, 23 March 1884.

25. See Best, *Temporal Pillars*.

26. Ibid.

27. *Canon Barnett*, Vol. I, p. 307.

28. LSE, Coll. Misc. 512, from Harrogate, 1 August 1880.

29. LSE, Coll. Misc. 512, from Harrogate, 6 August 1880.

30. *Justice*, Vol. I, 31 May 1884.

31. See Pimlott, *Toynbee Hall*.

32. Meacham, *Toynbee Hall and Social Reform*.

33. LSE Coll. Misc. 512, 19 September 1880.

34. *Canon Barnett*, Vol. I, p. 30.

35. See Meller, *The Ideal City*.

16: THE ESTABLISHED YEARS: SUCCESS AND FAILURE

1. Octavia continued to address meetings of the COS throughout the 1880s and 1890s; several drafts of her speeches are in the Ouvry papers.

2. See Ch. 18 for minutes.

3. CEM, p. 486, Miranda to Ellen Chase, 24 February 1889.

4. 'Letter to Fellow-workers', 1879.

5. 'Octavia Hill and Recreation'; talks given by Samuel Hamer and Sir William Hamer at meetings of the Association of Women House Property Managers, 21 October 1931 and 12 October 1932 (Royal Society of Arts), (Ouvry papers).

6. CEM, p. 247, to a friend, 4 October 1868.

7. For a while, around 1904, Olive helped in Octavia's housing work but she seems to have had constant health problems and Octavia frequently wrote offering money or holidays, rest or advice to her god-daughter. She died in 1910 and her ashes were scattered on Coniston Water.

8. 'No one who knew him can ever forget his purity, truth, unselfishness and tenderness . . .' Octavia recalled in a letter to young Sydney in 1905.

9. Notes by Mary Stocks, 1935 (Upcott papers).

10. Viscount Garnet Wolseley (1833–1913) was an immensely distinguished soldier. He fought successively in the Crimea, the Indian Mutiny, in China in 1870. In 1878 he was appointed High Commissioner in Cyprus, and was Commander in Chief of the expedition to Egypt in 1882. He was made a Viscount after the Sudanese campaigns of 1884–5, became a Field Marshal in 1894 and from 1895–1900 was Commander-in-Chief of the British army.

11. Alan Watts, 'Southwark Cottages', *The Lady*, 29 January 1976.

12. *Voluntary Service Gazette*, 1899.

13. H. W. Nevinson (1856–1941) was a renowned war correspondent and journalist. He was the father of Christopher Nevinson, the war artist.

14. Nevinson, ibid.

15. E. Sturge, *Reminiscences of my Life*, Bristol, 1928, pp. 45–52.

16. CEM, p. 470, letter to her mother from Loch Maree, 18 September 1886.

17. An elderly tenant told the author that her grandmother had brought up 14 children in a two-room apartment at Ossington Buildings.

18. Sir Patrick Geddes (1854–1932), town planner and social reformer.

19. P. Mairiet, *Pioneer of Sociology: Life and letters of Patrick Geddes*, London, 1957.

20. See Meller, *The Ideal City*.

21. See Outlook Tower Reports, 1907, 1911 (Upcott papers).

22. Edinburgh Social Union and Social and Sanitary Society, Report, 1912: memorial address on Octavia Hill by E. S. Haldane (Ouvry papers). Elizabeth Haldane (1862–1937) became the first Scottish woman JP.

23. CEM, p. 455, from Grisons, 7 June 1885.

24. CEM, p. 461, letter to her mother, 10 December 1885.

25. CEM, p. 463, 27 December 1885.

26. See J. Law, *Out of Work*, London, 1888, Ch. XV for a first-hand account.

27. CEM, 465–6, to Emily, 17 January 1886.

28. CEM, p. 464, January 1886.
29. CEM, p. 460, undated (probably November 1885).

17: THE ESTABLISHED YEARS: RECOGNITION AND NEW DIRECTIONS

1. LSE Coll. Misc. 512, 7 December 1888.
2. Information kindly supplied by Alan Crawford, (letter in V & A MSS Collection).
3. Cockerell papers, Marylebone PL, 2 April 1887.
4. April 1887; see *Friends of a Lifetime*, ed. Violet Meynell.
5. January, 1888; Violet Maynell, op.cit.
6. 19 January 1888; Sydney Cockerell copied it after Olive's death in 1910 and sent it to the family after Octavia's death.
7. See *The Best of Friends*, ed. Violet Meynell.
8. Letter to Cockerell, 2 May 1889, Marylebone PL.
9. 22 November 1893, Meynell, *Friends of a Lifetime*.
10. *Daily News*, 24 August 1900.
11. CEM, p. 517, 21 August 1891.
12. CEM, p. 519, 31 March 1892.
13. See Henderson, *William Morris*.
14. CEM, p. 501, letter to her mother, 28 April 1889.
15. *Sir J. F. Maurice, A record of his work and opinions*, London, 1913.
16. 'Letter to Fellow-workers', 1890. In January 1893 she wrote an article on the work for *Nineteenth Century*.
17. Stedman Jones, *Outcast London*, p. 328.
18. 'A few words to fresh workers', *Nineteenth Century*, September 1889.
19. OH to Jane Addams, 16 June 1896, Swarthmore College Peace Collection, Jane Addams Papers, Series I, supplement.
20. Jane Addams to Mary Smith, 22 June 1896, Swarthmore College Peace Collection, Jane Addams Papers, Series I, supplement.
21. Addams, *Twenty Years at Hull House*, p. 262 *et seq.*
22. Helen Gow (1860–1925) was the sister-in-law of the painter Alexander Mann. In later life she was for 23 years on the Southwark Board of Guardians whilst retaining her links with the WUS.
23. Letters published courtesy of Lady Pickthorn.
24. See Ch. 15, p. 223.
25. CEM, p. 488–9, 30 March 1889.
26. CEM, p. 507, 1890 (possibly in error for 1891).
27. Miss Pearson did accounts, but was not involved in the housing work. She was an aunt of Robin Barrington-Ward, editor of *The Times* (letter c. 1938, Upcott papers).
28. CEM, p. 514–5, letter to Mrs Durrant, 12 November 1890.

29. CEM, p. 533, 9 February 1895.
30. D. Garnett, *The Golden Echo*, London, 1953.
31. CEM, p. 522, to her mother, 4 September 1892.
32. Mary Booth, draft of foreword to a proposed publication by the COS in Octavia's memory (dropped from the final publication, for economy reasons); University of London, MS. 797/II/67/1 etc.
33. University of London, letter 21 February 1898.
34. The speeches were also printed in pamphlet form, but these quotations are from Miranda's notes.
35. It was Lord Goschen, who referred to her as the best Chancellor of the Exchequer we never had.
36. The Revd Alford conducted Miranda's funeral and was a firm family friend.
37. See Ch. 22, pp. 343–4 for sections of this speech.

18: THEORY: HOUSING MANAGEMENT

1. *The Life and Labour of the People of London*, Vol. III, London, 1892. Special subjects, part 2, Influence on Character.
2. Church Commissioners' records; Minutes of the Estates Committee, 25 November 1886.
3. Letter to Sir George Pringle, 10 December 1886; Church Commissioners' records, F. 65065 (1).
4. *The Architect*, Vol. XXVI, 1881, quoted in D. Olsen, *The Growth of Victorian London*, London, 1976. She made a very similar point in her answer to a question in the Select Committee on Housing, 1882.
5. See *The Reading Standard*, 23 February 1907.
6. Letter to an unnamed official of the Commission, July 1893; F. 65065.
7. See Lumsden, *Edinburgh Review*.
8. See Blunt, *Cockerell*, 16 December 1886.
9. Ibid.
10. Manuscript of talk given at the Portman Rooms to an unspecified audience (Ouvry papers).
11. Marylebone PL, 4 April 1903.
12. Marylebone PL, 28 May 1907.
13. From the Angel Hotel, Bury St Edmunds (where she was staying with the Poor Law Commission), 23 July 1907 (Marylebone PL).
14. To Janet Upcott, 4 July 1911 (Upcott papers).
15. Marylebone PL, 14 August 1907.
16. 'Letter to Fellow-workers', 1907.
17. Gaze, *Figures in a Landscape*, p. 49, (undated personal interview).
18. Nd, but post-1907 (Ouvry papers).

19. See Moberly Bell.
20. Janet Upcott, *National Trust Magazine*, No. 8, 1970.
21. Letter to Mary Booth, 27 February 1901 (University of London).
22. 'Letter to Fellow-workers', 1908.
23. To Carrington Ouvry, 2 November 1904 (Ouvry papers).
24. See Wohl, *Journal of British Studies*.
25. CEM, p. 527, 22 November 1893.
26. 'Letter to Fellow-workers', 1909.
27. 'Letter to Fellow-workers', 1911 (the final one).

19: POOR LAW

1. Charles Booth (1840–1916) was a Unitarian, born in Liverpool where he went into the family shipping firm. In 1871 he married Mary Macaulay, a cousin of the Potters, Kate and Beatrice (Webb). *The Life and Labour* was published between 1889 and 1903.
2. C. S. Loch, *Charity Organization Review*, 1912, Vol. XXXII, New Series, No. 190; 'In memoriam: Miss Octavia Hill'.
3. LSE, Coll. Misc. 512, 5 December 1905.
4. *Diary*, Vol. III, 29 November 1905.
5. Booth papers, University of London.
6. CEM, p. 564, 13 June 1907.
7. *Diary*, Vol. III; entry for 29 October 1908.
8. Letter to Mary Booth, 27 February 1908 (University of London).
9. Summarized in *The Times*, 22 August 1912.
10. Stedman Jones, *Outcast London*, p. 320.
11. Samuel Barnett, quoted p. 317, ibid.
12. Pamphlet of the Ecclesiastical Commissioners', 'Housing of the Working Classes London Estates', 1906. All quotes in following pages from this.

20: THE NATIONAL TRUST

1. *Cornhill Magazine*, 1914; obituary notice for Sir Robert Hunter by Canon Rawnsley.
2. Undated, MS in Ouvry papers.
3. Quoted Murphy, *Founders of the National Trust*, p. 103.
4. National Trust archives.
5. Ibid.
6. See Gaze, *Figures in a Landscape*, Ch. 2.
7. MSS, Acc. 34, National Trust archive.

8. Letter quoted D. Duff, *Princess Louise, Duchess of Argyll*, London, 1940. Nigel Bond was the Secretary 1901–11, and described by Lord Chorley (MSS. Acc. 34, National Trust archives) as a man of few words, always pessimistic.

9. CEM, p. 539, 28 July 1897.

10. National Trust archive, Acc. 6/2(b).

11. 25 November 1898, National Trust archive, Acc. 6/1(p).

12. Janet Upcott, *National Trust Magazine*, No. 8, 1970.

13. Appeal for funds, nd. (Ouvry papers).

14. 4 August 1896; National Trust archive, Acc. 6/29(a).

15. Quoted Gaze, *Figures in a Landscape*, p. 36.

16. 16 June 1898; report held in SPAB archives.

17. Marylebone PL, 7 April 1900.

18. Transcript of Ashbee's journal, 11–14 June 1901 from the Chelsea Hotel (Ashbee Journals, King's College, Cambridge).

19. 16 November 1900, Ashbee Journal entry from Pittsburgh, op. cit.

20. *John Bailey, 1864–1931; Letters and Diaries* edited by his wife, London, 1935, p. 81. Bailey also stood as a Conservative LCC candidate for Deptford, against Sidney Webb.

21. Author's tape-recorded interview with Romilly Ouvry.

22. *Nineteenth Century*, 23, No. CXXXII, February 1888.

23. The phrase is Dame Jennifer Jenkins's; tape-recorded interview, September 1988.

24. Ninth Annual Report, National Trust archive.

25. Letter to E. C. Ouvry, 8 September 1903.

26. Ibid., 27 December 1903.

27. Nigel Bond, quoted in W. Creese, *The Search for Environment*, New Haven and London, 1966, p. 223. Creese suggests that her views guided the choice of site and spatial layout of Hampstead Garden Suburb, Henrietta Barnett's foundation in the early 1900s.

21: THE LAST YEARS

1. For example, a ten-page review of a new biography of Joan of Arc, *Nineteenth Century* 37, 1895.

2. Her blind sister bought some of the St Katherine's Road properties in Notting Hill which turned out to be particularly difficult and only gave a 3% return. Mrs Bowen looked after property in Southwark, with Miss Bartlett; she went to look for it in 1948, to find the area terribly bombed.

3. Letter, 5 October 1948 (Upcott papers).

4. 24 June 1907 (Ouvry papers).

5. Letter to Elinor, 16 June 1907 (Ouvry papers).

6. CEM, p. 263, Maurice's own comments.

7. Letter to Barnett, nd., LSE Coll. Misc. 512 on subject.

8. See Prochaska, *Women and Philanthropy*, p. 229.

9. Marylebone D. Misc. 84/4; 7 August 1904. The comment may be compared to Florence Nightingale's 'While you have a Ward, it must be your *home* and its inmates your children.'

10. 31 August 1899, from Larksfield (Ouvry papers).

11. For example, her letter to Cockerell, 27 December 1873 (Marylebone PL), describing a Christmas spent with the MacDonalds: 'It is very bright and sweet here, in this large happy good family, so harmoniously joyous in themselves, so generously good to all around them.'

12. E. Sturge, *Reminiscences of my Life*, Bristol, 1928. She lived with the Hills for a while, finding them interesting ('an indescribable aroma of refinement pervaded the whole household and circle') but was glad to escape back to her family for light relief, away from an atmosphere 'where everyone was engrossed in business'.

13. 27 December 1909 (Ouvry papers).

14. B. Harrison, *Separate Spheres*, London, 1978.

15. Letter to Mary Booth, 27 February 1908 (University of London).

16. Charles was Member for St Pancras North from 1889 to 1891. He was on the Parks Committee. He also opposed the LCC's first-ever plan to build houses and cottages in Deptford (8 July 1889). No brother-in-law of Octavia Hill and staunch COS member (as he had been since 1876) was likely to support municipalization of housing (information from Andrew Saint).

17. CEM, p. 485, Caroline Hill to Miranda, 21 January 1889.

18. Hollis, *Women Elect*, pp. 307–8.

19. Ibid., pp. 306–317.

20. 20 December 1889, LSE Coll. Misc. 512.

21. GLRO; F/BAR/178; SB to his brother, Frank; 4 December 1897.

22. Ibid.,/187, 28 May 1898.

23. Ibid.,/209, 16 December 1899.

24. Ibid.,/282, nd. (1902?).

25. LSE Coll. Misc. 512, 6 December 1904.

26. LSE Coll. Misc. 512, 13 February 1905.

27. Quarterly Bulletin of the Society of Women Housing Estate Managers, No. VIII, January 1935.

28. A neat little plug for the first National Trust properties.

29. Report of meeting, 7 May 1897 (Upcott papers).

30. Notes in Upcott papers, also see M. Stocks, *My Commonplace Book*, London, 1970, pp. 56–7. In the latter account she contrasts the Hill household with that of Beatrice and Sidney Webb which she also visited. 190, Marylebone Road seemed 'rich dark brown' whilst the Webbs'

home was 'light grey-blue', the colour of bound volumes of Hansard. Mary Brinton, later Baroness Stocks (1891–1975) became principal of Westfield College.

31. 7 November 1903 (Ouvry papers).
32. Letter dated 6 May from Geraldine (Ouvry papers).
33. In fact Miss Mary Murray Schmitz, known to the family as 'Aunt' and 'Mica' from the Italian, 'amica'. She became Gertrude's companion in the 1890s, following Charles Lewes's death, and altered her name to Murray in the First World War, because of the difficulties of having a German (her father was Austrian, but naturalized British) name. She was 'more Scottish than the Scots', Romilly Ouvry remembers (letter to the author).
34. Letter from Gertrude, 7 May 1903 (Ouvry papers).
35. Letter in the possession of Romilly Ouvry, 26 August 1906. He was born at The Warren, his grandmother Gertrude Lewes's house, on 30 August 1905.
36. Born 13 March 1904, died March 1989. Miranda was one of his god-mothers.
37. Moberly Bell, p. 230.
38. See MacDonald, *Reminiscences of a Specialist*, p. 91.
39. 23 May 1910 (Ouvry papers).
40. Octavia wrote to Mary Harris, CEM, p. 500, 29 December 1889: 'I wish you could hear Mr Alford's sermons. No one, since Mr Maurice, seems to me so abundantly well worth hearing.'
41. Letter to Mary Booth, 9 July 1910 (University of London).
42. *Canon Barnett*, Vol. I, p. 32.
43. Ibid.
44. Letters dated between June and August 1910 (Ouvry papers).

22: AFTERWARDS

1. Hearing of Emma's death, C. R. Ashbee recalled in his Journal (King's College, Cambridge) how she 'shone out in her quaint shrivelled way at those dreary committee meetings, a curious living flame of enthusiasm and commonsense'.
2. Miss Moberly Bell states that a funeral at Westminster Abbey was offered but that the family turned it down.
3. C. R. Ashbee Journals, August 1912 (King's College, Cambridge).
4. 18 January 1914 from Blunt, *Cockerell*.
5. *The Times*, 17 August 1912.
6. 30 August 1912.
7. 31 August 1912.

8. Romilly Ouvry remembers his mother Elinor's fury at Emily's destruction of all matters of personal interest in the letters. He is sure that her love affair 'probably upset her a great deal more than was allowed to be revealed'.

9. 8 August 1912 (Ouvry papers).

10. Ruskin's literary executor.

11. Cockerell papers, Marylebone PL, 19 January 1913.

12. She was the sister-in-law of a present-day Crockham Hill resident.

13. Notes in *Crockham Hill Newsletter* (magazine of Holy Trinity church) December 1988, from an article by Margaret Shaen, loaned by Commander and Mrs Ouvry. Also letter to Janet Upcott from Harriot Yorke 1922 (Upcott papers).

14. Information from Romilly Ouvry, letter to author.

15. To Janet Upcott; from Eirene Cottage, Gainsborough Gardens, Hampstead, 12 November 1918 (Upcott papers).

16. Quotes from two tape-recorded interviews with Romilly Ouvry, 1986/8.

17. Sir Robert Hunter died in 1913, Canon Rawnsley in 1921.

18. For a detailed account, see Gaze, *Figures in a Landscape*.

19. See for example the obituary of Frances Fenter (1892–1989) who worked in Birmingham from 1925 as property manager and secretary of a slum housing project, COPEC House Improvement Society: the *Guardian*, 3 June 1989.

20. From the beginning it offered an Assistant's Certificate, awarded after twelve months' training.

21. The Royal Institute of British Architects accepted its first woman member in 1898 but until the 1920s no more than a handful of women trained as architects. Gillian Harrison became the first Fellow of the RIBA in 1931. Essay by Lynn Walker; *Woman Architects, their work*; RIBA exhibition catalogue 1984.

22. Irene Barclay (1894–1989), Kingsley Martin's sister, was the first woman chartered surveyor, qualifying in 1922. She had worked with both Miss Jeffery and Edith Neville – two of Octavia's most faithful followers – and became Secretary of the St Pancras Housing Association in 1925.

23. Miss Jeffery worked five days a week, from 10 to 5 for a salary of £80, helping on the Ecclesiastical Commissioners' estates.

24. The work here is described in a paper by Miss Charlesworth, originally published in *Housing*, 27 September 1919, and reprinted in *House Property and its Management*, 1921.

25. His sister Stella worked with Octavia; see Ch. 9, p. 153.

26. The COS had proposed it and H. L. Woollcombe, Secretary pursued the details.

27. One was Maud Galton, who with her sister Agnes was a central figure among the women housing professionals. Maud was a trained secretary and first worked at the Ecclesiastical Commissioners' Estate in Lambeth. On Octavia's death she took responsibility for a district called 'mixed Southwark' – an assortment of private property and that owned by Trusts. After her work in Barrow she managed property in Marylebone and, from 1929, the Chelsea Housing Improvement Society.

28. GLRO ref. A/FWA/C/C7/1.

29. In Rotherham, where Jean Thompson was appointed Housing Manager in 1928, the women's work was exclusively on problem estates. She produced a detailed report on the workings of the Octavia Hill system in Rotherham; see Brion and Tinker, *Women in Housing*.

30. Letter to Lord Sanderson, dated (?) 13 August 192-. GLRO, ibid.

31. Nancy Astor had taken her husband's Plymouth seat in 1919, becoming the first woman MP. The quote is from Margaret Wintringham's introduction.

32. It consisted of 345 houses and 10 hostels.

33. Later she became President of the Society of Housing Managers and was on the Council of the Housing Centre well into her eighties.

34. See Power, *Property before People*, quotation from LCC, Report of the Housing and Public Health Committee on Housing Management, March 1939.

35. Power, ibid., p. 237.

36. Power, ibid., points out that the increasingly institutionalized way in which tenants were picked was as intrusive and inappropriate as the most insensitive Victorian exercises in selection.

37. *Architects' Journal*, 4 April 1984, 'Town Hall Turnabout', Gillian Darley.

38. It incorporated the oddly titled 'Octavia Hill Club', founded by Miss Jeffery in 1928, and the Conference of Women Municipal Managers, founded the same year by Janet Upcott.

39. Power, op.cit.

40. For example the Lambeth Housing Movement (1927) and Liverpool Improved Houses (1928) – the latter renamed Merseyside Improved Houses, now one of the largest housing associations in the country with over 12,000 homes – were founded on the stated principle of following Octavia Hill's management practices. See National Federation of Housing Associations 'Album', published for its Jubilee 1935–1985.

41. My thanks to Marjorie Cleaver, Director of the Housing Centre until 1988, for this information.

42. December 1938 (Upcott papers).

43. Parker Morris is best remembered for the housing standards of 1961 which bore his name. In the late 1930s he was Town Clerk for Westminster. His daughter, Dame Jennifer Jenkins (coincidentally now

Chairman of the National Trust), remembered his interest in Octavia's work and his employment of a number of her trained housing managers (interview with the author, September 1988). See also Power.

44. Apparently the street was so notorious that 'desirable tenants were frequently hampered in obtaining good employment . . . for this reason Dr Schuster arranged to have it altered to Wilsham Street – named after his country place': from 'Some Account of the Horace Street Trust'.

45. Sir Reginald Rowe became the President of the National Federation of Housing Associations and wrote the introduction to Miss Moberly Bell's biography of Octavia. He regarded her 'as among the greatest of Englishwomen'.

46. Figures as of 31 March 1988 (Annual Report 1988).

Bibliography

Works by or relating to the Hill family:

BELL, E. MOBERLY, *Octavia Hill*, London, 1942

BOSANQUET, HELEN, notice on Octavia Hill, *Dictionary of National Biography*, London, 1927.

BOYD, NANCY, *Josephine Butler, Octavia Hill, Florence Nightingale*, London, 1982.

HILL, CAROLINE SOUTHWOOD, ed. Hill, Octavia, *Notes on Education*, containing 'Memoranda of Observations and Experiments in Education', London, 1907.

HILL, OCTAVIA, *The Homes of the London Poor*, London, 1875.

——, *Our Common Land*, London, 1877.

——, *Memorandum on the Report of the Royal Commission on the Poor Laws and Relief of Distress*, London, 1909.

HILL, WILLIAM THOMSON, *Octavia Hill*, London, 1956.

HORNE, R. H., *The New Spirit of Age* (Vol. I), containing essay 'Lord Ashley and Dr Southwood Smith', London, 1844.

LEE, AMICE, 'Recollections of Octavia Hill' in *Cornhill Magazine*, London, September 1936.

LEWES, MRS C. L., *Dr Southwood Smith, a retrospect*, Edinburgh & London, 1898.

LOCH, C. S., 'In Memoriam: Miss Octavia Hill', *Charity Organization Review*, October 1912.

LUMSDEN, MARY, 'Octavia Hill and the Housing Problem', *Edinburgh Review*, April 1913.

MAURICE, C. EDMUND (ed.), *Life of Octavia Hill*, London, 1913.

MAURICE, EMILY SOUTHWOOD (ed.), *Octavia Hill, early ideals*, London, 1928.

OUVRY, ELINOR SOUTHWOOD (ed.) *Extracts from Octavia Hill's Letters to Fellow-Workers*, foreword by Neville Chamberlain MP, London, 1933.

Society of Housing Managers Quarterly Journal, Vol. V, No. 8, fiftieth anniversary of Octavia Hill's death, special issue, October 1962.

In addition to these works relating to Octavia Hill there is a vast body of further material – her own published articles (reference to some of which appears in the Notes), letters to the press, and articles about her, both during and after her lifetime. The fullest bibliography is held in the Registry of the National Trust, and is available on request.

Selective bibliography:

ADDAMS, JANE, *Twenty Years at Hull House*, New York, 1910.

BARNES, JANET, *Ruskin in Sheffield*, Sheffield, 1985.

BARNETT, HENRIETTA, *Canon Barnett*, 2 Vols, London, 1918.

BAYLIS, L.; 'Emma Cons, the founder of the Old Vic' in Hamilton, Cicely M., *The Old Vic*, London, 1926.

BEST, G., *Temporal Pillars*, Cambridge, 1964.

BLUNT, WILFRID J. W., *Cockerell*, London, 1964.

BOOTH, CHARLES, *The Life and Labour of the People of London* (7 Vols), London & New York, 1892–7.

BRION, MARION and TINKER, ANTHEA, *Women in Housing*, London, 1980.

BURTON, HESTER, *Barbara Bodichon*, London, 1949.

BUTLER, BELINDA NORMAN, *Victorian Aspirations: the Life and Labour of Charles and Mary Booth*, London, 1972.

CHASE, ELLEN, *Tenant Friends in Old Deptford*, London, 1929.

COLLOMS, BRENDA, *Victorian Visionaries*, London, 1982.

COOK, SIR EDWARD, *The Life of Florence Nightingale* (2 Vols), London, 1913.

COOK, E. T. and WEDDERBURN, ALEXANDER, *The Library Edition of the Works of John Ruskin* (39 Vols), London, 1903–12.

DAVIES, EMILY, Intro. Howarth, Janet, *The Higher Education of Women* (1866) London and Ronceverte, 1988.

DAVIES, THE REVD J. LLEWELYN, *The Working Men's College, 1854–1904*, London, 1904.

EVANS, JOAN and J. H. WATERHOUSE, *The Diaries of John Ruskin* (3 Vols), Oxford, 1956–9.

FISHMAN, WILLIAM J., *East End 1888*, London, 1988.

GAULDIE, ENID, *Cruel Habitations*, London, 1974.

GAZE, JOHN, *Figures in a Landscape*, London, 1988.

HAIGHT, GORDON, *George Eliot*, Oxford, 1968.

HAIGHT, GORDON, (ed.), *The George Eliot Letters* (8 Vols), New Haven and London, 1954–6.

HARRISON, J. F. C., *A History of the Working Men's College*, London, 1954.

HILTON, TIM, *John Ruskin: the Early Years*, London and New Haven, 1985.

HOLLIS, PATRICIA, *Ladies Elect*, Oxford, 1987.

HOWITT, MARGARET, (ed.), *Mary Howitt. An Autobiography*, London, 1889.

JEFFREYS, SHEILA, *The Spinster and her Enemies*, London, 1985.

JONES, GARETH STEDMAN, *Outcast London*, Oxford, 1971.

LEWIS, RICHARD A., *Edwin Chadwick and the Public Health Movement*, London, 1952.

MACDONALD, GREVILLE, *Reminiscences of a Specialist*, London, 1932.

——, *George MacDonald and his Wife*, London, 1924.

MANTON, JO, *Elizabeth Garrett Anderson*, London, 1965.

MAURICE, F., (ed.), *The Life of Frederick Denison Maurice* (2 Vols), London, 1884.

MEACHAM, STANDISH, *Toynbee Hall and Social Reform*, New Haven, 1987.

MELLER, HELEN, (ed.), *The Ideal City*, Leicester, 1979.

MEYNELL, VIOLET, *Friends of a Lifetime, letters to Sydney Carlyle Cockerell*, London, 1940.

—— *The Best of Friends, further letters to S. C. Cockerell*, London, 1956.

MORRIS, MAY, *William Morris: Artist, Writer, Socialist* (2 Vols), Oxford, 1936.

MOWAT, CHARLES LOCH, *The Charity Organisation Society*, London, 1961.

MURPHY, GRAHAM, *Founders of the National Trust*, London, 1987.

NEVINSON, HENRY, *Changes and Chances*, London, 1923.

NOEL, G., *Princess Alice, Queen Victoria's Forgotten Daughter*, London, 1974.

NORMAN, EDWARD, *The Victorian Christian Socialists*, Cambridge, 1987.

OWEN, DAVID, *English Philanthropy 1660–1960*, Oxford and Cambridge Mass., 1965.

PARLIAMENTARY PAPERS; *PP. 1881, VII; 1882, VII*: Select Committee on Artisans' and Labourers' Dwellings' Improvement. *PP. 1884–5, XXX*: Royal Commission on the Housing of the Working Classes. *PP. 1909, XLII–XLIV; 1910, XLIV, LIII*: Royal Commission on the Poor Laws and the Relief of Distress.

PIMLOTT, J. A. R., *Toynbee Hall*, London, 1935.

POWER, ANNE, *Property before People*, London, 1987.

PROCHASKA, F. K., *Women and Philanthropy in 19th-Century England*, Oxford, 1980.

RAEPER, WILLIAM, *George MacDonald*, Tring, 1987.

RAWNSLEY, ELEANOR F., *Canon Rawnsley*, Glasgow, 1923.

SHAEN, M., *Memorials of Two Sisters*, London, 1908.

SIMEY, M., *Charitable Effort in Liverpool in the Nineteenth Century*, Liverpool, 1951.

TARN, JOHN NELSON, *Five Per Cent Philanthropy*, Cambridge, 1973.

TODD, MARGARET (Graham Travers), *The Life of Sophia Jex-Blake*, London, 1918.

UPCOTT, JANET, *Women House Property Managers*, St Albans, 1925.

VICINUS, MARTHA, *Independent Women*, Chicago and London, 1985.

VINCENT, A. and PLANT, R., *Philosophy, Politics and Citizenship*, Oxford, 1984.

WEBB, BEATRICE, (ed. MacKenzie, Norman & Jeanne), *Diaries, Vols. I–III*, London, 1982–1984.

WEBB, BEATRICE, *My Apprenticeship*, Cambridge, 1979.

WOODRING, CARL RAY, *Victorian Samplers, William and Mary Howitt*, Kansas, 1952.

WOHL, A. S. 'Octavia Hill and the Homes of the London Poor', *Journal of British Studies*, 1971, 10 (2).

——, *The Eternal Slum*, London, 1977.

WOODROOFE, KATHLEEN, *From Charity to Social Work*, London, 1962.

Index